HC244TRA

The Transition in
Eastern Europe

A National Bureau
of Economic Research
Project Report

The Transition in Eastern Europe

Volume
2

Restructuring

Edited by

Olivier Jean Blanchard,
Kenneth A. Froot, and
Jeffrey D. Sachs

 The University of Chicago Press

Chicago and London

OLIVIER JEAN BLANCHARD is professor of economics at the Massachusetts Institute of Technology. KENNETH A. FROOT is professor of business
administration at the Graduate School of Business, Harvard University.
JEFFREY D. SACHS is the Galen L. Stone Professor of International Trade
at Harvard University. All are research associates of the National Bureau
of Economic Research.

The University of Chicago Press, Chicago 60637
The University of Chicago Press, Ltd., London
© 1994 by the National Bureau of Economic Research
All rights reserved. Published 1994
Printed in the United States of America

03 02 01 00 99 98 97 96 95 94   1 2 3 4 5
ISBN: 0-226-05662-7 (cloth)

Library of Congress Cataloging-in-Publication Data

The Transition in Eastern Europe / edited by Olivier Jean Blanchard, Ken-
    neth A. Froot, and Jeffrey D. Sachs.
        p.   cm.—(A National Bureau of Economic Research Project
        Report)
        Includes bibliographical references and index.
        Contents: v. 1. Country studies—v. 2. Restructuring.
        1. Europe, Eastern—Economic conditions—1989-   —Congresses.
    2. Europe, Eastern—Economic Policy—1989-   —Congresses.
    3. Economic stabilization—Europe, Eastern—Congresses.
    4. Privatization—Europe, Eastern—Congresses.   I. Blanchard, Olivier
    (Olivier J.)   II. Froot, Kenneth.   III. Sachs, Jeffrey.
    IV. Series.
    HC244.T6989   1994
    338.947—dc20   93-36585
                                                                          CIP

⊚ The paper used in this publication meets the minimum requirements of
the American National Standard for Information Sciences—Permanence
of Paper for Printed Library Materials, ANSI Z39.48–1984.

Relation of the Directors to the Work and Publications of the National Bureau of Economic Research

1. The object of the National Bureau of Economic Research is to ascertain and to present to the public important economic facts and their interpretation in a scientific and impartial manner. The Board of Directors is charged with the responsibility of ensuring that the work of the National Bureau is carried on in strict conformity with this object.

2. The President of the National Bureau shall submit to the Board of Directors, or to its Executive Committee, for their formal adoption all specific proposals for research to be instituted.

3. No research report shall be published by the National Bureau until the President has sent each member of the Board a notice that a manuscript is recommended for publication and that in the President's opinion it is suitable for publication in accordance with the principles of the National Bureau. Such notification will include an abstract or summary of the manuscript's content and a response form for use by those Directors who desire a copy of the manuscript for review. Each manuscript shall contain a summary drawing attention to the nature and treatment of the problem studied, the character of the data and their utilization in the report, and the main conclusions reached.

4. For each manuscript so submitted, a special committee of the Directors (including Directors Emeriti) shall be appointed by majority agreement of the President and Vice Presidents (or by the Executive Committee in case of inability to decide on the part of the President and Vice Presidents), consisting of three Directors selected as nearly as may be one from each general division of the Board. The names of the special manuscript committee shall be stated to each Director when notice of the proposed publication is submitted to him. It shall be the duty of each member of the special manuscript committee to read the manuscript. If each member of the manuscript committee signifies his approval within thirty days of the transmittal of the manuscript, the report may be published. If at the end of that period any member of the manuscript committee withholds his approval, the President shall then notify each member of the Board, requesting approval or disapproval of publication, and thirty days additional shall be granted for this purpose. The manuscript shall then not be published unless at least a majority of the entire Board who shall have voted on the proposal within the time fixed for the receipt of votes shall have approved.

5. No manuscript may be published, though approved by each member of the special manuscript committee, until forty-five days have elapsed from the transmittal of the report in manuscript form. The interval is allowed for the receipt of any memorandum of dissent or reservation, together with a brief statement of his reasons, that any member may wish to express; and such memorandum of dissent or reservation shall be published with the manuscript if he so desires. Publication does not, however, imply that each member of the Board has read the manuscript, or that either members of the Board in general or the special committee have passed on its validity in every detail.

6. Publications of the National Bureau issued for informational purposes concerning the work of the Bureau and its staff, or issued to inform the public of activities of Bureau staff, and volumes issued as a result of various conferences involving the National Bureau shall contain a specific disclaimer noting that such publication has not passed through the normal review procedures required in this resolution. The Executive Committee of the Board is charged with the review of all such publications from time to time to ensure that they do not take on the character of formal research reports of the National Bureau, requiring formal Board approval.

7. Unless otherwise determined by the Board or exempted by the terms of paragraph 6, a copy of this resolution shall be printed in each National Bureau publication.

(Resolution adopted October 25, 1926, as revised through September 30, 1974)

Contents

Preface

This volume contains eleven papers that were prepared as part of a research project by the National Bureau of Economic Research on the transition in Eastern Europe. These papers examine the problems of restructuring, from fiscal reform, to labor market structure, to the design of privatization and bankruptcy mechanisms, to the role of foreign direct investment.

In addition to the papers in this volume, the project also includes studies of the experience of specific countries, including Poland, Czechoslovakia, Hungary, Germany, Slovenia, and the former Soviet Union, with emphasis on macroeconomic policies and performance. These studies are included in the first volume of this two-volume set.

The findings of NBER's Eastern Europe project were presented at a conference for economists, journalists, and policymakers from the United States and Europe. The conference was held in Cambridge, Massachusetts, 26–29 February 1992.

We would like to thank the Pew Charitable Trusts for financial support of this work.

Olivier Jean Blanchard, Kenneth A. Froot, and Jeffrey D. Sachs

8   What Direction for Labor Market Institutions in Eastern and Central Europe?

Richard B. Freeman

The telephone rings. It is the new minister of labor of the former Communist state of ———. "Professor, my first day in office and I'm at a loss. Prices are rising. Unemployment is growing by leaps and bounds. Output in the state sector dropped 20 percent. The finance minister says the budget hasn't a cent for workers. What can I do?"

The labor difficulties in the marketizing economies of Eastern Europe exceed those of competitive economies with stable labor institutions. Governments, ministers, laws, countries, change. Independent unions compete with successors to the old official unions to represent workers. The *nomenklatura* spin off profitable segments of state-owned enterprises. Managers with little knowledge of market economics struggle to run large state enterprises. Bankrupt state-owned firms seek government bailouts. Private firms develop their own employment relations. Westerners buy enterprises and introduce their nation's labor practices. Workers' councils pressure managers on wages and employment. Help!

When I told my colleague John Dunlop that I had agreed to analyze labor relations in the marketizing economies of Eastern Europe for this conference, he thought that I was mad: "It's chaos, young man. Any sane person would wait until the dust has settled. Then maybe you will have something sensible to say." Mad or not, I try in this paper to determine how labor relations and wage setting proceeded in Poland, Hungary, and Czechoslovakia during the

The observations that served as a basis for this study are derived from discussions with trade union and government officials and researchers in the various countries. In addition, the author benefited from the research assistance of Peter Orszag, from discussions with Mark Schaffer, Hartmut Lehmann, and Saul Estrin of the London School of Economics Centre for Economic Performance, and from written comments by David Laibson of the Massachusetts Institute of Technology.

1

initial phase of the transition to a market economy and to develop a framework for assessing how labor arrangements might affect that transition.

Section 8.1 reports surprising inertia in labor institutions despite new labor laws in all three countries. During the period under study, the successors to the old official unions remained in place at most workplaces; central authorities regulated wage setting through taxes on wage increases and minimum wages; tripartite bodies discussed labor issues but did not bargain over wages or other outcomes. Section 8.2 tells a different story about wages and employment. It shows sizable reductions in employment in *state-run enterprises* that mark a sharp break with behavior under "reform socialism" (Kornai 1986; World Bank 1987, 1990b). It also reports increased private-sector employment, widening industrial wage structures in Hungary and Poland, increasing differentials between managers and other workers, and falls in real wages and increasing unemployment. Section 8.3 assesses the effect of labor institutions on worker tolerance for the costs of reforms, on the ability of workers who lose in transition to conduct mass protests, and on whether the institutions provide "voice" feedbacks that may improve programs.

8.1   What's Happening to Labor Relations?

The starting points for the marketizing countries are the labor relations institutions of Communist dictatorships. Communist labor relations policies contributed greatly to the failure of their economies. They produced excess demand for labor, poor work effort, and distorted wage structures—all of which contributed to economic inefficiency. In addition, Communist governments sought to restrict labor mobility and occupational choice and enrolled all workers in official Communist unions that were "transmission belts" for authorities rather than the voice of the workers.

On the demand side, state enterprises hired labor to meet output norms subject to centrally determined "soft" budget constraints. In extreme form, demand for labor evinced "a tendency to grow without limits" (Kornai 1982, 27–28). Job vacancies were immense and responded perversely to economic changes. In Poland in the mid-1980s, for instance, vacancies rose as output fell (Freeman 1987)—presumably because enterprises cared little about labor costs in their desire to meet output goals. Indicative of this "noneconomic behavior," Lehmann and Schaffer (1992) report sizable gaps between estimated marginal productivity and wages in Polish enterprises in 1983–88 and find no evidence that firms expanded employment to close the gaps. Shortages of inputs and consumer goods also impaired labor market efficiency. Material shortages made it rational to hoard labor so that workers would be available when materials arrived. Shortages of consumer goods made nonmonetary remuneration, such as housing allotments or health care provided by the enterprise, critical in compensation, devaluing wages as a price and limiting the scope of labor and product markets. In 1988, as much as 80 percent of cars produced for the domestic market in Poland were supplied by allotment rather than sales (World Bank 1990b, 44). The individuals who received the allotments made roughly four years' pay at the free market resale value of the car (p. 45), while the producers had no price incentive to produce more cars.

On the supply side, the state made open unemployment illegal (in 1985, 7,000 people in Hungary served a prison sentence for idleness), tolerated poor performance by the employed, forbade those with entrepreneurial skills from establishing firms beyond a minimal size, and often sought to limit labor mobility, although with little apparent success.[1] With low pay and a guaranteed job, workers often "put in time" in the state sector while devoting themselves to second-economy jobs, using state materials or properties for their personal economic activities. Hungary's "work partnerships" meant that many would do little during the normal work day but work hard for shares of profits during after-hours production.

State wage and price setting compounded inefficiency. Low wages made labor "cheap," contributing to excess demand. Piece-rate systems were often "demoralized": in the mid-1980s in Poland, workers overfulfilled norms by 48–74 percent (Freeman 1987). Many enterprises paid workers largely with *add-ons* that made base rates a small component of pay and created significant divergences between wages and labor costs. In 1986, Polish coal miners received just one-quarter of their monthly remuneration through base pay. *Wage differentials* between nonmanual and manual workers were excessively narrow. In 1980, the relative earnings of nonmanual to manual workers was 1.05 in Poland and 1.13 in Hungary, compared to 1.44 in four West European countries (in 1978) (Redor 1986, 5). Differentials by industry were also narrow by world standards, save for favored heavy industries such as mining (Sziraczki 1990, table 6). At the same time, bureaucratic distribution of the right to purchase shortage goods produced a rationing system with great inequality.

Finally, the state *suppressed independent trade unions,* forcing workers into official "transmission belt" unions whose purpose was to carry out orders from the center. Unions owned considerable property (the Hungarian union Balatonfüred facilities shocked ILO visitors in 1984) and allocated subsidized vacations, pensions, and the like. The Party often placed its worst hacks in union jobs. Excess demand for labor and material shortages may have given local work groups "everyday power" to bargain with management (Kollo 1988) and allowed individuals to shift jobs despite legal sanctions, but overall the system made the most debilitating form of exit—halfhearted work effort—the main way of expressing discontent and ruled out productive "voice" methods of challenging workplace or national economic decisions.

In the 1970s and 1980s, nearly all Communist states attempted to reform this system, decentralizing some decisions and freeing some prices. However,

---

1. In some Communist countries, state restrictions on labor supply were more severe. The Soviet Union required permits to live in cities. China allocated school leavers to work sites.

in Eastern and Central Europe, these efforts failed (Kornai 1986; World Bank 1987, 1990a, 1990b; Sziracki 1990), just as did the longer-standing Yugoslav experiment with market-oriented worker management (Estrin 1991). Some reforms may have been misguided. Others were halfhearted. Poland freed many prices in the mid-1980s but failed to curb the power of branch ministries and enacted a workers' council law that nominally accorded great power to workers at the plant level but suppressed Solidarność. And so on. The ultimate cause of the failure of the reforms was not, however, their specifics but rather continued *nomenklatura* control of key decisions. When I visited Polish plants in 1986, managers shrugged at questions about the new reforms; they still relied on ministries to guide decisions, obtain supplies, and so on. Hungary's 1980s effort to engage labor in the productive process through enterprise councils failed to attract ordinary workers: 70 percent of participants in the councils were members of the Communist party. In Czechoslovakia, "by far the biggest obstacle for undertaking fundamental reform . . . was the almost total lack of interest of the labor force . . . alienated from the political leadership . . . [while] enterprise management, which had learned to manipulate the existing system to its own advantage, formed a powerful coalition of resistance" (World Bank 1990a, 40). Not until the late 1980s democratic revolutions was it possible to replace political domination of the economy with markets. With formal state controls lifted and the informal *nomenklatura* controls greatly weakened, management had to listen to a new drummer—the economic marketplace.

How far have Poland, Hungary, and Czechoslovakia moved from the Communist labor relations system by 1991–92? Which aspects of the Communist system have been replaced by more market-based practices, and which aspects persist, possibly slowing economic reforms?

8.1.1 Labor Laws

At the outset of the transition period, all three countries changed the rules governing labor in ways that brought them in line with Western practices (see table 8.1). They eliminated restrictions on labor supply, allowed freedom of association, accorded collective bargaining wide nominal scope in determining wages and rules of work (but in fact used taxes on increases beyond centrally determined rates to restrict wages in state-owned enterprises), gave workers rights to strike, replaced the guarantee (requirement) of work with unemployment insurance benefits, and introduced personal income taxes. In Czechoslovakia, the law on employment stipulates that employers inform trade unions and local employment offices about job vacancies and intended dismissals but gives employers full rights to hire and fire. In Poland, the obligation to list vacancies with state offices was abolished, then reinstated as unemployment rose. Each country devoted limited resources to active labor market policies.

Despite the general similarity of the new market-oriented labor legislation, there are differences in the laws that foretell different labor relations systems in the future. Czechoslovak law forbids lower-level bodies from bargaining for

Table 8.1   **Changes in Labor Laws in Transition**

A. Hungary

April 1989 Right to Strike Guaranteed

Extensive conciliation and mediation: 7-day conciliation period; allow 2-hour warning strike; if identity of employer cannot be determined, Council of Ministers shall appoint representative; no coercive measures to terminate employment; workers participating in lawful strike shall be entitled to all rights, save for wages or benefits; cannot strike if court has jurisdiction over issue or during agreement; safety or security of essential importance

Act II of 1989 on Right of Association

Questions regarding employment shall be regulated by collective agreements, but set up for SZOT

Employment Act (IV) of 1991

Establishes principles for collective bargaining; unemployment insurance from Solidarity fund; active manpower policies to be determined by triparite bodies

1991 Acts on Financing

11 July, on the Check-off System: workers to give written declaration to check off dues to union

12 July, on Trade Union Property and Equality of Opportunity in Workers's Organizing: requires unions to account for asset, with total to be distributed among unions by four-union group (LIGA, workers' councils, MSZOSZ, and one other) in proportion to support in election

B. Poland

Law on Unionization

April 1989: very similar to October 1982 law, which has been passed as compromise between government and Solidarność

Employment Law of March 1991

Provisions on dismissals, retraining, severance pay after 4 years of service; nominally gives unemployment benefits of 70% of pay for first 3 months of eligibility; 50% for next 6 months; 40% thereafter, but in fact limited to one-third of forecasted average pay (minimum wage)

Trade Union Act of 23 May 1991

No discrimination against union members; provision for multiple unionism (10 people); right to be heard by Sejm; responsible for health and safety laws; cannot divide income among members; role in social/housing funds; employer must provide information on wage, employment issues; premises and equipment for union activity; released time; compulsory mediation before strike; 14 days after dispute; can choose to go to social arbitration committee of court; chap. 4, art. 17.4: "When taking the strike decision, the union should ensure that demands are proportional to the losses connected with the strike"; majority vote if 50% vote; 5 days advance; 2-hour warning strike; participation is voluntary; employees retain rights during strike

C. Czechoslovakia

Strike Law/Act No. 83, December 1990

Amended labor code—Act on Association of Citizens abolished all restrictions on freedom of association; establishes unions who have to notify Ministry of Interior; illegal to give wages above those agreed by higher level—outlaws wage drift (sec. 4.2.c)

Collective Bargaining Act 1990 December, No. 2 of February 1991

Ministry of Labour and Welfare can extend contracts; Section 7; 1-year disputes—mediator required with shared costs; then arbitrator; 50% of labor force (not just those who vote) needed

Table 8.1   (continued)

C. Czechoslovakia

for strike; 3 days notice; essential services; no coercion; viewed as authorized leave of absence; mentions lockout

Employment Act of 4 December 1990/Effective as of February 1991
 Right to employment; employment services; unemployment benefits for job seeker, 60%, drops to 50% of net monthly income on basis of past job for those who work 1 year; 1 year max; 3-month advance notice on layoffs

Source: ILO (1990a, 1990b, 1991a, 1991b); "The Trade Union Act" (1991); *Rynek Pracy* (Ministry of Labour and Social Policy of Poland), no. 1 (January 1992).

wages in excess of those agreed on at a higher level, ruling out negotiated wage drift, and allows the Ministry of Labor to extend contracts to enterprises not covered in bargaining. These provisions set the stage for genuine centralized bargaining. The 1982 Polish workers' councils law gave considerable power to workers at the enterprise level, including the right to hire and fire managers, creating something akin to genuine worker-managed firms (Schaffer 1991). This has affected privatization (Federowicz and Levitas 1994), with the state forced to "buy off" the workers' councils by giving them seats on boards of directors and discounted shares as part of privatization. The Hungarian Communist regime gave unions veto rights over activities that contravene legal regulations or "offend socialist morality" (a power invoked in some 100–200 cases from 1980–87 [Hethy 1991, 65]), which has the potential of augmenting union power in the future along German workers' council lines, but which has had little effect on practices during the transition.

8.1.2   Rates of Unionization

While union-reported membership figures in the marketizing economies are undoubtedly exaggerations owing to the rivalry between old and new unions,[2] and while there are always problems interpreting membership data in different countries, the available information supports two observations.

First, union densities have fallen from the artificially high levels under communism. This is to be expected since Communist unions were more akin to government agencies than workers' organizations. Indeed, one could view densities under the Communist dictatorships as zero (save for Solidarność) and read the recent statistics as the growth of true unionism. The union-based figures in table 8.2 suggest densities that have plummeted to perhaps 35–50 percent in some of the countries as of late 1991. Membership is almost exclusively in state-owned enterprises, in their immediate successor enterprises, or among

---

2. The figures include pensioners, need not refer to dues-paying members in a given time period, and may include many inactive members.

Table 8.2   **Trade Unions in the Eastern Bloc (density or membership in parentheses)**

Takeover of Old Official Unions
  East Germany. Subsumed into West German DGB; many workers join IG Metall and other DGB unions

  Czechoslovakia (70% density). CS KOS formed in March 1991 as strike committees replace union; one-third of old officials reelected, but complete change at top; receive all property, but "cannot find its place in new market economy" (5,000,000)
  Confederation of Cultural Workers—intellectuals (300,000)

Dual Union Structure
  Poland (35%). OPZZ (4,500,000, including pensioners)—successor to Communists; opportunistic, allied with Communist party; branch structure; strong among professionals (associations); still controls all union properties
  Solidarnosc (2,000,000)—pro–market reform; related to government; elected to Sejm; regional structure with rivalries
  Some unaligned unions—miners and local strike groups

  Bulgaria (45%). Confederation of Independent Bulgarian Trade Unions (Association) (1,800,000)—reformed traditional unions
  Podkrepa (250,000)—pro–market reform; for big bang
  Edintstvo—early 1991 (250,000)

Multiple Unionism
  Hungary (60%) (September 1991). MSZOSZ—old official union SZOT declared independence 1988; dissolves 1990 (2,000,000)
  Breakaways from SZOT: Association for Intellectuals (90,000); Solidarity Association (150,000); Autonomous (350,000); Forum (750,000)
  Independent unions: LIGA—major opposition, aligned with Free Democrats; based on intellectuals (250,000); workers' councils—aligned with LIGA (45,000)

  Romania (65%). CNSLR (National Confederation of Free Trade Unions)—successor to Communists (2,500,000)
  Breakaways from old Communist: Aliate (1,000,000); Cartel-Alpha (1,300,000); Neafiliate (1,100,000); Hercules (300,000); Conosenerz (100,000)
  Independent unions: FRATIA—drivers; oil; teachers; scientists (500,000)

  Russia (100%?). Independent unions: miners union; air traffic controllers; pilots federation; SUTSPROF—largely intellectuals' unions; Confederation of Labor—social and political movement; strike committees
  Successor unions: GCTU—1989 declares independence; Russian branch becomes Federation of Independent Unions of Russia (FNPR); United Front of Working People—conservative union groups; Workers Unions in Moscow

Source: Hungary: *HUG,* 14 September 1991, 6; Reti (1991); Jones (1992); Gordon (1992b).

pensioners. For Hungary, household data from the International Social Survey Programme survey show a unionization rate on the order of 40–50 percent (Blanchflower and Freeman 1992), suggesting a greater fall in membership than indicated in the union-based numbers. For Poland, Federowicz and Levitas estimate that "in a typical firm 20–35% of workers joined Solidarity and 20–35% remained in OPZZ" (1994, 32), which suggests that, excluding pensioners, Solidarność may have similar membership to OPZZ.

The second and more surprising observation is the continued viability of the "successor unions" to the old official unions. Despite their checkered past, these unions remain the largest worker organizations. In table 8.2, I have categorized the trade union structure in the countries into three groups. The first is a "takeover pattern" in which the old unions were taken over by new leaders, as in Czechoslovakia, or where union members were absorbed into Western unions, as in East Germany. IG Metall initially intended to merge with the East German metalworkers' union but found that its East German pair was in fact a subordinate organization to the central Communist federation, with little real presence at workplaces. Instead, IG Metall enrolled 900,000 East German metalworkers (MacShane 1992). My second category is one of "dual union structures" where the successor unions compete with sizable free union confederations. It is found in Poland, Bulgaria, Albania, and Slovenia. My third grouping is one of multiple unionism, in which democratization has brought with it not only new independent unions but also breakaways from the old official confederation. Hungary and Romania are the prime examples, although Russia may also fall into this case, as successors to the old unions fragment.

Why, given freedom of association and the existence of new independent alternatives, have workers not "tossed out the scoundrels" or switched en masse to the newly formed democratic unions? Why have successor unions remained part of the new economic reality? Three factors appear to account for the persistence of the successor unions: the resources of incumbency; the weakness of new unions; and the ambivalence of the new governments toward reforming labor relations.

With respect to *incumbency*, the successor unions own substantial property—vacation and holiday facilities, buildings, newspapers, and so on— amassed under the Communist dictatorship; in many cases they continue to manage social fund expenditures in enterprises. They have experienced representatives in workplaces and large full-time staffs to communicate and organize activities. In Hungary, the successor unions often maintain close ties with management (managers were members of the union until 1990), which discourages the formation of rivals. The monthly *LIGA News,* put out by the new independent union movement from its offices in Budapest, reports cases of firings for new union activity in every edition. In Poland, the local leadership of OPZZ is in many cases made up of management.

The continued control by successor unions of assets obtained by taxing all workers is a major bone of contention. In Poland, OPZZ used financial chicanery to minimize the possibility that resources seized during martial law from Solidarność will be returned to that organization. In Hungary, the state enacted laws in July 1991 to prevent MSZOZ from dispersing union assets in ways that would allow the old Communist bureaucracy to maintain control of them. The 1992 meeting of independent unions in Gdansk made redistribution of trade union property and assets of the former Communist unions one of its three main declarations.

Incumbency advantages notwithstanding, had successor unions remained transmission belts of the state, their credibility among workers would have been zilch, and they would probably have collapsed. But, save in Czechoslovakia and East Germany, the official unions distanced themselves from the state in the closing days of Communist rule, if not earlier, as their leadership and the Communist party recognized that some autonomy was necessary for their operation. In Poland, OPZZ took a relatively independent stance after martial law, and many Poles came to view it as a genuine union rather than part of Communist repression. The Solidarność leadership has very negative views of its rival, but at lower levels OPZZ and Solidarność unionists often cooperate on workers' councils or in other labor activity (Dabrowski, Federowicz, and Levitas 1992). In Hungary, the old official unions protected workers at some workplaces and represented their interests in various forums (Noti 1987). "On several occasions branch unions were able to achieve far higher wage increases than originally planned by the government" (Kollo 1988, 27), often with the support of ministers whose incentive was to meet target outputs rather than to fight wage increases. In Russia, the official union declared itself independent of the Communist state in 1989 and led protests against the price increases of Yeltsin's reforms; as of this writing, it exists in the form of a federation of "independent" Russian unions.

There is often a sharp division between the position of local unions and the successor union central federation. Reformers may run some locals, while the central union bureaucracy is dominated by traditional Communist types; or, as in Bulgaria, reformers may control the central federation, while older-style officials remain ensconced in lower-level union positions. Opportunistic or amoral the leaders of the old unions may be, but, if they can run effective unions in the new environment, their organizations are likely to remain significant players on the labor scene.

On the other side, the *new unions* have weaknesses that limit their growth. Except for Solidarność, they are fledgling organizations with little financial resources and tiny professional staffs. LIGA, for instance, was formed in January 1990 with fourteen affiliates and 30,000 members. In the fall of 1991, it had just eight full-time staffers. Most of the new unions were initiated by medical, scientific, or artistic personnel (LIGA was founded by sociologists) and are dominated by intellectuals who may have difficulty relating to blue-collar workers. This contrasts with Germany after World War II, where experienced union leaders from the pretotalitarian period emerged to lead successor organizations to those banned under the Nazis. Solidarność, which has a longer organizational history, has a different problem: to transform itself from a national social movement with a regional structure (whose former head is president of the country) to a genuine trade union. Still, these unions often have considerable prestige in their countries and an influence that exceeds membership. In Russia, experts view their influence as being similar to that of the nominally much larger successor unions (Gordon 1992b).

The most serious problem the new unions face is developing an agenda and a message to attract workers in a period of massive economic restructuring. Solidarność and LIGA are liberal pro-market organizations that forthrightly recognize the costs of transition. Despite the potential for increasing union power, LIGA opposed eliminating taxes on wage increases in Hungary for fear it would create inflationary wage pressures (*LIGA News*, 1991, no. 2); Solidarność, by contrast, has opposed Poland's taxes on wage increases (*Solidarność News*, June 1991). Solidarność's link to the Walesa government has meant that some workers feel that they may be better represented by OPZZ, which has the option for demagoguery. Honesty about a depressing economic reality during transition is not a rallying cry for attracting workers to pro-reform unions.

Finally, governments have been slow to challenge the legitimacy of the old official unions. As of this writing, only Hungary has tried to reduce the successor unions' advantage of incumbency and to level the playing field for new unions. In July 1991, it passed legislation that required workers to sign a written declaration permitting dues checkoff, which had been automatically deducted and sent to the old official unions under legislation that the Communists introduced in 1988 to buttress those organizations. Given a choice between no union and a union that could affect their lives at workplaces, many workers chose to support MSZOZ, giving them a legitimacy they had lacked. A second law enacted in July 1991 set up an October 1992 election to divide the assets of all unions in proportion to their support among workers. The independent unions did reasonably well in this election.

Why have the new governments not tried to disestablish the traditional unions? One reason is to avoid state interference with union activity that would be mindful of Communist interventions. Another is that the governments' first concern is macrostabilization and privatization. Labor relations is a backburner issue, which governments would prefer to avoid for fear of precipitating a mare's nest of union rivalry and instability. Finally, some officials may prefer dealing with old unions with a history of subservience to the state and questionable legitimacy than with new representative bodies that could aggressively oppose stabilization programs. Some undoubtedly hope that unions will wither away. Given the need to enlist worker support for reforms and the potential contribution of unions to marketization, this is a shortsighted and risky strategy (see sec. 8.3 below).

8.1.3   Wage-Setting Institutions and Tripartite Organizations

Whereas marketizing economies have moved rapidly to market pricing of goods, they have maintained control of wages in the state-owned sector by levying high taxes on wage increases above a given level and by imposing minimum wage laws. In both areas, their policies mimic those of their Communist predecessor regimes. Reform Communist governments typically taxed changes in wages funds (= employment × wage) to discourage enterprises from raising wages. The policy innovation of the new regimes is to tax changes in average wages above a norm rate of increase dependent on expected inflation. The rules for taxing wage increases and for allowing catch-up when inflation exceeds expectations differ across the countries, as summarized in table 8.3, part A. In Hungary, enterprises with rapid increases in value added are allowed greater increases in wages before being taxed; in Czechoslovakia, the Ministry of Labor claims that taxes will be applied to wages funds (Riveros 1991, 11). Hungary and Czechoslovakia exclude from the taxes small state-owned enterprises, and all three countries exclude foreign-owned or private firms. Since large state enterprises employ the bulk of the work force, the taxation of wage increases in the state sector should determine the economy-wide level of increases from which private enterprises can be expected to deviate only moderately.[3]

The taxes on wage increases have not, however, controlled wage inflation. In Poland, wage increases fell short of the norms in the first half of 1990 and then rose to make up the deficit by the end of the year, when hundreds of enterprises paid the *popyvek* tax for increasing wages faster than the norm. In 1991, average wages exceeded the wage norm by a considerable margin (Schaffer 1992, 24), making the *popyvek* a major contributor to state budget revenue. In Hungary, the norm rate of increase in wages for 1990 was 14 percent (positing an inflation rate of 18 percent), whereas wages rose by 24 percent with an inflation rate of 29 percent. In Czechoslovakia, wages increased by less than the permitted rate in the first quarter of 1991 (Nesporova 1991, 18). That wage increases did not follow the tax-based norms does not, of course, mean that the policy was ineffective, but it does show that factors beyond the tax-based policy also affect wages.[4] In Poland, the limited increases in the first half of 1990 are ascribed to fears that wage increases might cause bankruptcies and loss of jobs, while the ensuing wage increases in the latter half of the year are attributed to a preelection weakening of government budget constraints.[5] Schaffer (1992) links the slackening of wage pressures in Poland in 1991 to the collapse of enterprise profits and the sharp drop in output (to which I would add rising unemployment) rather than to the *popyvek* per se.

3. At General Electric's Tungsram operation in Budapest, in the fall of 1991 wages were just 13 percent above those in the overall economy. The economy-wide minimum was Ft 7,000; the minimum at Tungsram was Ft 7,900; pay averaged Ft 14,000 in the economy and Ft 15,800 at Tungsram.

4. Absent a clear counterfactual, it is not easy to tell the effect of an incomes policy on wage setting. A spike in wage increases at the point where the tax "kicks in" may reflect its use as a norm for wage setting rather than the effect of the tax per se, perhaps causing enterprises that would have given smaller increases to give the norm increase. Increases greater than the norm may still be less than they would otherwise have been.

5. Calvo and Coricelli argue that the increase in wages was because firms realized that all enterprises were facing similar financial problems and thus that "policy-makers should try to devise ways to make the wage targets stick other than through sustained tight credit policy" (1992, 47).

What might happen if the taxes were eliminated and market and collective bargaining forces allowed free sway in wage determination in state enterprises? High unemployment in all three countries, continued central government influence on enterprise behavior, and harder budget constraints than in the past suggest that, even absent taxes on wage increases, wage inflation will be moderate. In January 1992, Hungary eliminated the tax on wage increases, providing a good test of this argument. With workers' councils having great power at many plants, Poland presumably would risk the most wage inflation by removing its tax, although the danger of job loss, uncertainty about future employment opportunities, and limited profits should still deter excessive wage increases. In 1992, it too began to consider elimination of the tax on wage increases. My assessment is that elimination will not produce massive wage-push inflation. If workers think that wage restraint will give their enterprise a possible future in a market economy, they should be relatively moderate in their wage demands, given poor outside economic opportunities. Only in enterprises where workers see no future will they be tempted to engage in endgame bargaining by putting all available funds into wages.

All three countries buttress the lower part of the wage distribution through minimum wage legislation. As can be seen in table 8.3, part B, the minimum is sufficiently high in Czechoslovakia and Hungary to have some "bite" on employment but is quite modest relative to average wages in Poland. The minimum in Czechoslovakia is indexed to rise with inflation greater than 5 percent (Riveros 1991, 12), but this appears not to have been implemented (Nesporova 1991, 18). The 1991 increase in the minimum raised the wages of 22 percent of the Hungarian work force (Lado, Szalai, and Sziraczki 1991, 23).

Hungary and Czechoslovakia have established tripartite consultative organizations consisting of union confederations, employer federations, and the government to discuss wage and related labor issues (table 9.3C), including the level of the minimum and taxation of wage increases. Such forums existed toward the end of the Communist era when official unions met regularly with government and management of the state-owned enterprises. In Hungary, the new National Conciliation Council brings together representatives of seven union confederations (including the successors to the old official unions), employer groups, and government officials. In Czechoslovakia, labor is represented on the tripartite forum by the leadership of the successor unions. As state-owned enterprises dominate the employers' federations and decision-making power resides with the government, the forums should not be confused with West European "social partners" negotiations. Some observers, including members of the forums, dismiss them as pro forma. In Czechoslovakia, the unions argued for higher minimum wages at tripartite meetings, but the government refused their demands. The 1991 General Agreement set measures to regulate the growth of wages, inflation adjustments, and the minimum desired by the government. In Hungary, employers and unions pushed successfully for elimination of the tax on excess wage increases earlier than the government

Table 8.3   **Wage Taxes and Minimum and Average Wages**

A. Tax-Based Incomes Policies

Poland. Popyvek tax based on wage bill in 1990, then on wages per worker. Penal tax of 500% of wage increase beyond norm, where the norm is based on expected change in inflation of retail prices with a modest indexation coefficient. The difference between expected inflation and actual is used to adjust the norm increase in later months. When enterprises give increases below the norm in a given period, moreover, they can give larger increases without being taxed in the future. Private firms are excluded from the tax.

Hungary. In 1990, 18% increase in wages were tax free; a tax of 43% is applied to wage increases between 18% and 28%; wage increases above 28% lead to a tax on the entire increment, producing a very steep rising price of wage increases just beyond 38%, which then falls as the increases continue since the big extra tax is the addition of the tax on the increment. There are exceptions for companies whose value added grows at twice the growth of the wage fund; small companies with a wage bill under Ft 20 million; joint ventures where foreigners own 20% or Ft 5 million of the capital.

Czechoslovakia. On 1 January 1990, enterprises were given freedom to set wages, but taxes on increases according to following schedule: no tax for increases 3% above the agreed norm; tax of Kčs 2.00 per korona for increases 3%–5% above the norm; and tax of Kčs 7.5 for increases more than 5% above the norm. At roughly average wages this implies that wage increases 3%–5% higher than the norm plus the 3% allowable extra increase will cost the firm twice the increase while increases over 5% above the norm (plus the 3% allowable extra increase) will cost 7.5 times the increase.[a] Does not cover firms with fewer than 25 workers or private-sector firms

B. Minimum Wage Regulations

Poland		
Minimum wage (Zl)	642,000	
Average wage (Zl)	1,800,000	
Ratio		.36
Hungary		
Minimum wage (Ft)	7,000	
Average wage (Ft)	11,000	
Ratio		.64
% at minimum		.22
Czechoslovakia		
Minimum wage (Kčs)	2,000	
Average wage	3,300	
Ratio		.60
% at minimum		.20

C. Tripartite Forums

Hungary: 1980s, Communist union and state/Party bargain behind closed doors; also establish Labour and Wages Council referred to in 1984 ILO report

1988, open bargaining with SZOT/management with National Council for the Reconciliation of Interests

1990, new government with set of unions under National Conciliation Council—"organ of competence to address issues" (Hethy 1991, 37); solved taxi drivers' strike; push for local-level wage settlements; ending tax on wage increases

(*continued*)

Table 8.3   (continued)

C. Tripartite Forums

Czechoslovakia. 1989, state sets up Council of Economic and Social Consensus
October 1990; Council for Economic and Social Agreement to reach general agreements on
wages above minimum in law January 1991; 20 employers' confederations deal with government
through Coordinating Council of Employers; council has 7 from unions, government, employers;
to recommend labor market policy and resolve disagreements.
    January 1991, agreement on wage increase far below inflation, sets minimum wages

Bulgaria. April 1990, National Council for Coordination of Interests
January 1991, signed agreement

Poland. 1989, establishes Confederation of Polish Employers; employer organization
dominated by public-sector employers; Polish Employers' Confederation—500,000 private
enterprises supposedly are members, but they employ just 10% of workers: 3,000 public but
90%; limited tripartite because state agency is one of two parties and because Solidarność and
OPZZ are not friendly.

Source: Malinowski (1991) Góra et al. (1991), and Nesperova (1991).
[a]For example, should an employer wish to raise salaries 10% from Kčs 3,000 to Kčs 3,300, the
cost to the employer would be Kčs 90 (or Kčs 390 total). A further 5% increase to Kčs 3540 would
cost the employer an additional Kčs 300 (or Kčs 690 total). And a further 5% increase to Kčs
3690 would cost the employer Kčs 1,125 (or Kčs 1,815 total), a cost so high that the raise is
essentially confiscatory.

desired. The Conciliation Council also played a role in ending the taxi drivers' strike in 1990. The animus between Solidarność and OPZZ has kept Poland from using such tripartite bodies to any extent, although the unions lobby in the Sejm in defense of their interests: "Parliament is the only place where NSZZ Solidarność can effectively defend workers' interests as long as the state remains the main employer" (*Solidarność News,* September 1991). Many of the other marketizing economies have also instituted tripartite forums for discussion of labor market issues. Absent federations of private employers and unionization of private employers, however, these forums are best viewed as places for public-sector workers' unions to negotiate with the state.

8.2   What's Happening in the Labor Market?

Measuring labor outcomes in the marketizing economies is difficult. Employment and wage statistics refer largely to the state-owned sector. Information is sparse on the sizable and growing shadow economies. Unemployment figures refer to people who apply for benefits rather than to respondents to a labor force survey. Price indices do not reflect shortages or the quality of goods. This said, the available data suggest substantial changes in economic behavior in the transition:

    1. State-owned firms have reduced employment, largely through attrition

and reduced hiring. Traditional job vacancies have disappeared, replaced by joblessness that can bankrupt incipient unemployment benefit systems.

2. Real earnings and living standards have fallen and the wage structure widened in Hungary and Poland but not in Czechoslovakia. Still, opinion poll data show that the costs of transition had not seriously taxed the population as of late 1991.

8.2.1   Employment and Vacancies

Employment in the socialist sector (corrected where possible for changes in form of employment as some enterprises became private) fell sharply in the initial phase of transition in all three countries. In Poland, socialized-sector employment fell by 15 percent from the first quarter of 1988 to the first quarter of 1991. In Czechoslovakia, employment dropped by 2.5 percent between 1989 and 1990, with the decline accelerating toward the end of the year (fourth-quarter 1990 employment was 5 percent less than fourth-quarter employment a year earlier) (Nesporova 1991, 5). In Hungary, employment fell by 23 percent from the first quarter of 1989 to the first quarter of 1991. By contrast, in each country, private-sector employment rose. In Poland, the share of the private sector in nonagricultural employment increased from 16 to 21 percent between 1989 and 1990 (Berg and Sachs 1992, table 14); in Hungary, it grew from 5 percent in 1983 to 11 percent in January 1990 (Lado, Szalai, and Sziraczki 1991, 11); in Czechoslovakia, it rose from 3 percent in 1990 to perhaps 7 percent in 1991 (Nesperova 1991, 6). As in the West, most of the fall in employment was accomplished through attrition. In Hungary, "enterprise managers systematically targeted elderly employees and working pensioners" (Lado, Szalai, and Sziraczki 1991, 9). In Poland, just 16 percent of the registered unemployed were involved in group layoffs (10 percent or more of the work force, or at least 100 persons, is laid off) in 1990. Information on hiring and separation rates in the state-owned sector in Poland shows that the drop in hiring was more important than rising separations in the reduction in employment of full-time employees (the figures in the following table are given in thousands):

	1986	1987	1988	1989	1990	% Change, 1987–90
Hiring	2,375	2,255	1,960	1,908	1,453	−36
Separations	2,377	2,361	2,178	2,417	2,594	10

Because the official data classify as separations retail trade workers who shifted from cooperative to private employment when their enterprises privatized, the role of separations is in fact exaggerated in the data. Adjusting for the change in classifications suggests that there were 2,195,000 separations in

1990, a 7 percent decline since 1987, making the fall in hiring the sole cause of the 1987–90 reduction in employment.[6]

Consistent with this picture of changed state enterprise behavior, the vacancies that had characterized Communist economies plummeted while previously "nonexistent" unemployment rose. In Poland in 1986, there were over a quarter of a million vacancies; in 1991, there were just 40,000–50,000. In Hungary, there were over 75,000 vacancies in the second quarter of 1986; in early 1991, 13,000. The ratio of unemployment to vacancies rose almost exponentially. By mid-1991, the ratio of unemployment to vacancies was nearly six to one in Czechoslovakia, eleven to one in Hungary, and thirty-three to one in Poland.

8.2.2   Relative Wages

Given the narrow wage distributions under communism, marketization should widen wage structures. There is evidence of widening in state-owned manufacturing in Poland and Hungary but not in Czechoslovakia (table 8.4) and evidence of rising skill differentials along various dimensions in Hungary.

In Poland, the widening of the interindustry wage structure roughly coincided with the change in regime at the end of the 1980s and was accompanied by rising dispersion of wages across firms related to profitability. In 1989, wages were essentially unrelated to enterprise profitability, whereas, in 1990, wages were higher in the more profitable enterprises (Schaffer 1991, 43). While competitive theory suggests that profitability and wages should be uncorrelated in a well-functioning market, in fact profitability and wages go together in many Western countries, such as the United States.

In Hungary, the interindustry coefficient of variation rose from .106 in 1981 to .162 in 1987, then jumped to .227 in 1990. The ratio of nonmanual to manual earnings rose 13 percentage points from 1978 to 1987; the earnings of small-scale private-sector producers went from 20 percent above national income per capita in 1982 to 55 percent above in 1987 (ILO 1990c, table 30); and income from work in the private sector rose from 6.5 percent of net income in 1980 to 14 percent in 1990 (Lado, Szalai, and Sziraczki 1991, 60). There is also evidence of sizable increases in the pay of managers relative to other workers in state-owned firms: between 1986 and 1990, the ratio of managers' pay to physical workers' pay jumped from 1.9 to 3.0 in the food industry, from 1.6 to 2.4 in textiles, and from 2.3 to 2.7 in engineering (Vanyai and Viszt 1992, table 6). In addition, earnings were higher in small than in large companies[7] and in private than in state-owned companies (Lado, Szalai, and Sziraczki 1990, 64–65). From 1989 to 1991, over two-thirds of managers, professionals, and skilled workers had increases in real earnings compared to half the less

---

6. The adjusted figures remove the increase in private-sector retail trade employment from reported separations. These data were provided by Mark Schaffer from the Polish *Statistical Yearbook.*

7. This is contrary to the results in virtually all other countries and may reflect the noneconomic size of the large state enterprises.

Table 8.4   Coefficients of Variation in the Interindustry Wage Structure: Manufacturing in the Socialized Sector, 1981–90

	1981	1984	1987	1988	1989	1990
Hungary	10.6	14.2	16.2	20.5	21.6	22.7
Poland	12.0	11.4	11.7	11.0	16.0	
Poland B					21.8	25.1
Czechoslovakia	12.0	12.3	12.2	11.9	11.4	

Source: All data based on 27 industries given in ILO *Yearbook of Labour Statistics* except for Poland B, where the data cover 23 industries from *Rocznik Statystyczny.* Hungarian wage figures prior to 1988 are gross earnings before income-tax deductions, whereas those after are net of income-tax payments. Industries are three-digit SIC codes.

skilled workers (Ferge 1991a, 12). The ratio of earnings between the top and the bottom decile in Hungary jumped from 5.0 to 6.0 largely "because the rich are getting significantly richer" (Ferge 1991a, 11). The college–high school differential in Hungary in 1986 was 1.53 compared to 1.29 in Czechoslovakia (1988) and 1.16 in Poland (1988).

In Czechoslovakia, the data show no rise in wage differentials by industry, but public opinion seems quite favorable toward increased inequality. A 1990 opinion poll reports that a majority answered "definitely yes" to the question whether differences in wages should be higher while 42 percent answered that it is right that really competent people should have lots of money, be it even millions (Stem Survey Organization, Prague, December 1990).

8.2.3   Unemployment

Contraction of the state-owned sector is an important step toward a market economy based on private ownership. If workers displaced from state jobs and new entrants to the job market quickly found employment in the growing private sector, we would proclaim the transition a roaring success. Data on private-sector employment and on unemployment show that this has not been the case. The private sector has not grown enough to absorb all the jobless, with resultant sizable rates of reported unemployment by 1991 and forecasts of even larger rates to come. By the end of 1991, unemployment approached 12 percent in Poland and 7 percent in Czechoslovakia and Hungary (Boeri and Keese 1992, chart 3). As unemployment refers to persons who apply for benefits, however, there is ambiguity about the magnitude and cost of joblessness. Some of the unemployed hold jobs in the shadow economy or are secondary earners in families where others are employed. Others are located in one-factory areas with little opportunity for irregular jobs. The experience of West European countries such as Spain in the 1980s makes it clear that rates of unemployment have very different implications for society depending on who is jobless, the social benefits paid the unemployed, and the ability of families to provide a private safety net, especially for the young. Through 1991, many East Europeans believed that many of the unemployed are working or not suffering greatly. In the fall of 1991, a Polish opinion survey asked, "If government spending must be reduced, which should be cut first?" and found that 40 percent were for reducing unemployment benefits, compared to 28 percent for reducing defense, 6 percent for reducing pensions, and 1 percent for reducing health spending (*Gaxeta Wyborcza, 29 October* 1991, cited in Malinowski 1991).[8] Polls in Czechoslovakia support the proposition that "unnecessary jobs should be reduced, even at the price of unemployment."[9] The vast majority of Poles surveyed viewed unemployment as too high, but 29 percent regarded it as a normal part of the market; 38 percent said that it should be fought, but not at any cost, compared to 29 percent who viewed it as impermissible. In Hungary, where one-third or so of work occurs in the shadow economy (Lado, Szalai, Sziraczki 1991, 18), a key issue is whether the unemployed obtain work there or whether they lose shadow economy opportunities that are associated with regular jobs because their regular job puts them into contact with potential shadow economy employers or clients.

8.2.4   Real Earnings and Living Standards

Measures of real earnings based on official wage and price statistics in the marketizing economies are likely to overstate income losses during the transition. Price indices fail to adjust for the shortages of goods under communism, the queuing for goods that reached shops, and the poor quality of goods. Wage figures fail to take account of earnings from the second or shadow economy. In Hungary, three-quarters of families had additional income from the second economy, and more than one-third of working time was allotted to jobs in that sector. According to Lado, Szalai, and Sziraczki, "The capacity of the second economy turned out to be sufficient to preserve previous standards of living even amid the worsening conditions of the 1980s" (1991, 6). In Poland, measured real wages in the final days of the Communist regime rose sharply, contrary to actual changes in living standards. During transition, GNP may have been as much as 10–15 percent higher on inclusion of second economy output. Still, no one would argue that the transition has been "smooth sailing" on the income front. Ferge (1991a) reports that the proportion of the Hungarians regarding themselves as poor or having difficulty managing their household budget rose markedly between 1987 and 1990. Berg and Sachs (1992) estimate that consumption in Poland fell by 7 percent during the initial phase of transition. Projections suggest continued economic troubles for some time in all three countries, which raises the question as to what form of labor relations

8. The responses are not due to the particular wording of the question. Asked which form of spending should be increased, 3 percent replied unemployment benefits, 3 percent defense, 17 percent health, and 21 percent pensions.

9. These polls are for June and December 1991, as reported by the Institute of Sociology of the Czech Academy of Sciences. The sociologist Siklova warned that "people [have] the feeling that the state and old civil servants are responsible for a citizen's having or not having a job [whereas] . . . unemployment is first of all evidence of their own incapacity" (1991, 2).

system might serve them best during the costly transition, to which I turn next.[10]

8.3   Designing a Labor Relations System for the Transition

In a fully developed capitalist economy, a labor relations system has three functions: to determine wages and working conditions through market forces or collective bargaining; to give workers a "voice" in the internal decision making of enterprises; and to provide a countervailing force to capital interests in the political system. The tasks for labor relations during the transition from a Communist to a market-driven economy are more complex and difficult. Labor institutions must remove the legacies of Communist labor relations described in section 8.1 (narrow wage distributions, reliance on the enterprise for commodities, low productivity and effort, politically chosen management, and moribund trade unions) and help create capitalist markets.[11] At the same time, those institutions must induce workers to accept the short-term costs of transition and guarantee that they share in future benefits. Trade unions also should protect members against management or government policies that may place excessive burdens on workers during transition.

The ability of labor institutions, particularly unions, to promote market reforms and convince workers to accept transitional costs while protecting them from the excesses of incipient capitalism and dying state firms will have a profound effect on the success of transition programs. In this section, I develop a general framework for analyzing how different labor arrangements might best carry out these important functions. My analysis is broad rather than specific, as economics does not have sufficiently compelling theory or empirical knowledge to answer questions about the institutional design of advanced capitalist economies,[12] much less of economies in transition. To keep from being overly abstract, I use the model to comment on the labor relations developments described in sections 8.1 and 8.2.

8.3.1   Costs of Transition and Worker Attitudes

Consider an economy that moves from a command system with a compressed wage distribution to a market-driven system with greater wage inequality. For simplicity, assume that, prior to transition, all workers earn a

---

10. Why the transition has been so costly in terms of falling output is an interesting question that goes beyond the scope of this study.

11. The Russian miners' union has stated, "We need to struggle for real businessmen to appear in our economy. And then or rather simultaneously to fight with these businessmen for real wages and worthy labour conditions" (cited in Gordon 1992b, 4). This parallels statements by Solidarnosc and LIGA.

12. Assessing the future of labor relations in marketizing economies would be much easier if there were a single recognized "best" set of labor institutions associated with market economies. But advanced OECD countries exhibit a wide spectrum of labor arrangements, which produce differing macroeconomic outcomes over time, all of which are basically "workable."

numeraire 0 and are employed by the state. A minority benefit immediately from the change in regimes (entrepreneurs, employees in private enterprises, the highly skilled). These "winners" obtain $W > 0$ after the reforms. The majority (losers) lose L through falling real wages or unemployment. Think of them as state employees, workers in heavy industry, the unskilled. Eventually, they will benefit from the change in regimes by moving into the winning group, but in the initial phase of transition their living standards fall. If p is the probability that a worker moves from the losing to the winning group at every time period and winning is an absorbing Markov state, the expected value of a worker's wage income during the first year of the reform is

(1) $pW - (1 - p)L.$

Similarly, the value of a worker's wage income in the second year is

(2) $[p + p(1 - p)]W - L(1 - p)^2,$

where $p(1 - p)$ is the proportion of first-period losers who moved to the winning group in the second period and $(1 - p)^2$ is the proportion who remain in the losing group.

The expected value of a worker's income in year t is

(3) $\left[p \sum_{i=0}^{t-1} (1 - p)^i \right] W - L(1 - p)^t = W - (W + L)(1 - p)^t.$

As t grows, an increasing proportion of workers are in the winning group so that the workers' annual (nondiscounted) expected income approaches W.

The continuous-time analogue of this expression from year 0 to t is

(3′) $W - (W + L)(\exp - pt).$

Since transition is costly, (3) is negative in early periods: at $t = 0$, expression (3) is $-L$. As time proceeds, however, more people become winners, and the gain approaches W. With interest rate r, the present value of the regime change is

(4) $W \int_0^t (\exp - rt) - (W + L) \int_0^t (\exp - rt - pt) =$

           $(pW - rL)/r(r + p),$

which must be positive for the change in regimes to be worthwhile. Here I assume infinite life solely for convenience and use different values of r to allow for the effects of differing years of work on (4). My assumption that all workers end in the winning group with wage W is also for convenience; allowing for differences in productivity among workers need not affect the argument.

Present-value formula (4) provides a useful framework for considering the benefits and costs of the new economic program. Since older workers have relatively few years to reap the benefits of the change, r is high for them. They will benefit less from reforms and thus be more opposed to the change than younger workers. This is, I believe, in accord with the observation that younger workers are more favorably inclined toward market reforms in Eastern Europe than older workers. More interesting, W and L enter (4) in such a way that even workers who initially lose from the transition may prefer more to lesser inequality of earnings ($W - L$). Losers will prefer a program that raises W by one unit to one that reduces the loss L by one unit whenever $p > r$. Why? Because they foresee high chances of becoming a winner and benefiting more from high W than from lower L. This is a variant of Hirschman's (1973) "tunnel effect," according to which people left behind in the early phase of a growth spurt tolerate their falling relative position if they believe that increases for others are a signal that growth will spill over to them. The analogy is with drivers in a stalled lane in a tunnel, who are happy when another lane moves because they think this means their lane will move soon also.

Most important, the model generates a distinct time pattern of changing support for reforms in a *fixed* population. Initially, everyone supports the transition because it has positive expected value. In period 1, there are p winners and $1 - p$ losers. The winners are happy with the program, but the expected benefits to losers fall owing to the reduced years for reaping benefits. In period 2, there are $p + p(1 - p)$ winners and $(1 - p)^2$ losers, whose benefits fall further. At some period T, the present value becomes negative for losers, who turn against the new regime, potentially producing massive opposition. Since p percent of the losers gain from the reforms in T (and succeeding years), however, overall support in the population bottoms out and rises thereafter. The result is a U-shaped "support curve" in which support falls (given some heterogeneity, the fall will be gradual) as winners and losers sort themselves out during transition, then rises as the benefits of the market economy reach the entire population (see fig. 8.1). The key period for the transition is at the bottom point of the support curve. If 50 percent or more turn against the program then, a democratic government might back away from a valid transition program—although, if it "stayed the course," support would rise.

The analysis is more complex when we allow for a population that changes, as new cohorts enter and older cohorts leave the work force. By assumption, new entrants expect to gain from reforms and thus add additional supporters of reforms to the group. As all the new entrants will be pro-reform while some older retiring workers will be against reform, there will be an upward tilt to the support curve. Thus, there are two forces at work affecting the aggregate proportion supporting reforms: the U-shaped curve of support for existing workers and the upward tilt due to the influx of new workers. If the vast majority of workers are in the group experiencing the U-shaped decline, the aggregate relation will still evince a U shape. But, if the groups are more evenly balanced, there may be no U shape in the aggregate.[13]

---

13. This can be seen in a three-period overlapping-generations model, in which the three cohorts are indexed by i, where $i = 1$ is the oldest cohort, $i = 2$ is the next oldest, and so on. The probabil-

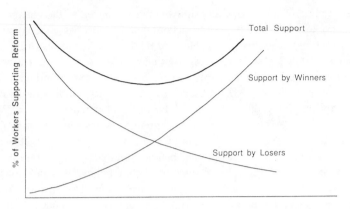

Fig. 8.1   Changes in the proportion of support for reforms

It is unlikely, however, that the costs of transition fall evenly on all cohorts. As pensioners seem to be major losers in marketizing economies, it is possible that even workers in the winning group may, on leaving the work force, oppose continued or further reforms if they see them as endangering payment of social security or pensions. If, moreover, costs of transition are concentrated among the young, as may also be the case, their attitudes toward reforms may not be accurately captured by the simple assumption that they uniformly favor reforms. All of this implies that additional information and analysis is needed to lay out the situations in which the U-shaped pattern that follows simply for a single cohort is also found in the aggregate.

8.3.2   Updating Expectations

The danger that a population will erroneously reject reforms during the transition process grows when we consider the way in which people may form

---

ity of getting into the winning group is .3 in each period, with the result that every cohort has a U-shaped support curve, with each new cohort supporting the program at rates of 100, 30, and 51 percent over time. That is, new cohorts will express 100 percent support in period 1 (since the present value of expected gains is positive), 30 percent support in period 2, and 51 percent support in period 3. But in period 1 there are two older cohorts. One possible assumption about them is that they have the same expectations as the youngest cohort. Then the following table shows the pattern of support over time:

	Cohort 1	Cohort 2	Cohort 3	Cohort 4	Cohort 5
Period 1	.30	.30	1.00		
Period 2		.51	.30	1.00	
Period 3			.51	.30	1.00
Period 4				.51	.30
Period 5					.51

expectations about their chances of benefiting from reforms. Assume a population consisting of two groups: those with a high probability of being in the winning group (p_h), for whom the expected return from the program is positive, and a smaller group with a low probability (p_l), for whom the return is negative. Initially, each group knows that the population is so divided, and each has the proper expectation of its chance of gaining in the reforms.[14] But individuals revise their expectations on the basis of their personal experience. Then, as time proceeds, losers from the high-p group may mistake bad luck for being a low-p person and erroneously choose to oppose the program. They will form erroneous expectations by updating their experiences. For instance, they might have the correct expectation of success of, say, $p = .25$ in period 1 but revise this expectation down to, say, .20 in period 2, to .16 in period 3, and then erroneously oppose the program.[15] This can readily produce a U-shaped support curve, as in figure 8.1, as support falls among high-p losers. The problem is that whenever losers weigh their *own* experiences more heavily than those of others with their same characteristics, they will understate their p and undervalue the program.

Finally, there is yet another way in which a population that forms expectations of gaining from reforms in a highly plausible and reasonable way can erroneously reject a beneficial reform program during a transitional period. Assume a world with a continuous distribution of unknown p's. Again, initially individuals have correct priors about their chances of advancing, but they update their expectations in each period on the basis of the proportion of the population that moves into the winning group (as opposed to their personal experience). Note that, in this case, more high-p than low-p people will move into the winning group in the first period with the result that the losing group will consist disproportionately of people with lower p's. High-p losers will erroneously reduce their expectations of gaining from reforms over time, as they adjust their p's toward the (falling) average. The result is once again an "erroneous" increase in the proportion of people opposing reforms among those who have not yet made the transit into the winning group.

These considerations highlight the importance of convincing losers in a transition to a market economy that in fact they will ultimately gain from reforms. In a world with different types of labor, losers may oppose reform unless they

---

If the cohorts are of equal size, 53 percent of the total population will support the program in period 1, 60 percent in period 2, and 60 percent thereafter. Only if cohort 3 makes up the largest share of the population will the aggregate support curve be U shaped.

14. An alternative model would be to assume that people do not know whether they are in the high- or low-probability group but have an accurate idea of the distribution of types. As losers from the high-probability group update their probability of winning on the basis of their experience, they will become increasingly confident that they are in the low-probability group. David Laibson has examined this model in a comment on this paper and shows that it too can give a U-shaped support curve (see Laibson 1992).

15. This follows if the individual updates her prior by the simple relation that $p_t = 1/(4 + t)$, where t is the number of periods in which she has failed to move into the winning group.

see persons like themselves benefiting from transition: blue-collar workers will expect gains only if they see blue-collar workers with whom they identify gaining, and so on. This suggests that workers in the private (winning) sector as well as in the public (losing) sector be in the same union organization. Unions limited to losing groups in the public sector, as in the marketizing economies, can endanger reforms. For a similar reason, support for reform will be strengthened if profitable enterprises are encouraged by policy or forced by collective bargaining to share economic rents with workers during the transition to a greater extent than they might otherwise do. Why? So that there will be clear examples of workers who benefit from the gains. This point has been recognized by pro-market unionists, who have noted that, "The union which wants to be actively involved in market-oriented reforms is facing a tough challenge. Persuading union members to adopt a different optical perspective—from wage demand to concerns about efficient production and market competition—will by no means be easy if the advantages of such a shift do not show up in the example of the most advanced enterprises" (*Solidarność News,* September 1991, 3).

The U-shaped curve of support has a further implication for the timing of government safety-net programs. It suggests that expenditures be concentrated in periods when support bottoms out rather than being spread over time (or, what may be worse, declining over time as the fiscal costs of interventions become clearer, as appears to be the case in Eastern Europe). With respect to specific interventions, even "bribes" or subsidies that keep alive unprofitable enterprises may enhance the reform process if they buy additional time for painful reforms or are easier to earmark for the crucial period when support is near its minimum level than other forms of social expenditures. Taxing winners and paying off losers is an obvious intervention to preserve support, but in East European marketizing economies many winners are in small private firms, in some cases in the shadow economy, which makes taxing them difficult.

8.3.3   Collective Action

Labor institutions can also affect the success of a transition program through the potential for collective action and social upheaval. Consider what might happen in a marketizing economy when support for reforms falls sharply along the U-shaped curve of figure 8.1. Many people have lost faith because they have been losers. Specific groups of workers—miners, workers in heavy industry—may see an opportunity for demanding substantial "gains" or special treatment for their sector that will seriously impair the transition strategy. If the government continues on course, the danger to reforms is the "hot spring" or "angry autumn" of mass protests, strikes, etc., about which many in marketizing economies worry, or the coups that have plagued Latin America. Such collective action can become a self-fulfilling prophecy of failure: if people had greater tolerance for the costs of transition, the program would work, but if losers are sufficiently aggrieved to protest, the program may fail. Alternatively, the government may decide to back away from its reform program. The danger that collective actions based on short-term costs could overturn or destroy a reform program argues for labor arrangements that make broad collective action difficult in the transition period and thus for policies that restrict union activity or powers in ways that would be undesirable in a fully functioning capitalist system.

A fragmented or divided union movement, of the type found in most marketizing economies, offers one institutional model for reducing the threat of collective action. In Poland, if OPZZ organizes protests against a transition program, Solidarność may sit on its hands, and vice versa. Or both unions may accept the logic of certain reforms, while informal groups of workers do not. But, lacking wide support, the informal groups will be unable to force changes in policy. Unions with a legacy of Communist leadership, like MSZOZ in Hungary, may be able to organize protests, but many citizens will distrust their activities. And so on. But fragmentation based in part on the persistence of successor unions is not without its problems. The leadership of successor unions could manipulate discontent in ways inimical to the reform program. A labor system that encourages enterprise-level unionism or democratically elected workers' councils and discourages wider union groupings might be a more desirable way to reduce the risk of mass collective action.

Finally, there are examples of suppression of free trade unions—Korea, Singapore, Taiwan, Franco's Spain, Pinochet's Chile—accompanied by economic growth to make a strategy of suppression attractive to some with a limited commitment to democratic rights. If a 1960s-1970s Korean-style authoritarian labor relations system and dictatorship could guarantee a 6–8 percent annual growth of real wages to Eastern Europe for two decades, many in the marketizing economies would readily sign on. But comparisons of the economic success of dictatorships (which invariably suppress unions) and democratic regimes in developing countries show that suppression is neither sufficient nor necessary for successful stabilization or economic growth (World Bank 1991, chap. 7). And who wants General X or Colonel Z running the show if he cannot guarantee growth? East European tolerance for such regimes after the failure of Communist dictatorships may be quite low.

8.3.4   Collective Voice and Labor Input into Transition

If reforming governments had reliable blueprints for the transition and acted solely in the "public interest," one could support a labor relations system based on weak institutions for the transition period. However, no one—not even economic experts—knows for certain the correct road to a market economy, and no government, however well intentioned, is immune to the aggrandizement of some groups at the expense of the rest of society. Even the best constructed stabilization and transition programs can, and do, go wrong. Inflation costs may be higher than expected. Unemployment and output losses may be bigger. Workers, pensioners, or children may suffer more than anticipated. The greater the uncertainty about the blueprint, and the more removed officials and experts are from the lives of the citizenry, the greater is the need for labor institutions to provide feedback about the real effects of programs and to pressure politicians to change the cost or benefit structure of those programs.

The most efficacious labor relations system for carrying out this voice/pressure function would be an all-encompassing union confederation with the resources to assess and criticize transitional programs and the incentive to internalize distortionary costs in favor of a broad national economic perspective. On the information side, such a union body would provide a reality check on government programs that may be sorely needed by technocrats and politicians attuned to the world financial community. Had Poland's advocates of rapid privatization developed plans with greater attention to workers' council power at local workplaces, the pace of privatization might have been much faster (Federowicz and Levitas 1994). A strong union movement would also provide workers who lose during transition with an institutional mechanism for carving out a share of gains in the future through "tripartite pacts" or centralized wage-setting arrangements. The inefficiency losses due to union monopoly power stressed by economists may be of second-order importance if that power promises labor a share of the future and thus "buys" support during the critical transition. Explicit profit sharing or distribution of stock to workers in firms undergoing privatization or of national bonds can also offer losers options to benefit from the future gains of reforms.

Centralized labor relations systems are not, however, easy to institute or maintain, as the decentralization of bargaining in Sweden shows. The labor movement must be strong and unified. It must have the credibility to vouch for reform programs to workers and the strength to win gains or transfers for losing members, particularly those who may suffer for long periods of time. Czechoslovakia and Hungary have tripartite councils designed in part to centralize labor relations, but the union movements in both countries would have to be much stronger and, in the case of Hungary, less divided for a genuine social pact to emerge. The division between OPZZ and Solidarność makes it unlikely that Poland could develop along these lines. Finally, note that a strong centralized labor organization would have the potential for massive collective action, which contravenes the desire to minimize the chances of such action against a valid transition program.

8.4   Conclusion

The preceding analysis has described the evolution of labor relations institutions and outcomes during the initial phase of marketization in Poland, Hungary, and Czechoslovakia and developed a model of changing support for reforms during the transition to a market economy. The examination of institutions and outcomes has revealed surprising stability in labor institutions in the first stage of transition to a market economy but dramatic changes in labor outcomes. Successor unions to the official trade unions remained on the union scene. Central governments taxed wage increases so that enterprises would not give increases that matched or exceeded inflation, enacted minimum wage legislation, and instituted tripartite forums to seek consensus on labor issues—as they had done under reform communism. By contrast, labor market outcomes changed greatly. State-owned enterprises reduced employment even absent privatization, producing sizable joblessness and eliminating massive vacancies. The dispersion of wages increased substantially in Hungary and Poland, although not in Czechoslovakia.

The model of changing support for reforms predicts a U-shaped curve of support for a successful reform program, with support falling among those who fail to advance rapidly in the new economic environment. It has shown that such a pattern is likely under a range of "reasonable" assumptions about the gains from reforms and individual expectations of those gains. Given this pattern, I examined three criteria for assessing labor arrangements in marketizing economies: whether they increase workers' tolerance for the costs of transition, whether they are conducive to organizing mass protests by those who suffer from transition, and whether they provide information flows to governments about program failures and pressure governments about potentially valuable changes in the direction of programs through worker "voice."

While a system of tripartite agreements that creates a social consensus during transition has the greatest appeal for dealing with the problems of transition, my examination of the development of labor relations institutions in the marketizing economies suggests a very different outcome: weak and fragmented unionism, concentrated in the public sector, and little or no unionism in the growing private sector, save in large joint ventures. This will minimize the probability of mass protests but is unlikely to increase tolerance for the costs of transition (so that other government policies may be needed to keep enough popular support) and is unlikely to provide the optimal information flow or voice to the political system that might lead to more realistic and successful marketizing strategies.

References

Berg, A., and J. Sachs. 1992. Structural adjustment and international trade in Eastern Europe: The case of Poland. *Economic Policy*, no. 14 (April): 118–73.
Blanchflower, D., and R. Freeman. 1992. Unionism in the United States and other OECD countries. In *Labor market institutions and the future role of unions*, ed. M. Bognanno and M. Kleiner. Cambridge, Mass.: Blackwell.
Boeri, T., and M. Keese. 1992. Labour markets and the transition in Central and Eastern Europe. Paris: OECD. Mimeo.
Calvo, G., and F. Coricelli. 1992. Stagflationary effects of stabilization programs in reforming socialist countries: Enterprise-side and household-side factors. *World Bank Economic Review* (January).

Dabrowski, J., M. Federowicz, and A. Levitas. 1992. Polish state enterprises and the properties of performance: Stabilization, marketization, privatization. Mimeo.

Estrin, S. 1991. Yugoslavia: The case of self-managing market socialism. *Journal of Economic Perspectives* (Fall), 187–94.

Federowicz, M., and A. Levitas. 1994. Poland: Councils under Communism and neo-liberalism. In *Works councils: Consultation, representation, cooperation,* ed. J. Rogers and W. Streeck. Chicago: University of Chicago Press. Forthcoming.

Ferge, Z. 1991a. Marginalization, poverty, and social institutions. A paper prepared for the Roundtable on Social Institutions for Economic Reform in Central and Eastern Europe, organized by the International Institute of Labor Studies, International Labor Organization, Geneva, and the Research Institute for Labor, Budapest, in Balaton-füred, 29 September–1 October.

———. 1991b. Unemployment in Hungary. Budapest. Mimeo.

Freeman, R. 1987. If it doesn't work, fix it . . . if you can: Reforming the labor market in socialist Poland. Report to the World Bank, Washington, D.C.

Góra, M., I. Kotowska, T. Panek, and J. Podgórski. 1991. Labour market, industrial relations, and social policy: A report on Poland. Paper delivered at the ILO OECD-CCEET Conference on Labour Market and Social Policy Implications of Structural Change in Central and Eastern Europe, Paris, September.

Gordon, L. 1992a. The independent workers movement in the USSR (an analysis of experience of 1989, 1991). Mimeo.

———. 1992b. Labour movement in days of difficult reforms: To suppress or to support? Mimeo.

Hethy, L. 1991. Social institutions for economic reform: The industrial relations institutions. Paper delivered at the Conference on Social Institutions for Economic Reform in Central and Eastern Europe, Blatonfüred.

Hirschman, A. 1973. The changing tolerance for economic inequality. *Quarterly Journal of Economics,* vol. 87 (November).

International Labor Organization (ILO). 1984. *The trade union situation and industrial relations in Hungary.* Geneva.

———. 1990a. Hungary: Right to strike. *Labour Law Documents* (January), 41–43.

———. 1990b. Poland: Trade unions. *Labour Law Documents* (January), 101–5.

———. Committee on Employment. 1990c. *Wages, labour costs, and their impact on adjustment, employment, and growth.* Geneva, November.

———. 1991a. Czechoslovakia: Collective bargaining act. *Labour Law Documents* (February), 1–12.

———. 1991b. Czechoslovakia: Employment act. *Labour Law Documents* (February), 13–24.

Jones, D. 1991. The Bulgarian labor market in transition. *International Labour Review,* vol. 130, no. 2 (February).

———. 1992. The transformation of labor unions in Eastern Europe: The case of Bulgaria. *Industrial and Labor Relations Review* 45, no. 3 (April): 452–70.

Kollo, J. 1988. Without a golden age—Eastern Europe. Paper presented at Harvard University.

Kornai, J. 1982. *Growth, shortage, and efficiency.* Oxford: Blackwell.

———. 1986. The Hungarian reform process: Visions, hopes and reality. *Journal of Economic Literature* 24: 1687–1737.

Lado, M., J. Szalai, and G. Sziraczki. 1991. Recent labour market and social developments in Hungary. Paper delivered at the ILO OECD-CCEET Conference on Labour Market and Social Policy Implications of Structural Change in Central and Eastern Europe, Paris, September.

Laibson, David. 1992. Comments on East European Paper. Massachusetts Institute of Technology. Mimeo.

Lehmann, H., and M. Schaffer. 1992. Productivity, employment, and labour demand in Polish industry in the 1980s: Some preliminary results from enterprise-level data. Working Paper no. 91, rev. Centre for Economic Performance.

LIGA News. 1991. Budapest, vols. 1–8.

MacShane, D. 1992. Workers and their unions in Eastern Europe—May 1991. *Labour/ Le Travail* 29 (Spring): 211–20.

Malinowski, T. 1991. Unemployment family policy and social assistance. Paper prepared for the Conference on Social Costs of the Political and Economic Transformation of the CSFR, Hungary and Poland, Vienna.

Nesporova, A. 1991. Recent labour market and social policy developments in the Czech and Slovak Republic. Paper delivered at the ILO OECD-CCEET Conference on Labour Market and Social Policy Implications of Structural Change in Central and Eastern Europe, Paris, September.

Noti, S. 1987. The shifting position of Hungarian trade unions amidst social and economic reforms. *Soviet Studies* (January), 63–87.

Redor, D. 1986. Différenciation des rémunérations et incitation au travail: Une comparaison internationale. Paper presented at the International Workshop on Wages and Payment Systems and the Socioeconomic Environment, Siófok (Sofia), September.

Reti, Tamas. 1991. East European trade unions and labour representation. Budapest. Mimeo.

Riveros, L. 1991. Wages and employment policies in Czechoslovakia. Policy Research and External Affairs Working Paper no. 730. Washington, D.C.: World Bank.

Schaffer, M. 1991. A note on the Polish state-owned enterprise sector in 1990. Discussion Paper no. 36. Centre for Economic Performance.

———. 1992. Poland. Working Paper no. 183. Centre for Economic Performance.

Siklova, J. 1991. Unemployment: The Czech way. *Literary Newspaper,* 29 August.

Solidarność News. 1991. Coordinating Office of NSZZ *Solidarność,* Belgium.

Sziraczki, G. 1990. Economic adjustment, pay structure, and the problem of incentives in Eastern European labor markets. Labour Market Analysis and Employment Planning Working Paper no. 46.

The trade union act, 23 May 1991: The act of 23 May 1991 respecting employers' organizations; The act of 23 May 1991 respecting settlement of collective disputes. 1991. Available through the International Labor Organization, Geneva.

Vanyai, J., and E. Viszt. 1992. Human resources and structural change in the Hungarian industry. Budapest: Research Institute of Industrial Economics, Hungarian Academy of Sciences. Mimeo.

World Bank. 1987. *Poland: Reform, adjustment, and growth.* Washington, D.C.

———. 1990a. *Czechoslovakia: Transition to a market economy.* Washington, D.C.

———. 1990b. *Poland: Economic management for a new era.* Washington, D.C.

———. 1991. *World development report, 1991: The challenge of development.* Washington, D.C.

Comment   Fabrizio Coricelli

The paper deals with a central issue for economies in transition, namely, how labor market institutions can support or jeopardize sustainable market reforms.

After reviewing the behavior of labor market institutions and labor market variables during the initial phase of transition in three countries—Czechoslovakia, Hungary, and Poland—Freeman discusses the role of labor market institutions in ensuring support for reforms.

As to the behavior of labor market institutions and variables, Freeman presents interesting evidence pointing to institutional inertia, combined with rapid changes of labor market variables. There seems to be a parallel with the inertia of the overall political structure. While the breakdown of the old regime has given unprecedented powers to the new governments, there has been significant continuity in political institutions—the *nomenklatura* is still very powerful in Parliament (see Poland and Romania, e.g.); traditional trade unions are still very influential (again, see Poland). While this has not proved to be an obstacle at the very beginning of the reform programs, it may nevertheless prove to be a major obstacle for the sustainability of reforms. Indeed, after a short initial period of "free hand" for the new governments, the old political institutions may be an obstacle to the creation of long-lasting political support for reforms. This may be particularly relevant when external shocks—like the collapse of the CMEA (Council for Mutual Economic Assistance)—occur after the launch of reform programs and sharply increase the costs of transition (for a discussion of this aspect in the case of Poland, see Johnson and Kowalska [1992]).

To summarize, while labor market institutions do not seem to have played a crucial role in the aftermath of stabilization-cum-reform programs, they are likely to be a key factor in determining the speed of reforms and even their success. Within these broad trends, however, the comparative aspect remains largely unexplored in the paper. While it is shown that labor market institutions and the behavior of labor market variables vary significantly across countries, there is no explicit attempt to draw some conclusions on the linkages between labor market institutions and performance of the labor market.

Freeman suggests important institutional reforms—related to the structure of bargaining, the structure of trade unions, and rules for profit sharing—that may ensure the necessary support for the reforms.

These suggestions arise from a simple framework that attempts to establish precise criteria for judging labor market institutions during the transition. The framework is interesting. It is based on the assumption that, while the majority of workers will benefit in the long run from reforms, they will lose in the short run. Since there is uncertainty about the distribution of these losses, ex ante workers will support reforms. However, once the initial results are revealed, the majority may turn against reform.[1] Poland is a case in point: the initial strong support evaporated slowly, and, by mid-1991, the majority seemed to

---

1. That uncertainty on the distribution of losses across individuals may create a reversal of the support to a reform program has been shown for the case of trade reform by Fernandez and Rodrik (1991).

be against the program (see opinion polls reported in Johnson and Kowalska [1992]). According to Freeman, this might have been caused by workers attaching too much weight to their own experience and not to the experience of workers successfully concluding the transition to the winning group (e.g., the private sector). Here the paper may be weighing too much the role of Hirschman's "tunnel effect" and neglecting the possibility of congestion effects. Indeed, the transition probability for each worker may decline as the number of workers trying to move to the winning group increases. An important issue is therefore that of balancing the rate of absorption, or creation of jobs, in the private sector with the rate of destruction of jobs in state-owned enterprises. This naturally raises the issue of the speed of reforms, which is not touched on by the paper. A big bang approach, like the one followed by Poland, may create the sort of congestion described above. In contrast, a more gradual approach may push workers in a staggered manner into the race to the winning group. This implies that state-owned firms reduce output and release employment more gradually. The process may involve a less traumatic shock to state enterprises initially, through a supporting fiscal policy and/or a more accommodative credit policy. Note that ex post it is not obvious that this more gradual approach is more costly in terms of fiscal balance than a big bang approach.[2] Production inefficiencies may be larger. However, these have to be weighed against an increased credibility and support for the overall reform program. This is perhaps the central dilemma, entailing the choice of the overall stance of macroeconomic policies. The role of labor market institutions stressed in the paper may be of secondary importance in the short run. Nevertheless, the role of examples of successful transitions remains important. Important as well are mechanisms, such as the distribution of shares in firms undergoing privatization, that may front-load future benefits. It seems that increasing worker participation through distribution of shares up front and the use of revenues from privatization for social safety nets are the best options to "invest in political support."

To conclude the discussion of the model on the cost of transition and the support for reform, I would raise a note of caution on the use of models that take the variables determining the losing and winning positions (wages and unemployment) as exogenous. Indeed, some of the policy recommendations, which seem appropriate to ensure the necessary support of the workers, may be highly undesirable if one takes into account that these measures affect wages and unemployment, the variables determining the degree of support for the reforms.

The paper concludes by discussing the issues of collective action and collective voice. One puzzle that remains unanswered is the fact that, despite large shocks to wages, unemployment, and living standards, which, according to

---

2. Dewatripont and Roland (1991) actually argue that the fiscal costs of gradualism are far smaller than those of the big bang.

Freeman, have thrown, at least for the moment, the majority of workers into his loser category, no significant episodes of labor unrest have arisen.

References

Dewatripont, M., and G. Roland. 1991. The virtues of gradualism and legitimacy in the transition to a market economy. Discussion Paper no. 538. Center for Economic Policy Research.
Fernandez, R., and D. Rodrik. 1991. Resistance to reform: Status quo bias in the presence of individual-specific-uncertainty. *American Economic Review,* vol. 81, no. 5.
Johnson, S., and M. Kowalska. 1992. The transformation of Poland, 1989–91. Washington, D.C.: World Bank. Mimeo.

Comment   Anthony Levitas

Richard Freeman's paper first summarizes labor relations under communism. Freeman argues that since 1989 there has been relatively little change in the institutions that regulate labor markets in Eastern Europe: wages are still centrally controlled; the old Communist unions have proved surprisingly strong; the new unions remain relatively weak; and little attempt has been made to integrate organized labor into the reform process as a whole. He then goes on to show that, while labor market institutions have proved remarkably stable, there has been rapid and dramatic change in labor markets: unemployment has risen dramatically; real wages have fallen; and wage differentials are increasing. Finally, he reflects on the implications of this gap between the rate of institutional change and the rate of change taking place on labor markets.

Unlike many others, Freeman argues that this gap poses severe problems for the long-term viability of reform. On the one hand, he points out that the persistence of the gap may incline short-term losers to unravel sound economic policies through mass protest. On the other hand, he suggests that it may also permit unsound economic policies to go unchanged until the population rebels. Disturbed by both possibilities, Freeman proposes three criteria by which we might judge the contemporary institutional efforts to reform labor markets in Eastern and Central Europe: Do these reforms increase the tolerance of workers for the costs of transition? Do they give workers sufficient voice to inform governments that their policies are pushing people past the breaking point? Do they help facilitate intolerance by making it too easy for "voice" to become mass protest?

Using these criteria, Freeman then outlines four developmental possibilities. The first gives workers too much voice, leading to Peronism and the slow death of market reforms. The second suppresses labor's voice now, in the name of an economic success that, as Freeman takes pains to point out, may or may not come later. The third allows the current, confused situation to persist, perhaps making it possible for reform to muddle on, but sufficiently distorting people's voices so that feedback to the state is unclear and the threat of explosion remains ever present. The fourth calls for nurturing unions responsible enough to negotiate the balance between current costs and future gains with the state while strong enough to compel their members to accept the fruits of these negotiations.

Normatively speaking, Freeman hopes that this last strategy will be pursued, although he concludes by saying that he would be "mad" either to predict outcomes or to recommend particular solutions. Thus, while it is hard not to sympathize with Freeman's intent, it is also hard not to feel a little shortchanged by the open-endedness of his conclusions. Indeed, I think that the language of voice and tolerance that Freeman uses to set up the problem of institutional reform, and to justify it as a political project worthy of an economist, does more to confuse the issues than resolve them. On the one hand, it tends— despite disclaimers—to reduce the problem of reforming labor market institutions to a problem of either convincing short-term losers to bide their time or providing the government with feedback mechanisms so that it will know when its time is running short. On the other hand, it does not provide us with the conceptual tools necessary to distinguish between the responsible neocorporatism that Freeman desires and the Peronism that he fears.

In short, the economic problem presented by labor market reform is not really about improving either workers' or the state's perception of things. Rather, it is about recasting institutions so that they might provide people with better opportunities to improve their life chances on the market. Moreover, the question is not just about arriving at some macroeconomic modus vivendi with organized labor—although this would be nice—but of creating a framework for a microeconomic modus operandi in which organized labor has an institutional role.

Indeed, it is seems to me that only by enlisting organized labor in local, institutional efforts to improve people's life chances could either the pressure for or the temptation of Peronist macroeconomic policies be decreased. And, while I agree with Freeman that there are no generalizable blueprints for such a scheme, I think that we can go farther in specifying the principles on which such an attempt might be made. First, unions ought to be institutionally supported since without them there is no way of actively enlisting labor in reform efforts. This support, however, should be focused at the local level, both by giving unions control over new resources (such as the disbursement of unemployment checks) and by requiring them to take part in the joint administration of active manpower programs. Second, more resources must be invested in creating such programs. This means founding training institutes, redeploying and reforming existing educational facilities, and providing start-up capital to new enterprises.

Third, and most important, the institutions responsible for these programs should be run by tripartite councils composed of local government, union, and business representatives. Local unions, in other words, not only should be forced to confront the problems of marketization but should also be given an institutional stake in and a responsibility for finding solutions. Fourth, unions should be encouraged to support privatization by using a percentage of the proceeds to create development funds at least partially controlled by union locals. Finally, unions should be enlisted in the effort to restructure the region's industrial dinosaurs. So far these efforts have been painfully slow, not only because governments have been reluctant to negotiate plant reform or closings with labor, but also because governments have been naively hoping that the market would resolve these problems for them.

Discussion Summary

Tom Kolaja disagreed with the conventional wisdom that individual success stories encourage workers to have confidence in the reform process. He said that jealousy was the overriding sentiment, adding that Poles tend to believe that corruption is behind most success stories. He cited the case of ABB, a Western company that purchased a Polish turbine plant. This joint venture was extremely successful until envious workers in an associated state-owned enterprise effectively sabotaged the new company.

Kolaja also discussed the development of a work ethic in Poland. He noted that, in Warsaw, a number of all-night stores that pay relatively high wages have had difficulty finding people to staff the night shift. He said that workers need to be convinced that it is worth working hard to get better pay.

Simon Johnson criticized the timing of the Polish reform program. He said that, at the beginning of the liberalization, workers and unions showed amazingly high support for radical change. At that point, nobody knew who the winners and losers would be. Six to nine months later, individual outcomes became much clearer, stratification occurred, and reform fatigue syndrome set in. However, some of the reforms were postponed until this time. Johnson felt that more of the reforms should have been implemented when there was still very high initial popularity.

Pentti Kouri provided several anecdotes about production techniques in Eastern Europe and Russia. He emphasized that these countries have plenty of skilled labor but a devastating lack of efficient production techniques. The average wage in Russia is $16.00 per month, but Russian industry still cannot compete. He cited the example of Russia's main car manufacturer, where an assembly line set up by Henry Ford is still in use.

Richard Layard noted that, even though there has been little change in the structure of labor market institutions, there has been a dramatic change in the way those old institutions function. For example, wages used to be set at a national level, but now wages are set at an enterprise level. Layard stressed the importance of preventing the leapfrogging practices associated with decentralized wage bargaining.

Jan Winiecki warned that it is unrealistic to rely on the emerging private sector to generate enough "winners" to make the reforms popular. If workers rely exclusively on the private sector, they will have to wait a very long time. Winiecki proposed that the government mollify workers by giving them control rights over state-owned firms and/or promising them some of the (future) privatization revenues.

Richard Freeman agreed with Levitas's suggestions about extending the domain of union activity. Freeman added an extra task: the management of pension funds. In the United States, union-managed pension funds own 15 percent of U.S. equities. Freeman warned, however, that unions would require some technical assistance and Western aid to develop the required expertise to undertake all the new activities that he and Levitas had proposed.

Freeman concluded by questioning whether it was appropriate to try to develop a stronger work ethic in Eastern Europe. He was not bothered by the fact that Polish workers did not want to work late at night. He said that Western economists should not force everyone to look like Americans.

9 Fiscal Policy during the Transition in Eastern Europe

Roger H. Gordon

The transition in Eastern Europe from centrally planned to market economies inevitably will be a complex and lengthy process. Virtually every aspect of these economies will need to change, and at every stage in the process fiscal policy will be a major concern. Several of the East European countries started the transition process with large government deficits and rapid inflation. Raising government revenue and reducing expenditures in order to eliminate these deficits have therefore been immediate priorities in reform efforts. The initial reform process has also involved a substantial relaxation of direct government control over the allocation of resources, allowing firms, individuals, and local governments to respond to prices rather than directives from the central government. As a result, distortions to the incentives faced by these units created by national tax and regulatory policies suddenly mattered, and these distortions were often severe—the inherited tax systems differed dramatically from those prevailing in market economies. In addition, whereas the government previously maintained direct control over trade patterns, economic reform at least in Poland involved an immediate opening of the border to private trade. As a result, tax and regulatory distortions to trade patterns suddenly started to matter as well.[1]

Privatization inevitably occurs more slowly during the process of reform, but it is essential for a successful transition. If firms are sold, the result is immediate revenue for the government and an immediate drop in nonstate funds available for investment. Privatization also means that the government loses dividends from privatized firms in the future. The resulting changes in

The author thanks Olivier Blanchard, Barry Bosworth, George Kopits, Michelle White, and conference participants for comments on an earlier draft, Annette Brown for research assistance, and Yolanda Kodrzycki Henderson for sending data on the Polish economy.
1. Because of these distortions, Czechoslovakia felt obliged to close its borders prior to price reform, in order to stop the outflow of subsidized goods.

the time pattern of government revenue will require continual readjustments in fiscal policy.

Throughout the reform process, there will be many new demands for government subsidies and expenditures. The newly unemployed hope for support payments; struggling firms and farms hope for subsidies, cheap credit, and trade protection; the need to invest in infrastructure is enormous; the rise in inequality creates demands for redistribution; etc. Yet the taxes needed to finance these expenditures may be so high as to stifle economic development.

In this paper, I try to provide an overview of the fiscal pressures on East European governments during the transition and what responses might be called for. In each case, I start by describing the conventional wisdom concerning how best to deal with such pressures in a developed market economy. East European countries are not developed market economies, however, so I will also discuss the implications of various idiosyncratic features of these economies for fiscal policy. Given the lack of experience and research on economies undergoing such an economic transition, these latter arguments are inevitably somewhat speculative.

9.1   Fiscal Policy prior to the Reforms

In the past, the tax systems in Eastern Europe resembled those in market economies, at least superficially. Table 9.1, taken from Mihaljek (1991), describes the revenue flows reported from the major forms of taxes. The East European governments collected 43.2 percent of GDP in explicit tax revenue on average, compared with an average figure of 38.1 percent of GDP in the OECD countries. The composition of this revenue was quite different, however. Profits taxes played a much more important role in Eastern Europe, while personal income taxes were much less important.

Profits taxes in Eastern Europe differed in fundamental ways from those in use in OECD countries. To begin with, statutory tax rates were much higher—in Poland prior to the reforms, for example, the tax rate was 65 percent, while in Czechoslovakia it was 75 percent. In addition, firms did not necessarily have the right to retain their depreciation allowances, and a firm's assets were often subject to separate taxes.[2] More important, the government was free to modify a firm's tax obligations ex post, with the result that the explicit tax rules were of little substantive importance. Furthermore, after-tax profits could simply be taken by the government, and as a rule losses would be covered in full by the government. Even if some profits remained with the firms after taxes, firms were not free to spend these funds without approval of government ministries; if approval for expenditures was obtained, financing came with it.[3]

---

2. Hungary and Poland imposed a tax on the balance sheet value of fixed assets. For further details, see Gray (1990).

3. This financing could take the form of low-interest loans, cheap prices for capital and other needed inputs, or simply direct transfers.

Table 9.1   **Composition of Tax Revenue in Central and Eastern Europe, 1989**

	Enterprise Profit Tax	Personal Income Tax	Turnover/ Sales Tax	Trade Taxes	Social Security Contributions	Tax Revenue/ GDP
Bulgaria	47.3	8.3	22.7	1.6	19.5	49.3
Czechoslovakia[a]	34.3	9.6	30.1	4.4	13.2	50.7
Hungary	14.3	10.2	35.9	8.2	29.2	49.0
Poland	27.7	9.2	24.2	3.0	23.6	36.8
Romania	26.2	16.0	34.7	2.4	20.5	42.4
Soviet Union	32.0	11.5	30.7	16.1	9.2	41.0
Yugoslavia[a]	14.8	21.4	20.8	9.3	22.0	33.2
Average	28.1	12.3	28.4	6.4	19.6	43.2
OECD	7.9	31.8	30.2	—	24.4	38.1
LDCs[b]	41.4		38.8	15.1	—	—

Source: Mihaljek (1991).
[a]1988.
[b]Unweighted average for 12 middle-income LDCs, 1985.

Without explicit government controls on the allocation of resources, these high implicit tax rates would have created overwhelming distortions to allocation decisions. Allocation decisions were made primarily by government ministries, however. The government simply assigned inputs to firms and ordered the delivery of particular outputs. Prices for each were set by the government. Firms were obliged in principle to fulfill the production plans ordered by the government, even if doing so resulted in a loss in financial profits. In sum, taxes served mainly an accounting role—direct controls rather than taxes were the primary means used for allocating resources.

Taxes could still have some indirect effects on allocation decisions. While these decisions were made primarily by government ministries, they would be based on information conveyed to these ministries by firms. Firms could attempt to manipulate these decisions in response to the implicit incentives they faced. In addition, firms could control the degree to which they in fact fulfilled the production plans ordered by the government. While tax distortions could therefore still have some net effect on allocation decisions, the nature of these effects was far different from those that would arise in market economies.

Not only did taxes have only indirect effects on the allocation of resources, but they also had little effect on the distribution of income. While personal income taxes did not normally exist, the government could still tax workers indirectly through ordering a reduction in wages, through raising the prices of consumer goods, or simply through reducing production of consumer goods, with queues or explicit rationing used to absorb the increased scarcity. Similarly, interest rates were set extremely low, implicitly creating very high taxes on financial savings but subsidies for firms receiving credit. The government controlled firm profits not only through the tax law and the allocation of cheap credit but also through its control over output and input prices.

Since the government controlled the allocation of resources directly, taxes were not even the primary means of collecting revenue for government operations. The government could simply order the delivery of goods, paying for them at prices far below their market value. These goods were often then resold at quite different prices, generating trading profits or losses, depending on the government's objectives. Many of these implicit taxes and subsidies are not even reported in the accounts of government revenues and expenditures. Since firms were state owned, the separation between the government's budget and firm budgets was of little importance in any case. In sum, given the limited role of the tax system prior to the reforms, the tax law could and did take a form entirely incompatible with the successful functioning of a market economy.

9.2   Effect of the Reforms on Government Revenues and Expenditures

With economic reform, allocation decisions are no longer made directly by government ministries; instead, they are made by firms, individuals, and local governments. Prices, wages, and to some degree interest rates and exchange rates are set by market forces rather than by the government. This reform process will have fundamental and pervasive effects on the allocation of resources and the distribution of income. This section focuses on the implications for government revenues and expenditures.

9.2.1   Effect on Government Revenues

The reform process has both immediate and long-lasting effects on government revenue. To begin with, the immediate jump in prices when prices are decontrolled and the likely continuing inflation have complicated effects on reported profits and business income-tax payments, even if real activity and the tax law were to remain unchanged. The immediate jump in prices raises firms' revenue but does not affect many of the firms' deductions. For example, depreciation deductions, deductions for goods taken out of inventory, and interest deductions are all tied in the very short run to the low prices that prevailed prior to the reforms. The result is an immediate jump in taxable profits and in profits-tax payments, with the result that firms at first appear far more profitable than they really are. Poland's recent experience illustrates this. The reported average profit rate of Polish firms jumped from 19 percent in 1988 to 45.5 percent in 1989, the year of Poland's explosive rise in prices. Profits continued at the relatively high level of 29.4 percent in 1990, in spite of the sharp recession in Poland during that year.[4] Eventually, however, the high nominal interest rates required to compensate for inflation led to an understatement of

---

4. These figures, taken from table 1 in the 1991 *Statistical Bulletin* published by the Polish Ministry of Finance, measure the ratio of accounting profits to accounting costs, as defined under Polish accounting conventions.

true profits, as nominal interest payments were deducted from real incomes.[5] As a result, the reported average profit rate fell to 8.3 percent during the first three months of 1991 and should continue to fall further.

As seen in table 9.2, Poland's business income-tax revenue in real terms followed a similar time path, growing moderately in both 1989 and 1990, but then collapsing during the first eight months of 1991.[6] This collapse in income taxes in 1991 almost entirely explains the sharp fall in aggregate government tax revenue that occurred in 1991.

Inflation-induced biases in the measurement of profits are not the only explanation for this collapse in business income-tax revenues. The recession that began with the initiation of reforms in 1990 certainly caused true profits to fall.[7] In addition, with the reforms firms acquired the ability to alter their decisions so as to reduce their tax liabilities. For example, heavily taxed state firms could set up lightly taxed private "subsidiaries" (or joint ventures) and shift their taxable profits to these lightly taxed firms through use of transfer prices. If sidewalk vendors are more lightly taxed than businesses operating out of a storefront, commerce can and has simply moved onto the sidewalk. Tax evasion will also become much more of a problem under the reforms. With the decentralization of prices and decision making, auditing of firms becomes far more difficult. Financial records will be inadequate, in part because use of financial intermediaries is limited, which eliminates an independent source of information. In addition, there are not yet enough trained accountants (or accounting standards) to provide any effective oversight. When prices are so much in flux, it is even difficult to judge the plausibility of reported transactions.

Firms also have an incentive to increase their wage payments, resulting in a fall in taxable income. Prior to the reforms, wage rates were very low, particularly for skilled workers, owing to implicit taxes on these workers. With the end of direct controls over wages, firms are under competitive pressure to raise wages to market levels.[8] Poland has attempted to prevent this jump in wages

5. Inflation creates other biases in accounting measures of profits that cause profits to be overstated since depreciation and inventory deductions are based on historic cost. Gordon (1984) shows that, even at U.S. inflation rates, inflation causes on net a reduction in taxable profits.

6. Nominal figures for tax revenue come from the 1991 *Statistical Yearbook,* supplemented by figures for 1991 from the *Statistical Bulletins* in 1991. Income-tax revenues were defined to include dividends received by the government from state enterprises. These figures were deflated using a price index for industrial production, constructed from data in the *Statistical Bulletins.* In particular, the annual data for each year are deflated back to June 1988 using an average of the monthly price indices in each year. (These deflators equaled 1.005 for 1988, 3.252 for 1989, 23.208 for 1990, and 32.900 for the first eight months of 1991.) These deflated figures undoubtedly overstate real revenue, particularly in 1989, since they assume a constant real flow of revenue, whereas firms often postponed tax payments in order to make them with a deflated currency.

7. Initial drops in output under the reforms have been substantial. For example, industrial production in the state sector in Poland fell by 25 percent in 1990, compared with the previous year.

8. In fact, state firms acting in the interests of their workers should be willing to raise wages above workers' marginal products.

Table 9.2   Real Government Revenues and Expenditures in Poland,
                   1988–August 1991, (trillions of Dec. 1988 zloty)

	1988	1989	1990	1991:1–8
Revenues				
Total	10.04	9.26	8.46	5.94
Business income tax	3.79	4.00	4.21	1.87
Turnover tax	3.20	2.71	1.71	1.71
(On alcohol)	(.94)	(.72)	(.34)	(N.A.)
Wage taxes	1.25	1.03	1.15	1.20
Customs duties			.16	.36
Taxes on nonstate				
firms	.70	.77	.49	N.A.
Expenditures				
Total	9.96	10.36	8.35	6.79
Subsidies to:				
Socialized sector	3.31	2.98	1.42	N.A.
Goods	2.41	2.45	.70	.32
Housing/services	.48	.40	.45	.20
Investment	1.23	.98	.70	.41
Social insurance	.30	.45	.42	.86
Deficit	.08	−1.10	.10	−.85

Note: N.A. = not available.

through high taxes on "excess" wage payments. These conflicting pressures have resulted in sharp fluctuations in reported real wages during the transition period to date.[9]

The economic reforms also have important implications for revenue from the turnover tax. The shift from controlled to market prices causes a price jump. But revenue from the turnover tax should not change in real terms as a result if this revenue is deflated using the actual prices at the stage where the tax is collected. This is true only for ad valorem taxes, which collect some percentage of sales revenue, however. Some turnover taxes, primarily those on alcohol, were ad rem, and these payments remain fixed in nominal terms and therefore fall in real terms owing to inflation. In addition, revenues fall when production drops. As seen in table 9.2, turnover tax revenues in Poland fell moderately in 1989 but then dropped dramatically in 1990.[10]

The relative growth of the private sector should also result in a fall in tax revenue relative to GDP. Collecting revenue from private firms is difficult since

9. According to the data in the *Statistical Bulletin*, if wages in 1988 equaled 100, then real monthly wages in trade were 120 in 1989, dropped to 82 in 1990, but jumped back to 122 during the first eight months of 1991. These figures ignore many forms of supplementary payments made to workers both in kind and through parallel private firms.

10. The drop in tax revenue from beer and alcohol explains roughly 40 percent of this overall drop.

their activity is very hard to monitor. Whatever mechanisms did exist for monitoring private firms prior to the reforms were substantially weakened as part of the attempt to eliminate the barriers restricting private activity.[11] In part because of the inadequate financial sectors in these countries, private businesses are likely to operate primarily through cash transactions, making auditing extremely difficult. At least to begin with, effective tax rates on these firms are likely to be much lower than those on state firms, regardless of the relative statutory tax rates. As seen in table 9.2, tax revenue from the private and household sectors has always been small, and it shrank after the reforms started in spite of the entry of thousands of new private firms.

A basic part of the reforms has inevitably been a reduction in both profits and turnover-tax rates, in order to lessen the efficiency losses resulting from tax distortions. The resulting direct loss in tax revenue only adds to the losses that would have occurred in any case.

All these factors lead to a reduction in tax revenue. Decentralized allocation decisions should result in an increase in efficiency, however, and part of this increase will go to the government in increased tax revenue. Many of these effects can occur very quickly. For example, allocating goods among consumers on the basis of cash sales rather than queues results in an efficiency gain and extra revenue. The increased interest rates paid on bank deposits should induce individuals to put their savings in banks rather than continuing to hoard foreign currency or stockpile real commodities. Unlike other forms of savings, bank deposits free resources for productive investment, generating an efficiency gain and additional tax revenue. While efficiency gains raise the absolute size of tax revenue, however, they should not have much effect on the share of tax revenue in GDP.

The net effects of all these pressures on tax revenue can be substantial. In China, where we have ten years of information on the reform effort, government revenue fell steadily from 34.4 percent of GNP in 1978 to 20.4 percent in 1988,[12] for many of the reasons described above. Unless their tax policies change dramatically, governments in Eastern Europe should forecast a steady decline in their tax revenues as a fraction of GDP.

9.2.2 Effect on Government Expenditures

The likely drop in government revenues that results from reform will create substantial macroeconomic pressures unless the reforms also cause a comparable fall in government expenditures. The reforms are likely to cause government expenditures to fall for a variety of reasons, although not necessarily at the same time or to the same extent as the fall in government revenue.

The initial reform process should involve a cut in subsidies to both consum-

---

11. For example, prior to the reforms, Polish farmers could sell only to a state marketing agency, but afterward they could sell directly to consumers.

12. For further discussion and documentation, see Blejer and Szapary (1990).

ers and firms, in order to improve the incentives that these groups face when making allocation decisions. As seen in table 9.2, the drop in subsidies to firms in Poland was quick and dramatic; the drop in subsidies to the household sector was also dramatic, although it occurred more slowly. This cut in subsidies in Poland was complicated by the increasing importance of loss-making firms resulting from the recession. While the government no longer covers their losses directly, the government-controlled banking system may well support these firms through extending further credit that is unlikely to be repaid, simply shifting the subsidies to another part of the government's budget. Documenting the extent of any such subsidies is difficult.[13]

Government-financed investment expenditures should also drop under the reforms. Previously, the government financed essentially all new investment out of government revenue. Under the reforms, investment will be increasingly financed by firms out of their retained earnings or by the banking system using household deposits, allowing the government to reduce its investment expenditures.[14] As seen in table 9.2, government-financed investment in Poland has in fact been falling quickly.

Other factors lead to increased demands for government expenditures, however. To begin with, governments can no longer order delivery of goods at below-market prices—even if revenue as a percentage of GDP remains unchanged, the resources that these funds can buy may be sharply diminished. In addition, the reforms have been accompanied by a sharp growth in unemployment and therefore in expenditures on unemployment and other social insurance benefits.[15]

In the intermediate term, privatization will have important implications for government revenue. The government may receive revenue initially if it sells ownership rights rather than giving them away, but in the future it loses the stream of dividend payments from privatized firms.[16] The result can be sharp fluctuations over time in government receipts.

On net, the government deficit in Poland has fluctuated substantially during this period. It grew substantially during the inflation in 1989, as subsidies rose to maintain various prices at their historical values, in spite of the inflation. The initial reform package intentionally cut expenditures by enough to result in a net surplus, so as to stop this inflation. But in the resulting recession a large deficit has again reappeared and is growing quickly.

13. Net reported government revenue from the financial sector increased under the reforms, owing presumably to the sharp increase in the spread between borrowing and lending rates. Bad debts will show up in the accounts only when default occurs.

14. In China, investment as a fraction of GDP held steady under the reforms in spite of a sharp drop in explicit government financing. For further discussion, see Naughton (1988).

15. Prior to the reforms, unemployment was avoided by forcing firms to hire otherwise unemployed individuals. As a result, unemployment benefits previously showed up in the budget in the form of reduced profits of state firms. Now they are reported directly.

16. For an extended discussion of the revenue and macroeconomic effects of the privatization process, see Gordon (1991).

9.3   Macroeconomic Fiscal Policy during the Reforms

Given these fluctuations in the government deficit that inevitably accompany the reform effort, preventing future inflation (or deflation) will be a serious challenge. Yet inflation is likely to be much more costly in these countries than it would be in developed market economies. Decentralized decision making requires a price system in which prices accurately and clearly convey the value of each good and service. Inflation inevitably erodes the information conveyed by prices. The East European countries have not begun to develop the institutions that exist in the West to lessen the costs created by inflation. Even such basic responses as penalties for late payments often do not exist. Many prices, for example, interest rates, do not yet respond quickly and flexibly to market pressures, with the result that inflation can quickly lead to rationing and even to trade outside established institutions, in order to avoid price restrictions.[17] One major cost of inflation is that it makes accounting information about firm profitability very misleading, for reasons described above. The misleading accounting information makes allocation of credit much more difficult, it makes the firm's own analysis of investment opportunities difficult, and it leads to tax payments that have little or no relation to economic profits, creating larger and more pervasive distortions to incentives than would occur without inflation.[18] On net, tax revenue is likely to fall substantially owing to inflation.[19] Stabilizing market prices should therefore be a key priority at the beginning of the reform process, as it was in Poland.

Put simply, stopping inflation requires stopping the (excessive) printing of money, thus bringing government cash flow back into balance. East European governments are now under immense political pressure to raise expenditures. To avoid inflation, they are therefore under immense pressure as well to raise financing for these expenditures through some means. The alternatives are raising taxes or borrowing either at home or abroad. Given the low initial tax base and high initial tax rates, raising taxes will be very difficult without a major reform of the tax system. Such tax reforms take time. Without a tax reform, higher business income-tax rates at the beginning of the reform process will sharply discourage new investment, particularly in the private sector, where investors are committing their own funds, thereby undermining one of the key

17. Uncertainty concerning future inflation rates also makes bonds paying a nominally fixed interest rate very risky. To lessen this risk, bonds could pay a floating interest rate, with frequent revisions in the interest rate. Indexed bonds are another alternative, but this option would be much more complicated given the difficulty of creating a reasonable price index in the face of rapidly changing relative prices and consumption bundles. Another option is to issue bonds denominated in a more stable currency, although this still imposes exchange rate risk on purchasers.
18. For further discussion, see Auerbach (1988).
19. Double-digit inflation rates can undermine a conventional income-tax system, as nominal interest deductions overwhelm real profits of firms. Even in the United States, Gordon and Slemrod (1988) found that nominal interest deductions were large enough to more than wipe out all tax revenue from the return to capital.

objectives of the reform process. This occurs not only because the high tax distortions reduce after-tax earnings on new investments but also because high tax payments (including payments to the government for firms being privatized) reduce current consumption relative to future consumption. These factors raise the implicit rate of return that new investments must earn to be attractive. High tax rates also exacerbate the inevitable distortions created by the mismeasurement of economic income and by differences in effective tax rates by industry or commodity.

Balancing the government budget period by period through changes in tax rates would also require large short-term fluctuations in these rates, in order to avoid large short-term fluctuations in money creation and therefore in prices. Selling off state-owned firms, for example, results in a one-time jump in revenue, owing to the sale. But these fluctuations in tax rates can create severe distortions in their own right. Unexpected fluctuations in these tax rates make new investment more risky and lead to costly attempts to shift income and deductions across time to minimize tax payments. Once rates are clearly expected to fall, however, taxes make new investment unusually attractive since the start-up expenses can be deducted at the initially high tax rates while the income from the investment will be taxed at the lower rates expected to prevail in the future. All these responses reduce taxable income when rates are high and increase it when rates are low, forcing even larger fluctuations in tax rates to maintain budget balance period by period, which further distorts economic incentives.

As Barro (1979) has argued, efficiency argues for stable tax rates, with the level of rates set so that the government's budget is balanced only in present value rather than period by period. This calls for borrowing to smooth out temporary differences between revenues and expenditures. In the East European context, this policy requires that governments borrow during the early years of the reform process when fiscal pressures are great and pay back these loans in the future. In principle, the government could borrow either at home or abroad. But borrowing at home undoubtedly crowds out loans to finance business investment and business restructuring. As a result, this borrowing directly slows the transition process and so is also very costly.

This leaves the alternative of borrowing from abroad. Standard theory argues that a country that is small relative to the world capital market should borrow from abroad (or lend abroad) until the domestic interest rate equals that prevailing in the world market (after correcting for the effects of anticipated exchange rate changes).[20] Given the initially low rate of private savings in many of these countries and the many demands for capital, this would imply substantial capital flows from abroad.

20. Of course, the demand for capital by the East European countries, and particularly by the Soviet Union, will be substantial, so technically the optimal level of borrowing may be somewhat smaller, to avoid driving up the interest rates they face. For a formal analysis, see Gordon and Varian (1989).

But most of the East European governments are already heavily in debt to foreign lenders. Given the resulting risk of default, they will find it very difficult to borrow yet more from abroad. Of course, if individuals and firms could borrow from abroad, the government could then borrow on the domestic market. These capital flows from abroad could take the form of loans from branches of foreign banks to individuals or firms or of corporate direct investment in new or existing firms. So far, however, such capital flows from abroad have also been very limited. Many explanations might be given. Foreigners find it very difficult to screen loan applicants, they rarely find effective collateral available for these loans, and they can have little confidence in how the legal system will end up dealing with loan defaults and individual or firm bankruptcies. Corporate direct investors face not just the fundamental uncertainty concerning which industries, firms, and managers will be successful but also uncertainty concerning future government policy. To what degree will the government support union pressure on foreign-owned firms, change the tax law in adverse ways, impose restrictions on competition with domestic firms or conversion of currencies, etc.? Even if the government seems committed now to maintaining a favorable business climate for foreign direct investment, these policies are time inconsistent—the new businesses will be an attractive source of tax revenue in the future. Given the large overhang of foreign debt inherited from past policies, this threat of high future taxes should be of real concern. Anticipating the possibility of adverse policy changes, potential entrants have a strong incentive to wait until the uncertainties have been reduced before committing funds or at least to focus primarily on very short-term projects. But these delays slow down the recovery process and undermine the reform effort.[21]

One way to reduce these uncertainties is for Western countries to make credit conditional on adoption and maintenance of government policies that are conducive to economic growth. Only international organizations such as the IMF and the European Bank for Reconstruction and Development or foreign governments are in a position to impose such conditions and credibly commit to imposing "punishments" on a country that does not meet them. These implicit threats are actually in the interests of the borrowing countries since they increase the credibility of government promises concerning future policy. As a result, foreign investors should have less fear about adverse changes in policy, making investing in the countries more attractive. One essential step in reassuring investors concerning the possibility of adverse policy changes is to set up a tax structure and tax rates that will raise sufficient revenue to balance the government's budget in present value, given its budgetary commitments, without requiring future changes in tax rates.

Therefore, a major tax reform may be essential quickly, even if short-term government financing will come from foreign loans. Since relying primarily on foreign loans to help finance current expenditure needs seems unrealistic,

21. For one attempt to model this process more formally, see Laban and Wolf (1991).

the pressure is that much greater to reform the tax system immediately, to enable the government to finance current expenditures through additional taxes, without unduly distorting the allocation of resources.

9.4   What Changes in the Tax Structure Are Most Urgent?

In the past, effective turnover and business income-tax rates in Eastern Europe were very high. In addition, the government often intervened ex post to alter the net tax payments, covering the losses of some firms and expropriating excess cash reserves of others, raising effective tax rates yet further. Given the past government controls over firm behavior, firms were not in much of a position to react to the resulting tax distortions, which limited their consequences. With the reforms, however, decision making is being decentralized. These tax distortions are large enough to alter allocation decisions substantially, imposing large excess burdens on the economy. The result is substantial pressure to reduce tax rates. There is also substantial pressure, however, to raise more revenue quickly. The only way to accomplish both is to broaden the tax base considerably. The problem is how to do this quickly.

Initial reforms will be constrained by what can feasibly be implemented in a short time period. Tax reform is always a complex and time-consuming process. Inevitably, the solution will be a sequence of tax reforms, starting with what can be done quickly, and evolving toward a tax system that would be preferred in the long run. In designing a sequence of tax reforms, however, it is important to minimize the windfall gains and losses that occur during later steps in the reform process. To begin with, large windfall losses create strong political constituencies that oppose the reforms. Grandfathering past decisions to lessen these windfalls, however, greatly complicates further reforms and slows the reform process. In addition, individuals will attempt to anticipate ex ante the possibility of such windfalls and alter their behavior accordingly. Therefore, if tax changes that create windfalls will be essential in the near future, then the actual distortions created by the sequence of tax structures may be quite different than they would appear simply analyzing the tax statutes at any date. In discussing immediate reform needs, I therefore discuss as well what further reforms should follow.

9.4.1   Reform of the Turnover Tax

Traditionally in these countries, turnover-tax rates varied dramatically by good. There were several hundred if not several thousand different turnover-tax rates, allowing the government to set consumer prices that prevented undue rationing while maintaining producer prices at arbitrary values. Once production decisions are decentralized, however, these differences in tax rates by good create severe distortions to both the pattern of production and the pattern of trade and make enforcement far more complicated. Also, collecting tax on output rather than on value added creates an artificial incentive to integrate vertically in order to avoid turnover taxes on purchased inputs.

Reforming this traditional system of turnover-tax rates is probably the highest priority in tax reform (and one that was often undertaken well before the current wave of reforms). To begin with, the range of tax rates needs to be narrowed substantially both by good and by firm. Poland, for example, moved very quickly toward equalizing turnover-tax rates, and the same should be done quickly in all these countries. Complete equalization of rates would make administration of the system easiest. While some rate variation may be desirable on equity grounds, it would be best to start with a uniform rate and then introduce rate variation if appropriate at a later date when the tax administration is in a position to enforce it.

In the past, turnover taxes were imposed on domestic production. In principle, no tax was due when goods were exported, but tax was due on imported goods. Maintaining such border corrections is essential, once tariff and nontariff barriers to trade are reduced as part of the reform effort. Any difference in the taxes on imported versus domestically produced goods or any unrebated taxes on exports create incentives to import goods that are taxed more heavily if produced at home and export goods that are relatively subsidized.[22] Given that the effective turnover-tax rate on a good depends on the degree to which intermediate goods are traded between taxed firms and the degree to which production takes place in firms subject to the tax, differences in effective tax rates can easily become important. Any remaining differences in the effective tax rates should be eliminated in the early stages of the reform process. Once industries develop in response to these distortions, eliminating them will become far more costly.[23]

More time consuming will be reform of the basic structure of the tax. In the past, turnover taxes were normally imposed at a single stage in the production process, when firms involved in manufacturing sold to customers outside the manufacturing sector. As a result, there was an incentive to shift activity to the retail sector in order to avoid these taxes. Under this traditional system, it is difficult to determine the appropriate rebate when goods are exported since there is no information concerning taxes previously paid on inputs purchased by the firm. There are two alternative directions to go in reforming the system. One would be to shift to a tax only on sales to final consumers, as is done with U.S. sales taxes; the other is to shift to a value-added tax (VAT), as is used in

22. Only relative tax distortions matter here—if the effective surtax rates on domestically vs. foreign-produced goods were all equal, then the exchange rate would simply adjust to offset this distortion.

23. One problem faced, however, is evasion of the tax on imports by small traders, encouraging excessive entry into commercial activity by such traders. One response, other than tightening the controls on the border yet further, is to impose a presumptive tax in the form of a license fee to offset the expected evasion of turnover taxes.

Western Europe. In theory, the two approaches are completely equivalent. The latter approach has many administrative advantages, however. For one, enforcing tax collection is much easier at the production stage, where there are a few large firms, than at the retail stage, where there are many small firms and individual traders. Under a VAT, tax is collected at each stage, with the result that evasion at the retail level implies loss of revenue on only the value added at that last stage rather than loss of the entire revenue. In addition, at earlier stages in production, the European-style VAT is almost self-enforcing. In order to document a rebate for value-added taxes previously paid on inputs purchased, a firm needs to provide an invoice proving that value-added taxes have been collected, and how much, on the goods purchased. If taxes had been evaded on this sale, then the rebate would be disallowed to the purchaser; evasion therefore has no net effect on tax revenue. Furthermore, it would be much easier to move from the existing system to a VAT than to a retail sales tax. Currently, primarily firms involved in production are subject to turnover taxes. The first step in a transition to a VAT could involve taxing all firms involved in production and then granting rebates to these firms for turnover taxes paid on inputs that they purchase from other such firms, a step that should take only a year or so to organize. More difficult will be to extend the coverage of the tax to firms in the commercial and retail sectors. Far more firms would be involved, and each firm is far smaller and harder to monitor. In Poland, small firms rely heavily on cash transactions and keep poor records. Adequate enforcement of a tax on these firms may have to wait until cash transactions have been replaced by use of the banking system, allowing accounting and tax auditing to focus on bank records. Presumptive taxes (e.g., license fees or surtaxes on inputs they purchase) might be used instead.

9.4.2   Reform of the Profits Tax

Explicit taxes on business income are a major source of government revenue in Eastern Europe and the Soviet Union, much more so than in the OECD countries. At least until very recently, average tax rates were extremely high. The economic reforms now give firms much more discretion over their actions and eliminate the offsetting subsidies that previously made the investment projects chosen by the government profitable. As a result, existing tax distortions will become far more costly than they had been previously, inducing firms to change their behavior so as to reduce their tax liabilities.

The most immediate problem that needs to be dealt with is the effect of the high inflation rates and rapid relative price changes in many of these countries on the tax base used for the business income tax. As in most countries, inflation has dramatic effects on the measure of taxable income, holding real income constant. Nominal rather than real interest payments are deductible, depreciation deductions are based on historic costs of capital equipment rather than replacement costs, and deductions for use of materials are based on historic cost, uncorrected for inflation that occurred since these goods were purchased.

Inflationary effects on measured income can easily overwhelm real factors, given the range of inflation rates seen in these countries. For example, as noted above, reported profits for firms in Poland rose dramatically during 1989 and continued to be high in 1990 in spite of the economic slump that followed the initiation of the economic reforms. The explanation is simply that the tenfold increase in prices during 1989 virtually wiped out interest, depreciation, and material expense deductions for these firms, all leading to a sharp increase in measured profits. Yet the continuing inflation is likely now leading to a sharp downward bias in measured profits since deductions for the high nominal interest payments offset any taxable profits being earned by these firms.[24]

These sharp fluctuations in taxable profits not only imply sharp fluctuations in the government budget but also create substantial distortions to investment incentives. Correcting the definition of taxable income for inflation and relative price changes, however, would add substantial complexity to the tax code. The cost of this complexity is high enough that even OECD countries have not adopted such corrections.[25] A simpler solution is to shift to a different definition of taxable income that is not vulnerable to these effects of inflation. A value-added tax base, for example, measures all flows using current rather than past prices and is therefore not vulnerable to the effects of inflation. While other alternatives would be available, moving toward a value-added tax base would eventually allow both the turnover tax and the profits tax to be replaced primarily by a value-added tax, greatly simplifying the tax structure.

The key changes in the definition of taxable income in order quickly to eliminate the current vulnerability to inflation would be the following:

1. *Eliminate the taxation/deductibility of interest income/payments.* This would be the most critical change in the definition of taxable income. Under a conventional income tax, nominal interest payments are deductible, and nominal interest income is taxable. If interest payers and recipients face the same tax rate, and if the economy is closed, then net taxes collected remain the same if both interest deductions and the taxation of interest income are eliminated, as occurs with a VAT. Differences in tax rates, however, lead those in high tax brackets to borrow from those in low tax brackets, with the result that eliminating the taxation/deductibility of interest leads to a jump in tax revenue. Avoiding the taxation of interest income in the future would also prevent any tax incentive to invest abroad in foreign bonds so as to avoid domestic taxes.

24. Take, for example, the situation where capital is in fact earning a 15 percent taxable rate of return while the real interest rate is zero. Even if only 50 percent of new investment were financed by bank loans with a nominal interest rate of 30 percent, to compensate for a 30 percent inflation rate, reported profits would be zero. In fact, the nominal interest rate was higher than this in Poland in 1990, to compensate for the continuing high inflation rate, with the result that such a firm would report large losses.

25. Brazil, Chile, Mexico, and Israel have all attempted to correct their definitions of taxable business income for inflation, in response to their much higher inflation rates. These countries were in a much better institutional position to handle the required sophistication in accounting practices than are the East European countries, at least for the immediate future.

Given the physical proximity of the East European countries to West European financial markets and the number of East European families with friends and relatives abroad, the threat of capital flight is a very real one.

2. *Replace depreciation deductions with immediate deductions for new capital purchases.* If any deductions allowed for new investment can be taken immediately, then inflation does not deflate the value of these deductions.[26] When capital purchases are allowed as a deduction in full and interest payments are not, as under a VAT, then no taxes are collected in present value on marginal investments, and investment decisions are undistorted. The government simply pays a fraction of any expenses of new investment equal to the tax rate and collects that fraction of the income derived from the investment. If the investor breaks even in present value, so does the government. The government does tax any above-marginal returns on new investments and taxes the gross returns from existing capital.[27] Allowing a smaller initial deduction, as proposed in Auerbach (1980), does result in a net tax discouraging capital investment, but one whose value is still unaffected by inflation. In theory, a small open economy should invest until the marginal product of new investment equals the cost of funds on the world capital market, even given the need to raise revenue through distorting taxes.[28] Allowing a full deduction for the purchase price of new investment results in the desired level of investment and corresponds to the tax treatment of new investment under a VAT.

3. *Deduct materials when purchased rather than when used.* Similarly, if the amount spent on purchases of materials is deductible and sales revenue is taxable at the same rate, then there is no distortion to marginal investments in inventories. If, instead, a deduction is allowed only when the materials are used, then the *nominal* return from investing in inventories is subject to tax, causing inflation to raise effective tax rates. For the same reason that a small open economy should not discourage investment in capital, however, it should not discourage investment in inventories. Again, the tax treatment under the VAT achieves the desired outcome.

On net, these changes are likely to broaden the tax base substantially, allowing the government to raise more revenue while reducing tax distortions. Using U.S. data for 1983, Gordon and Slemrod (1988) found that introducing the changes outlined above under both the corporate and the personal income tax systems would result in a net increase in tax revenue. This occurred because the revenue gained by eliminating interest deductions more than offset the

26. At high enough inflation rates, postponement of tax payments within the tax year can substantially reduce real tax payments. This was a serious problem in Poland during 1989. Avoiding it requires timely payment of taxes throughout the tax year.

27. One transitional issue is whether to allow the continued depreciation of existing capital. Eliminating these deductions for existing capital imposes windfall losses on firms. Since most firms are owned by the government, these windfalls should not be of much policy concern. In Poland, at least, these deductions were largely wiped out in any case by the inflation in 1989.

28. This result dates back at least to Diamond and Mirrlees (1971). For further discussion, see Gordon (1985) or Razin and Sadka (1989).

losses that arose from eliminating the taxation of interest income and shifting to the expensing of new investment.[29] Given the much higher inflation rates in most of the East European countries and the fact that they have not in the past taxed interest income, the revenue gain from these tax changes should be much more dramatic there.

Any delay in introducing these changes will result in continued gyrations in tax revenue and misallocations of new investment. These proposed changes would make the business tax easier to administer[30] while leaving the basic structure of the tax unchanged and should therefore not be complicated to introduce. One potential drawback to these changes, however, is that foreign investors in the country may no longer be able to claim a credit for these tax payments against the income taxes that they owe in their home country because the tax looks like an indirect tax rather than an income tax. This is unlikely to be an important consideration at the current time. To begin with, a number of European countries (e.g., France and the Netherlands) do not tax foreign-source income and so do not grant credits for taxes paid abroad. Many firms based in the United States have excess credits available already and so gain little from further credits. In any case, taxes are owed in the home country only when profits are repatriated, and repatriation can be postponed indefinitely.

Another potential problem with existing business taxes is that any differences in effective tax rates by industry create trade distortions—imports will be encouraged in industries facing high effective tax rates, and conversely. Since small open economies should not distort trade patterns, they would gain by eliminating the trade distortions created by a business income tax. Given the high business income-tax rates and the large number of tax-exempt sectors, these distortions are of dominant concern. As before, it is important to eliminate them before industries develop to take advantage of them. One approach is simply to choose the same effective tax rate in all industries. This is undoubtedly infeasible, given the problems in taxing agriculture, the financial sector, services, etc. A simpler approach would be to exempt from tax the revenue from exports and to impose a tax on imports, as would occur under a VAT.

The changes in the business income tax proposed above would not eliminate evasion by smaller firms. These firms engage heavily in cash transactions, particularly given the primitive state of the existing commercial banking sector, making enforcement virtually impossible. If the expected value added by these firms is roughly proportional to their inputs (e.g., retail sales are proportional to wholesale purchases), then one option is to impose a presumptive surtax on inputs purchased by these firms, at a rate reflecting the expected value added within the firm. In principle, small firms could have the option of paying the

---

29. On net, revenue went up even if dividends and capital gains income were also made tax exempt.

30. With these changes, no records need to be kept over time concerning the prices paid for existing capital, for existing goods in inventory, or for financial assets purchased or sold.

presumptive tax or submitting to an approved audit and paying the resulting VAT obligation.

9.4.3   What about the Introduction of a Personal Income Tax?

Given the important role of the personal income tax in other countries, it would be natural for East European countries to try to set up a personal income tax quickly as well. This probably should not be a major priority. Taxes imposed on individuals are much more difficult and expensive to enforce than taxes on firms since so many more entities are involved. Since these taxes have not existed in the past, their introduction will be time consuming and complicated. What should be done in the meantime? How quickly should a personal income tax be introduced?

The bulk of the tax base under a personal income tax is wages and salaries earned by workers. Under a conventional income-tax system, wages are deductible under the business income tax but then are taxable under the personal income tax. If the tax rates under the two taxes were the same, then eliminating the deductions for wage payments under the business income tax and not taxing wage income further at the individual level would be equivalent. Eliminating the deductibility of wage payments under the business income tax is an easy change administratively and can be done far more quickly than introducing a personal income tax. This explicit tax on labor income would replace the implicit tax that existed previously through direct controls on wage payments. This approach to taxing labor income is exactly that used under a VAT.

An alternative advocated by McLure (1991), one that is not much more difficult to administer, is to continue wage deductions under the business-level tax but to have businesses deduct a tax from each employee's wage income. Under this alternative, labor income could be taxed at progressive rates, but all taxes would still be collected at the firm level. The extra complexity that this change involves may well seem appropriate on equity grounds in the long run, but it should probably be postponed in the short run, given the time needed to introduce such administrative procedures. Another drawback of McLure's proposal is that the GATT rules may not allow border adjustments under his proposal, whereas they are allowed under a VAT.

In addition to taxing wages and salaries, a conventional personal income tax would also attempt to tax income earned from savings. Prior to the reforms in these countries, financial savings were subject to virtually confiscatory taxation since the only available forms of financial savings were bank deposits or perhaps government bonds and the interest rate paid on these forms of savings was sharply negative in real terms. Since individuals could not save effectively through financial securities, they saved instead through investing in consumer durables, housing, other storable commodities (e.g., canned goods), or perhaps foreign exchange. The statistics rarely reflected these forms of savings since purchase of most of these goods would be reported as consumption while acquisition of foreign exchange was often illegal and thus unreported. These forms of savings do not free resources for productive investment, however.[31] In the past, the government compensated by providing all the financing for business investment.

Substantial new investment is essential for the success of the reform effort. Given the budgetary pressures on the government and the difficulty of borrowing more abroad, it is essential that the reform process create incentives for individuals to save through financial assets rather than through consumer durables, foreign currency, or other forms of investment that do not free resources for new productive investment. This requires a dramatic reduction in the effective tax rate on financial savings. To begin with, this requires paying nonnegative real interest rates on bank deposits, so that financial assets earn at least as high a rate of return as the zero rate of return earned on real commodities or foreign currencies.[32] Such a rise in the rate of return on financial assets should lead to a one-time jump in financial deposits as well as a continuing growth in financial deposits as new savings are invested. In particular, those holding foreign currency should quickly be willing to deposit these funds in an interest-bearing account, facilitating their productive investment either at home or abroad. Similarly, those holding stockpiles of real commodities would have the incentive to sell them off and invest the funds in financial assets. Given that much of the savings done previously showed up in the statistics as consumption, this change should also lead to a dramatic rise in the reported savings rate. In China, for example, reported household savings grew from 1.6 percent of disposable national income in 1978 to 12.0 percent in 1986,[33] allowing the national investment rate to remain very high in spite of a sharp fall in the amount of investment financed by the government.

These gains could easily be undermined if any attempt were made to tax the return on financial assets. Until equity markets develop, financial assets will primarily be interest-bearing securities and bank deposits. Given the high inflation rates in these countries, even minor tax rates can quickly cause after-tax interest rates to be negative. In addition to inducing individuals to invest in the types of untaxed assets used previously, such taxation would now also induce individuals to circumvent the banking system by lending directly to private firms.[34] At times, this may be appropriate because individuals sometimes have better information than banks about the likely success of some firms or because the banking system is reluctant in general to lend to private firms.[35] In

31. Another alternative available to individuals was to send savings to relatives abroad who could then invest in foreign financial securities. This allowed the individuals to earn a real return on their savings but also did not finance investment at home.
32. To the extent that individuals can invest abroad in foreign bank accounts, domestic rates would have to be competitive with those paid abroad.
33. For further details, see Naughton (1988).
34. Such loans would very likely avoid taxation, owing to the difficulty that the government would face in monitoring them.
35. To facilitate these personal loans, modifications in contract law may also be needed, to assure investors that they are in a position to enforce payment in the event of default.

most cases, however, these direct loans to businesses are less well informed and more costly to negotiate than bank loans—banks are valuable financial intermediaries. It is therefore important to avoid financial disintermediation through imposing taxes on financial assets. Given the high efficiency and administrative costs of taxes on financial assets, they should be avoided, at least for the immediate future.

9.4.4   What about Border Taxes?

One other source of revenue that is also much more important among the East European countries than among OECD countries is trade taxes. Political pressures for tariff protection have been strong. Given the need for additional tax revenue, can a case be made for tariffs on these grounds alone?

The simple answer from the public finance literature is no.[36] In a small open economy, an optimal tax structure should not distort trade patterns. As argued above, however, taxes on domestic production in themselves distort trade patterns to the extent that they distort relative prices of domestically produced versus foreign-produced goods. For example, taxing domestic manufacturing but not domestic agriculture encourages exports of agricultural goods and imports of manufactured goods. These distortions can be offset, however, by a counterbalancing tariff on imports that is set to equal in size the tax on domestic production, good by good, and a subsidy on exports of each good that implicitly rebates the domestic tax on that good. These counterbalancing taxes and rebates are a basic part of a value-added tax. Eliminating trade distortions under other tax systems is more complex and will likely violate GATT rules.

9.5   Other Tax Reform Issues in Eastern Europe during the Transition

This discussion of tax policy has made little mention of the enormous transformation that these economies are undergoing. What complications does this transformation process create for fiscal policy? The models used to justify the types of tax policy outlined above presume that the economy would operate efficiently were it not for tax-induced distortions. But there are likely to be important market failures affecting each step in the process of economic transformation. The first key requirement of a successful transformation, for example, is the entry of large numbers of new firms. But the success or failure of a new firm provides important information to other potential entrants, implying inadequate incentives for new entry.[37] These firms also likely face credit constraints since banks cannot tell legitimate from fraudulent new entrants and may prefer lending to established firms in any case. The second key requirement of the economic transformation is that existing inefficient firms need to

---

36. For a recent reference, see Gordon and Levinsohn (1990).

37. This is just a variant of the arguments concerning incentives for research-and-development activity. The recent endogenous-growth literature (e.g., Romer 1986; and Lucas 1988) argues that these externalities may play a fundamental role even in developed economies.

be shut down. But there is a large literature pointing out ways in which the incentives faced by firms near or in bankruptcy can be badly distorted. Third, workers leaving inefficient firms and searching for employment in new firms likely face spells of unemployment in between. Again, there is a large literature describing how incentives faced in employment are distorted.

All these distortions exist to some degree in OECD countries as well. In cases where corrective policies have developed to lessen the distortions, the problem is simply to import these policies into East Europe. More commonly, however, these distortions remain uncorrected but are of minor consequence since these economies have been very stable and distortions affecting the entry and exit of firms therefore do not affect much the economies' overall performance. In Eastern Europe, however, these distortions can in principle have major effects on the transformation process. In this section, I explore to what degree a case can be made for some further fiscal intervention to lessen these costs.

9.5.1 Positive Externalities Generated by New Businesses

During the transformation process, there will inevitably be major changes in the types of goods produced; the technology used to produce them; the size, location, and internal organization of and incentive schemes used by the firms; the means used for marketing goods; the nature of interfirm contractual relations; the means used for financing firms; etc. No one is yet in a position to describe clearly how these economies will look a few years from now. Investors face a strong incentive to wait until more is known before committing their funds to any particular project, hoping to learn from the experience of others what works and what does not. But this learning is a form of externality generated by the initial entrants. If a firm succeeds, others will quickly try to imitate those aspects of the firm that worked best; if it fails, others will know better what to avoid. Given that virtually nothing is yet known concerning the future design of these economies, every new firm is in effect an experiment.

In theory, the right response is to subsidize whatever specifically is generating an externality. Since there is uncertainty concerning the appropriate design of virtually every aspect of these firms, however, it is difficult to pinpoint a specific action generating externalities. Inevitably, much of the experimentation will be done by small new firms that initially invest little in order to "test the waters" before investing further. Changes by existing firms are likely to be much more limited. Replacing old technology with newer but well-tested imported technology, for example, should not generate much information of use to others.

This suggests some form of subsidy limited to new firms, the reverse of the favoritism traditionally shown for state firms. But what form should such a subsidy take? Many developing countries have adopted tax holidays, under which new firms are exempt from corporate income taxes during their first few years of operation.[38] This tax exemption often has little direct value, however, since new firms normally have little or no net income during their first few years of operation. As shown in Mintz (1990), its value can also vary dramatically depending on detailed aspects of the tax law, for example, whether loss carry-forwards are allowed, making it very difficult to set the desired subsidy rate.[39] The size of the subsidy depends on the capital intensity of the firm.

Yet the size of the externality need not be closely related to capital intensity. An alternative that is neutral with respect to a firm's capital intensity would be to subsidize firms on the basis of their value added during the first few years of operation. This cannot be done simply by assigning a firm a lower VAT rate during its first few years in operation, however.[40] In addition, when a firm's tax rate changes over time, timing of deductions becomes important, whereas this timing can be ignored when the rate remains constant over time. For example, allowing expensing of capital investment at the initial low VAT rate and then taxing the later income generated by this capital at high rates discourages new investment, contrary to the intent of the subsidy. An effective subsidy would spread these deductions over time to correspond in timing to the income generated from these expenditures.[41]

Foreign subsidiaries may generate particularly large externalities since they can introduce local managers to information about the internal operations of successful foreign firms. In addition, they provide externalities to other potential foreign investors, who may wait to observe the outcome from earlier foreign investments before committing their own funds. The argument for subsidizing also applies to foreign subsidiaries.

The size of externalities should diminish over time, as the economy reaches a new equilibrium, since in a stable economy less would be learned from new entrants. As a result, any subsidies based on these externalities would also diminish rapidly over time. This declining subsidy gives firms an incentive to enter sooner rather than later, as desired. The effect will be stronger if the declining time pattern of the subsidy rate is agreed to in the initial legislation.

Even in a stable economy, some case can be made for such subsidies. To some degree, they do exist even under U.S. tax legislation. Certainly there are

38. For a summary of these tax provisions and a discussion of the incentives created by these holidays, see Mintz (1990).

39. One problem that exists with any such subsidy scheme is that firms not qualifying for the subsidy have the incentive to shut down and then reopen or to open new subsidiaries in order to qualify for the subsidy. Administrative rules might be used to limit this abuse, e.g., limiting the fraction of capital or labor in a new firm that comes from any given existing firm.

40. Doing so results in a rebate of the value-added taxes paid at a higher rate on the inputs it purchases, in which case the subsidy is tied to the firm's gross sales to final consumers rather than its value added. Similarly, a lower VAT rate provides a subsidy for output sold domestically but not for output that is exported, which again seems inappropriate.

41. One mechanism to spread out these deductions is to grant a deduction each year equal to the market interest rate times the historical cost of the capital in use. If tax rates were to remain constant over time, this is equivalent in present value to allowing expensing. Inflation still leads to a "front-loading" of deductions, however.

tax incentives for research and development. But, in addition, small firms and noncorporate firms face lower tax rates.[42] New entrepreneurs also receive an important part of their compensation in the form of capital gains on the value of their business, and these capital gains have also been subject to favorable tax treatment.

If externalities generated by new firms are not adequately internalized through subsidies, then any policy that affects the rate of entry of new firms should take into account the welfare consequences of this effect. For example, selling off state firms reduces the amount of funds that investors have available to start up *new* private businesses. If new businesses generate greater externalities than do state firms after privatization, as seems likely, then this crowding out imposes important social costs.[43]

9.5.2 Credit Constraints

The entry of new firms in these countries has been quite limited so far, in part because credit has been very difficult to obtain. To some degree, the banking system has simply continued to focus on the large state firms with whom it has had a working relationship for many years. The problems are more basic, however. New firms have no track record to use to demonstrate their creditworthiness, and new owners may have few personal assets to pledge as collateral.[44] Some of the potential borrowers may also be fraudulent, simply intending to disappear with the borrowed funds. Given banks' limited ability to screen loan applicants, they may rationally anticipate receiving a below-market rate of return on loans to new firms. The social rate of return on such loans can be much higher, however, since the funds lost to fraudulent borrowers from a social perspective are a transfer rather than a waste of resources.

Even if banks could successfully screen out all fraudulent borrowers, there may still be too little lending to new firms. Even if the expected economic rate of return on the invested funds at least equals the opportunity cost of funds, for example, the return to the bank can be much lower since it bears all the losses on bad projects that default but receives only the interest rate on projects that succeed. Without asymmetric information, equity financing would not be subject to this problem. But equity markets do not yet exist in these countries.

Asymmetric information problems are far less important with existing firms, since the past experience of the firms provides substantial information about their viability. From a social perspective, there will therefore be too little lending to new firms relative to existing firms. But how can policy be used to increase credit allocations to new firms? One simple approach is simply to require that at least some percent of each bank's lending go to new firms. If the

---

42. New entrants are normally small and normally subject to taxes at noncorporate rates for their first few years in business.

43. For further discussion, see Gordon (1991).

44. In any case, the law may make it difficult for the bank to seize these assets in the event of default.

banks in fact lose money on these loans, then the result is a higher equilibrium interest rate on loans to existing firms and/or a lower rate paid on deposits. Competition with foreign banks may limit the banks' ability to pass on the losses on new loans to other customers of the bank. An alternative would be to reduce the bank's tax rate as a function of the fraction of its loans going to new firms.

Just as asymmetrical information will limit the amount of credit extended by domestic banks to new firms, it will also likely limit the amount of funds invested by foreigners in these countries. Foreigners do not know which firms are good risks—they do not even know which countries are good risks. In theory, they will invest until the ex ante marginal return is the same as that available elsewhere. But if the country gains at the margin from additional funds, even given the rate of return charged on these funds, then it has the incentive to intervene to increase the size of capital imports. Under what conditions would it gain at the margin? If foreigners received the economic return from their investments, free of tax, and those who sold the assets to the foreign investors broke even on the sale, then there is no direct net gain to the country from the marginal investment. With asymmetrical information, however, domestic sellers may often succeed in selling "lemons" to foreigners and would not knowingly undercharge for assets, so on average they gain from sales of assets to foreigners. In addition, the domestic government gains not only from taxes known at the time of the investment but also perhaps from additional taxes enacted in the future. If the country gains at the margin from additional capital inflows, the appropriate response is a subsidy to capital inflows chosen so that on net the country breaks even on the marginal capital inflow.[45]

Another response to asymmetrical information problems is to redesign the tax system so as to leave more funds in the hands of the better informed, who face fewer asymmetrical information problems when they invest these funds. The better informed are primarily the new private entrepreneurs who by self-selection have been willing to commit their time and savings to their new businesses. Not only do taxes on these businesses distort marginal incentives, but they also worsen the problems created by asymmetrical information by reducing the cash holdings of the better informed.[46] Making negative tax liabilities on tax losses incurred during the first few years of operation of a business refundable, for example, provides an extra source of finance for these firms. Another approach is to allow immediate deductions for new investment rather than spreading these deductions out over time. A credit-constrained firm will gain from these accelerated deductions even if the present value of the deductions is unchanged.[47]

As long as credit constraints remain important, any policies that affect the

45. For a similar argument, see Doyle and van Wijnbergen (1984).
46. For further discussion, see Greenwald and Stiglitz (1989).
47. An example would be replacing depreciation with a one-time deduction at the beginning equal in present value to the depreciation deductions, as advocated in Auerbach (1980).

amount of credit going to new businesses must take into account the welfare consequences of this effect. For example, financing a government deficit through borrowing from the banking sector reduces the amount of financing that banks can provide to new businesses. This reduction is particularly costly if too little was being loaned to new businesses to begin with.

9.5.3   Distortions to Layoff Decisions

Inevitably, during the rapid economic transformation in Eastern Europe, many existing firms will lay off some of their workers. Yet layoff decisions are badly distorted, even under the institutions in use in the OECD countries. Policies there have evolved over time to lessen these problems, but many distortions remain. The institutions now being set up in Eastern Europe are likely to lead to worse distortions, at least initially. Given the importance of layoffs during the transition process, any distortions to incentives are of concern.

Even ignoring unemployment insurance programs, there are some distortions to layoff incentives. When an additional worker is laid off and starts competing with other unemployed workers for new positions, these workers are made worse off since their chances of being hired have been somewhat reduced; the layoff therefore creates a negative externality. Firms, however, may find it slightly easier to fill vacancies owing to the larger pool of unemployed workers. Unemployment insurance introduces important further distortions. If it is financed out of general tax revenues, as it now is in Poland, then it simply provides a subsidy to unemployment. As a result, firms are too quick to lay off workers and too slow to hire them on efficiency grounds.

In Eastern Europe, economic transformation necessarily involves a large-scale movement of workers from inefficient firms and unprofitable industries to efficient firms and profitable industries. Yet workers may cling to low-paying jobs in existing firms, in spite of the substantial potential benefits of finding a better job elsewhere, because their low savings may be insufficient to tide them over until they can find a better job. The "safety net" provided by unemployment insurance may be essential to induce workers to move and to induce worker-controlled firms to lay off existing workers.

Given these conflicting pressures, how should an unemployment-insurance program be structured? Aid specifically to the unemployed cannot easily be defended on redistributional grounds. Whether the tax system taxes consumption or income, it would already attempt to treat the poor more generously than the rich. But, given their current income (consumption), why should the unemployed be treated better than other individuals with the same current income (consumption)? Just because of their previous employment, the currently unemployed should be better off than others with the same current income (consumption). The key problem is that the unemployed may have little savings. They cannot plan ahead adequately owing to the unanticipated nature of layoffs, they cannot buy insurance ex ante to protect against the financial stress created by unexpected layoffs, and they cannot borrow ex post against their presumed future earnings. These problems arise from adverse selection, compounded by the primitive nature of the financial sector in these countries.

The U.S. unemployment-insurance program attempts to provide a "safety net" to laid-off workers ex post while still not distorting the incentives faced for *temporary* layoffs. In particular, this program taxes each firm on the basis of the rate at which benefits have been paid in the past to its workers. In equilibrium, the firm basically ends up paying the unemployment-insurance benefits of its former workers while competition in the labor market implies that the ex ante costs are passed on to workers through a wage reduction to reflect their expected future unemployment benefits. In principle, therefore, the program corresponds to an insurance policy.[48] If the program provides full insurance to workers, then the firm faces roughly correct incentives when deciding whether to lay off or rehire a worker—the firm bears all the financial implications of its decisions, and workers are fully insured against the implications of these decisions.[49] Workers, however, have an incentive to remain unemployed too long since accepting a job means loss of further benefits. Since firms make rehire decisions, this distortion is unimportant with temporary layoffs but is important if the layoffs are permanent.

The U.S. program was designed in a setting where most layoffs are temporary. But this will not be the case during the next few years in Eastern Europe, where most of the firms laying off workers will be in the process of shutting down. These workers will have an incentive to search too long for new employment. In addition, since a U.S.-style system does not attempt to tax a firm's residual assets for the cost of the unemployment benefits received by the firm's former workers, failing firms do not bear the cost of the unemployment benefits received by their former workers, and firms will therefore shut down too quickly.[50]

If an unemployment-insurance program were financed out of general revenues, as in Poland, then even temporary layoff incentives would be distorted. The program simply subsidizes unemployment, encouraging firms to lay off workers and discouraging new firms from hiring them—the only way an individual can receive these benefits is to be unemployed. Paying for the program through general taxes in addition exacerbates the distortions created by these general taxes.

An alternative design for a "safety net" would be to lend money to the unemployed. Government loans to the unemployed avoid the adverse selection problem faced by private lenders since the government would be lending to all the

---

48. In practice, however, the link between taxes and future expected benefits is hardly complete. One problem emphasized by Feldstein (1974) is that there are maximum and minimum tax rates; firms at these constraints pay nothing at the margin when they lay off an extra worker. For further discussion, see Brown (1981).

49. For a formal presentation of this story, see Baily (1978).

50. This distortion is compounded by the fact that employed workers face high social insurance tax rates.

unemployed. These loans provide the liquidity that workers may need to be willing to quit and search for a better job, hastening the transition. As long as the loans are repaid by the worker in the future, there are no resulting distortions to incentives.[51] These loans would be appropriate whenever borrowing constraints seem to be important. Laid-off workers would normally face binding borrowing constraints, but so would workers who had previously been self-employed who choose to look for a different job. A good example would be Polish farmers driven out of business by cheap imports. One administrative way to run such a program would be to tax the firm hiring an unemployed worker for the past benefits paid to this unemployed worker. The firm would in equilibrium pass on these costs to the new employee either through reduced wages or through explicit payments to compensate for the costs imposed on the firm.[52] The change from a U.S. program appears small—in the United States, the firm that lays off a worker rather than the firm hiring a worker is taxed on the basis of the benefits received by this worker—yet the differences in incentives can be very important.[53]

There will still be a moral hazard problem. Individuals may accept these loans even though they have no intention of finding future employment and thus have no prospect of repaying the loan. Conditions on eligibility (e.g., past commitment to the labor force or limits on length of eligibility) could well be appropriate to limit the problems. Although some individuals would still receive loans without repaying them, the incentives are better than under the existing Polish program, where *no* individuals pay back the loans they receive.

9.5.4 Distortions Affecting Bankruptcy Decisions

When firms are on the verge of bankruptcy, their incentives can be badly distorted. Managers in principle act in the interests of a controlling subset of creditors, be they the equity holders in Western firms or the firm's workers in East European state enterprises. When a firm is not near bankruptcy, actions in the interest of a controlling subset of creditors should also be in the interest of creditors as a whole since these outside creditors would continue to be repaid in full. Near bankruptcy, however, any actions that increase the risk of bankruptcy or reduce the value of the assets left given bankruptcy will harm outside

---

51. This still leaves a lack of insurance, ex ante, for the losses that result from being unemployed. The loss should be small relative to lifetime income, however, so that the gain from insurance is likely to be much less important than the gain from relaxed borrowing constraints.

52. Given the possibility of future quits and layoffs, a firm will be under competitive pressure to pass on immediately to that worker any taxes that it pays. As a result, these taxes should be spread over time, to allow the credit-constrained worker to maintain a smooth consumption path. If the worker does leave the new firm, any remaining liabilities should be transferred to the following employer.

53. Administration of the program becomes more complicated, however, since the net payments to each worker must be kept track of, rather than simply the net payments to workers from each firm.

creditors. Yet managers have no reason to take this harm into account in their decision making, leading to the possibility of inefficient decisions.[54]

One way to limit the importance of these adverse incentives would be to limit the debt that state firms carry with them into the transition period, particularly when they are privatized. In principle, eliminating a given amount of debt from the balance sheet of a state firm should induce investors to pay that much more for the firm. In fact, the increase in the sales price for the firm may be more than enough to cover the cost of the debt assumed by the government since the reduced risk of bankruptcy is valuable to those who purchase the firm.

9.6 Conclusions

Prior to the economic reforms, the tax systems in use in Eastern Europe served primarily just an accounting role. The allocation of resources was determined in large part through negotiations between firms and the planning ministries. Income distribution was determined in large part through direct government controls over wages, prices, and the supply of consumer goods rather than through the tax law. Serving simply this accounting role, the tax law could and did end up taking a form completely incompatible with the successful operation of a market economy.

Under the reforms, governments in Eastern Europe are faced with many pressing expenditure needs, ranging from heavy investment demands for firm restructuring and improved infrastructure to social insurance benefits for the newly unemployed. Yet the existing tax system already has very high tax rates, making it very difficult and costly to raise further taxes to finance these needed expenditures. In addition, the tax base has been shrinking both because firms now have the ability to alter their decisions so as to reduce their tax liabilities and because inflation causes a drop in the tax base due primarily to the deductibility of nominal interest payments from some approximation of real income.

As a result, tax reform is essential. Since this reform must occur quickly if large misallocations and large deficits are to be avoided, proposed alternative tax systems must be simple and quick to implement. One alternative for both the current turnover tax and the current business income-tax is a tax on each firm's real value added. This alternative tax would result in a much broader tax base and would be easy to implement and easier to administer than the existing tax system.

Revenue needs are only one of the problems that will be faced by fiscal policy during the economic transformation in Eastern Europe, however. This economic transformation will inevitably be a long and difficult process. This is true in part because there are many market failures inhibiting the speed of each step of this transformation. The first key requirement of a successful

54. For further discussion, see White (1989, 1990).

transformation, for example, is the entry of large numbers of new firms. But new firms are likely to face severe credit constraints and are likely to generate important information spillovers of value to other potential entrants, on net resulting in too slow a rate of entry of new firms on efficiency grounds. The second key requirement of the economic transformation is that existing inefficient firms need to be shut down. But there is a large literature pointing out ways in which the incentives faced by firms near or in bankruptcy can be badly distorted, resulting in misinvestment and too slow a rate of exit. Third, workers leaving inefficient firms and searching for employment in new firms likely face spells of unemployment in between. While some form of unemployment insurance is essential to facilitate this movement of workers, existing programs provide a large subsidy to becoming and remaining unemployed, resulting in an excessive rate of unemployment.

These distortions exist to some extent in all economies but are particularly important in Eastern Europe given the rapid rate of firm entry and exit that needs to occur there and the great uncertainty that exists now concerning the future design of these economies. As a result, there are strong economic grounds for further fiscal intervention. Given the presumption that the rate of entry of new firms and the rate of exit of existing firms will be inadequate, that resources will be used poorly by failing firms, and that the unemployment rate will be too high, based on efficiency criteria, any policies that move these decisions in the desired direction should take these benefits into account. Some possible approaches are suggested in the paper. Any such interventions must be designed with great care, however, given the potential for the old planning ministries to reassert their control over the allocation of resources.

References

Auerbach, Alan J. 1980. The first-year capital recovery system. *Tax Notes* 10:515–23.
———. 1988. Inflation and the tax treatment of firm behavior. *American Economic Review* 71:419–23.
Baily, Martin Neil. 1978. Some aspects of optimal unemployment insurance. *Journal of Public Economics* 10:379–402.
Barro, Robert. 1979. On the determination of the public debt. *Journal of Political Economy* 87:940–71.
Blejer, Mario I., and Gyorgy Szapary. 1990. The evolving role of tax policy in China. *Journal of Comparative Economics* 14:452–72.
Brown, Eleanor P. 1981. "Experience rating for unemployment insurance taxes." Ph.D. diss., Princeton University.
Diamond, Peter, and James Mirrlees. 1971. Optimal taxation and public production: I, Production efficiency; II, Tax rules. *American Economic Review* 61:8–27; 261–78.
Doyle, Chris, and Sweder van Wijnbergen. 1984. Taxation of foreign multinationals: A sequential bargaining approach to tax holidays. World Bank/University of Amsterdam. Mimeo.

Feldstein, Martin S. 1974. Unemployment insurance: Adverse incentives and distributional anomalies. *National Tax Journal 37*: 231–44.

Gordon, Roger H. 1984. Inflation, taxation, and corporate behavior. *Quarterly Journal of Economics* 99:313–27.

———. 1985. Taxation of corporate capital income: Tax revenues vs. tax distortions. *Quarterly Journal of Economics* 100:1–27.

———. 1991. Privatization: Notes on the macroeconomic consequences. Mimeo.

Gordon, Roger H., and James Levinsohn. 1990. The linkage between domestic taxes and border taxes. In *Taxation in the global economy*, ed. Assaf Razin and Joel Slemrod. Chicago: University of Chicago Press.

Gordon, Roger H., and Joel Slemrod. 1988. Do we collect any revenue from taxing capital income? *Tax Policy and the Economy* 2: 89–130.

Gordon, Roger H., and Hal Varian. 1989. Taxation of asset income in the presence of a world securities market. *Journal of International Economics* 26:205–26.

Gray, Cheryl W. 1990. Tax systems in the reforming socialist economies of Europe. Working Paper no. WPS 501. Washington, D.C.: World Bank.

Greenwald, Bruce, and Joseph E. Stiglitz. 1989. Impact of the changing tax environment on investments and productivity: Financial structure and the corporate income tax. *Journal of Accounting, Auditing, and Finance*, n.s., 4:281–304.

Laban, Raul, and Holger C. Wolf. 1991. Wholesale privatization during incredible reforms. New York University. Mimeo.

Lucas, Robert E. 1988. On the mechanics of economic development. *Journal of Monetary Economics* 21:3–42.

McLure, Charles E., Jr. 1991. A consumption-based direct tax for countries in transition from socialism. Stanford, Calif.: Hoover Institution. Mimeo.

Mihaljek, Dubravko. 1991. Tax reform in socialist economies in transition. Washington, D.C.: World Bank. Mimeo.

Mintz, Jack. 1990. Corporate tax holidays and investment. *World Bank Economic Review* 4:81–102.

Naughton, Barry. 1988. Macroeconomic management and system reform in China. University of California, San Diego. Mimeo.

Razin, Assaf, and Efraim Sadka. 1989. International tax competition and gains from tax harmonization. Working Paper no. 3152. Cambridge, Mass.: NBER.

Romer, Paul. 1986. Increasing returns and long-run growth. *Journal of Political Economy* 94:1002–37.

White, Michelle. 1989. The corporate bankruptcy decision. *Journal of Economic Perspectives* 3: 129–51.

———. 1990. Bankruptcy issues in Eastern Europe. University of Michigan. Mimeo.

Comment   Barry Bosworth

Roger Gordon's paper is very useful in providing some sensible advice, gained from the experience of OECD countries, on the primary measures that East European countries will need to take to establish viable tax systems to support public expenditures. I fully agree with his analysis of the potential large benefits from moving as quickly as possible to convert the turnover tax to a value-added tax and reducing the degree of reliance on the business profits tax, restructuring it as a cash-flow tax. However, I am bothered by some of the more minor themes of the paper. In addition, I feel that it is mistitled since it really emphasizes issues of taxation with very little discussion of the pressures that these countries will face from the expenditure side.

First, the need to adopt a long-term horizon for fiscal policy that considers the costs of unfunded future liabilities has been a popular theme in the policy debate of the industrialized countries in recent years. Translating that discussion into a recommendation that economies in transition move away from a focus on the cash-flow budget to a concept of balancing the budget on a present-value basis seems to me to be a serious mistake. Basing current policy on projections of tax revenues and expenditures several years in the future seems foolhardy given the uncertainty of the economic environment in which they are operating. Plus, as we know from our own experience, budget projections are subject to enormous political manipulation. Furthermore, I would encourage these countries to avoid reliance on foreign indebtedness in the early stages of reform when it is difficult to instill the discipline needed to ensure repayment. Grants are always good, and these countries definitely need trade credits and foreign equity investments; but there are already excessive political pressures to use foreign debt to finance government consumption.

Second, I would be less opposed than Gordon to the introduction of a personal income tax. While the value-added and business cash-flow taxes should be the primary revenue sources, small business, the self-employed, and agriculture are essentially untaxed under his scheme. On the basis of the experience in Poland, they become a significant portion of total employment within a short time period. Plus, there will be a need for some method of introducing a progressive tax somewhere in the system. There are various means of taxing agriculture, the most efficient being to rely on a presumptive tax on agricultural land.

Third, given the fiscal pressures that these countries face in the early stages of the transition, I do not share Gordon's opposition to tariffs as long as the number of rates is very limited and maintained in the range of 10–20 percent. One could easily make infant-industry-type arguments for a transitional period of tariff protection. It is a very simple tax to collect, and the administrative structure is already in place.

Fourth, while I would agree with Gordon that inflation can lead to severe distortions with an unindexed corporate profits tax, he may give too much emphasis to inflation in explaining what happened in Poland in 1990–91. I would have liked to see some analysis of the extent to which the gap between accounting profits and economic profits accounted for the swing in corporate tax revenue versus changes in the rate of economic profit itself. I thought that economic profits went up in the early months of 1990 as firms with considerable market power raised prices and cut output, holding on to the profits because of enormous uncertainty. As the year progressed, they began to pay out the profits in the form of large wage increases. By early 1991, the economic rate of profit was low because of weak advocacy for a return to capital and because the real rate of interest was highly positive.

Fifth, I believe that the subsidy for new businesses is precisely the sort of cute fiscal program that should be avoided. It would be subject to potential abuse without a very strong tax administration system, something that is certain to be in short supply. If the problem is a bias in the allocation of credit between new and existing firms, it should be dealt with directly in the design and supervision of the financial system, rather than indirectly through a tax subsidy that is only loosely related to credit needs.

Finally, I think that Gordon's suggestion of a loan program for the unemployed in which employers would be taxed for the previous unemployment-insurance payments to a new hire is not practical. Given the starting point of the near absence of a functioning labor market, I would prefer to emphasize the positive aspects of an unemployment-insurance system of encouraging workers to move and to promote necessary layoffs in firms with excess workers and weak management control. These countries would be better advised to establish an unemployment-insurance system, similar to that of Western Europe, with a focus on a low insurance payment and a conversion of the long-term unemployed into a general means-tested welfare program. I agree that there are distortions of the type that Gordon mentions, but these countries have limited administrative resources, they cannot afford experiments, and they should focus their attention on the big problems.

Discussion Summary

Kemal Derviş said that domestic borrowing had been overlooked as an important source of government finance. He felt that domestic borrowing could be particularly successful in Poland and Hungary. Attracting private saving would reduce the need for monetary financing, helping stabilize the inflation rate.

Geoffrey Carliner addressed Bosworth's criticism of government programs that provide credit to new firms. Carliner said that, even though programs like the Small Business Administration may have been a failure in the West, such programs might be useful in Eastern Europe. Banks in Eastern Europe are closely tied to big state enterprises, and these banks have little experience in analyzing the creditworthiness of new firms. As a result, new firms do not have access to formal credit.

Simon Johnson cited survey evidence that suggests that many new firms do have access to credit but that they choose not to borrow because of high nominal interest rates. Johnson agreed with Bosworth that tax holidays generate gaming: firms close down and reregister in sectors where tax breaks are available.

Jan Winiecki also criticized tax holidays. He warned that a three-year tax holiday for new firms would be very costly since such a holiday would effectively rule out tax revenue from the private sector. As an alternative to tax holidays, he favored the proposal that new firms be able to write off investment immediately.

Jacek Rostowski supported Gordon's recommendation that East European governments should emphasize indirect taxes like wage taxes and the VAT. However, Rostowski said that too much stress was being put on changing the tax system and not enough on the question of administration. He noted that Poland already has a tax system that is like a VAT, so it really does not matter that a pure VAT has not been introduced. He said that getting people to pay, particularly people in the private sector, is the real problem.

Olivier Blanchard agreed with Gordon's resistance to rapid development of an income tax. Blanchard noted that, because of the complexity of income tax administration, such taxes should be implemented only if the government feels a strong need to make the tax system more progressive. He believes that this is not a short-term priority.

Pentti Kouri said that the public sector in Russia has a substantial asset base and low debt and should therefore be able to borrow abroad. *Jeffrey Sachs* added that the Russian government could raise "significant amounts" by issuing deutsche-mark-denominated notes at an interest rate 2 percentage points higher than the German rate.

Sweder van Wijnbergen felt that Gordon's paper did not devote enough attention to the issues of tax administration and the associated implications for tax structure. Wijnbergen said that it takes time to build an effective administrative system, even in relatively sophisticated countries like Turkey. He concluded that, over the short run, the government will need to rely on "easy" taxes, like the VAT and temporary tariffs.

Wijnbergen noted that temporary tariffs are also useful because of their effect on the balance of trade. At least for the short run, the East European countries will not have access to Western credit markets and therefore will not be able to run large trade deficits. He said that tariffs will make it easier to sustain balanced trade. *Dani Rodrik* added that tariff policy is one of the few areas in which gradualism—in this case, phasing out tariffs *slowly*—is better than shock therapy.

10   Pension Reform in a Transition Economy: Notes on Poland and Chile

Peter Diamond

Like other countries in the process of converting from centrally planned to decentralized market economies, Poland has a pension system that is undergoing change.[1] This paper explores issues that arose in considering the problems and proposals for change in the Polish pension system. Since one of the proposals is to imitate the Chilean system and replace part of the Polish system with individual retirement accounts, it seems useful also to discuss the Chilean system as well as a partially similar proposal made for the United States.

Before the start of transition, the Polish pension system was a defined-benefit system, with benefits based on years of service and earnings in the last twelve months of work. No records on individual workers were kept by the social insurance institution, which relied on information provided by employers. It is widely understood that a decentralized economy cannot base a social insurance system on a short earnings record. The incentives for both legal and illegal manipulation are too great. Thus, it is essential that a set of earnings records be built up as quickly as possible and that the pension system not rely too heavily on the short earnings records that will become available in the near future. The current situation also involves great tension between the severe budget shortfall of the government and the low level of income of many retirees (and future retirees). Thus, there is great need to concentrate benefits on those most in need, recognizing that the system should evolve as longer earnings

The author is grateful for helpful discussions about the situation in Poland with many people. He would particularly like to thank Marian Wisniewski for his thoughts and time. The content of this paper was formed in large part by the need to understand and react to Wisniewski's work with Wojciech Topinski. The author is also grateful to Salvador Valdes-Prieto for information about Chilean pensions. He has also received valuable help from Andrew Berg, Olivier Blanchard, Martina Copelman, Eduardo Engel, Yolanda Henderson, and John Micklewright. He has benefited from the comments of Barry Bosworth at the conference.

1. For other discussions of pension change in Eastern Europe, see Atkins (1991), Deutsch (1991), Hambor (1992), Jenkins (1991), and Kopits (1991).

records become available and as the budget situation and income levels evolve. The current system also has excessively easy access to disability benefits, a defect widely seen to be in need of correction.

It has been proposed that part of the current defined-benefit system be replaced by a privatized defined-contribution system, partially imitating Chile's. However, the Chilean system involves a great deal of regulation of the privatized fund managers, a level of regulation that may be beyond the regulatory abilities of Poland. In any case, one can ask whether the regulatory abilities might not be better allocated to the banking system. In addition, the Chilean system currently costs about 15 percent of tax revenues per year in administrative costs. This is far higher than the costs of administration of the current system. It is not clear that privatization will bring benefits that exceed this cost. Moreover, one can consider a defined-contribution system that is not privatized. This might have many of the advantages of the proposal with fewer complications. Whether privatized or not, high interest rates in a defined-contribution system represent an increase in government implicit and explicit liabilities relative to those in a continued defined-benefit system. Unless the change in pension system affects other taxes or government spending so as to increase investment, a high interest rate may be harmful for society even though it is good for those who will receive higher benefits from the government budget. The paper presents these issues, along with a considerable number of additional issues in the design of pension systems.

The discussion of retirement and disability pensions is divided into three groups of questions. The first group considers incentive and insurance aspects of pensions and the distribution of pensions while holding constant the aggregate level of expenditures. I will refer to this as the microeconomics of pensions and discuss some of these issues in section 10.1, along with a presentation of recent Polish legislation. The second group of questions relates to the aggregate budget for pension expenditures, and these questions are discussed in section 10.2. The third group of questions has to do with funding, involving the role of funding in the intertemporal pattern of consumption cuts to finance benefits, the effect of funding on other government expenditures, and the effect of funding on the politics of pension determination in the future. These issues are discussed in section 10.3 along with a Polish proposal to create individual funded accounts, a proposal for reform of Social Security in the United States, and the experience with individual accounts in Chile. The possible roles of public pension funds in the privatization of firms and in the development of the capital market, as well as issues of the private annuity and private pension markets, are raised in section 10.4.

10.1   The Microeconomics of Pensions

To start the discussion of the microeconomics of pensions, I give a rough description of the workings of the current Polish pension system, with some mention of the previous system.[2] This description is approximate because the system is complex and in the midst of reform, with some grandfather clauses in the new legislation. Moreover, there is the possibility of further change. In December 1990, pensions for those over age eighty were reformed. In November 1991, a new law changed the basic pension calculation for all workers and retirees.

10.1.1   Description

The pension system inherited from the pretransition regime was very generous relative to wages, although the low level of real wages means that many pensioners are living in poverty. The old system relied heavily in its functioning on the role of state enterprises in the economy.[3] The pension system is *administered* by ZUS (Zaklad Ubezpieczen Spolecznych, the social insurance institution). ZUS maintains no records on active workers. For pension recipients, ZUS does preserve in its records the elements relevant for the determination of benefits in the benefit formula. There are four elements. First is whether the pension is a retirement pension or a disability pension. Second is the final wage level of the benefit recipient. Third is the calculation of the number of years of work. Fourth is the particular industry of the worker if that is relevant for either benefit determination or benefit eligibility. In the new law, the dependence of pension benefits on industry was largely eliminated.

For *financing*, there is a payroll tax levied on the aggregate payrolls of enterprises. At present, the tax rate is 45 percent, with 43 percent going to ZUS and 2 percent for unemployment benefits that are not distributed by ZUS.[4] In 1990, contributions covered about 88 percent of expenditures. The deficit is financed from general revenues. In 1990, benefits made up 19.6 percent of aggregate disposable income, with 49 percent of the benefits being for retirement and survivor pensions, 23 percent for disability pensions, and the remaining 28 percent for family allowance, maternity, sickness, and work injury benefits. Administrative costs run 4 percent of benefits, half of which went to the post office for hand delivery of benefits (Tymowska and Wisniewski 1991).

The age of *eligibility* for retirement benefits is sixty-five for men and sixty for women. However, workers can become eligible for benefits at a younger age if they have worked for a sufficient number of years in a designated industry. As a result of the various ways of becoming eligible for benefits, the average age of new retirees is fifty-eight for men and fifty-seven for women (Tymowska and Wisniewski 1991). Eligibility for disability benefits is based

---

2. In this description, I am drawing on Barr (1991) and Henderson (1991) as well as conversations with Polish economists.
3. In addition to the pension system for industrial workers, there is a separate, sizable pension system for the agricultural sector and a system for priests, neither of which I discuss. In June 1991, there were 6,137,000 recipients of labor pensions and 1,765,000 recipients of pensions for farmers (Central Statistical Office, Warsaw, August 1991).
4. There are some deviations from this structure, which I ignore.

on the certification by a doctor of inability to work. The system recognizes three different levels of disability: level 1 is an unambiguous inability to work, level 3 an unclear inability to work, and level 2 in between. In 1990, nearly 40 percent of benefits in force were disability benefits (Topinski and Wisniewski 1991a). It was believed by analysts that the standards for disability were not adequately policed. Benefit calculations are different for the different levels of disability. Benefit eligibility also depends on the cessation of full-time work.[5] Under the new law, no benefits are paid to those eligible for benefits but still earning more than 120 percent of the national average wage; benefits are reduced by 24 percent of the national average wage for those earning between 60 and 120 percent of the national average wage. Survivor benefits are paid to children, the surviving spouse, and, sometimes, surviving parents. There is a family supplement of 10 percent of the national average wage. Benefits are fully subject to income tax, having been increased just enough to offset the basic income tax rate.

Before the start of the transition, the *benefit formula* was in nominal terms; the very high levels of inflation that occurred in the 1980s resulted in periodic adjustments of benefits for those already retired. These adjustments often involved raising the minimum benefit, resulting in cohorts of workers receiving the same benefit level. The current reform is designed to restructure the pension system on the basis of previous earnings records rather than simply adjusting for the most recent inflation without adjusting for the somewhat arbitrary corrections for earlier inflation. Thus, benefits are based on the earnings records, with *indexing of records* for the determination of benefits for those newly retired and *indexing of benefits* after retirement. In both cases, the index used is the national average wage. Benefits in force are *adjusted quarterly*, if the adjustment is at least 5 percent. There is also a *minimum pension* of 35 percent of the national average wage.

The formula in the new law is that the worker receives 24 percent of the national average wage plus 1.3 percent per year "worked" of the individual's "final" wage adjusted for the increase of the national average wage since the year that the individual's final wage was earned.[6] In formula terms, the pension can be written as

$$e_{it} = aW_t + bn_i r_i W_t,$$

where e_{it} is benefits for person i in year t, W_t is national average wages in year t, n_i is "adjusted" years of work for person i, r_i is the average of w_{is}/W_s over the relevant averaging period, w_{is} is wages that were earned by person i in year s, and a and b are constants.

---

5. However, under previous law, working 90 percent of full-time did not bar individuals from receiving either disability or retirement benefits. Such years of additional work after retirement resulted in a new (higher) benefit calculation.

6. This law has been found unconstitutional. Nevertheless, it remains useful to see the shape of legislation that can be passed by Parliament.

In the debate over pension reform, the Sejm first passed a law with a equal to 25 percent rather than 24 percent and a b of 1.5 percent rather than 1.3 percent. The calculation of "adjusted" years worked includes adjustments for education, military service, and child care. For a noncontributory year, the benefit calculation uses the factor 0.7 percent (0.9 percent in the first plan) rather than 1.3 percent. In terms of the formula as written above, adjusted years of work include 7/13 times the number of allowed noncontributory years. Thus, a retiree with twenty-four working years and six allowed noncontributory years would have 27.2 adjusted years, 90.7 percent of the adjusted years of someone who had worked thirty years. This is fairly close to a calculation based simply on age. The years used for calculating the individual's final wage are initially the best consecutive three calendar years out of the last twelve. The number of years used in calculating the individual average wage increases by one per year until it reaches ten (out of the last twenty).[7] The length of the averaging period depends on the year of retirement, not the year of eligibility (or date of birth).

The formula for disabled retirees is basically the same, with an inclusion in the formula of years until "retirement" (twenty-five years of service or age sixty) treated the same as the noncontributory years in the retirement benefit formula.[8]

There is also a *cap on benefits* that comes from a ceiling on the final wage usable in the benefit formula, with the cap equal to 2.5 times the national average wage (three in the first plan).

10.1.2   Discussion

The image of the system held by analysts with whom I talked was that replacement rates (the ratios of benefits to wages) were very high by Western standards, but, with very low wages, the living standards of many of the retirees were very low.[9] This contributed to the perceived need for a highly redistributive formula.

It was widely recognized among the pension authorities with whom I talked that a final wage formula based on a short averaging period is not viable in the kind of private economy that Poland is evolving into. There are three obvious problems for final wage systems that will lead some of the people to have very high final wages and so very high pension benefits. One element is direct fraud and misreporting of final wages. This is relatively easy in a system where ZUS maintains no records and one goes to one's employer for documentation of final earnings (taxes paid by enterprises have been paid on the total wage bill without any reporting separately of wages by individuals). The second element

7. Under previous law, benefits were based on earnings in the last twelve months of work.
8. While the special supplementary pension for particular industries was eliminated, miners receive more than one year of service for benefit calculations per year of service under ground.
9. Average replacement rates were reported to be 80 percent in Poland, in contrast to 41 percent in the United States (Hambor 1992). In 1991, the average benefit (disability and retirement) was Zl 1,050,000 ($95.00) per month, equal to 62 percent of the national average wage (Atkins 1991).

is the rise of implicit contracts that will result in workers getting very high final wages presumably taken implicitly out of earlier earnings or the earnings of younger workers. This will again make the pension system very expensive and uneven across workers depending on the extent of their access to such an implicit contract. The third element is the possibility of additional work, for example, overtime, to boost the earnings of workers in their last year or last three years.

In thinking about the magnitude of these problems, it is useful to recognize that, with an annuity based on final earnings, the return to shifting earnings is very large. One would even find it profitable to report very high wages in circumstances where high wages were subject to both income tax and payroll tax because the return would be so substantial. As a rough calculation, with a three-year averaging period, each additional zloty of earnings yields $bn_i/3$ additional zlotys in benefits in the first year, with the amount indexed to national average wages for the rest of the retiree's life (plus the possibility of a survivor's benefit). With a b of 1.3 percent and an n_i of 30 (roughly the average), the return is a wage-indexed 13 percent per year for the rest of life.

Moreover, the effect of pensions based on final average wages on the use of overtime by older workers is clearly illustrated by experiences in the West. For example, the MBTA (bus and subway system) in Boston has such a pension system, one based on a four-year average. Also in the union contract is the right of senior workers to claim available overtime if they want it. As a result, workers in their sixties at the MBTA work very long hours and get large pensions. This came to the attention of the public in 1978, when a Green Line train plowed into another train at the Arlington Street station, injuring twenty-one persons. The driver had worked twenty-five straight hours, had six hours off, and had gone straight back to work. It was reported that he averaged seventy-five hours a week during 1977 (*Boston Globe*, 19 January, 6 and 10 May 1978).

The use of a formula combining years of work with a relatively short averaging period creates an unattractive pattern of work incentives across workers of different ages. For workers who are merely contributing a year toward the benefit calculation, the tax is a deadweight burden on their labor supply without any offsetting benefit for marginal hours worked. On the other hand, for workers in a year that will go into the benefit calculation, the incentive for additional labor supply from the benefit calculation can easily exceed the cost from taxes, resulting in another distortion. That is, there is a double distortion involved in the use of a short averaging period. For years that will not enter the averaging period, the payroll tax is a pure tax on the margin, generating the usual deadweight burden. For years that do count for averaging purposes, the value of additional benefits less taxes will be positive, again generating a deadweight burden. Thus, if one is to maintain a system with a defined-benefit calculation of pension levels, the longer the averaging period and the less importance given to late years, the fewer the distortions that will be associated with labor supply.[10]

In addition to the effect on incentives of the use of a short earnings period in determining the average wage, this use also has implications for the fairness of the system and its success in fulfilling its role of giving a sensible pattern of replacement rates. In a private enterprise economy, individual earnings are highly stochastic.[11] The fraction of the population with smoothly growing annual earnings is not large.[12] Thus, the use of a short earnings period results in a highly random distribution of pensions. This is not fair under many conceptions of fairness. In addition, if replacement rates are meant to relate to the standard of living to which individuals became accustomed, the use of a short averaging period defeats this purpose since a short period of earnings is not a good proxy for lifetime income and therefore the standard of living.

ZUS has discussed the need to develop a computerized system of tracking individual earnings but does not seem to feel that such a system is urgently needed. This was in contrast with the tax authorities, who are hard at work on a computerized system felt to be necessary for collecting taxes under the new income tax scheme. Thus, it would make sense to have ZUS piggyback on the large investment that the tax authorities are making, yielding an earlier tracking of earnings records than would occur with a delayed start. Taking a subtotal of earnings subject to ZUS taxation would not be a problem for the tax authority's computer system being installed. Moreover, direct linking of tax and ZUS records would affect the incentive to underreport income for tax purposes. With taxable income eventually becoming the basis for pension receipt, there is less incentive for income-tax evasion. Again, there is an interaction between incentives for tax evasion and the length of the averaging period. Even with a ten-year averaging period, the incentive for tax evasion among younger workers remains high since there is no benefit payoff for any reporting above the minimum necessary for receiving credit for a year of service. This combining of tax and insurance contribution records also represents a structure for beginning to inform workers about the value of benefits to be received as well as taxes paid and therefore, it is to be hoped, for altering the behavioral response to ZUS taxes and with it deadweight burdens.

The current reform is a change in benefit calculation, staying within the structure of the defined-benefit formula used previously. The legislated increase in the averaging period for determining final wages represents a steady cut in benefits since a high average is used for the calculation. That is, selecting the three best years of the last twelve is very likely to yield a higher average wage than selecting the best four of the last thirteen. In order to determine how

10. Of course, in the short run with very high anticipated unemployment during the transition, this issue needs to be framed differently than in the standard Walrasian model.
11. I do not know how much earnings variation there was in Poland before transition.
12. For the United States, see Consultant Panel (1976).

much of a benefit cut is implied, one would need a stochastic model of the age structure of earnings.[13]

As employment records grow, it will become appropriate to rethink the benefit formula, both the values of the constants a and b and the structure of the formula. Now, the formula includes a flat benefit term and a term that is a product of years worked and a final average wage, calculated over a short period. The growth of the length of the averaging period raises the question of the appropriateness of changing the relative sizes of the flat benefit term and the earnings-related benefit term in the formula. Moreover, once there are long earnings histories, it might be appropriate to change from a formula based on such a product to one based simply on average earnings, with years out of the labor force represented by zeros that go into the averaging calculation. Partial weight for years of child bearing, education, or military service could be included in such a formula, as at present, by imputing a wage level for such years for benefit calculation purposes. This could be done on a flat basis or proportionally to individual earnings in other years. That is, one can ask how the contribution to pension benefit of a year of military service should vary with the level of nonmilitary earnings.

With increased years available in earnings records, there is less randomness in the relation between benefits and lifetime earnings. This represents one reason for a phased transition in the benefit formula with more reliance on individual earnings and less on average earnings. Moreover, it is appropriate to consider a phased transition to a different degree of progressivity as the economy becomes richer. It might be useful to consider explicitly a time-varying benefit formula such that the constants a and b in the formula change by a rule designed to preserve the cost of pensions for a given cohort (based on age, not retirement date). One would also want to think about adjusting the minimum pension as part of the same reconsideration.[14]

The steady increase in the length of earnings records raises the further question of whether lengthening the averaging period and otherwise preserving the structure of the benefit formula is the best mature structure. In particular, once one had a long earnings record for individuals, would one still want the same level of importance given to years of service? Consider two individuals with the same earnings level for the averaging period, which also equals the national average wage. Then each of them will receive $.24 + .013n_i$ times the average wage. Differences in earnings outside the averaging period do not affect benefits, although the number of years with earnings (or counting toward earnings)

---

13. Such a model was estimated for the United States precisely to calculate the implications of a lengthening averaging period (see Balcer and Diamond 1977; and Consultant Panel 1976).

14. In the United States, there is a legislated phase-in of a delay in the "normal retirement age." This is a legislated phase-in of decreased benefits; the age of eligibility for benefits was not changed.

does matter. There does not seem to be a clear case for this way of treating different years.[15]

In order to consider the question of redesigning the formula, it might be useful to rewrite it in a mathematically equivalent form, but one that might be more helpful. Consider listing the earnings of an individual for all the years of his life up to retirement age. There will be many zeros for years for which there is no credit. There will be many years with actual wages. There will be years that count as noncontributory years. The first step in the procedure is to select the years used to calculate the final wage. For these years, the actual wage is left for calculation purposes. For other years with positive earnings (that count toward years of service), the actual wage is replaced by the final wage. For noncontributory years of service, the wage attributed is seven-thirteenths of the final wage. The remaining years are left as zeros. Then an average is taken of all these years. This method gives the same calculation as the present one (up to a linear transformation). Thus, one is imputing to a year worked but not counted in the average for final wages a wage equal to the final wage. Thus, one is imputing to a noncontributory year a wage equal to 7/13 times the final wage. Taking this approach toward actual benefit calculations represents another way of thinking about both the transition and the final structure. One can then use a system where every year will count toward benefits, but not necessarily by taking a straight average. Having every year count should help ease the deadweight burdens from taxes used to finance the formula as well as helping with tax evasion and providing increased fairness.

Under the income tax law that came into effect 1 January 1992, pension benefits are fully taxable under the income tax. Given the lack of a tight historical link between benefits and past earnings, this seems an appropriate step in having a suitable distribution of after-tax pension incomes. As the system evolves, and as private pensions grow up, it may become necessary to rethink the tax treatment of pensions to reflect fairness issues on a life-cycle basis as well as on a short-run-needs basis. Fairness issues depend on the tax treatment of payroll taxes for pensions, on tax treatment of both contributions for and benefits from private pensions, and on the tax treatment of the return to savings generally.

The earnings test described above has cliffs rather than a smooth decrease in benefits with respect to earnings. It also makes no exception for advanced ages. This limits the incentives for work beyond the retirement eligibility age that comes from anticipation of future benefits. In the United States, it is also true that Social Security benefits are (partially) subject to income taxation, and there is an earnings test (for beneficiaries under seventy). The combination of tax and earnings test further concentrates net benefits not only among

---

15. The fact that private firms commonly use a final average wage and years of service formula does not imply that it is appropriate for a social insurance benefit formula.

those with low incomes but also among those with low earnings (beyond the progressivity present in the benefit formula). The underlying logic behind having two separate bases for implicit and explicit taxation of benefits is that benefits are meant to replace lost earnings and to be concentrated among the currently poor. Insofar as we think of the pension system as an insurance system as well as a forced savings system, this approach provides insurance against a short working life. With the rise of the income tax and the fact that benefits are taxable under the income tax, there is a mechanism in place for having a smoothly varying earnings test.

Consideration of the link between continued work and pension benefits also raises the question of the role of actuarial adjustments of benefits, that is, the variation of the level of benefits with the age at which they are first claimed. The current system has credits for years of service, and this implies that an extra year of work increases benefits. With a final benefit formula based on a short period of earnings, there is also the possibility of a sizable increase in the final wage for benefit calculation purposes as a result of an additional year of earnings. However, the increase in the averaging period based on the date of claiming benefits offsets this increase for some workers. Thus, there are two routes to increased benefits as a result of continued work, through years of service and through the calculation of the final average. Neither route involves an adjustment of the flat benefit part of the formula. The question here is whether delayed benefits should be partially compensated by increased benefits in a different way. With the lengthening averaging period, the incentive for continued work will decrease over time. With a benefit formula depending on fuller earnings histories, one can consider the incentives to continued work (and earlier work) implicit in actuarial adjustment as well as the question of the timing of paying benefits that have the same expected present discounted value. Insofar as one is trying to insure length of working life, optimal insurance principles call for a less than full actuarial adjustment for delayed retirement.

The current system has special rules for particular industries, although far less than previously. In Western economies, it is common for private pensions to differ in anticipated retirement ages even when the social insurance program does not distinguish. Given the presence of labor mobility between industries and occupations, it seems appropriate to relegate this differential to private pensions. In addition, with the current system financed by uniform taxes, industry-varying benefits imply a redistribution toward some industries that seems unlikely to have good efficiency effects.

A rethinking of disability standards is obviously an important part of a reform of the overall pensions system. The force of the importance of such a rethinking can be seen from the fact that, in 1990, nearly 40 percent of beneficiaries were receiving disability pensions. For the short run, one needs to recognize the role of disability benefits in lieu of long-term unemployment benefits. It would not be surprising if there were a concentration among older workers of the long-term unemployment caused by the transition to market capitalism.[16]

10.2   Aggregate Budget for Pensions

There are two dimensions to a consideration of the determination of the aggregate level of benefits. One is the familiar normative economic calculation trying to contrast the shadow value of resources in the hands of the government with the importance of additional benefits in the hands of retirees. This dimension needs to be considered both in the short run, where there is a serious overall budget problem for Poland, and in the longer term, where demographic developments will increase the burden of a fully wage-indexed social insurance system.[17] The second dimension is the political economy of budget determination, as it is affected by the design of institutions.

While the Polish replacement rate is extremely high by Western standards, the standard of living is extremely low, with the result that many retirees are living in poverty. This combination of factors makes one think that the level of progressivity in the system could properly change significantly over time as the economy grows; preservation of a high minimum pension to avoid poverty could go with a pattern of change in the benefit formula that will result in a steady shift over time in the degree of progressivity. Real growth relative to the minimum pension would represent some decrease in pension costs relative to the economy. Similarly, designing a system with progressivity in replacement rates that is not fully indexed to wages could help the long-run fiscal problem if there is real economic growth. Such a shift will not happen automatically, however, if the system is indexed on the wage, as indeed it should be in the short run, given the unpredictability of the behavior of real wages in the near term during the transition. This again raises the question of alternative structures for the benefit formula, both for the short run and as a planned transition.

It is also important to recognize the role of indexing in protecting pensions against inflation. During the 1980s, difficulties in the overall Polish budget contributed to the rise of inflation. With unindexed pensions that were adjusted incompletely and periodically, a considerable amount of the redistribution from inflation fell on pensioners. With pensions now indexed, the scope for such transfers is considerably reduced, although lags in the recalculation of pensions would imply redistribution from inflation, particularly if inflation rates are very high. In addition to considering the link from the budget to pen-

---

16. More generally, one needs to recognize that disability evaluation is subject to both type-I and type-II errors. For evidence from the United States of the significant fraction of workers denied disability benefits who never work again, see Bound (1989). For a discussion of the principles behind selecting disability and retirement benefit levels in recognition of the errors in disability eligibility determination, see Diamond and Sheshinski (1992).

17. The ratio of workers to retirees changes from 2.20 to 1 in 1990 to 1.76 to 1 in 2020 (Topinski and Wisniewski 1991a).

sions through inflation, it is natural to ask about possible planned real changes as the budgetary picture changes: To what extent does one want to change the earnings test as part of changing progressivity? Is there a case for changing benefit determination for those already retired to price rather than wage indexing at some point in the future? Should there be phased benefit cuts in advance of the demographic changes coming early next century?

In addition to considering normative issues in the determination of the level of aggregate expenditure on benefits, it is important to consider the interaction between the organization of the pension system and the politics of pension determination, beyond the role of indexing in the effect of inflation. The present payroll tax is levied only on enterprises and is not normally seen by workers. Thus, it is natural to consider changing the system along the lines of the change that was done to incorporate the income tax, making workers aware of the presence of the income tax. In the case of the income tax, on 1 January 1992 the wages of all workers were raised to offset the fact that they are now subject to income tax. The plan was to leave workers approximately in the same position as before.[18] A similar move could be made to shift the basis of ZUS taxation from being fully on the employer to being partially on the employee, with half and half a common, but not universal, Western number (U.S. Department of Health and Human Services). This would have no short-run economic effects but would matter in the longer run if it affected the perceptions of workers and therefore the political pressures in the pension determination process. I think that there is every reason to think that there would be such an effect and that such a change would have a moderating effect on the determination of expenditures for the pension system.

10.3 Funding

The Polish pension system does not have its own fund. In the past, the payroll tax exceeded the expenditures of ZUS, with the surplus going into the general budget. At present, the payroll tax is inadequate to cover the expenditures of ZUS, and the deficit is coming out of general revenues. There has been serious consideration in Poland of partially imitating Chile and creating individually funded pension accounts managed by private firms (see Topinski and Wisniewski 1991a, 1991b). Unlike Chile, where the entire social security system was replaced by this new system, the proposal for Poland is to preserve the current benefit formula up to 120 percent of the national average wage and to replace the benefit levels between there and the cutoff of 2.5 times national average earnings by a funded system.

One can envision a strictly pay-as-you-go pension system, where either ben-

---

18. Since the payroll tax rate was not changed at the same time as wages were increased, this represents a sizable increase in the tax being paid by enterprises.

efits or taxes or some combination is adjusted on a year-by-year basis so that the earmarked tax revenues exactly equal benefit payments (plus administrative costs). I am not aware of any use of such a system. Thus, while it is common to refer to pension systems without substantial funds as *pay as you go*, they are not in a strict sense pay-as-you-go systems. Instead, they are systems with defined-benefit rules, earmarked revenues, and reliance on a political mechanism to deal with the implications of differences in the annual rates of flows of benefits and taxes. The crisis in social security that occurs from time to time in different countries is generally a political crisis, not an economic one. It comes from this structure and the political difficulty of either raising taxes or cutting benefits. Such crises would not happen if there were a truly pay-as-you-go system or an adequately funded and planned system.[19] From the perspective of avoiding crises and of figuring out how the government will respond to the ones that do occur, it is natural to ask about the implications of having an explicit fund that grows at a rate equal to the difference between earmarked taxes and expenditures plus the value of some interest rate times the level of the fund. Such a fund will not start with a zero balance if there is a plan for a transition to a new benefit formula that starts by endowing either individual accounts or an aggregate fund. Such an endowment can come either from giving the fund government debt (perhaps debt specially designed for this purpose) or from giving the fund claims on assets being privatized.

There are many dimensions to the implications both of having a fund and of having different ways of relating benefits and taxes to the presence of a fund (either de jure or de facto). In order to separate out the different factors, I proceed in the following sequence of steps. In section 10.3.1, I briefly describe a concrete proposal that has been made for Poland to make clear the relevance of the materials that follow. In section 10.3.2, I focus on the microeconomic implications of the use of individual accounts for the determination of benefits. For this purpose, I consider how a mature system with such a funded basis might work. For purposes of concreteness, I consider a proposal for the United States put forward by Boskin, Kotlikoff, and Shoven (1988). In section 10.3.3, I turn to describing the system in Chile. I ask about the role of a fund in affecting the level of other government expenditures and the response of aggregate pension expenditures to aggregate shocks. A further question that arises in this context is the extent to which having individual accounts creates a difference from just having an aggregate fund. Because part of the logic behind proposals for creation of a fund is to decrease the role of the government, it is appropriate to consider issues of alternative methods of portfolio management and of organization of annuities for the retired. Considering Chile also raises issues of

---

19. Each year in the United States, costs and revenues of the retirement system are forecast for the following seventy-five years. Of course, such planning alone has not been sufficient to avoid crises.

alternative ways of dealing with the transition from the previous system to a newly designed system. Such a transition could be purely for new entrants into the labor market. However, proposals generally assume a much more rapid development of the new system by incorporating in it all individuals below some age, generally somewhere between forty and fifty. This raises the question of the design of the transition, which can naturally be either backward looking or forward looking. In section 10.3.4, I review transition considerations in Chile and in the Polish proposal, recognizing in particular the complexities in the Polish context that come from the absence of individual earnings records.

10.3.1 The Polish Proposal

The Polish reform passed in November has a cap on benefits from the cap on final average wages set at 2.5 times the national average wage. It does not contain any comparable cap on wages subject to taxation, although the introduction of such a cap would not represent any significant change in the design of this system, merely a decrease in revenue and progressivity. The reform that was proposed by Topinski and Wisniewski (1991a, 1991b) would replace part of the earnings levels subject to the current benefit formula by an alternatively funded system. The proposal is to continue to use the existing defined-benefit formula up to a wage level of 1.2 times the national average wage.[20] This would include the full earnings of approximately 75 percent of the work force. Similarly, the revenue from the payroll tax on earnings up to this level would go to ZUS. For earnings above 1.2 times the national average wage (perhaps up to some alternative cap), the existing benefit formula would not apply; additional benefits would instead be based on the outcomes associated with individual funded accounts. Individuals over age fifty-five would remain subject to the existing system. Individuals under fifty-five would get an initial fund level based on their age and earnings in the year of transition. The calculation for the determination of the individual fund is forward looking, based on putting the individual at the same benefit level as with the current formula if the forecasted wage growth and interest rate patterns hold and the actuarial factors come out as projected. Actual fund accumulation would depend on actual earning levels above 1.2 times the national average wage and realized rates of return on the investments selected for the individual accounts. It is proposed to follow the Chilean pattern and have some number of regulated private portfolio managers to handle fund accumulation and investment. Individual accounts would be insured by the government. Some of the income would be used to purchase life and disability insurance policies for the workers; the rest would be accumulated for retirement. It is proposed that conversion of the fund to an annuity or individual phased withdrawal would happen at age sixty-five without any

20. It is proposed to lower this cutoff slowly over time as the economy grows richer.

earnings test.[21] Moreover, borrowing against the account would be allowed for approved purposes.[22]

Thinking about such a proposal, one needs to recognize that this is a compulsory savings program, with limited insurance elements apart from the conversion to an annuity, and with the capital accumulation forced to flow through the designated intermediaries. With individuals having forced savings rather than lower taxes, some will save more than they would have otherwise, which can be evaluated in terms of the usual paternalism that underlies much of social insurance. From the perspective of an individual who would have saved otherwise, by and large the payroll tax will come out of the savings that would have happened anyway, so we are getting a redistribution of the flow of capital accumulation through these intermediaries rather than through whatever alternative allocation mechanism might have been employed. This system presumes that the level of redistribution arising from the current benefit formula in the basic part of the pension system is sufficient and envisions no further redistribution through the mechanism of the individual accounts. Of course, there would also be a chain of derivative effects on wages, employment, and interest rates that I will not discuss. This proposal differs in many ways from the continuation of the current structure. My purpose in this presentation is to isolate some of the differences by considering comparisons having only some of them.

10.3.2   The U.S. Proposal

In a thumbnail description, in the United States at present, there is a payroll tax on individual earnings up to a maximum level that covers full earnings for over 90 percent of the labor force. The revenue finances disability insurance, survivor insurance for both children and spouses, and retirement benefits. The benefit system is based on families rather than individuals, but without record sharing. That is, there are explicit spouse benefits, with individuals receiving the higher of the benefits that they would receive as a spouse or as an individual. Receipt of retirement benefits is based on a combination of age and earnings. Between sixty-two and seventy, one can receive benefits if one's earnings are sufficiently low. Beyond seventy, benefits are paid independently of earnings. Benefits are partially taxable. The level of initial benefits depends on the age at which they are first claimed and the earnings history. A piecewise linear formula relates benefits to the average of wage-indexed earnings in the thirty-five best earnings years, with declining marginal rates for progressivity. Notice

---

21. The annuity would include survivor benefits. This approach, based on marital status at the time of retirement, is different in its treatment of divorce and remarriage from the American proposal described below, which is based on marital status at the time of taxation. After a divorce, there is no good reason to have a benefit dependent on the continued life of a former spouse, as in the U.S. proposal. On the other hand, the Polish proposal does little to protect divorced spouses.

22. Chilean law attempts to prevent borrowing against the individual account. Allowing borrowing for some purposes results in a more open door for proposals to allow borrowing for other purposes, threatening to erode the paternalistic requirement of adequate savings for retirement.

in this structure that paying benefits independently of age at some point is an important part of the incentive for individuals who want to go on working until an advanced age.

The proposal for the United States was designed to stay rather close to the existing U.S. structure. As such, the system was envisioned as a wholly government-run and -organized system, with investment strictly in Treasury debt. In contrast with the defined-benefit approach of current law, the personal security account plan of Boskin, Kotlikoff, and Shoven (1988) is a defined-contribution approach. Moreover, the approach treats the family at the time of taxation as the basis for future benefit receipt from that year's taxes. Thus, the first step is to determine the taxes to be paid on the basis of aggregate family earnings. These taxes are then allocated separately and equally to husband and wife. The second step is to redistribute across individuals so that taxes that are the basis for future benefits are not the same as taxes paid. Low earners are credited with more than they paid, high earners with less.[23] Boskin, Kotlikoff, and Shoven consider no explicit redistribution between single individuals and married couples, although such a redistribution could also be done at this step. The credits available for an individual are then allocated to several uses. One is the purchase of five-year term disability insurance. Another is the purchase of survivor insurance for children. Another is the purchase of survivor insurance for the spouse. The rest goes for the purchase of a real annuity that will begin payment at age sixty-two.

In order to calculate the amount of this year's contribution to the future real retirement annuity, one needs a life table and a real interest rate (or a sequence of interest rates). The life table is presumably the current life table (or possibly some projected life table based on trends in mortality improvement). The interest rate could be simply a market rate taken from the Treasury yield curve. Such an approach would require adjustment of taxes over time to balance the budget as taxes, interest rates, and demography develop. That is, there is an aggregate risk associated with interest rates and demography. This risk must be borne somewhere in the economy.

This risk could be viewed as a problem for the income tax, with the risk shifted from the social insurance fund to the general fund. Alternatively, the social insurance system could be viewed as self-contained. Then the payroll tax would need to respond to these changes. Such induced tax changes would, in turn, result in additional benefit credits and thus further tax changes. To avoid having the system driven in this way, the authors propose that the interest rate be chosen to reflect the projected position of the social insurance fund, with taxes and benefits projected to balance. With a sizable actual fund to absorb short-run fluctuations and to smooth projected long-term changes, smooth adjustment of the interest rate should be possible to keep the social insurance

---

23. Thus, redistribution is done repeatedly on an annual basis, rather than once on a lifetime basis, as with a redistributive formula based on lifetime accumulation.

fund in rough balance at the level (of taxes or benefits) desired. Once an annuity has been allocated to an individual, that amount is not changed in response to future developments. Rather, the forecast of future conditions made in some year is the only basis for future benefits based on that year's earnings. That is, the social risks that arise later are spread among future benefit promises and future taxes, not past benefit promises.

Some of the differences between this proposal and current U.S. practice are compatible with the current defined-benefit approach and are not part of my discussion. For example, equal sharing between husband and wife of their total annual earnings is something that has been repeatedly proposed for and is compatible with the existing system (see, e.g., Congressional Budget Office 1986).[24] The two elements that I consider are the role of an earnings test and the determination of benefits for the newly retired.

Earnings Test and Actuarial Adjustment

Under the current U.S. system, benefits are reduced by one-third (for sixty-five to seventy-year-olds) or half (for sixty-two to sixty-five-year-olds) of the excess of earnings above an allowable amount.[25] Thus, the system works to give larger benefits to people who have shorter careers. This is a separate mechanism from relating the size of initial benefits to the date at which they are first claimed. Both these mechanisms are designed to provide insurance on the length of working life, an otherwise uninsurable event. Moreover, to the extent that length of working life for a given individual is independent of length of actual life, reflecting risks associated with job availability rather than health, the risk has a twofold nature: a shorter working life represents both a shorter time for the accumulation of income for retirement and a longer retirement period that needs to be financed. Thus, this seems a dimension of risk well worth consideration in the design of a social insurance program. Of course, any attempt to insure length of working life by observing actual period of earnings involves a deadweight burden through the disincentive to additional work. Optimal insurance/tax considerations suggest there should be some positive implicit tax on further work. Given the presence of an income tax already, this theorem, which is based on no taxation in the absence of an implicit tax from the insurance program, is not directly applicable but needs to be confirmed in the context of the actual income-tax level.

It is useful to consider the question of the relation between benefit level and age at which benefits are first claimed in a series of steps. Assume that one has an annuity that begins at age sixty-five. One could then consider allowing

24. Further differences relating to family structure are also ignored. For example, the current U.S. system provides survivor benefits for children out of the general revenue pool. The Boskin, Kotlikoff, and Shoven proposal would deduct the expected cost of survivor benefits for children from the retirement benefits of their parents.

25. $6,840 for sixty-two- to sixty-five-year-olds and $9,360 for sixty-five- to seventy-year-olds in 1990.

individuals to select a different age at which to start the annuity. Individuals feeling a liquidity pinch at an earlier age could receive an actuarially reduced pension at an earlier age. (Of course the paternalism that underlies a forced savings program should limit the minimum age at which such a claim can be made.) Alternatively, individuals who are not feeling a pinch at age sixty-five might prefer to delay receipt of this pension. Since the private annuity market is very imperfect (high markups and limited indexing), an individual might prefer having a larger annuity starting later rather than starting an annuity now, which includes the option of taking the payments and using them to buy further annuities. The obvious difficulty with simply allowing such a choice is the adverse selection problem associated with life expectancy: those with longer life expectancy would be more likely to delay the start of benefits in return for increased benefits once started. Considering both earlier and later starting dates for benefits, one can ask about limiting choice based on an earnings test. That is, one might only allow an early start of benefits for retired workers, and one might require the start of benefits once retired beyond some age. Thus, allowing the claiming of benefits by workers age sixty-two to seventy can be viewed in one of two different lights. First, it is a form of paternalism requiring workers to wait to receive higher benefits. Second, it relates to adverse selection that the trade-off between earlier benefits and higher benefits will be selected by workers in light of their life expectancies. Without the use of the earnings test, choice of date to start benefits will depend on the shadow interest rates for individual calculations, which are no doubt related to earnings flows as well as wealth levels. The presence of an earnings test therefore seems to be a useful supplement to the incentives and the deviation of the change in benefits from a purely actuarial pattern, even if the actuarial adjustment is deliberately different from actuarially fair.

Defined-Benefit and Defined-Contribution Formulas

In this context of a government-designed and -run social insurance system, the differences between defined-benefit and defined-contribution approaches lie in the differences generated by the types of formulas likely to be used and the differences in the ways the two systems are likely to be adapted to changing circumstances. In terms of typical formulas, there are four differences that are worth noting. A defined-benefit formula is normally related to past earnings, while a defined-contribution formula is normally related to past taxes. The conventional defined-benefit formula begins by calculating an average lifetime wage and thus aggregates nominal wages in different years by a wage index. The defined-contribution formula aggregates by means of an interest rate. The defined-contribution formula aggregates all years with positive taxes, while a standard average earnings approach calculates an average over some number of years (thirty-five in the United States). The approach to redistribution in a defined-benefit approach is by progressivity in the benefit formula, usually designed from consideration of the wage-related replacement rate; the defined-contribution approach could redistribute on the basis of the size of accumulated funds, but seems less likely, politically, to do so. In Chile, redistribution is in the form of a guaranteed minimum pension. However, the minimum pension is financed from general revenue, not social security revenue. With only part of the labor force included in the social security system, it seems appropriate to have a broader tax base for redistribution purposes.

While I have focused on the differences in the two approaches, it is perhaps useful to notice that in a mature system, in a smooth, stable economy, the differences may be small. In particular, if tax rates do not change, there is no difference between relying on wages subject to tax and relying on taxes paid. It is probably not a bad approximation of many mature economies that the wage growth rate and the nominal interest rate are roughly equal on average. In a transition economy, however, one would expect large differences between the interest rate and the wage growth rate. There are probably small differences across people in the implications of extending the averaging period a few more years. Thus, the major difference is accommodation to shocks and transitions. There is also a difference in the likely response to foreseen changes, such as the demographic swing coming early next century. I will return to this issue in the next section, where the role of funding is discussed in relation to shocks and transitions.

In terms of promised benefits, both approaches can be seen as specific simplified approximations to a more general benefit determination function. That is, consider determining the benefits for a new retiree as a function of the entire history of both the individual and the economy up to that date; the benefit depends on the full history of earnings subject to tax, the history of tax rates, the history of interest rates, and any other variables that one might like to add to an expanded conception of the design of an insurance mechanism responsive to both individual risks and social risks. It is not clear what elements would go into deciding which of the two common approaches is a better approximation of an optimal design. Of course such a question cannot be answered without a prior determination of what an optimal design might look like, a question that has not been addressed in the literature as far as I know. In particular, the literature typically ignores issues involving the general health of the economy. In practice, the state of the economy often results in ad hoc adjustments of general benefit levels. Of course this opens up the level of descriptive complexity (and, often, mismanagement) that comes with repeated ad hoc adjustments of benefit levels.

10.3.3 Chile

In 1981, Chile introduced a new, fully funded social security system with individual accounts.[26] Retirees and older workers were kept on the old system;

---

26. I have drawn on several descriptions of social security in Chile, including Cheyre V. (1991), Iglesias and Acuna (1991), Mesa-Lago (1989), and Vittas and Iglesias (1992).

younger workers switching to the new system had special government bonds allocated to them and have their payroll taxes go into their accounts. This funding pattern meant an enormous expense for the government, financed out of general revenues. The deficit in the pension system increased from 2.2 percent of GDP in 1980 to 6.6 percent (including borrowing from the new pension funds) in 1986 (Mesa-Lago 1991). The new system is a mandatory defined-contribution system (with contributions only from workers) for old age, survivor, and disability benefits (although a guaranteed minimum benefit was retained). These funds are managed by private firms, called AFPs (Administradoras de Fondos de Pensiones). At present, there are thirteen, with the four largest having 75 percent of the insured. The AFPs are heavily regulated and meant to compete. The set of allowable investments and the portfolio fractions allowed in riskier investments have grown slowly over time. The government guarantees a minimal return of the lesser of (1) the average return on all funds less 2 percent and (2) half the average return on all funds.[27] Workers are free to switch their accumulated funds between AFPs every three months. On retirement, the accumulated funds are used to purchase indexed annuities, or they can be taken in a phased withdrawal (or a combination of the two).

The experience of these funds to date has been very favorable for workers. The annual average real yield for all invested assets for the period 1981–90 was 13 percent (Vittas and Iglesias 1992). The return for 1991 is about 30 percent. While it would be tempting to attribute these high rates of return to the power of competitive markets, I think that this attribution would be misplaced. The funds have been heavily regulated, no doubt reflecting the Chilean experience with the collapse of their banking system, which was bailed out by the government even though the funds were not guaranteed. Overwhelmingly, the funds have been in government bonds and in bank liabilities, both deposits and mortgage bonds. Investment in shares did not exceed 1 percent of the portfolio until 1984 and reached 8.1 percent in 1988 (Mesa-Lago 1991) and 20 percent in 1991. There is a committee to select the set of stocks in which AFPs can invest. Thus, the high returns have reflected high real interest rates generally rather than excellent investment decisions. It is important to remember that, when the portfolio is in government debt, a high rate of return is an increase in government obligations. That is, if the rate of return is higher than the rate that would have resulted in approximately the same aggregate pensions as under the previous defined-benefit system, then there is an increase in government obligations beyond what would have been present under the previous system. Only when the portfolio is invested (directly or indirectly) in real assets does a higher rate of return represent a greater sum of resources for the economy.

27. Each fund has a reserve fund, and the government has a fluctuations reserve fund to finance this guarantee. So far, one pension fund has been liquidated for failing to maintain the minimum return.

The pattern of portfolio holdings also makes it clear that having individual accounts does not necessarily translate into a more positive government budget balance. In order to know what has happened to government budget balance, one needs to infer the implications of individual accounts for other tax increases or expenditure cuts to finance the benefits that are no longer directly financed by the taxes now flowing into individual accounts. The experience probably does show how defined-contribution pensions are likely to show a different growth over time than defined-benefit pensions, although one wants a longer time series before reaching conclusions on long-run effects.

The rate of return on the portfolios held by the AFPs does not translate directly into the return on taxes for workers since there are commission costs that must be paid and are deducted from the account or bundled with monthly payments. The structure of these costs is regulated.[28] Net commissions are currently around 15 percent of contributions, down from 23 percent in the early years (Vittas and Iglesias 1992). The marketing and sales costs amounted to 39.8 percent of total operating costs exclusive of depreciation and amortization in 1982 and 30 percent in 1983 (Arellano 1985, cited in Mackenzie 1988). Currently, marketing costs are estimated to run in the range from 30 to 40 percent of operating costs (Vittas and Iglesias 1992). In contrast with these numbers, administrative costs for the cash benefits portion of U.S. Social Security were 0.9 percent of benefits paid in 1990 (U.S. Department of Health and Human Services, *Social Security Bulletin* 54, no. 9 [1991]: 19), and, as noted above, administrative costs in Poland are currently 4 percent, including 2 percent for the post office for delivery of benefits. Instead, the privatized system has costs that resemble those of life insurance markets.

The Role of Funds

There are two dimensions to building up individual funds. One dimension relates to a possible decision to have a time shape of taxes that generates a fund that is different from a time shape that does not generate a fund. Obviously, any change in the time shape of taxes represents a redistribution across generations and across individuals in the same generation with different lifetime earnings patterns. When a fund is being created that did not otherwise exist and there is no particular plan to make taxes in the future different from what was originally planned, then we are not considering this dimension of the effect of building up a fund. Rather, we are converting an implicit liability into an explicit one, changing the characteristics of the obligation as a result.

First, such a changeover affects the politics of social insurance expenditures. Second, there is the question of the extent to which funding, both in the short run and in the long run, affects the expenditures on the rest of the budget. This

---

28. The design of this structure has important distributional implications. The mix of charges per account, per peso deposited, and per peso on deposit affects the returns on taxes of workers with different earnings levels and different histories. The choice of mix has been a source of controversy in Chile.

depends a lot on the nature of the political process and the role of different measures of the budget deficit in that determination. It is to my mind an open question whether the use of individual accounts has a further effect on this outcome beyond the role of funding in the aggregate. A third question that is addressed below is the role of individual accounts and private management in the workings and development of the capital market.

The presence of an aggregate fund is likely to have a significant effect on the politics of the evolution of a social insurance system. In considering such effects, it is natural to think in terms of a two-by-two matrix. One dimension relates to whether earmarked taxes are above or below the benefit flows. The other dimension refers to social insurance expenditures and other government expenditures. (In addition, one should consider the effect of a fund on legislation in advance of short-run difficulties.) I do not know of solid empirical work on political responses to fill in the elements in this matrix. But it is useful to state the questions that arise in the four boxes. Assume that the earmarked tax flow exceeds the current benefit flow. Does the presence of a fund (into which the excess flows rather than flowing into general revenues) affect the continuation of the current levels of earmarked taxes and benefits? Would taxes be more likely to be cut or benefits more likely to be raised if the excess did not flow into a fund? Considering the politics of the full budget, rather than just the social insurance budget, an excess of earmarked taxes over current expenditures is probably powerful protection against a cut in benefits even when the rest of the government budget is in trouble. In the adjoining entry in the matrix, the question is the extent to which this surplus flow affects other government taxes and other government expenses. My own impression of the process in the United States is that recent Social Security annual surpluses have indeed had some effect on other government expenditures even though the money was flowing into a fund. That is, it is not clear how much larger the deficit on the rest of the budget would be if the Social Security surplus went to general revenues rather than to a fund. Whether having the money flow into a fund limited the size of other expenditures is too subtle to be inferred from the casual evidence at hand.

In the row where earmarked taxes do not cover current benefits, the presence of interest on a fund and the presence of the fund itself seem likely to affect the behavior of the social insurance account. That is, the state of the fund has an independent political effect. The effect of such a continued short-run deficit on other expenditures is more difficult to have a feeling for. One also needs to examine the role of a fund in the likelihood that the social insurance system will be in such a position. That is, a fund that appears to be in trouble, now or in the future, contributes to the possibility that benefits, at least benefits out in the future, will be reduced below then-legislated levels and that increases in the earmarked taxes will also be voted in advance.

Given the desirability of lead times for pension planning, the forward-looking politics generated by a fund is good. Contrasting a sufficiently funded system so that large changes can be introduced with sizable lead times with a strictly defined pay-as-you-go system, there is a general consensus that one wants to protect the retired from sudden changes in benefit levels. Moreover, it is difficult (although not impossible) to design a sequence of benefit changes in response to short-run fiscal positions so that they add up to a sensible overall design.

I suspect that having individual accounts rather than an aggregate fund contributes to the protection of social insurance benefits from short-run fiscal difficulties. This protection is only limited, however. The opportunity to change tax treatment of benefits represents another way of altering benefits, at least up to the point where benefits are taxes on the same basis as other income (a situation that already holds in Poland). This is probably a natural barrier to the height of taxation of social insurance benefits. Tax treatment of the interest earnings of individual funded accounts is another way of altering benefits. Similarly, there is the possibility of requirements to invest in low-yield socially preferred assets.[29]

The focus in this discussion has been on the response of the social insurance system to short-run difficulties. Given the demographics of a steadily aging population, true in Poland as it is in Chile and the United States, it is also appropriate to ask how the presence of a fund affects the politics of adapting the social insurance system to this ongoing phenomenon. A fund represents a mechanism for adapting to such a change in a different way than a sequence of simultaneous tax and benefit changes. The presence of a fund may contribute to advance legislation for dealing with such a problem. Thus, in the United States, legislation to cut benefits (by delaying the normal retirement age but not the age of eligibility for benefits) beginning in 2000 was passed in 1983. This was without doubt an easier problem for the legislature than would occur with a later response. Moreover, one can expect that, on average, decisions taken with less time pressure will be better and better integrated.

Fund Management

In Chile, individual accounts are partially invested in the economy, and that investment is handled by private portfolio managers.[30] There are three sorts of questions that come to mind when considering investment of the fund in the economy. One is the extent of real effects on the allocation of capital. Presumably, the less well developed the capital market, the larger the effects of directed investment. That is, in the United States, it is likely that general portfolio adjustments would make the shift of a Social Security fund from Treasury debt to stock market holdings somewhat offset by private portfolio adjustments.

29. In the United States, there have been repeated calls to move the Social Security trust fund partially out of Treasury debt and into direct investments in infrastructure. It is not clear how this generates revenue for pension payment.
30. Another model of funds being invested in the economy can be found in some Asian economies.

The small changes in interest rates on different types of assets would probably not have large effects on the U.S. economy. Of course it remains the case that any differences in rates of return will affect benefits determined by a defined-contribution formula and may affect the legislated level of benefits in a defined-benefit formula. In a less well-developed capital market, the final incidence of investment plans will be much closer to the initial incidence. Thus, there is room for a significant effect on capital allocation. This is discussed further below. Second, one must ask the question of the response of the system to the bearing of risk that is a natural counterpart of investments in riskier assets than Treasury debt. To what extent will the political process de facto insure the investments being made. If this is indeed the case, as experience in Chile and elsewhere with the banking system suggests, then the general capital allocation process and the role of government guarantees needs to be thought through.[31]

The question of asset choice for funds must also face the question of the transfer of funds between different fund managers. The presence of a significant part of a portfolio in terms of assets that are not readily evaluated by the market opens up the possibility of runs. Having significant movement out of some fund at a point of time raises the problem of the effect on the market of the sale of assets on well-organized markets as well. Purchases by the funds to which accounts are moved need not coincide with sales by the funds losing accounts. If this movement is not regulated in some way, there could be significant gains and losses associated with such movements, as a forced sale is combined with an unforced set of purchases. This can happen even when all assets are regularly traded if funds are large relative to the market, as they are in Chile. Possibly, one should consider the option of transferring divisible assets rather than their value. The possibility of runs is not restricted to individuals who monitor the performance of their funds closely. As experience in Ohio has shown, there can be runs by normally passive investors when some event has raised the question of the safety of the funds in a salient way.[32]

The third question is the role of portfolio managers and their regulation. We know that even the most highly regulated capital markets in the world today are subject to criminal behavior that involves sizable losses of funds. It is natural to wonder whether similar problems would happen with these funds. In Chile, portfolio decisions are very tightly regulated by the government, with the majority of funds necessarily invested in government securities or bank deposits. The process of development of the funds has reflected a very slow widening of investment opportunities. It seems to me unlikely that private forced savers can be relied on to do much in the way of serious overseeing of funds; in fact,

31. The likelihood of government guarantees in case the funds do not have earnings rates as high as were forecast has been recognized by Topinski and Wisniewski (1991a).
32. In Ohio, there were runs on sound banks because the deposit insurance fund was thought to be inadequately financed. For a description of a recent run in Missouri triggered by rumors of a takeover by the FDIC, see *New York Times*, 3 April 1992, D1.

there is probably a serious cost associated with trying to rely on the market in this case.

This concern with the costs of private markets starts with the expenses that will be associated with attempts by portfolios managers to compete for handling of the funds. Advertising and sales commissions are a natural part of the expense associated with insurance markets and portfolio management of funds. As noted above, returns on portfolios are not the same as returns on taxes paid. In this case, the presence of large numbers of inexperienced investors suggests that the aggregate selling costs will more closely resemble that for individual policies in insurance markets than it will selling costs for portfolio management in well-developed capital markets like the United States. If that is the case, then a sizable fraction of the value of the funds will be eaten up in the competitive process. There is an obvious internal contradiction between having a forced savings system based on a lack of reliance on individuals to save adequately for their own retirement and the empowering of these people to control the management of their portfolios. In particular, the implicit high discount rate of such workers raises questions as to whether they will respond to solicitation to change managers in a way that will overweight the current blandishments of solicitation relative to the possible long-run effects on the value of the account. I am told that, already in Chile, running shoes are being given out to workers switching between funds.[33] This is reminiscent of the time in the United States when interest rates were regulated and banks competed by giving out toasters to people opening accounts. An even closer parallel is the report of a school in England, where there are education vouchers, that "offered a discount on shower units as an incentive to parents to enroll their children there" (*New York Times*, 7 January 1992, 1). The cost of private firms pursuing individual fund account holders may be very large, and there is an important role for regulation to avoid such an equilibrium. I think that it is natural to be very suspicious about the efficiency of the competitive market in this type of intertemporal transaction involving large numbers of inexperienced investors.

Another problem arises with the conversion of accumulated funds into annuities. The annuities market is a relatively underdeveloped market even in advanced economies. There is no reason to think that this market will work with reasonable efficiency on the basis of individual purchases. Of course there is a range of alternative interventions for organizing this market besides simply having the government do it. This is discussed further below.

10.3.4 Transition

When setting up accounts for existing workers at the start of such a program, there are two bases for selecting account levels. One is to be backward looking,

---

33. Such incentives for switching are illegal. Regulation of the marketing process is an important component of the regulation of portfolio management.

giving individuals an approximation of what they would have had had the new system been in place. The alternative is to be forward looking, giving individuals a sum that will yield approximately what the existing system would yield. This can be done with a sum that can be invested or with bonds that come due at retirement age. In Chile, bonds that grew at a real rate of 4 percent per year were allocated to individual workers. The underlying logic was forward looking, aiming at a Pareto improvement.[34] In Poland, the proposal is to be forward looking. The calculations that have been made imply that men under forty-five and women under forty would not lose from the changeover and would receive no initial compensation. Older highly paid workers would receive compensation, with the amount drawn from a share of the value of enterprises being privatized (Tymowska and Wisniewski 1991). This assumes not only a satisfactory projected basis for compensation but also a reasonably accurate valuation of the shares being distributed.

One complication, of course, is the absence of earnings records for individual workers in Poland. Thus, the proposal keys off a single year's earnings at the time the funds are set up. This is highly random in its implied redistributions and highly subject to manipulation. An alternative approach would be to make use of additional years of earnings as they become available. There are probably a number of different ways of doing this that should be explored. The current proposal gives an individual an initial allocation that is a multiple of earnings (above the threshold) determined in the year the accounts are started, with the multiple depending on age. Instead, the multiplier could be allocated to a number of the remaining years until retirement age. For example, instead of giving someone an initial allocation of twice the level of earnings above the threshold in the first year of the transition, the individual could be given half that sum the first year and an additional amount the following year equal to the amount of the following year's earnings, less that year's threshold. This second number could be adjusted for interest. This pattern would both be fairer and have a better incentive structure.

10.3.5   An Alternative Proposal

The current Polish law is based on a defined-benefit formula that may be easily manipulated and that has limited long-run appeal. The proposed reform is focused on a privatized role in asset markets. The problems of regulating such a privatized system may be severe. If one considers a defined-contribution system that invests only in government debt, it may be possible to design a system that is politically acceptable, has some effect on fiscal discipline, and has better incentives. The following simple proposal is put forward to show how such an approach might work, perhaps thereby stimulating development

---

34. One problem was the absence of a complete set of records for individual workers. Bond levels were calculated on the basis of the average of declared income for three years (1977–79).

of more detailed proposals that fit with Poland's political and economic constraints. The current benefit law has two parts, a flat benefit and an earnings-related benefit. Consider earmarking part of the payroll tax for defined-contribution pensions. Consider dividing the earmarked tax between a general account and individual accounts. The general account finances the flat benefit. The individual account finances the earnings-related benefit. Either or both benefits can be subjected to an earnings test. To implement this system, one needs a rule for selecting an interest rate and an actuarial formula for converting an accumulated fund into an indexed annuity.

This approach lends itself to a straightforward transition that does not rely on individual records. Each eligible worker can be credited with an indexed benefit to begin at the same time as the flat benefit. The indexed benefit would depend solely on age at the time of transition. An algorithm is still needed to determine the structure of this benefit. One could be constructed along lines parallel to the analysis done for the proposed reform.

With individual accounts in place, in the future one could consider privatizing part of the accumulation of individual accounts, once there were better understanding and skills for regulating privatized accounts. Contrasting this proposal with both current law and the proposed reform highlights the many different pieces relevant for design of a pension system.

10.4 Relation to Private Institutions: Capital, Annuity, and Pension Markets

Returning to the discussion of Poland, it is natural to think about the role of this pension reform in the development of the capital market and in the privatization of state enterprises. It also seems useful to mention issues in organizing the annuity and private pension markets.

10.4.1 The Polish Capital Market

Economies converting from central planning to decentralized markets do not have well-developed capital markets. To my way of thinking, the most critical missing piece is a set of intermediaries. The creation of pension funds seeking to invest does not directly do anything about the lack of experience and capacity in the allocation of funds. Since the development of mutual funds is a (probably small) piece of the development of the range of intermediaries, one can count the creation of such institutions by this proposal as a contribution to institution development. However, government-regulated, and probably implicitly insured, funds with a large number of small investors is probably not the best environment for the growth of such institutions. It would probably be better to have private market mutual funds receiving deposits from a smaller number of larger investors. It is probably also true that direct investments have greater importance when intermediaries are weak. Thus, it is appropriate to wonder whether the nonintermediated investment that will be displaced by this forced saving program might not have greater efficiency.[35] Restating this point in a different vocabulary, the question is whether to let the demand for mutual funds respond to market opportunities or to generate demand in order to induce a larger supply of intermediaries. Of course, there is room for foreign assistance in intermediation, limiting concern about pushing too fast.

A further set of issues arises when one starts to contemplate the kind of investments, other than government securities, that these funds might hold. Obviously, the prime purpose of having such a program is to support new investment. Thus, direct loans from these funds to large firms is one possibility, although it is a possibility fraught with all the same difficulties that are present in the inadequacy of the banking system in channeling funds directly to firms. The alternative that is natural with developed capital markets, of having the funds invest in the securities market, is much less attractive in this setting. The securities market is extremely underdeveloped, suggesting that a large fraction of the funds flowing into the market will go into bidding up the prices of existing securities and so be transfers to existing securityholders rather than being a flow into new investment. (One could consider restricting investment to the purchase of new issues—including those associated with privatization—although there is unlikely to be an adequate flow of new issues to supply many good securities for such investment.) Second, some of the funds will flow into manipulation and outright theft. Only a fraction of the funds will go into encouraging investment. My uninformed prior is that the fraction is rather small and that direct general investment stimulation by the government would be a superior mechanism.[36] Creating a suitable environment for (possibly foreign) private mutual fund creation is probably a better route to institution creation than creating a forced demand for such institutions and hoping to create their supply simultaneously, with a larger government obligation for protection of investors. Presumably, there is a great shortage of experienced regulators of financial intermediaries in Poland. One question that must be addressed by the proposal for individual funded accounts is whether the regulation of the firms handling such accounts is the best use of limited regulatory abilities.

10.4.2   Transition to Private Ownership

Like other centrally planned economies converting to a private market organization for the bulk of the economy, Poland faces the problem of redetermining the ownership of firms. It seems useful to divide this problem into three pieces. One is the creation of some private ownership in order to create the ownership part of the ownership-management relationship, which deter-

---

35. On the role of direct lending to friends and family, see Ben-Porath (1978).
36. Case-by-case direct stimulation is subject to the same potentialities of fraud and mismanagement.

mines the rules and incentives under which firms are managed. A second issue is the ownership of future income. Since one does not need to allocate all of ownership to have enough ownership to create a relationship with management, these two issues are clearly separable. The third issue is to develop institutions for the ongoing role of ownership in policing management. This ongoing role includes bankruptcy, sale of ownership, takeovers, etc. This third step is clearly slower and of less initial importance and compatible with a variety of other institutions.

It is natural to inquire into the role of a public pension system in filling each of these roles. An active role in overseeing management must involve either explicit institution design for overseeing (such as public representatives on boards of directors) or ownership shares (either individual or aggregated) that have enough of a stake in a firm to oversee management. Thus, it is commonly felt that a widespread individual distribution of share ownership would not easily generate any concentrations of ownership sufficient to overcome the free-rider problem and so have relatively efficient overseeing of management. It is therefore frequently proposed that mutual funds be used to aggregate ownership shares and so have an incentive (and obligation) to oversee management. Pension plans can clearly be used in this role in place of mutual fund companies. In terms of ownership shares and obligations, the two institutions seem similar in the short run.

For the longer run, there are several differences in the way the two institutions might work. Since the payout of pension plans is based on retirement behavior of workers having claims on the assets of the funds, this could be used as a device to transfer shares into the pool of individually owned and traded shares slowly. This would contribute to the third aim, of a slowly growing private market. Second, there is a fiscal problem for the Polish government. By substituting the funding of some pension obligations for the one-time general gift of ownership, there should be a reduced claim on the government budget in the future. This could be done in a way that tends to place the risk of success of Polish enterprises either on the benefit claimants or on the government. With political pressure to move ownership out of the hands of the government, it might be sufficient to move it to an earmarked use, as in pensions. Such an allocation opens up the issue of the age-related structure of the allocation of this wealth to individuals. While a direct giveaway could have any age structure, the use of pension funds naturally structures this question while leaving room for a variety of answers, depending in part on the offset from other government pension obligations that are part of the package. For example, the proposal discussed above had an allocation based on a forward-looking replacement of part of pension obligations. Whether shares are allocated to individual accounts or to an aggregate fund is open. Individual accounts could be used to create another level of incentive in the presence of multiple funds. However, such allocation does place individuals at additional risk. There is also a serious problem of valuing these assets if they are being used as part of some "compensation" of workers for a change in the pension system, as in the Polish proposal described above. The use of the vocabulary of compensation may affect the likelihood of later government compensation in the event that the assets prove to be worth less than anticipated.

10.4.3   The Annuity Market

Another issue that is raised by individual accounts is the problem of conversion of accumulated funds to annuities at the time of retirement. The individual annuities market does not function very well anywhere in the world, as we can expect from the theory of adverse selection.[37] Thus, this market would need to be organized and regulated by the government if the pension system is to work well. Since to date few pensions have been received out of the new system in Chile, there has not been so much concern about how well the annuities market functions.[38] There are a variety of ways for the government to organize this market that lie between full reliance on the private market and government provision of annuities. A variety of regulatory schemes have been proposed for health insurance, which could be adapted for annuities.[39]

10.4.4   Regulation of Private Pensions

Unless the social insurance system is so large that there is little room for private saving for retirement, it is natural to expect that employer-provided pensions will arise as an institution.[40] This is an institution that needs serious regulation. One of the worst possible outcomes would be unfunded private pension promises where the workers did not save because they believed excessively in the likelihood of collecting on these promises, while firms and shareholders did not save because of a recognition that the risk-adjusted expenditure needs were not very large. This combination would depress capital accumulation and do little to deal with retirement needs. Thus, it is a common phenomenon for governments to worry about the funding of pension promises, an issue that arises particularly with defined-benefit pensions. More generally, the history of private pensions is a history of the need for consumer protection legislation. Pension promises are very complicated assets. Individual workers are not

37. Adverse selection can be a problem when individual retirees choose between phased withdrawal or annuity purchase on the basis of asymmetrical information on life expectancy. Adverse selection can also be a problem when insurance companies particularly seek out those with shorter life expectancies, incurring additional marketing costs. From a social insurance perspective, one needs to consider the optimal degree of cross-subsidization between groups with different life expectancies; those with longer retirement periods are, in one sense, poorer.

38. There are independent brokers charging sizable fees for counseling retirees on annuity choice.

39. One could, e.g., consider mandatory grouping of individuals into risk pools with private market bidding on the groups. Such a proposal has been made for health insurance in the United States (Diamond 1992).

40. The proposed reform described above would allow individuals to contribute voluntarily to their individual fund accounts on a tax-deferred basis. Similarly, in Chile, there is favorable tax treatment for additional contributions to the individual account by the employer.

generally sophisticated enough to appreciate the risks associated with these assets. Thus, there has arisen in the United States a set of rules designed to protect the expectations of workers that are taken to be legitimate.

With a defined-contribution pension, individuals are promised whatever annuities their accumulated funds will purchase when they reach retirement. The retirement implications of such funds are somewhat difficult to describe to workers because they depend on projections of interest rates and actuarial factors, which one does not project with certainty. However, defined-contribution pensions have the obvious advantages that they are more readily perceived as having the same value to both sides of the promise and involve no portability difficulties when there is to be labor mobility. Defined-benefit pensions are easier to describe to workers in large part because the description focuses only on the circumstance of the worker staying with the same firm until retirement, the firm doing well, and the worker having steady wage increases. Introducing the various other scenarios, such as worker mobility, firm bankruptcy, and low future wages because of industry or firm difficulties, makes this much more complicated to describe. Also complicated to describe is an adequate level of funding. In an economy that does not have a well-developed actuarial profession, it is implausible that funding for defined-benefit pensions can be adequately policed. If the government is to enter this arena by allowing tax recognition for the development of pension funds, then serious thought needs to be given to the class of pension systems that will get tax-favored treatment. Restricting tax-favored treatment to defined-contribution pensions is a way of avoiding a host of potential difficulties. In other words, the issues appropriate for comparing defined-benefit and defined-contribution pensions are very different when considering private market pensions and social insurance pensions. The latter can be based on employment records throughout the economy and do not have to adapt to the needs of labor mobility. Moreover, the risks associated with the ability to pay pensions are different for governments and individual firms. On the other hand, the process of adapting the system to a changing environment is driven differently by a political process and a market process (whether collective bargaining or not).

In the United States, the government also enters directly into guarantees to workers about some of the funds available for their pensions. Insurance against some risks associated with fund accumulation by intermediaries is a widespread aspect of well-developed capital markets. Thus, it is common for there to be insurance provided by either the government or the industry against well-defined criminal activities involving stealing funds. Because it is very difficult for individuals to police this issue themselves, this is a natural role for some sort of collective institution. The question is the extent to which the government should go beyond fund-based guarantees to look at promise-based guarantees. It is very easy for such guarantees to turn into a basis for political manipulation, and such redistribution was indeed a major part of the development of ERISA in the United States. Moreover, the design of the guarantee mechanism can encourage behavior that adds considerably to the magnitude of the risk borne by taxpayers (see, e.g., Bodie 1992).

10.5 Concluding Remarks

This has been a long paper, rambling through a wide variety of policy issues. It would serve no point to recapitulate all of them. An underlying theme of my approach may be worth recapitulating. Poland faces serious short-run financial difficulties both in general and with its social insurance system. Like many other countries, Poland faces a large demographic swing early in the next century with long-run financial consequences. Poland also faces a major need to develop institutional design of its pension system. It is difficult for the political process to separate out the three elements of short-run financial concerns, long-run financial concerns, and institutional design. One can only hope that a balance among these elements will be struck in the process of reform.

References

Arellano, Jose Pablo. 1985. Politicas sociales y desarrollo—Chile, 1924–84. Santiago: CIEPLAN.
Atkins, G. Lawrence. 1991. Social security and pension reform in Central Europe. Paper prepared for the meeting of the Institut für die Wissenschaften vom Menschen, Vienna, November.
Balcer, Yves, and Peter Diamond. 1977. Social Security benefits with a lengthening averaging period. *Journal of Risk and Insurance* 44, no. 2:259–65.
Barr, Nicholas. 1991. Poland: Description of the cash benefit system. Washington, D.C.: World Bank. Typescript.
Ben-Porath, Yoram. 1978. The F-connection: Families, friends, and firms, and the organization of exchange. Report no. 29/78. Institute for Advanced Studies, Hebrew University of Jerusalem.
Bodie, Zvi. 1992. Federal pension insurance: Is it the S&L crisis of the 1990's. Boston University. Typescript.
Boskin, Michael J., Laurence J. Kotlikoff, and John B. Shoven. 1988. Personal security accounts: A proposal for fundamental Social Security reform. In *Social Security and private pensions*, ed. Susan M. Wachter. Lexington, Mass.: Lexington.
Bound, John. 1989. The health and earnings of rejected disability insurance applicants. *American Economic Review* 79, no. 3:482–503.
Cheyre V., Hernan. 1991. *La prevision en Chile ayer y hoy.* Santiago: Centro de Estudios Publicos.
Congressional Budget Office. Congress of the United States. 1986. Earnings sharing options for the Social Security system. Washington, D.C.
Consultant Panel on Social Security to the Congressional Research Service. 1976. Report. Washington, D.C.
Deutsch, Antal. 1991. One pension system in transition: The case of Hungary. Vancouver: International Studies Association. Typescript.

Diamond, Peter. 1992. Organizing the health insurance market. *Econometrica* 60, no. 6:1233–54.

Diamond, Peter, and Eytan Sheshinski. 1992. Economic aspects of optimal disability benefits. Working paper. Massachusetts Institute of Technology.

Hambor, John. 1992. Issues in Eastern European social security reform. Washington, D.C.: U.S. Treasury Department, Office of Economic Policy. Typescript.

Henderson, Yolanda. 1991. Translation of Jaka dostaniesz emeryture by J. Koral. Boston: Federal Reserve Bank. Typescript.

Iglesias P., Augusto, and Rodrigo Acuna R. 1991. *Chile: Experiencia con un regimen de capitalizacion, 1981–1991.* Santiago: CEPAL/PNUD.

Jenkins, Glenn. 1991. Privatization and pension reform in transition economies. Paper prepared for the International Institute of Public Finance Congress.

Kopits, George. 1991. Social security in transition economies. Paper prepared for the International Institute of Public Finance Congress.

Mackenzie, G. A. 1988. Social security issues in developing countries: The Latin American experience. *IMF Staff Papers* 35, no. 3:496–522.

Mesa-Lago, Carmelo. 1989. *Ascent to bankruptcy: Financing social security in Latin America.* Pittsburgh: University of Pittsburgh Press.

———. 1991. Portfolio performance of selected social security institutes in Latin America. Discussion Paper no. 139. Washington, D.C.: World Bank.

Topinski, Wojciech, and Marian Wisniewski. 1991a. Pensions in Poland: Proposals for reform. University of Warsaw. Typescript.

———. 1991b. [Untitled.] University of Warsaw. Typescript.

Tymowska, Katarzyna, and Marian Wisniewski. 1991. Poland's social security system. University of Warsaw. Typescript.

U.S. Department of Health and Human Services. Social Security Administration. Office of International Policy and Office of Research and Statistics. 1990. Social security programs throughout the world—1989. Research Report no. 62. Washington, D.C.

Vittas, Dimitri, and Augusto Iglesias. 1992. The rationale and performance of personal pension plans in Chile. Washington, D.C.: World Bank. Typescript.

Comment   Barry Bosworth

The establishment of a pension system in Eastern Europe and the former Soviet Union is a very important issue. The proportion of the population of these countries that is retired or disabled is very high, yet they lack a functioning tax system that can provide sufficient revenues to finance the costs. The old system is very inadequate to deal with the issues of tax compliance, work incentives, equity, and corruption that will arise with the operation of a public pension program in a decentralized economy. In practical terms, these countries will have to start from scratch in designing new pension programs, and the question addressed in Peter Diamond's paper is what that new system should look like. The choice is between a defined-benefit program, similar to that of most industrial countries, and a defined-contribution program, like that of Chile. A choice must also be made between a publicly and a privately managed system.

The paper covers a very wide range of issues relevant to establishing a social security system in Eastern Europe. To begin with, it provides a great deal of background information about the existing defined-benefit system and the problems that will be faced in an attempt to extend it in the future. I think that that material is valuable in laying out the primary issues associated with operating a conventional defined-benefit program.

Subsequently, a major portion of the paper is devoted to evaluating a specific reform proposal that combines a flat minimum benefit payment, financed out of general revenues, with a privately managed, defined-contribution plan, similar to that of Chile. From a macroeconomic perspective, a defined-contribution program is attractive as a potential means of augmenting national saving; it is a funded system. From a microeconomic perspective, it avoids some of the political problems of keeping benefits at affordable levels.

Most articles on the Chilean program emphasize the high rates of return earned by the funds. Diamond's analysis was a major surprise to me in pointing out two serious problems of the Chilean system that have not attracted much prior attention. First, the high rate of return is a simple reflection of the fact that the Chilean stabilization program has driven the real rate of return on riskless investments to extremely high levels. The funds invest nearly all their portfolio in government bonds, where the real interest rate has been in excess of 10 percent. Chileans may feel good when they look at the earnings on their funds, but they should be a little concerned as taxpayers who have to pay those rates of return on government bonds. Private equity investments have been a very small share of the overall portfolio.

The second surprise is that the administrative charges by the fund managers represent an amazingly high percentage of contributions. It is hard to understand how these fees can be justified. If the funds were investing in an open market at global rates of return, the administrative fees would be sufficient to wipe out the interest return, and the realized yield of the contributors would be negative.

A final problem is that the fund accumulation will ultimately have to be converted to a private annuity at retirement. Annuities are a surprisingly poor bargain even in sophisticated American markets, and it is difficult to design them in a fashion that protects the retiree against inflation.

One issue that will be important in Eastern Europe—one that is not fully examined in this paper—is the effect of a Chilean-type social insurance fund on national saving. The extent of reliance on public debt in the portfolios of the Chilean pension funds suggests that their effect on national saving is ambiguous. The funds create a ready market in which the government can sell a larger volume of debt instruments than would otherwise be possible. If the existence of this debt market has made it easier for the government to finance budget deficits, any gain in private saving may have been lost at the national level.

The net effect of this paper is substantially to alter my previous favorable view of private defined-contribution programs as an alternative social security system in countries without advanced financial market institutions. I agree with Peter Diamond that financial markets may not be sufficiently developed in Eastern Europe to support such a system. Furthermore, the Chilean experience is not as favorable as previously reported.

The East European countries are probably better advised to establish a defined-benefit plan similar to those of Western Europe and the United States. Furthermore, for the time being, the compressed nature of the wage structure suggests that they could use a simple flat benefit payment for existing retirees. In the future, however, it is imperative that they establish an administrative system that maintains records on the contribution history of future retirees and relates workers' benefits to past contributions. Furthermore, the idea of a funded system is very attractive as a source of increased saving, but it will be very difficult to accomplish because of the large existing number of retirees who must be provided for.

Discussion Summary

Boris Pleskovic noted that many privatization plans assume that pension funds will play a major role in the privatization process. He said that pension funds are expected to receive 10–20 percent of the equity in the newly privatized firms and that many planners hope that the funds will therefore take an active oversight role on the boards of directors of these new firms.

Simon Johnson warned of the problems of loopholes in pension schemes. He said that one of the largest firms in Czechoslovakia employs 500 workers, of which only two are *officially* employed. The rest are registered as individual entrepreneurs. He noted that this setup enables the firm to avoid paying the social security and wage taxes that are equal to 60 percent of the wage of official employees.

Mark Schaffer said Poland's relatively high social insurance costs partially reflect the fact that the Polish system has indexed benefits to wages instead of simply indexing to the price level. The rise in real wages has driven real pension expenditures up and contributed to the deterioration in the budget.

Peter Diamond did not agree that pension funds should be relied on to play a significant oversight role as equityholders of newly privatized firms. Diamond wondered if there was any advantage to locating this oversight capacity in pension funds. He said that, even in the United States, pension funds do not appear to be particularly sophisticated, as evidenced by their consistent pattern of relatively poor financial performance. *Olivier Blanchard* was also critical of the idea of giving pension funds a large equity stake in privatized firms. He said that it is contradictory to set up a social insurance system that relies on such extremely risky assets.

Comment   George Kopits

The papers by Roger Gordon and Peter Diamond deal with key fiscal policy issues confronted by postsocialist economies. Although their primary focus is the reform of Poland's tax structure and pension system, respectively, both papers have relevance for neighboring countries, including the former Soviet republics. These remarks intend to address issues of potentially broader relevance, rather than those that are specific only to Poland.

In his paper, Gordon seeks to explain fiscal developments (in particular, revenue developments) since 1988 and to recommend tax reform measures. This explanation would be, of course, incomplete without a discussion of the overall fiscal relations that prevailed between the government and state-owned enterprises (SOEs) and between the government and households under socialist central planning. Such a discussion provides the necessary backdrop for formulating appropriate tax measures and broader systemic reforms for the transition to a market economy.

From the outset, it is worth noting that, in the past, SOEs traditionally operated under a soft budget constraint and without exposure to bankruptcy risk, in the pursuit of an ill-defined objective function. Accordingly, the government budget, as well as extrabudgetary accounts controlled by industrial branch ministries, constituted simply a channel for redistributing financial resources from profitable to loss-making SOEs, to meet rigid volume targets prescribed in the plan. Financial resources were collected in the form of negotiated tax liabilities on profits, assets, depreciation, and various earmarked contributions or through outright confiscation of profits. In turn, these resources were distributed as producer subsidies or as capital transfers. Meanwhile, households faced fixed retail prices to satisfy merit wants, as defined by the plan; differences between retail prices and producer costs resulted in either product-specific turnover tax rates (positive wedges) or consumer subsidy rates (negative wedges). Likewise, foreign trade tax rates and subsidy rates were determined residually through domestic price controls and product-specific foreign exchange coefficients. In addition to these fiscal wedges, there were implicit taxes and subsidies determined by controls on wages and bank deposit rates.

With the possible exception of payroll taxation for social security, taxes were neither parametric (across products, across enterprises, or over time) nor transparent. Statutory tax rates and tax bases had little, if any, meaning. Thus, international comparisons, such as the one in Gordon's table 9.1, would make more sense if all budget revenue from SOEs (including entrepreneurial income and other transfers) was shown. A similar comparison should be provided, on the expenditure side, of all direct subsidies and other transfers to SOEs, to reflect the redistributive role of the budget. By the same token, a discussion or com-

The views expressed do not necessarily reflect those of the International Monetary Fund.

parison of turnover tax revenue needs to be accompanied by references to outlays on consumer subsidies (see Kopits 1991).

Reform of Poland's tax system toward uniform and fixed rates, phase-out of subsidies, the associated hardening of the budget constraint for SOEs, and the dramatic adjustment in relative prices, interest rates, and exchange rates faced by SOEs and households—all of which took place almost simultaneously—render an interpretation of changes in the real tax revenue more difficult than suggested in the paper. Indeed, revenue fluctuations at constant prices, especially in 1989–91, reflect not only output and price changes but also changes in the tax system and accounting conventions.[1] The effect of setting fixed turnover-tax rates at the beginning of 1990 needs to be separated from the effects of output and price changes, to explain the revenue changes discussed in section 9.2. The rise in expenditures in 1989 and the fall at the beginning of the adjustment program can be attributed, as noted in the paper, to a large extent to the rise and then to the cut in subsidies. However, an additional explanation for the fall in other outlays in 1990 lies in the enforcement of cash limits on the budget—a feature common to the initial phase in several East European adjustment programs—to ensure budget balance for stabilization purposes. The subsequent relaxation of these limits, the rising claims on social assistance, and the adverse effect of the collapse of CMEA (Council for Mutual Economic Assistance) trade on both the revenue and outlay sides all contributed to the widening fiscal imbalance in 1991.

The author flags the difficulty of balancing the budget and explores various forms of nonbank financing of the deficit to contain its expansionary macroeconomic effect. Unfortunately, the scope for external financing is very limited in most postsocialist countries, including Poland. As indicated in the paper, given the low initial tax base, resorting to high tax rates would be counterproductive. A related problem in the initial tax reform, starting with Hungary, has been the proliferation of tax preferences that required compensatory tax rate hikes. In this regard, it is worth stressing the need to broaden tax bases so as to permit moderation in tax rates and a larger and more elastic revenue flow.

The central question raised in the paper is the design of a fiscal system that meets a number of objectives, subject to microeconomic constraints during the transition. The objectives are familiar: allocative neutrality, fairness, incentives to work and to save, and stabilization. The micro-level constraints consist of inadequate administrative capacity, accounting illiteracy, and continued confusion over ownership rights, goals, and management responsibilities in SOEs. The value-added tax (VAT) and, under certain conditions, the cash-flow tax on enterprises,[2] apparently advocated by Gordon, meet the neutrality objective.

---

1. The accounting data underlying the average profit rates reported in sec. 9.2 are probably quite unreliable and would need further elucidation to explain revenue developments.

2. For an assessment of the cash-flow tax proposal for economies in transition, see Kopits (1992b).

Whereas the cash-flow tax has the virtue of administrative simplicity, the VAT requires some administrative sophistication, which is greatly compounded on the introduction of multiple rates for equity reasons—an approach suggested in section 9.4. Instead, the equity objective can be pursued more efficiently through means-tested social assistance to low-income households, supplemented with some progressivity in personal income taxation. Admittedly, both the progressive personal income tax and targeted assistance also entail a minimum administrative capacity, which takes some time to develop. In fact, at the outset, it is necessary to resort largely to withholding taxation, possibly accompanied by presumptive techniques for self-employment income, as the economy is privatized.

Perhaps the most elusive goal during the transition is macroeconomic stabilization, in view of the difficulties in financing the deficit from domestic nonbank and external sources and in raising tax rates. These difficulties would be exacerbated by a considerable net revenue loss associated with the shift from a profit tax to a cash-flow tax on enterprises. Moreover, fledgling private enterprises engage in outright tax evasion, while SOE managers and employees collude to raise wages, nonwage remuneration, and bonuses at the expense of profits. Also, in anticipation of possible privatization, SOE managers resort to asset stripping and insider deals—partly through joint-venture arrangements. In addition to adverse revenue implications, this behavior leads to considerable wage pressures that must be contained for stabilization reasons. Thus, until the profit-maximizing goal of SOEs is clarified and collective bargaining evolves or the fear of layoffs materializes, it is necessary to rely temporarily on the taxation of excess wage increases at highly progressive marginal rates. This has been the function of such tax-based incomes policy rather than containment of "competitive" wage increases, contrary to the assertion in section 9.2 of the paper. The adjustment of wages to market levels through increased wage differentiation—in line with marginal productivity differentials—has not been prevented by this tax, which in both Poland and Czechoslovakia was triggered by excessive increases in the enterprise's wage bill (including manager's bonuses) while allowing high salaries for skilled and productive workers at one end and the layoff of redundant workers at the other end of the spectrum. These wage pressures in SOEs certainly cannot be averted simply with equal tax rates on their profits and wages[3] since employees do not formally own shares in these enterprises.

Therefore, consistent with incentive, allocative, administrative, and revenue considerations, every effort should be made during the transition to adopt—quite apart from a temporary tax on excess wage increases—broadly based taxes mainly on profits, personal income, and value added, at moderate rates. Also, as a temporary revenue-raising measure, consideration can be given to

---

3. In early 1992, Russia and Ukraine introduced the nondeductibility of wages from taxable profits (conceptually equivalent to a VAT) in addition to a formal VAT.

the adoption of a nondistortionary import tax, levied at a uniform rate—in conjunction with a realistic exchange rate—above and beyond the VAT to be also imposed on imports under the destination principle. At the same time, tax preferences, such as those applied earlier in Hungary and Poland, must be quickly eliminated. A predictable level playing tax field would be far more helpful in inducing domestic or foreign private activity than any attempt to fine-tune subsidies—in order to offset credit constraints or induce positive externalities—to possible "winners," as distinct from "losers," especially given that the planning instinct is still alive and well in these countries. For parity, the same tax rate and definition of the base should be applicable to private enterprises and SOEs, but, in addition, SOEs could be subject to a required dividend payout to the budget (much like in Hungary and Poland) just as private enterprises are expected to yield an adequate rate of return to their owners.

The paper by Diamond is an informative analysis of Poland's pension reform that should be useful for policymakers in Poland and other postsocialist economies. The author correctly points to the flaws in the benefit formula, the lack of tracking of contributions and underlying earnings of beneficiaries, the lack of any connection between social security administration and tax administration, and questionable industry-specific differences in benefits. Although Poland's system has a number of superior features (taxation of pensions, linear accrual formula, higher official retirement age), it suffers from shortcomings comparable to those of neighboring countries.[4] Partly on the basis of these shortcomings, as well as mounting pressures for using disability pensions and early retirement pensions as covert unemployment benefits—in lieu of relying on transparent unemployment compensation—the financial cost of the system is likely to rise significantly in the period ahead.

Failure to correct these deficiencies (including misuse of disability and early retirement pensions) and to enhance the cost effectiveness of the system will inevitably lead to further increases in contribution rates as it has been the case elsewhere. The need for such increases is compounded, of course, by unfavorable demographic trends in the medium to long run. Statutory contribution rates in Bulgaria, Czechoslovakia, Hungary, and Ukraine range between 50 and 60 percent. With the hardening budget constraint on SOEs and the emergence of private enterprises, this tax burden is being resisted through an accumulation of contribution arrears by the former and evasion of contribution payments by the latter and through a narrowing of the contribution base (with increased nonwage remuneration of employees) by both. This, in turn, adds pressure to raising contribution rates further, making virtually inevitable the recourse to budgetary transfers for financing benefits.

In addition to recommending corrective measures under the present system, the paper explores the relevance of the Chilean model for Poland. This model has been held up as an example by various authors for other economies in

4. For an assessment of social security schemes in postsocialist countries, see Kopits (1992a).

transition (see Hanke 1990; and Deutsch 1991). In the same vein, a recent proposal for the United States is also examined. Undoubtedly, the basic approach is in many ways appealing from the perspective of these economies and deserves scrutiny. Diamond's investigation is thorough and the evaluation of key characteristics of the proposed approach persuasive. On balance, two essential conditions for the successful adoption of a Chilean-type approach in economies in transition are missing, namely, an appropriate regulatory apparatus and financial markets. Moreover, the treatment of claims by existing beneficiaries poses a difficult transitional issue under the reform proposal outlined in the paper. Any solution involving the transfer of ownership of privatized SOEs to the new funds or to the beneficiaries is unlikely to provide the anticipated security for old-age retirement given the questionable value and lack of marketability of enterprise shares. Ultimately, this could result in a considerable claim on the budget. In any event, if Poland or the other postsocialist countries were able to accumulate reserves—largely by rationalizing the benefits—these reserves should be translated, in the first place, into contribution rate cuts.

References

Deutsch, A. 1991. One pension system in transition: The case of Hungary. Paper prepared for the International Studies Association, Vancouver, 21 March.
Hanke, S. H. 1990. Reflections on Yugoslavia's transition to a market economy. Paper presented at the Cámara de Comercio e Industria, Madrid, 13 November.
Kopits, G. 1991. Fiscal reform in European economies in transition. In *Transition to a market economy*, ed. P. Marer and S. Zecchini. Paris: OECD.
———. 1992a. Social security. In *Fiscal policies in economies in transition*, ed. V. Tanzi. Washington, D.C.: International Monetary Fund.
———. 1992b. Tax reform in Eastern Europe: Comment. In *Proceedings of the 84th Annual Conference on Taxation of the National Tax Association*, ed. F. D. Stocker and J. L. Staton. Columbus, Ohio.

11 The Government Budget and the Economic Transformation of Poland

Alain de Crombrugghe and David Lipton

Poland's budgetary position shifted dramatically from 1989 to 1991. A large deficit emerged in 1989, there was a huge swing to surplus in 1990, and a deficit reemerged in 1991. These shifts resulted, first, from the collapse of the Communist fiscal system and, then, from the macroeconomic and structural forces set in motion by the economic transformation process.

Poland's fiscal system, designed during the Communist period primarily as an instrument to reallocate resources, collapsed when macroeconomic pressures mounted in 1989. The Communist government was unable to cope with falling revenues or to reduce sufficiently the budgeted subsidies and social spending, and a large budget imbalance (of about 7 percent of GDP) resulted. The deficit was financed by central bank credit, which contributed to an avalanche of money printing and, by August 1989, an explosive inflation.

The Solidarity government began the economic transformation by launching a program of stabilization and liberalization at the beginning of 1990. This program produced a huge budgetary correction, about 10 percent of GDP in 1990, as the profitability of enterprises was restored and subsidies were cut drastically (see app. table 11A.1). Over time, however, the stabilization correction eroded, mainly because the process of economic transformation had unfavorable effects on the management of the budget. The liberalization of economic activity produced qualitative and quantitative changes in the nation's tax base and changes in spending priorities. For example, enterprise profits taxes, which had been a major source of revenues, fell as a result of the decline of the state enterprise sector. In addition, pressure mounted for improvements in public services and increases in social safety net spending.

At the same time, budget management has been constrained by financial

The authors would like to thank Andrew Berg, Kalman Mizsei, Jeffrey Sachs, Joakim Stymne, and Staci Warden for their helpful comments and suggestions, and the World Institute for Development Economics Research for funding the research..

realities. Since the economic transformation began, the government's room to maneuver has been restricted by the need to avoid budget deficits of a scale that would jeopardize the effort to stabilize prices and the exchange rate. So far, the government has avoided a budgetary erosion of dangerous proportions, although the emergence of a deficit has prevented a decisive victory in the anti-inflation battle. The deficit reached about 4 percent of GDP in 1991, and, as a consequence, the government was unable to reach its aim of bringing inflation down to 1–2 percent per month. Nonetheless, the deficit was financed by the banking system without a loss of monetary and financial control.

With the anti-inflation battle always in the foreground, Poland's post-Communist governments have begun major reforms of the fiscal system. Poland is now creating a fiscal system better suited to a modern, market economy, with much less emphasis on directing the allocation of resources. The new priorities must be to support macroeconomic stabilization and foster the development of a market economy. In time, the reform of the fiscal system will include tax reform, a reevaluation of spending priorities, civil service reform, the revamping of social insurance programs, and the creation of a public investment program.

This paper explores the challenge of managing budgetary policy during Poland's transition to a market economy. The focus is on the case of Poland, but much of what is discussed has been or will be faced by other countries in Eastern Europe and the newly independent states of the former Soviet Union.[1] The paper begins with a description of the shortcomings of the Communist fiscal system. This is followed by an examination of the effect of the economic transformation on the budget and an explanation of the budget swings that have taken place since the economic transformation began. The next section describes the role of the budget in a market economy and discusses the major changes that will be necessary to fulfill this role. Finally, the paper offers some comments about how budget targets can be set in the transition to a market economy and illustrative targets for the main budgetary aggregates in the short and long run.

11.1   The Breakdown of the Communist Fiscal System

During the Communist period, the government budget was primarily an instrument for resource reallocation. Under this approach, fiscal policy was used differently than in market economies, where policymakers aim to support macroeconomic balance and to provide public goods. Budget policy under Poland's Communist governments involved the administration of turnover taxes, enterprise profits taxes, tax reliefs, and subsidies to support an extensive system of

---

1. For descriptions of fiscal developments and budgetary policy issues in Hungary, Romania, and Czechoslovakia, see Boote and Somogyi (1991, 21–24), Demakis and Khan (1991, 26–27), and Aghevli, Borensztein, and van der Willigen (1992, 10–11).

consumer and producer price controls. In fact, neither the tax nor subsidy schemes were fixed regimes (i.e., with established parameters on which economic agents can base their decisions), as is the case in the West. In practice, taxes and subsidies were negotiated, with enterprises seeking to achieve their desired level of post-tax-cum-subsidy profits and the government seeking to maintain price controls and clear commodity markets.[2]

Although Poland's governments had sought other budgetary objectives, maintaining macroeconomic balance was not among them. The tax system was managed to achieve incomes policy objectives, targeting the growth of state enterprise wages and then using these wages as the base for social insurance benefits and government-sector wages. Although the state investment budget included some infrastructure projects executed by government ministries, it was designed primarily to channel resources to state enterprises, to support their industrial investment projects and profitability.

Thus, a complicated network of resource transfers rested on a shaky foundation, Poland's very narrow tax system. The tax system relied primarily on turnover taxes and the enterprise profits tax (see app. table 11A.2). These two taxes provided revenues of about 23 percent of GDP in the mid-1980s, roughly two-thirds of all state budget revenues. Most of the turnover-tax revenues were from three products (gasoline, alcohol, and tobacco), and the base was not broad; in fact, exemptions were plentiful.

The macroeconomic effects of budget policy on aggregate demand were not given much consideration. This was possible because the prevalence of price controls and subsidies bottled up domestic imbalances and the lack of exchange rate convertibility restricted the spillover of imbalances into economic relations with the rest of the world. When the macroeconomy started to veer off course, budgetary policy was not adjusted.[3] During the buildup of the imbalances in 1988 and 1989, real wages in state-owned industry rose by 28 percent. Since this was far in excess of productivity gains, enterprise profitability slumped. This slump produced a corresponding decline in government tax revenues in 1989. As the revenue crisis materialized, spending was not reduced sufficiently, mainly owing to an effort to maintain enterprise profitability and consumer price controls in the face of growing aggregate demand.

Ultimately, the government was unable to bring about an adequate fiscal adjustment. In August 1989, the last Communist government raised food prices by 150 percent. This was a last-ditch attempt to strengthen the budget and also to prepare the way for a greater role for market forces. Meaningful

2. Balcerowicz (1989) explained that, in Poland, the governmental authorities "heavily tax enterprise gross profits but then channel them—to a large extent in an arbitrary way—back to enterprises. . . . The problem is that a great deal of fiscal assistance flows to enterprises in financial difficulties, and that practically all such enterprises are bailed out."

3. Poland's earlier episode of macroeconomic imbalances, in 1981 and 1982, led to a harsh budgetary adjustment and a sharp reduction in real wages under conditions of martial law. For a general discussion of the reasons why budgets in socialist economies turn toward deficit during periods of economic reform, see Kornai (1992, 337–43).

fiscal adjustment, however, would have required the rethinking of many related policy areas—including consumer and producer price controls and the operation of the trade and exchange system—something the Communist reformers were politically and technically incapable of doing. The budget deficit for the year was about 7 percent of GDP. Since almost all the budget finance came from loans from the banking system, the deficit led to a huge increase in base money and fueled Poland's hyperinflation.

11.2   The Economic Transformation and the Budget

11.2.1   The Stabilization Correction

The first Solidarity government launched a stabilization and liberalization program at the beginning of 1990. The measures introduced at that time produced a nearly 10 percent budgetary correction that year (see app. table 11A.1) and resulted in a surplus of about 3 percent of GDP. This stabilization correction resulted mainly from the following four aspects of the program.

First, the liberalization of economic activity—the freeing of prices and the liberalization of domestic and international trade—gave the government the opportunity to cut subsidies to consumers and enterprises sharply. With prices set by supply and demand, the government no longer had to intervene with subsidies to maintain desired price levels. Instead, enterprises were expected to manage their own profit positions. In the course of the budget crisis of 1989, subsidies had been reduced to about 12½ percent of GDP from the 16 percent level that had prevailed in the mid-1980s (see app. tables 11A.3 and 11A.4). The 1990 liberalization measures permitted a sharp cut in explicit subsidization to about 7 percent of GDP. The effort to slash explicit budget subsidies continued in 1991, with subsidies falling to only 4 percent of GDP.

Second, the stabilization program restored enterprise profitability. The most important factor in the restoration of enterprise profitability was the reversal of the real wage increases that had occurred in 1988 and 1989. These real wage increases were unwarranted in the sense that they far exceeded productivity growth. To a degree, however, the measured increases in real wages were symptomatic of the growing excess of aggregate demand. Wages were rising in comparison with controlled prices, but these controlled prices were increasingly irrelevant, as the availability of goods at official prices diminished. In 1990, the real wage dropped by 27 percent in 1990 in comparison with the previous year. In part, wages fell back into line with productivity, and, in part, price liberalization led to the comparison of wages with prices that more closely reflected the scarcity and value of goods and services.

Another factor in restoring profitability was the establishment of a unique, convertible exchange rate. Convertibility removed the long-standing antiexport bias of the old exchange rate system and permitted many Polish enterprises to be competitive in world markets. Yet another factor was the one-time increase in enterprise taxation resulting from nominal asset revaluation. The rapid inflation and nominal devaluation (and their effects on asset values) in early 1990 created taxable profits. In 1990, enterprise profits taxes rose by 4 percent of GDP to reach 14 percent, a level that exceeded even those of the mid-1980s (see app. table 11A.2).

Third, Poland was able to reduce substantially its external debt service burden. Shortly after taking office in September 1989, the new government stopped making interest payments on medium- and long-term external obligations and announced its intention to seek a permanent reduction of Poland's debt service burden. Much of Poland's debt service had been rescheduled during the 1980s, but, in September 1989, the government sought debt forgiveness. In early 1990, official creditors agreed to a generous rescheduling of debt service falling due that year and, in early 1991, to a permanent 50 percent reduction of all eligible debt. Poland continues to negotiate with commercial bank creditors for comparable treatment of their claims.

The immediate effect of Poland's debt service reduction was cash-flow relief for the budget and reduced pressure on the monetary system and balance of payments. In the short run, the cessation of interest payments permitted Poland to reduce debt service payments to $0.7 billion in 1990 from $1.6 billion the year before (a reduction of about 1½ percent of GDP).[4] The rescheduling provided relief not only for the balance of payments but also for the budget. This resulted from the reduction in inflationary finance that had been funding government purchases of foreign exchange for debt service.[5]

Fourth, state budget support for investment reached an all-time low. Many investment projects were stopped in 1990, and there were almost no new government investment projects. Budgetary expenditures for investment, which had fallen by 1½ percent of GDP in the two years prior to the reforms, dropped another ½ percent of GDP to about 3½ percent (see app. table 11A.3).

11.2.2   The Transformation and Emerging Budgetary Pressures

The effects of the stabilization effort were not all positive. While the positive effects dominated at first, certain effects placed a greater burden on the budget from the outset. The sharp decline in production, employment, real wages, and retail sales in the state sector depressed the level of tax revenues linked to those

---

4. For years, because of earlier reschedulings, Poland had been paying only a fraction of the nearly $7 billion of interest and principal falling due. The 1990 payments represented a smaller fraction than in earlier years.

5. In addition to cash-flow relief, the permanent 50 percent reduction in Poland's debt burden has probably eliminated Poland's debt overhang (presuming that the debt reduction granted by official creditors is followed by a comparable deal with commercial bank creditors). Had debt service merely been rescheduled rather than permanently reduced, doubts would have remained regarding the government's ability to generate the resources for debt service in the future (when the rescheduled obligations would fall due). The risk of a renewal of inflationary finance and renewed balance-of-payments problems would have made it all the more difficult for the government to reestablish its creditworthiness.

activities. Turnover taxes and wage-related taxes combined fell by 3 percent of GDP. Moreover, some modest compensation for subsidy cuts was extended to the population in the form of income support, rising government expenditures on health (related to purchases of medicine), and changes in social insurance benefits (primarily for housing).

As Poland's program of transformation has progressed, several aspects of the process have had important and sustained negative effects on government revenue and have forced the government to constrain its spending tightly. In most cases, these negative effects stem from the nature of the post-Communist transformation and are undoubtedly important factors in other countries in transformation.

Revenues

The most important development was the reversal of the initial improvement of enterprise profits and profits taxes. In 1991, enterprise profit tax revenues fell by 7½ percent of GDP to a level well below what had prevailed in the mid-1980s. With a tax system heavily dependent on this particular revenue source, the effect on total revenues was large and not easily remedied.

The fall in enterprise profits taxes can be traced to three aspects of the transformation process.

First, by its very nature and design, the liberalization of prices and economic activity exposed the fact that an important segment of Poland's capital stock would prove unprofitable in an environment of market-determined prices. The pattern of capital accumulation had been shaped by central planning and, then, supported by subsidies, low energy prices, and the protected CMEA market. The low value (and in some cases worthlessness) of much of this capital was exposed by the liberalization of the economic environment. Over the long term, new investment will lead to a reorientation of the capital stock and will support new business activities (for the most part private business activities). New capital will provide a basis not only for economic growth but also for the collection of corporate profits taxes. In the short run, however, the fall in the profitability of old capital has had a direct, negative effect on enterprise profit tax revenues.

Moreover, the enterprise profit tax system has not been effective in collecting revenues from new private businesses. Poland is now accumulating profitable "new capital" in thousands of new private businesses, mainly in the service sector, but also in manufacturing, transport, distribution, and construction. So far, however, the share of taxes paid by the private sector has not risen with its growing share in total business activity (see table 11.1).

Second, wage pressures reemerged in late 1990 and were not adequately resisted. As mentioned earlier, the fall in the measured real wage at the outset of the program had contributed to the restoration of healthy profit levels. By late 1990, workers began to seek a greater share of these profits in the form of wage increases, and state enterprise managers for the most part did not resist. As a result of the absolute absence of central authority over state enterprise

Table 11.1   **Poland: Shares of the Tax Burden, 1991**

	Socialized Sector	Private Sector
Total sales	72.4	27.6
Total taxes paid	90.2	9.8

Source: Central Statistical Office, Warsaw.

Note: The data cover the 20,700 largest employers (with 50 or more employees in construction and industry and 20 or more in other sectors), and the period is the first three quarters of 1991. These data undoubtedly lead to an understatement of the role of the private sector in sales (because of the employment cutoff level) and an overstatement of the share of taxes paid by the private sector (because of tax avoidance by small enterprises). Figures given are percentages of total.

managers, there were no effective owners to oversee management decisions and no effective resistance to wage increases within the industrial structure.

The government was aware that the prevalence of state ownership and decentralized decision making would lead to weak control over enterprise costs, particularly wages. For this reason, the government instituted a tax-based incomes policy aimed at curbing wage growth at the beginning of 1990. The instrument of policy was an excess wage tax, under which wage payments above a putative norm would give rise to a tax liability for the enterprise equal to several times the excess of wage payments.

One inherent difficulty with this type of policy is establishing the level of the wage norm. Poland's excess wage tax was not binding in the first half of 1990 because real wages remained below the preset norm. This left room for untaxed wage increases later on that were not fully warranted by macroeconomic circumstances or the financial position of particular state enterprises. In the second half of the year, when the wage norm was binding in most cases, many enterprises chose to raise wages and pay the tax.

Wages began to rise in the fourth quarter of 1990, and enterprise profits and profits taxes began to fall accordingly. There was also automatic upward pressure on budget-sphere wages and pensions, which were linked to industrial wages. The rising trend of wages continued in 1991. In retrospect, it was unrealistic to place too much weight on a tax-based incomes policy; the incentive problems of the state enterprise sector could not be rectified by a tax on excess wages.

In fact, the real culprit in the wage saga is the sluggishness of the privatization program. The Polish Treasury technically remains the sole owner of most large state enterprises. Of course, the government no longer has the will or the mechanisms to exert direct influence over state enterprise behavior. Until enterprises are commercialized and privatized, industry will remain in the hands of state enterprise managers and their labor councils, neither of which are subjected to much outside scrutiny. In this transitional state, enterprise managers have no particular incentive to seek to make a profit, apart from an ill-defined motive to accumulate some resources for investment. The main consequence of higher profits is higher profits taxes; therefore, enterprise managers find ways to spend their resources and avoid profit tax liabilities.

This failing has had important consequences for the budget and, thus, for the management of the macroeconomy. When viewed from the vantage point of the consumer, wage growth in 1991 does not seem excessive, as it was only slightly higher than the increase in the consumer price index. When viewed from the vantage point of enterprise profitability, however, the situation was actually grave. Wages rose by 24 percent more than producer prices in 1991 and contributed to the sharp fall in profitability in that year.[6]

The third blow to profit tax revenues was the scrapping of the CMEA (Council for Mutual Economic Assistance) trading system at the end of 1990. Under this system, the Soviet Union and the East European countries had exchanged goods on the basis of a clearing arrangement denominated in the unit of account called *transferable rubles*. The decision to end this system coincided with a crippling balance-of-payments crisis in the Soviet Union, related to the collapse of its political and economic system. In the midst of the crisis, the Soviet Union was unable to provide an effective foreign exchange system or payments mechanism for its enterprises. Thus, trade between Poland and the Soviet Union collapsed, as did trade between the Soviet Union and the rest of Eastern Europe. Poland's exports to the Soviet Union under the clearing arrangements fell by 92 percent in 1991 (as only transitional transactions occurred as the system was wound up), and very little of the trade was converted to a hard currency basis.[7]

The Soviet trade shock brought on a profound collapse of profits and profits taxes in Polish industry. The principal effect of the trade collapse was the sharp drop in the demand for exports from those enterprises with traditional links to the Soviet economy. The effect on the enterprise sector was broader, however, because real zloty input prices (for oil, natural gas, electricity, and iron ore) rose universally. This increase in input costs need not have been borne entirely by profits, for the real product wage could in principle have fallen to absorb part of the shock. But, as mentioned above, the real product wage rose sharply, and, as a result, enterprise profits and profits taxes declined sharply for much of the Polish state enterprise sector in 1991.[8]

Another feature of the transformation that lowered budget revenues was the sharp reduction in import tariffs that constituted part of the strategy to liberalize external trade. Tariff revenues fell in early 1990, fortunately coming at a

6. Consumer prices rose by 60 percent in 1991, while producer prices rose by 36 percent. The difference is accounted for by the sharp increase in the relative price of services.

7. For a description of trade developments with the former CMEA countries and an analysis of the quantification of trade between Poland and the Soviet Union, see Rodrik (chap. 18 in this volume).

8. For a detailed analysis of the effects of the CMEA collapse on Polish industry, see Berg and Sachs (1992).

time when the budget had been strengthened by the stabilization correction. The tariff system was revamped in July 1991, and tariffs were set at an average level of about 15 percent. Revenues in 1991 were 1.7 percent of GDP, down about ½-1 percent of GDP from the mid-1980s.

The privatization program, on the other hand, was expected to provide greater support for the budget. Little was expected from this source in 1990 because it was necessary to put privatization legislation through Parliament and design a privatization program before collecting revenues. The program was expected to be under way in 1991, however, so the 1991 budget included an estimate of Zl 15 trillion (about 1.5 percent of GDP) from privatization revenues. The privatization effort was intended to include many components, including initial public offerings (IPOs) and auctions of shares for individual enterprises, a mass privatization program to distribute ownership claims to the population via investment funds, and a sectoral privatization program aimed at the restructuring and sale of enterprises in key industrial sectors. The elements of the privatization effort that were expected to provide revenues for the state were the sale of enterprises through IPOs and auctions. In the end, these two elements turned out not to be practical avenues for privatization, and revenues turned out to be well below initial expectations.

Expenditures

The most important change in the pattern of budget expenditures arising from the economic transformation is in the area of social safety net spending. Unemployment, virtually unknown in Poland before 1990, rose steadily after the program began in 1990. An extrabudgetary labor fund was created to administer an unemployment scheme and a job retraining and relocation program. The government initiated the unemployment scheme with high replacement rates (70 percent for the first three months), no time limitations on benefits, and broad eligibility criteria. In 1991, the expenditures of the labor fund rose to 1.4 percent of GDP, as the rate of unemployment rose to 12 percent by the end of the year (see app. table 11A.5).[9] Unemployment should decline over the course of the transformation, but, as in any market economy, frictional unemployment will remain, and an appropriate social insurance scheme must be maintained.

Social security benefits paid by the social insurance funds—sickness, maternity and family benefits, and pensions—also increased sharply. This resulted mainly because the government inherited from the Communist period a social

9. Group layoffs from state enterprises account for less than 25 percent of the registered unemployment in 1990 and 1991. The rise in registered unemployment was probably accelerated by the fact that the initial unemployment benefit scheme adopted in 1990 was generous and did not have as eligibility criteria that individuals were job leavers or were engaged in an active job search. In early 1992, the scheme was revised, benefit eligibility was limited, and the government began to strike individuals from the unemployment rolls (for further discussion of this subject, see Berg and Sachs 1992).

security system with comprehensive and universal benefits. In time, this system must be reformed to make it suitable to the conditions of a market economy and sustainable from a fiscal point of view. In the first two years of the economic transformation, however, the government attempted to maintain the comprehensiveness of the social security benefits carried over from the Communist period. Where real benefits had been allowed to erode through the lack of inflation adjustment, the government revalued benefit packages. Where the link of pensions to the average industrial wage had been allowed to slip, the government restored a stronger link. Expenditures of the two social insurance funds rose to 14.2 percent of GDP in 1991 from 10.7 percent of GDP in 1989. Rising public expectations about social insurance benefits have made it difficult to contain benefit levels and the scope and coverage of benefits.

11.3   The Budget in a Market Economy

As Poland's market economy takes hold, the government will have to reassess its role in Polish economic life. There is a continuing demand for modern and effective public services. In addition, the social insurance system is facing mounting demands from many segments of the population asking for greater income support and social protection. As mentioned earlier, unemployment benefits will remain a permanent feature of Poland's market economy, even after the temporary budget burden of transitional unemployment has passed.

In addition, new demands for budget resources will arise from the need to overcome the heritage of the Communist system. To meet them, the government will have to reform its own administration and trim the size of the overstaffed civil service. At the same time, the government will have to revamp the civil service wage structure to overcome the heritage of egalitarianism and to attract qualified staff. In addition, the government will have to develop a public investment program to build a modern infrastructure, clean up the environment, and recapitalize the banking system.

To create a revenue base that will make all this possible, Poland will need to complete the ambitious tax reform agenda that has already been drawn up. Finally, the tax system will have to be supported by an improved system for budget finance that removes the dependency of the budget on banking system credit. The following subsections describe briefly these long-run imperatives of budgetary reform.

11.3.1   The Public Investment Program

To modernize its infrastructure, which at present is not adequate for a growing, capitalist economy, Poland must develop a public investment program. Billions of dollars of investment are required to upgrade transport and communications systems alone. In addition, the Communist economy produced extensive environmental degradation, which has led to adverse effects on health and the quality of natural resources. Estimates of the environmental cleanup costs vary, but they range as high as the Ministry of Environment's estimate of $260 billion.

The abundance of public investment needs and the shortage of budgetary resources mean that public investment criteria, now virtually absent, must be developed. The many potential projects must be evaluated and compared, and a selective public investment program must be drawn up that is based on a careful assessment of rates of return. In all likelihood, public investment expenditures in the state budget will have to rise from about 2 percent at present to 6–7 percent of GDP.[10] This range would not be atypical for a country with a similar income level (even ignoring Poland's particular environmental problems). The financial implications of boosting the level of public investment by this magnitude will be discussed in the section on budget finance. But it is clear that a sustained increase in public investment can be managed only by some combination of an improvement in government savings, domestic bond finance, and substantial recourse to external finance.

Unfortunately, Poland, like other countries in the region, does not have a tradition of a well-defined public investment program based on sound economic selection criteria. In the Communist past, investment expenditures in the state budget were devoted only in part to building infrastructure and more often to channeling resources to particular industries and sectors to finance enterprise investments. In fact, no distinction was drawn between the provision of public goods and private goods in the selection of state-funded investment. Moreover, when the state has chosen to fund investments, there have been no clear and acceptable procedures for the evaluation of the return on these investments. Interestingly, in 1990, when the new government considered which of the unfinished investment projects to complete, the only data available were the nominal amounts spent to date (without correction for inflation) and the total expenditures required for completion. No rate-of-return calculations were made at the outset, nor were calculations made regarding the return on project completion. In order to develop an effective public investment budget with an adequate spending level, the government must develop investment evaluation rules that are based on concepts of public goods provision and appropriate rate-of-return requirements.

11.3.2   Commercial Bank Rehabilitation

Poland will probably have to recapitalize some of its state commercial banks in order to privatize them. Attempts to privatize banks that do not have an adequate capital base may prove impossible and will certainly not lead to a strong banking system. Thus, recapitalization will have to come first. If this is carried out in connection with privatization, the budgetary contribution will

---

10. Public investment by local and municipal authorities amounted to about 1 percent of GDP in 1991. General government investment of 6–9 percent of GDP is in line with what is found in comparable developing countries.

not be wasted by a continuation of inappropriate state enterprise management.

The budgetary burden of the recapitalization is likely to be modest, but not inconsequential. The government is now in the process of preparing nine large state commercial banks for privatization. The banks have been audited, and estimates of bad loans in their portfolios range from 10 to 30 percent. Nonetheless, the financial position of the banks is still in flux because the underlying condition of the state enterprise borrowers has not stabilized. Thus, the market value of these banks is not yet known and will not be known until the large state enterprises are either closed or privatized. When the state commercial banks are privatized, some estimation of their market value will emerge, but in all likelihood certain banks will not have an adequate capital base to make privatization possible.

Recapitalization could take many forms, but one illustrative possibility would be to place government bonds at these banks to strengthen their assets positions. In this case, the annual budgetary effect of the recapitalization effort would be the interest burden of the bond placements. The domestic portfolio of the banking system stood at Z1 170 trillion at the end of 1991 (or about 18 percent of GDP). A recapitalization effort equivalent to only 10 percent of this portfolio would involve the placement of bonds of about 1.8 percent of GDP. The magnitude of the interest burden stemming from bond placements of a recapitalization would depend on interest rate developments. If stabilization efforts succeed in bringing the interest rate down to 25 percent per annum, the recapitalization could add Z1 4 trillion (or ½ percent of GDP) to budget expenditures.

11.3.3 Social Spending

Poland has begun to reform its social insurance system, which was designed during the Communist period and, thus, embodied the strong Communist preference for care for the social needs of all citizens. Polish society continues to place a high priority on the government's role in social support, but this priority must now be weighed against others. In the coming years, the government may want to shift its emphasis away from the "care" of social needs and toward the creation of "opportunities" for the Polish people. This will require less support in the form of social insurance and more support for education and the creation of human capital. Moreover, the development of the market economy will require that social insurance spending be sustainable from a fiscal point of view and be structured so as to minimize the disincentives and distortions for the population.

11.3.4 Tax Reform

Poland has begun a process of fundamental tax reform.[11] The reform has several aims. First, the new tax system will be less distortionary, mainly be-

---

11. For a more detailed discussion of tax reform issues, see Gordon (chap. 9 in this volume).

cause the selectivity and exemptions of the old tax system will be replaced by broadly based taxes. Second, the new tax rates and tax bases will be sufficient to generate the revenues needed to support an acceptable level of spending. This is of paramount importance in light of the many competing demands for government resources and the need to limit budget deficits to levels that can be financed in a noninflationary manner. Third, the new tax system will be more fair. Private and state enterprises will be treated alike, and all individuals' incomes will be treated uniformly under the personal income tax.

In brief, the taxes inherited from the Communist period will be replaced with several broadly based taxes modeled on Western tax systems. In January 1992, the government introduced a personal income tax, expected to raise about 5½ percent of GDP in revenues. A value-added tax has been designed to replace the selective turnover-tax system, but it has not yet been passed by Parliament because of political conflicts over the question of whether construction and agricultural value added should be exempt. In the meanwhile, the base for the turnover tax has been broadened as a stopgap measure. The reformed company profits tax is now comparable to those used in the West.

The authorities expect that the introduction of the new taxes will in time lead to a substantial recovery of tax revenues as a fraction of GDP. In the short run, however, there will be an inevitable loss of revenues, stemming from the difficulties of taxpayer education and tax administration.[12] The personal income tax administration relies on a system of estimated tax payments to collect revenues from the hundreds of thousands of new, private businesses. The procedures are unfamiliar in the Polish context and difficult to enforce.

11.3.5 Budget Finance

The main source of budget finance in Poland has been credit from the banking system, which has led for the most part to the monetization of budget deficits. An important goal of budget policy, therefore, will be to limit the reliance of the budget on the banking system to amounts of credit that are consistent with low rates of inflation, declining in time to European levels. Because the economic transformation relies so heavily on the maintenance of a stable macroeconomic climate, its success depends on giving the inflation goal top priority and shaping budget deficit targets accordingly.

At the end of 1991, high-powered money in the banking system amounted to Zl 89 trillion, or about $8 billion. To bring the rate of inflation down toward European levels (or at least to the neighborhood of 10 percent per annum), high-powered money could be allowed to grow by about Zl 9 trillion, or about 1 percent of GDP, per year to accommodate the rise in nominal money de-

---

12. A recent journalistic account quoted the head of Poland's tax inspection office, who explained that he was "still trying to figure out all the ways that people can evade [the new personal income tax]. I don't think we will replenish the budget overnight. Germany has 11,000 tax inspectors, France has 16,000, and Poland has 1,524" (Battiata 1992).

mand.[13] Setting the amount of banking system credit granted to the government with this limitation in mind will make the low inflation target attainable.

This does not imply that the budget deficit must be limited by the credit available from the banking system. In light of Poland's investment and environmental cleanup requirements and the need for improved public services and social insurance benefits, over the next several years the government may need to accept budget deficits that exceed the amount of credit from the banking system. The first step toward making this possible is to develop a domestic bond market.

To date, Poland does not have a functioning bond market. The government issued bonds in late 1989 as it attempted to reduce the inflationary effect of the budget deficit in preparation for the introduction of the Balcerowicz program. At that time, inflation was running at more than 20 percent per month, and there were great uncertainties about the government's ability to introduce a suitable economic program. The bonds carried very high yields to maturity (to improve their acceptability), and the government incorporated conversion options, under which the bonds could be used to buy assets in future privatizations and to pay future taxes. In the end, the bond sale amounted to only a small fraction of 1 percent of GDP, and the instruments did not provide a suitable basis for establishing a functioning domestic bond market. Since mid-1991, the central bank has begun to create a market for short-term Treasury bills that it auctions to commercial banks as an instrument for monetary absorption. Although this instrument represents an improvement in the management of monetary policy, its use has been limited, its term is four to twenty-six weeks, and the bills are held only by commercial banks.

It should be possible for the government to issue longer-term bonds—without conversion options or other novelties—that can be sold to the nonbank public and form the basis for a domestic bond market. This should be achievable, given the low initial level of domestic government debt and the lack of financial assets for the nonbank public (i.e., alternatives to savings deposits in state commercial banks). There should be little difficulty or fiscal risk in selling bonds equivalent to 1–2 percent of GDP per year, as is done in many other countries around the world. After all, provided that economic growth in Poland resumes at even a modest rate, borrowing on this scale would not lead to a rising debt-to-GDP ratio.

Budget finance could also be augmented from foreign funds. Uncertainties regarding Poland's economic prospects will probably continue to restrict access to commercial credits in the West in the coming years, and access will improve only gradually. Therefore, Poland's external borrowing strategy may have to focus on multilateral and bilateral official credits, such as World Bank

---

13. Of course, if inflation were brought down to a low level, the real demand for money might be somewhat higher and the base for the inflation tax greater.

loans to support sectoral adjustment efforts, the public investment program, and the environmental cleanup activities.

Quantitatively, the most important potential source of external finance may be export credits and credit guarantees from Western export credit agencies. Poland already has commitments from Western governments for credits exceeding $8 billion, very little of which has been used to date. And it is likely that additional commitments could be secured from Western export credit agencies because of their desire to support the exports of their domestic companies. To date, there have been many obstacles to the utilization of export credits, including the reluctance of the government to guarantee state enterprise borrowing for projects of uncertain return. Moreover, few export credits have gone to support the budget because of the paucity of capital import requirements among the investment expenditures included in the state budget.

During the transition to a market economy, it should be possible to make much greater use of export credits for budget support. An ambitious public investment program would increase the scale of capital imports by the public sector. But more important, the government can channel to the budget much of the finance extended by export credit agencies in connection with nongovernment imports. The government can assist Polish enterprises in importing capital equipment from the West to obtain export credits but also require that a large portion of the imports be paid for by these enterprises out of their own funds. In essence, by not passing along foreign finance to Polish importers, the finance can be diverted to support the budget.

11.4 Targets for Budgetary Aggregates

11.4.1 The Long Run

An illustration of long-run budgetary targets can give an idea of the direction and magnitude of the budgetary changes still required in Poland over the coming decade. Of course, future policy choices and macroeconomic developments will have a direct bearing on the desirability of any particular budget target. Nonetheless, this subsection presents a view intended to take into account the many demands for budgetary resources and financing constraints facing the government.

First, it will be necessary to boost government revenues to the neighborhood of 30 percent of GDP (see table 11.2).[14] This level of revenues is lower than what was consistently collected by the state budget in the mid-1980s and

14. The numerical examples that follow refer to the state budget and exclude the extrabudgetary funds and local governments. It is presumed that the division of responsibilities between the state budget and the extrabudgetary funds and local governments is not changed again, that the extrabudgetary funds are placed on a self-sustaining basis, and that the local government budgets are balanced.

Table 11.2   Poland: Budget Aggregates

	1991	Target Budget
Revenues	23.4	30.0
Current spending	24.9	27.0
Government saving	-1.5	3.0
Investment	1.9	6.0
Surplus (minus indicates deficit)	-3.3	-3.0

Source: Ministry of Finance, Warsaw.
Note: Figures given are percentage of GDP.

would represent a scaling back of government claims on the resources of the economy.[15] However, revenue levels of even 30 percent of GDP will represent a substantial recovery from the 1991 level of 23 percent of GDP. A recovery of revenues of this scale is necessary to support the expenditures that Poland will need to make. This should be possible once tax reform is complete and transitional losses have been overcome. Moreover, the intrusion of government via the tax system will be greatly reduced in comparison with the Communist period because tax reform will eliminate most of the arbitrariness and selectivity of the tax system.

Second, current expenditures will have to be kept to about 27 percent of GDP. This limit would represent a decline in expenditures of about 8 percent of GDP compared to the mid-1980s but is consistent with the reorientation of government activity away from subsidization and resource reallocation. The need to improve education and health services, to raise civil service salaries, and to reform social safety net programs will make this limit difficult to attain. On the other hand, this level would represent an increase in current spending of more than 2 percent of GDP in comparison with the compressed spending level experienced in 1991.

Achieving these targets for revenues and current expenditures would reverse the pattern of government dissaving that emerged in 1990 and 1991. The main reason to aim for government savings of about 3 percent of GDP is to provide the resources for an enhancement of public investment expenditures. If public investment is boosted to the neighborhood of 6 percent of GDP, half the amount could be financed by government saving and the rest by government borrowing. As argued above, the Polish government need not attempt strictly

15. Total revenues of the state budget averaged about 39 percent of GDP over the period 1983–86 and then declined to about 35 percent of GDP over the period 1987–88. To compare these data with the target proposed in the text, it is necessary to adjust for the fact that, in the 1980s, state budget revenues included certain funds that were collected by the state and then transferred to local governments. Beginning in 1991, local governments were allowed to retain revenues to cover local expenditures, and in that year these governments retained revenues of about $3^{1}/_{2}$ percent of GDP.

to balance the budget in the next decade. There are limits, however, to the amount of budget finance that can be achieved in a noninflationary manner, and there are limits to the amount of public debt that can be taken on. It is reasonable that the government could run budget deficits of about 3 percent of GDP over the coming decade without adverse consequences. Domestic bank credit, domestic bond sales to the nonbank public, and foreign credits could each provide finance equivalent to about 1 percent of GDP.

11.4.2   The Short Run

The transition to a sustainable budget position is proving difficult for Poland. As these difficulties stem from the nature of the transformation process, the Polish experience may be instructive for other countries attempting the transformation to a market economy.

For some years, revenues are likely to remain below an acceptable long-run target. The revenue base remains weak because the state sector remains in crisis and the private sector has not yet become the predominant force in many areas of the economy. And revenue collection remains weak because tax reform is not yet complete and will involve transitional revenue losses and because tax administration is still being improved.

Similarly, expenditures are difficult to control during the transition. Some of the remnants of the old system, such as subsidies, have not been fully jettisoned. Some elements of the economic transformation, such as the transitional surge in unemployment, place temporary burdens on the budget. And the population is eager for rapid improvements in public services and expanded social benefits.

In weighing budget choices during the transition, the government's financing constraints dictate what is an acceptable budget deficit. Budget financing must be guided by the stabilization objective because of the importance of a stable climate to nourish the new private sector. To create such a climate, the government will have to reduce domestic inflation toward European levels. As explained above, this will require limiting budgetary recourse to banking system credit to about 1 percent of GDP. There is some greater leeway in the areas of domestic bond finance and foreign finance in the short run. Domestic bond sales could probably reach 2 percent of GDP or so if a concerted effort were made to develop the instruments and the market.[16] Foreign finance could provide another 1–2 percent of GDP, combining what might be available from the IMF, the World Bank, and export credit agencies.

The 1992 draft budget has been at center stage in Poland's political arena for most of the first half of 1992. The government put forward a draft budget

16. Of course, domestic borrowing on this scale inevitably places pressure on the nongovernment sector, by depriving it of much of the available domestic financial savings and, thereby, bidding up interest rates. This pressure must be weighed against the transitional pressures limiting budget revenues and elevating budget expenditures.

calling for a deficit of 5 percent of GDP.[17] This deficit is near the upper bound of what might be financed in a noninflationary manner. For this reason, political attitudes toward the draft budget have proved to be a litmus test on Poland's anti-inflation program.

To reach its target, the government has proposed measures both to boost revenues and to curtail expenditures. Among the measures to boost revenues, the turnover tax has been extended to previously exempted goods, such as food, clothing, and construction materials. Modifications in social security contributions, some public-sector price increases, and the new personal income tax are also expected to play a positive role. Among the measures to curtail spending, the revaluation of pensions would be postponed, family allowances and disability pensions would be restricted, and housing subsidies to cooperatives would be cut.

To keep the deficit below 5 percent of GDP over the next two years will require emergency efforts to boost tax revenues by several percentage points of GDP from the low level of 23 percent of GDP collected in 1991. Tax revenues must be raised quickly toward the level that must be restored over the long run. Several options (beyond what is already being proposed by the government) might be considered.

One option is to introduce a value-added tax with an elevated tax rate for two years or so. The elevated rate would compensate in part for the transitional losses of switching from the turnover tax. Another option would be to tax the enterprise sector more heavily. The tax burden on this sector accounted for most of the fall in revenues in 1991, and it is doubtful that revenues can be substantially restored unless more revenues flow from the enterprise sector. Recent signs point to some recovery in production and to continued strong exports. Thus, it should be possible to restore in part the tax contribution of the enterprise sector, even though important segments of the state enterprise sector remain in crisis.

In the long run, the answer to the enterprise taxation question is to privatize and introduce a new company profits tax. In the short run, the dividenda, a tax on enterprise capital assets, could play a role. State-owned enterprises are prone to profits tax avoidance, which is less of a problem with a capital tax. The dividenda is unpopular and has been reduced, not increased, in the past two years, mainly because it cannot be evaded. The dividenda will be paid by healthy enterprises. Unhealthy enterprises that do not pay should suffer sanctions, in the form of either wage controls or outright intervention.

On the expenditure side, reducing the budget deficit will require an aggressive effort to eliminate or sharply reduce remaining subsidies. And social in-

---

17. The budget as presented does not take into account the implications of two decisions of Poland's constitutional tribunal invalidating limitations that had been placed on the growth of pensions and budgetary-sphere wages in the course of 1991. The effect of these decisions will oblige the government to make expenditures equivalent to at least 4 percent of GDP. At present, it remains unclear whether these expenditures will be made in 1992 or later.

surance benefits, health, pension, and education must be contained to a level consistent with a reasonable budget position, until the revenue system begins to perform adequately.

11.5 Conclusion

Poland faces the immense task of reorienting the role of government in the economy to support its emerging market economy. To facilitate this transition, the government will have to support allocative efficiency, invest in and supply public goods, and provide an appropriate social safety net. To play these new roles effectively will require sweeping tax reform, a reevaluation of spending programs, the development of a public investment program, a comprehensive privatization effort, and the development of improved techniques for budget finance. These tasks are being undertaken in the difficult environment of economic transformation. If Poland is to sweep away the remnants of the Communist fiscal system, it must shoulder the burden of the enduring costs of the Communist period (such as pollution, bankrupt banks and state enterprises, and inadequate infrastructure). This will prove a difficult agenda because, at the same time, Poland's government must fulfill its most important new function, to provide a stable macroeconomic environment.

Appendix

Table 11A.1   **Poland: Budget Summary, 1987–91 (in percentage of GDP)**

	1987	1988	1989	1990	1991 (est.)[a]
Total revenue	34.3	35.6	29.7	32.5	22.8
Turnover tax	10.6	10.9	8.8	6.5	6.6
Profit tax	11.5	12.9	9.7	14.0	5.8
Other	12.1	11.9	11.2	12.0	10.4
Total expenditure	37.8	37.0	35.7	31.9	27.3
Wages, goods, services	12.9	12.4	13.4	14.7	12.2
Subsidies	15.4	16.0	12.5	7.1	3.7
Transfers to social funds	1.5	1.5	2.3	3.3	4.7
Investment	5.6	5.3	4.1	3.6	1.9
Other	2.5	1.8	3.3	3.2	4.7
State budget balance	−3.5	−1.4	−5.9	.6	−4.5
Extrabudgetary funds					
balance	2.7	1.4	−1.2	2.1	−.5
Local government balance	. . .	. . .	. . .	. . .	.5
General government:					
Revenue	48.2	49.0	41.8	44.6	37.4
Expenditures	49.0	49.1	48.9	41.9	41.8
Balance	−.8	−.0	−7.1	2.7	−4.4

(*continued*)

Table 11A.1   (continued)

	1987	1988	1989	1990	1991 (est.)[a]
Financing	.8	.0	7.1	−2.7	4.4
Change in arrears	.0	.0	1.9	−.3	.9
Domestic banks	.0	.0	5.0	−2.6	4.4
Other domestic financing	.0	.0	.5	.1	.0
Foreign financing	.0	.0	−.3	−.7	−.1
Other	.8	.0	.0	.7	−.9

Sources: The 1991 Statistical Yearbook of Poland and the Ministry of Finance.
[a]Local government operations were excluded from the state budget for the first time in 1991. In 1991, local government revenues and expenditures amounted to 3.5 percent of GDP.

Table 11A.2   **Poland: Budget Revenue, 1987–91 (in percentage of GDP)**

	1987	1988	1989	1990	1991 (est.)[a]
Total revenue	34.3	35.6	29.7	32.5	22.8
Tax revenue	31.5	33.4	26.0	30.2	20.6
Turnover tax	10.6	10.9	8.8	6.5	6.6
Profit tax	11.5	12.9	9.7	14.0	5.8
Dividends	.0	.0	1.7	2.1	1.2
Payroll tax	3.6	3.5	3.3	3.0	1.8
Excess wage tax	.3	.7	1.7	1.4	2.9
Foreign trade taxes	2.4	2.0	.0	.6	1.8
Other	3.0	3.4	.8	2.5	.5
Nontax revenue	2.8	2.2	3.7	2.4	2.2
Privatization	.0	.0	.0	.0	.2
Profit transfers	.5	.5	.7	1.6	.7
Other	2.2	1.7	3.0	.7	1.3
Memorandum Items					
Tax revenue	31.5	33.4	26.0	30.2	20.6
From socialized sector	29.3	31.0	23.6	28.1	20.0
From nonsocialized sector	2.2	2.4	2.5	2.1	.6

Sources: The 1991 Statistical Yearbook of Poland and the Ministry of Finance of Poland.
[a]Local government operations were excluded from the state budget for the first time in 1991. In 1991, local government revenues and expenditures amounted to 3.5 of GDP.

Table 11A.3   **Poland: Budget Expenditures, 1987–91 (in percentage of GDP)**

	1987	1988	1989	1990	1991 (est.)
Total expenditure	37.8	37.0	35.7	31.9	27.3
Current expenditure	32.2	31.7	31.6	28.3	25.3
Science and culture	.6	.8	.7	.6	.9
Education	3.6	3.4	4.3	4.7	3.5
Health, sport, tourism	4.0	3.9	4.2	5.0	4.7
Administration	.8	.7	.8	.9	.7
Justice, police, defense	3.9	3.6	3.3	3.6	3.1

Table 11A.3   (continued)

	1987	1988	1989	1990	1991 (est.)
Subsidies	15.9	16.0	12.5	7.1	3.7
Transfers to social funds	1.5	1.5	2.3	3.3	4.7
Financial costs	.1	.1	1.3	2.0	1.7
Other	1.8	1.7	2.0	1.2	2.4
Capital expenditure	5.6	5.3	4.1	3.6	1.9
Memorandum items					
Salaries	3.0	3.0	4.3	4.1	4.9

Sources: The 1991 *Statistical Yearbook of Poland* and the Ministry of Finance of Poland.
Note: Local government operations were excluded from the state budget for the first time in 1991. In 1991, local government revenues and expenditures amounted to 3.5 of GDP.

Table 11A.4   **Poland: Budget Subsidies, 1987–91 (in percentage of GDP)**

	1987	1988	1989	1990	1991 (est.)
Total subsidies	15.9	16.0	12.5	7.1	3.7
Subsidies to the population	10.0	10.0	8.1	3.8	2.3
Foodstuffs	3.4	4.9	3.6	.2	.0
Meat products	.8	1.4	1.1	.0	.0
Dairy products	1.4	2.1	1.5	.2	. . .
Cereals	.9	.9	.5	.0	.0
Consumer goods	.7	.4	.2	.1	.1
Coal and coke	.7	.4	.2	.0	. . .
Private agriculture inputs	1.0	.9	.9	.2	.0
Passenger transportation	.8	.8	.9	.4	.3
Housing	3.6	2.5	2.4	2.7	1.7
Medicine (imported)	.3	.5	.1	.0	.0
Books	.0	.0	.0	.0	.0
Other subsidies to private agriculture	.1	.1	.1	.1	.1
Subsidies to enterprises	5.9	6.0	4.4	3.3	1.4
Inputs and transportation	1.0	1.1	3.2	1.5	.5
Coal	.9	1.0	3.2	1.5	. . .
Transfers of goods	.0	.0	.0	.0	. . .
Foreign trade	2.5	2.2	.2	.0	.0
Socialized agriculture	.6	.5	.2	.1	.0
Other subsidies to enterprises	1.0	.3	.1	.9	.6
The banking system	.0	1.2	.0	.0	.0
Other economic units	.8	.7	.6	.8	.3
Road maintenance	.4	.3	.3	.3	.0

Sources: The 1991 *Statistical Yearbook of Poland* and the Ministry of Finance of Poland.

Table 11A.5   Poland: Operations of Extrabudgetary Funds, 1987–91 (in percentage of GDP)

	1987	1988	1989	1990	1991 (est.)
Total revenues	16.9	16.6	16.9	17.9	15.7
Direct revenues	13.9	13.4	12.0	12.1	11.0
Transfers from state budget	3.0	3.2	4.8	5.8	4.7
Social Insurance Fund	10.1	9.1	9.7	9.5	12.0
(of which transfers)	(.7)	(.7)	(1.3)	(1.5)	(2.4)
Social Insurance Fund for Farmers	.9	.9	1.1	1.4	1.6
(of which transfers)	(.7)	(.7)	(1.0)	(1.2)	(1.5)
State Labor Fund	.1	.1	.1	.8	1.3
(of which transfers)	(.1)	(.1)	(.1)	(.6)	(.8)
Central Fund for Development of	1.2	1.4			
Science and Technology[a]			1.0	1.4	...
(of which transfers)	(.0)	(.2)	(.1)	(.0)	
Foreign Debt Service Fund[a]	1.2	1.2	1.0	1.6	...
(of which transfers)	(.0)	(.0)	(.9)	(1.5)	
Export Development Fund[a]	.0	.0	1.0	1.3	...
(of which transfers)	(.0)	(.0)	(.0)	(.0)	
Other	3.1	3.9	2.9	2.0	.8
(of which transfers)	(1.5)	(1.5)	(1.5)	(1.1)	.0
Expenditures	14.2	15.2	18.1	15.8	16.2
Social Insurance Fund	8.3	8.4	9.7	8.5	12.4
Social Insurance Fund for Farmers	.9	.9	1.0	1.3	1.7
State Labor Fund	.1	.1	.1	.6	1.4
Central Fund for Development of	.9	1.4			
Science and Technology[a]			1.0	1.1	...
Foreign Debt Service Fund[a]	1.2	1.0	3.2	1.5	...
Export Development Fund[a]	.0	.0	.9	1.0	...
Other	2.8	3.5	2.2	1.9	.8
Balance	2.7	1.4	−1.2	2.1	−.5
Social Insurance Fund	1.9	.7	−.1	1.0	−.4
Social Insurance Fund for Farmers	.0	−.0	.1	.1	−.0
State Labor Fund	.0	.0	.0	.2	−.1
Central Fund for Development of	.3	.0			
Science and Technology[a]			−.1	.3	...
Foreign Debt Service Fund[a]	.1	.3	−2.1	.1	...
Export Development Fund[a]	.0	.0	.1	.3	...
Other	.4	.4	.7	.1	−.0

Sources: The 1991 Statistical Yearbook of Poland and the Ministry of Finance of Poland.
[a]Liquidated in 1991.

References

Aghevli, Bijan, Eduardo Borensztein, and Tessa van der Willigen. 1992. Stabilization and structural reform in the Czech and Slovak Federal Republic: First stage. Occasional Paper no. 92. Washington, D.C.: International Monetary Fund.

Balcerowicz, Leszek. 1989. Polish economic reform, 1981–88: An overview. In *Economic reforms in the European centrally planned economies,* Economic Studies, no. 1. New York: United Nations.

Battiata, Mary. 1992. In Poland, the wages of capitalism. *Washington Post,* 15 April 1992.

Berg, Andrew, and Jeffrey Sachs. 1992. Structural adjustment and international trade in Eastern Europe: The case of Poland. *Economic Policy,* no. 14 (April): 118–73.

Boote, Anthony, and Janos Somogyi. 1991. Economic reform in Hungary since 1968. Occasional Paper no. 83. Washington, D.C.: International Monetary Fund.

Demakis, Dimitri, and Mohsin Khan. 1991. The Romanian economic reform program. Occasional Paper no. 89. Washington, D.C.: International Monetary Fund.

Kornai, Janos. 1992. *The socialist system: The political economy of communism.* Princeton, N.J.: Princeton University Press.

Comment   Michael P. Dooley

The paper by Alain de Crombrugghe and David Lipton provides a frontline account of the enormous difficulties faced by governments in transition economies. Their focus on the fiscal implications of the transition is consistent with the traditional view that monetary stability is necessary for the transition and that the fiscal deficit is the fundamental determinant of monetary growth.

The transitional "fiscal" problem is easy enough to identify, but I am less convinced that privatization and the reform of tax and spending programs are an adequate response to the problem. Although their paper provides a valuable description of a number of important determinants of the fiscal position, two factors stand out. On the revenue side, the inherited tax system relied heavily on a profits tax on state-owned enterprises. As the central government lost control over the enterprises, labor has protected its income in the face of falling output at the expense of profits. On the expenditure side, reduced spending on price supports and capital expenditures has been partially offset by rising expenditures for the social safety net.

The authors emphasize the positive role that privatization could play in dealing with the current situation. The revenues from privatization might help balance the budget in the short run, but, perhaps more important, private ownership would provide market discipline for wage demands. The importance of better corporate governance is underlined by the access of state-owned enterprises to credit. It is not hard to imagine that, once profits have been squeezed, labor might continue to press wage and employment demands, resulting in increased losses covered by borrowing from state-owned domestic banks.

The difficulty with privatization as a policy response to this dilemma is that it is hard to find a case where the pace of privatization is not much slower than expected. A part of the problem might be that the central government does not clearly own all the property rights that go along with the sale of a firm.

The enactment of a broadly based income or value-added tax is also a reasonable policy prescription, but like privatization one that takes considerable time to yield the significant share of national income needed to match government expenditures. Thus, a significant amount of foreign assistance may be necessary in order to reduce the government's resort to the inflation tax.

In the interim, it may be necessary to recognize that workers in state-owned enterprises are government employees and that state-owned commercial banks are a part of the fiscal system. It seems obvious that some restraints must be placed on the economic behavior of these institutions during the transition.

Discussion Summary

Mark Schaffer pointed out a puzzle in the Polish budget statistics. He noted that the payroll tax fell by over a third in 1991 even though real wages rose. *David Lipton* responded that the payroll tax is collected primarily from the state sector and that the number of state-sector employees fell in 1991. However, Lipton noted that the decline in workers can explain only a portion of the revenue collapse.

Andrew Berg asked whether the authors' reported revenue estimates for 1991 include arrears. Lipton did not know, but Schaffer said that a quick comparison of the numbers in the paper with the numbers in the *Polish Statistical Bulletin* suggests that the numbers in the paper are actual receipts. Schaffer added that there are substantial arrears associated with the excess wage tax.

Kalman Mizsei contrasted the "bad news" that the Polish government has had difficulty collecting taxes with the "good news" that government expenditure is less than 40 percent of GDP. He said that indirect taxes can be used to make up the temporary shortfall between expenditures and receipts. Mizsei said that such stopgap measures would be needed only for two years.

Lipton noted that the government will face difficulty restraining spending. He said that social benefits, which were pared back in 1991, could explode in 1992. The threat comes from a pair of constitutional tribunal decisions in which the 1991 cutbacks were declared unconstitutional. Lipton concluded that, if the government can hold the line on spending, then the remaining degree of freedom will be foreign official finance coming from the World Bank, the European Bank for Reconstruction and Development, and already committed but unutilized export credits. He said that the availability of these sources for one or two years might put Poland in a position where some of the longer-term adjustments to the budgetary position can take hold.

Lipton also discussed the government's labor policy. He said that, in negotiations with labor, the government should discuss the costs of the high real wage instead of publically acting as if Poland does not have a real wage problem. He suggested that the current government effort indirectly to lower the real wage with a nominal devaluation will fail because the policy was developed without the cooperation of labor.

Berg criticized the authors' proposal that the dividenda tax be used in the short run. Berg recommended that a higher payroll tax be used instead. He said that the dividenda tax is arbitrary because it depends on unreliable official measurements of each firm's capital stock.

Lipton defended the temporary dividenda tax. He noted that the dividenda tax is nondistortionary because it is based on an input that is fixed in the short run. Moreover, he emphasized that the healthy state enterprises are capable of paying the dividenda tax since they have a lot of financial resources at their disposal that they are carelessly spending on excess wage payments and other unnecessary expenditures.

12   Privatization in Russia: First Steps

Andrei Shleifer and Robert W. Vishny

On 3 July 1991, the Russian legislature passed a law that mandated privatization of most state firms and prescribed methods for doing so. The work on implementation of this law was slow at first and was interrupted by momentous changes in the government in August. Starting from mid-November 1991, the new government resumed work on the privatization guidelines. On 27 December 1991, the Supreme Soviet passed an elaboration of the 3 July law, called the "Fundamental Positions of the Privatization Program." In January 1992, this document was supplemented by several decrees signed by Yeltsin, which explained the various steps of the process. Finally, in late March 1992, the government produced the actual privatization program that it offered to Parliament for approval. Since the privatization itself has not really begun, these documents represent the first steps toward privatization in Russia. Our paper discusses the state of Russian privatization up to the end of March 1992, including the proposed program. In particular, we focus on one key issue that the privatization process confronted: how to reconcile the conflicting claims of the de facto "owners" of assets that must be privatized.

The issue of the initial allocation of property rights in state firms, before they are privatized, rarely receives attention. In many cases, it simply does not arise. For example, in the U.K. privatization, the government clearly owned the shares it sold, so there was no question of who was selling the shares, only how and to whom. Even in the context of Eastern Europe, it is often simply assumed that the government owns the shares and then has to sell or distribute

---

Between March 1992, when this paper was written, and January 1994, when it went to press, Russia privatized over a third of its industry using the privatization program described in this paper. Boycko, Shleifer, and Vishny (1993) presents an update on the progress of privatization. In all this work the authors have benefited from the collaboration with Maxim Boycko, Jonathan Hay, and Dmitri Vasiliev of the State Committee on the Management of State Property (GKI).

them to the population. The questions that generate intellectual and practical excitement are, first, who should be the eventual owners of the shares and, second, how to sell or allocate the shares from the government to these eventual owners to maximize efficiency? Both these questions presume that the seller of shares is clear, namely, the government.

Yet, as the experience of Poland illustrates, the workers of the companies do not agree that the shares are the government's to distribute as it wishes. Failure to appreciate this point is undoubtedly the most important cause of the delay of privatization in Poland. More generally, companies in Eastern Europe in general, and Russia in particular, do not have an unambiguous de facto ownership structure, in which the government owns the shares. On the contrary, many "stakeholders" have existing ownership rights, in the sense of being able to exercise control rights over assets effectively. Moreover, these stakeholders take both economic and political action to defend their rights. Unless these stakeholders are appeased, bribed, or disenfranchised, privatization cannot proceed.

In Poland and Hungary, the important stakeholders are the workers and the managers. In Russia, they also include the local governments and the branch ministries. These stakeholders correctly see privatization as a redistribution of property rights rather than as a gift from the government. In this paper we ask how the center can reconcile the control claims of these multiple de facto owners and, in particular, how it can reduce the damage they do while competing for the pie? Our answer is to pay off some stakeholders with dividends and privatization proceeds so that they give up the control rights that conflict with those of others.

We develop this answer in several steps. Section 12.1 briefly discusses our theoretical approach to property rights and privatization. Section 12.2 surveys the distribution of property rights in enterprises under socialism and shows how the relatively clear distribution of these rights collapses when socialism does. The decline of the power of the state and the ministries has created an "ownership vacuum" in Russia that was filled by new effective owners: the workers, the managers, and the local governments, whose control rights are often in conflict. Section 12.3 looks at spontaneous privatization, which is essentially a way to cut out the Russian government from its ownership claim. Section 12.4 discusses ways to reconcile the conflicting claims. Section 12.5 examines the likely future of privatization in Russia. Section 12.6 sums up.

12.1   The Theoretical Framework

Coase (1960) has made the profound observation that, once property rights over assets are completely defined between a set of agents, in most circumstances these agents will negotiate an efficient way to use these assets. Coase also argued that many inefficient uses of assets stem from poorly defined property rights. He did not explain what to do when property rights are indeed poorly defined. He also argued that, so long as property rights are in fact well defined, it does not matter exactly how they are delineated. Grossman and Hart (1986) showed, in contrast, that the allocation of property rights is not neutral, as Coase argued, but matters for the ex ante investments that agents must make in human capital complementary with these assets. Thus, a possibly unique efficient allocation of property rights does indeed exist. Grossman and Hart did not treat the case where property rights are not well defined.

This paper focuses on situations with poorly defined property rights. It therefore pays to specify more clearly what that means. When property rights are poorly defined, no agent has unambiguous control rights over assets in uncontracted for circumstances. There are no clearly defined rules of the game about who decides what to do with the asset. As a result, default rules come to be used. One such rule is, First come, first served: the agent who gets to the asset first gets to use it, at least for a time, as he likes and can exclude all the others from using it. Another such rule is that no agent can use the asset, since every agent can exclude others from using it; therefore, the asset stands idle. Hart and Moore (1990) called this arrangement *joint ownership*. A variation of this rule is that no agent can use the asset in a new way, so some status quo other than idleness prevails. A third default rule is that all the agents try to use the asset simultaneously in ways they see fit and cannot exclude others from using it. Some Nash equilibrium in agent's actions obtains in this case. These default rules do not typically lead to an efficient use of the assets. Defining property rights would replace them by efficient negotiations, but can this be done?

State firms in Russia, like elsewhere in Eastern Europe, exemplify assets with multiple owners with overlapping control rights and no procedures for resolving conflicts. The workers, the managers, the ministries, the local governments, and the central government all have some cash-flow and control rights over particular uses of these assets, and in many cases these rights overlap. In this situation, the Coase theorem predicts an inefficient outcome.

Privatization is a way to define the property rights between these various claimants so that efficient bargains could subsequently be struck. The means of doing so is to bribe the various parties by giving them cash-flow rights when they give up some of their control rights that conflict with those of other stakeholders. The workers and the local governments, for example, might be given payments if they commit not to interfere with layoffs. Thus, local governments might be given a share of privatization proceeds in exchange for abandoning their interference with business. Or the workers might be given a percentage ownership in exchange for letting the managers determine employment and wages. Privatization is a mutually acceptable redistribution of both control rights and cash flows between the various claimants.

Overlapping control rights are very costly to the Russian economy, for, while some control rights over assets have been defined informally after central control has collapsed, other control rights are still in dispute. Without settling these disputes, privatization cannot proceed. Moreover, the prospect of reallocation of property rights during privatization gives the stakeholders an incentive to take actions that would increase their ownership claims during privatization even if these actions reduce the size of the total pie. These actions include signaling and positioning to show toughness that would cause the center to give the relevant stakeholder a higher ownership claim. For example, workers might strike and local governments turn off electricity supply to the firm to show how tough they are. Stakeholder activities that destroy value to enhance their ownership rights—perhaps through a large delay of privatization—are an important cost of ambiguous property rights.

This paper tries to describe plausible ways to allocate cash flows and control rights to reduce some of the costs associated with the current disagreements. We first explain, in the context of Russian privatization,who the relevant stakeholders are, what decisions they have control over, and what damage they can do and have done if their ownership claims are not respected. We then propose a way to allocate cash flows in order to contain, if not eliminate, the value-reducing activities of the unhappy stakeholders. We discuss how to pay off the local governments, the managers, and the workers to go along with privatization and restructuring. Importantly, we discuss not optimal schemes but rather schemes that can be easily introduced into the law and therefore guide privatization.

12.2   Ownership during Socialism and after Its Collapse

12.2.1   Ownership under Socialism

Under socialism, the state supposedly owns all the means of production, including the firms. This notion of ownership, however, is not particularly revealing. Ownership consists of a claim to residual profits as well as to residual control rights (Grossman and Hart 1986). The Treasury has some claim on profits or losses of state firms. But there is no "state" that has control rights. These rights instead are shared by the managers of the firm and the bureaucrats in the ministry that oversees the firm. The ministry bureaucrats are probably the more important owners, in the sense of having most of the power to dictate the decisions of the firms. Legally, the ministry bureaucrats have the right to choose the top managers, to determine the production and investment, to set prices, to allocate inputs and buy outputs, to determine the general growth rate of wages, and so on. They do not make micro production decisions, but they control most of the other ones. Most rights of the ministry bureaucrats are enforced through central control, but they also maintain these rights through complete control over the delivery of scarce inputs.

How do the ministry bureaucrats translate these control rights into cash flows for themselves? The ministry bureaucrats use their rights to extract surplus from the firm, subject to attaining some minimal level of profits (or maximal level of losses) for the Treasury. One way to do it is to extract presents and services from the firm. Another way to extract surplus is to underprice the supplier's and the firm's output. By intentionally making the inputs scarce, the bureaucrats can extract bribes from the firm in exchange for deliveries; by making outputs scarce, they can do the same with the firm's customers. Pervasive shortages under socialism result from this profit-maximizing exercise by the bureaucrats of their effective ownership rights (Shleifer and Vishny 1992).

Under socialism, managers of the firm also have some control rights. They have the know-how and the connections to solve the problems of pervasive shortages and breakdowns. This gives them some control over production, investment,and employment decisions as well as over most micro decisions of firms. Their knowledge also makes them valuable to the bureaucrats and hence enables them to collect some of the rents from the firm.

In contrast, workers own nothing under socialism—Marx and Lenin notwithstanding. Workers own the firm only to the extent that they have an influence over its policies or a claim on its cash flows. In Communist Russia, workers' ability to strike and otherwise exercise control rights was severely limited by the central government. They certainly had no control over wages or employment. Also relatively unimportant were the local governments: any attempt by them to exercise control over the firm was certain to invite retribution from the center. With full control over local budgets, the center had local governments under its thumb. The relevant owners, then, were first the ministry bureaucrats and second the managers.

12.2.2 Ownership during the Transition

The control rights over the decisions of firms have changed radically in Russia since 1988, as socialism and central control collapsed. Starting in 1988, the government implemented a range of reforms that transferred many of the decisions over output mix, output level, customer choice, and wages to enterprise managers. The ministries also lost their right to appoint managers, although it is not clear who gained it (the workers began to have some input). The 1988 reforms kept the prices fixed but at the same time allowed firms to sell a small portion of their output at free prices. The reforms also kept most of the input allocation centralized, thereby letting the ministries keep most of their effective control rights.

Over the subsequent three years, the ability of the center to enforce the planned allocation has collapsed. The Communist party enforced deliveries to the state, and that mechanism simply failed. As a result, enterprises refused to deliver their products to the state at low prices and instead began selling them at market prices to whomever they pleased. What began as a Chinese-style experiment with capitalism on the margin transformed itself into a collapse of the central allocation mechanisms. This collapse of socialist coordination greatly damaged state enterprises and may have led to aggregate output declines in 1990 and 1991.

These changes deprived the ministries of most of their control rights. First, they could no longer dictate to firms what to do, and, even if they tried, they had no law or force to support their orders. More important, when the ministries lost control over the outputs of some enterprises, they also lost control over firms for which these outputs were inputs. When the ministries could no longer assure supply deliveries, managers had to find inputs, which often meant barter and other market transactions. To the extent that the control rights of the ministries depended on supply assurance, these control rights have diminished a great deal.

The control rights of the ministries have not disappeared completely. Because ministries still have control over some industry assets, such as research institutes, information networks, and export licenses, they continue to exercise control over firms. Perhaps more important, branch ministers from the old regime continue to sit on the council of ministers and in fact have more votes in the aggregate than do the members of the reform team. They use this power to influence the course of privatization in two main directions. First, they argue that many state firms are too vital to be privatized or even to be transferred to the jurisdiction of the local governments. The ministries want to keep government control over assets because control brings the ability to extract cash flow and services from these firms in the future as well as continuation of ministerial jobs. Second, if privatization is to take place, the ministers want it to take the form of free distribution of shares along vertical production chains so that firms own shares in their suppliers and customers. The ministers prefer, but do not insist, that they actually supervise this allocation of shares. The ostensible reason for such privatization is to preserve supply links and to avert the further collapse of the economy. It is obvious, however, that preserving the existing supply relations through cross-holdings is largely a way to preserve existing industrial structures and ministerial oversight. The ministers thus accept privatization only if it preserves their control over firms.

Some of the arguments that the ministers make to slow down privatization seem absurd yet are sustained by the political process. In one meeting, the food minister argued that yeast factories, while quite small and numerous, should remain under central jurisdiction lest the politicians in the areas where these firms are located force them to refuse to sell the yeast just to blackmail the rest of Russia. The minister of publishing demanded that all the publishing houses should remain in state hands because "publishing is our ideology" and hence cannot be given up either to the private sector or even to the local governments. And the construction minister has insisted that all the trucks used in construction remain in state hands because they are critical to the war mobilization effort. Even more radical have been the proposals of the minister of industry, who wants to distribute 70 percent of enterprise shares along the vertical production chains. Despite these efforts to stop reforms using both influence over firms and votes in the government, the power of the bureaucrats is nowhere near what it used to be.

As the bureaucrats partly lost their control over enterprises, who gained it?

In Russia, this control has reverted to stakeholders who previously had virtually no power. These stakeholders include the workers of the firm, the managers, and, perhaps most important, the local governments. To understand who de facto owns the firms before privatization begins, we must clarify the control rights of these stakeholders.

Consider first the workers. Today, the workers have influence over employment, wages, and the choice of managers. After liberalization, the workers got a right to negotiate collective bargaining agreements and to strike. This and the influence over the choice of managers gives them control over employment and wages. Even where the workers do not select the managers, managers recognize that privatization will in many cases formally allocate voting rights to the workers tomorrow. This, of course, gives the workers many effective control rights today.

In addition to these economic sources of worker power, workers represent a substantial number of voters, in the Russian as well as local elections. The democratic political process thus naturally favors the allocation of the control rights over the firms' assets to the workers. An important political formation in the Russian Parliament supports workers' rights. Compared to the regime prior to reforms, changes in Russia have led to a large increase in the control rights of workers—similar to although not as dramatic as what has occurred in Poland. Workers are beginning to exercise these control rights. They have started to strike, particularly in the coal and other natural resource industries, demanding not only higher wages but also explicit ownership rights to the assets with which they are working. In many firms, workers have voted to replace the managers by those who are more sympathetic. The extraordinary wage explosion in Russia since 1988, in which most of the extra profits of enterprises were passed on to the workers in higher wages, is clear evidence of the increased power of the workers. The surprising slowness of layoffs in Poland and Czechoslovakia after the reforms is also strong evidence of the control rights of workers. East Germany, where the managers and the foreign buyers kept the control rights, provides a striking contrast because layoffs have been huge.

Workers are also expressing clear claims on the assets of the state firms. Worker groups have demanded complete ownership of the assets of their firms. Larisa Pyasheva, the head of Moscow City privatization, has formally endorsed this strategy as rapid and fair. The 3 July privatization law allows for a sale of some government shares to workers at a 30 percent discount, but that is clearly considered to be insufficient. The initial demands have been much more extreme. An interesting illustration along these lines is VAZ, the giant automobile manufacturer that has been negotiating a sale of 33 percent of its shares to Fiat for a price between $1 and $2.5 billion. The proceeds from the sale are to be invested in upgrading VAZ. In late November 1991, the workers of VAZ addressed an open letter to Yeltsin and the prime minister of Italy, demanding that they immediately get a 51 percent share in VAZ before any discussions of sale take place and that some of the revenues from the sale be allocated to them as shareholders. They have also threatened industrial action should their demand be rejected. Since the Fiat investment is the best hope for these workers regardless of whether they own any shares, their demands are a clear illustration of the vastly increased control rights of the Russian workers. Interestingly, as of this writing, the VAZ deal is still up in the air.

The control rights of managers have also increased tremendously. First, the existing law gives managers a lot of discretion over what to produce, what price to charge, and to whom to sell the output. The legal control rights over firms are therefore largely theirs. Second, even when the ministries have retained legal rights, they are no longer obeyed, and hence the control rights by default revert to the managers. Managers also have some control rights over employment and wages, which conflict with those of the workers on these decisions. Third, the managers have the network of contacts and the personal relationships that are essential for barter and for the procurement of inputs. They have thus inherited from the bureaucrats their most important control right. Like the workers, managers have been trying to use their political influence, with the local governments and especially with Parliament, to translate the effective control into the ownership of cash flows as well. They favor worker-management buyouts at low prices, where they often get large ownership stakes in exchange for promising high wages to the workers. They also prefer these buyouts to take a partnership rather than a corporate form, mostly to avoid possible control challenges in the future.

Last but not least, the local governments also gained many new control rights. After the demise of the Communist party and of the central control over government more generally, the local governments have found tremendous room to govern their localities. Because the local governments are typically democratically elected, they have some legitimacy as representatives of the local population. In addition, they have received control over some key local assets, such as electricity, water, and other utilities, and can translate this control into influence over firms.

Not surprisingly, the local governments have demanded a share of the revenues of the enterprises in their areas, particularly in the oil and other natural resource rich areas. They have also demanded and received a say over those with whom the firms can enter joint ventures, what they can produce, and what they can barter. Many localities went on to demand that large state enterprises be made responsible for the procurement of foodstuffs for all the residents in their areas. They have also attempted to change firm policies toward pollution and other public goods. Many of the control rights of the ministries have thus been transferred to the local governments.

In the privatization area, the local governments have demanded both the right to privatize and the revenues from privatization. Since December 1991, the Moscow and the Russian governments have fought over the speed and the mechanism of privatization in Moscow. In demanding all these control rights, the local governments realize the inability of the center to enforce Russian laws. They also make effective threats: to turn off water and electricity at factories that do not cooperate. Even more effective are the threats from the republics on the Russian territory inhabited by ethnic minorities to declare independence unless they receive control over firms on their territories. But the most serious problem is that the local governments often do not want to privatize at all. Instead, they want to use prospective privatization as a mechanism to transfer control over firms from the ministries to themselves so that they can continue the *upravleniye,* or management, on their own. In many cases, the ability of the local governments to assure the supplies of goods to their areas, as well as power and bribes for themselves, relies on retaining control over firms rather than privatizing them.

The remaining stakeholder in the Russian firms is the Russian "state," the nominal owner of these assets. Traditionally, the state exercised its control rights through the ministries and the Communist party. In light of the decline of both, "the state" has no clear residual control rights at all, although it nominally has all the residual cash-flow rights.

Formally, the state is represented in the privatization process by GKI, the State Committee on Property. This committee is supposed to oversee privatization and take care of the state property before it is privatized. While the committee is quite small, it is supposed to have regional representatives who do its job in various regions. In practice, the local governments have already demanded control over appointing the local representatives of GKI, even though GKI is an explicitly federal organization. The functioning of the local GKIs is severely handicapped by such intergovernmental conflicts. This is only one example, of course, of the ruinous conflicts between the stakeholders.

The greatest power of the state comes, as always, from its ability to make general laws and enforce them in some cases. This, in fact, is what the privatization program as written by GKI is. Even so, most realistic privatization schemes, including the one that is being introduced in Russia, institutionalize the actual fact of nonownership by the center. Luckily, the people running the privatization program in Russia accept the decline of the control of the center over firms, although they do not want local governments to step in its shoes.

In summary, the situation in Russia early in 1992 fits nicely into the general model of multiple owners with overlapping and conflicting control rights. Unfortunately, the cost of these conflicts is the delay of privatization since a typical consequence of disagreement between the stakeholders is inaction. When privatizations do occur, they look a lot like theft, as our next section illustrates. The immediate objective of government policy, then, is to compensate the stakeholders to reconcile these conflicting claims and so to allow legal privatization to proceed.

12.3   Spontaneous Privatization

Spontaneous privatization in some forms began in earnest in Russia in 1988, when the state relaxed the close monitoring and direction of enterprises. Initially, it took the form of simply diverting the profits from the firm so that the government could not capture them. An enterprise manager sets up a parallel private firm or a cooperative next to the state firm or even inside it. That private firm then buys the output of the state firm at the official controlled price and resells it at the market price. The profits are in part kept by the managers, who of course are the owners of the private firm, and in part distributed as higher wages to the workers.

The enormous recent growth of cooperatives in Russia largely reflects this mechanism for diversion of profits from the state and their distribution as wages, not the private productive initiatives that many Westerners hoped to see. The formation of these private ventures to syphon off profits from the state was made possible by lax enforcement of laws and state orders by the center since output could be sold only on the market if it was not delivered according to the plan. The process was speeded up by paying off local authorities, who frequently shared in the spoils of theft from the center. Informal reports indicate that most state enterprises that produced desirable output have engaged in at least some form of such profit diversion. Gains for all parties at the expense of the central government made spontaneous privatization very popular in Russia.

While the initial spontaneous privatization has focused on the diversion of profits, more recently, as the control of the center has deteriorated further, it evolved into the transfer of state assets to private firms and cooperatives. Initially, these transactions took the form of leasing, where buildings or machines were leased part time from the state firms but were in fact used full time and more extensively than the lease allowed. More recently, the private daughter firms set up by the managers have begun simply to buy "redundant" assets from the state firms at negligible prices, often using the profits earned earlier from leasing. Of course, these assets often turned out to be not redundant at all but in fact quite essential. In this respect, asset diversion has naturally followed output diversion.

This type of spontaneous privatization, initiated by the managers with consent by the workers in exchange for higher wages, has accelerated sharply in 1991. These deals are usually accompanied by purchases of approval from the local governments and sometimes the ministries in Moscow as well. Rumored bribes in Moscow average 10 percent of the value of diverted assets and are often taken in dollars. Spontaneous privatization thus partially recognizes the ownership rights of the ministries and the local governments while transferring wealth from the Russian "state," which cannot monitor these transactions.

The more complete form of spontaneous privatization, which is beginning to appear in Russia, is a worker-management buyout (W/MBO) at the book value of assets. Book values of most assets in Russia are extremely low relative to their market values, a fact that has become even more extreme thanks to the rapid recent inflation. In a typical MBO, managers raise some funds from other state firms or from commercial banks that get their capital from state firms, add a trivial amount of their own and worker's money (perhaps R 10,000 altogether for a R 10 million firm), and buy their firm's assets at book value. In such a deal, managers might own 30 percent of the stock and the workers 70 percent. In many cases, the assets of the firm include a large amount of liquid funds, which are not typically counted in the calculation of book value. Because the book value is so low, and because many of the firm's assets are not even counted, the privatized firm can typically repay the loans within a few months, if not immediately. The managers and the workers then end up with the assets of the firm in exchange for a close to zero commitment of their own funds. These MBOs are virtually never contested, especially if the right local and federal officials are paid off. Moreover, the assets are usually acquired through a closed company (*tovarischestvo*) that does not have traded shares. As a result, once the loan is repaid, the control of the managers—and to some extent the workers—over the assets of these companies is complete. Until now, only a few managers in Russia have begun to take advantage of this way to privatize, but the practice is likely to grow.

Spontaneous privatization has many benefits. It gives the managers and the workers financial interest in the firm and therefore solves some of the incentive problems that state firms cannot overcome. In particular, manager-owners have a tremendous personal incentive to find foreign or other partners to help them restructure the firm. Spontaneous privatization is extremely rapid, especially if the local government officials are bribed to go along, since the managers themselves initiate and push forward the transactions. Spontaneous privatization also separates the firm from the state and hence hardens the budget constraint. Last but not least, it respects the ownership claims of all the stakeholders other than the Russian government or bribes the ones whose control rights are diminished to go along. At best, the Russian government gets the extremely low book value of assets and no control rights. Of course, the whole point of spontaneous privatization is to reduce the Russian government's claim.

The low prices and nontransparent deals endanger spontaneous privatization because it will become wildly unpopular as soon as some organizers openly become very rich. This problem is especially severe in Russia, where the privatization law explicitly states that firms must be sold through competitive processes, such as auctions. In spontaneous privatizations, in contrast, no competition for assets ever takes place. As the experience of Hungary demonstrates, popular backlash can derail the whole privatization process, not just spontaneous privatization. In fact, the talk of reversal of the deals of the last two years is already quite loud in Russia. For this political reason, spontaneous privatization is dangerous.

It may also be inefficient. First, the ownership stake that workers get in these transactions is typically very large, which might preclude efficient layoffs and wage control. Second, these deals typically isolate the managers of a privatized firm from all capital market pressures since there are no shareholders or effective bankers to monitor them. Of course, product market competition and ownership incentives still provide a lot more incentives than government control. Nonetheless, complete entrenchment is too much to give the managers in privatization. Third, only the better companies are typically involved in spontaneous privatization. The real losers that need to be shut down remain in state hands and are not restructured.

In sum, spontaneous privatization represents one way in which the competing ownership claims can be reconciled, namely, by a substantial exclusion of the nominal owner from privatization. Spontaneous privatization will remain very important in Russia, for, even if this process is somewhat regularized and firms are put up for competing offers, potential bidders will usually have to make peace with the incumbent management. The smaller firms will eventually go to the managers and the workers at very low prices anyhow. The relevant question, which we address below, is how to make this process more efficient and sustainable politically.

12.4   Privatization Strategies

The previous section has described the conflicting ownership and control claims of the stakeholders of Russian companies. For many important decisions, such as employment, wages, product sales, the appointment of managers, and investment,more than one stakeholder wants to influence the decision. In many cases, their interests conflict, particularly when decisions concern the restructuring of their companies. In the current situation, no clear rules for resolving these conflicts exist.

The present status quo has two implications for privatization. First, the usual way of resolving disagreements now is to do nothing. Each stakeholder has an effective veto power over any changes. In the context of privatization, this means that any proposal is vetoed and privatization delayed. What makes this problem worse is that some stakeholders, such as the local governments and many corporate managers, are quite happy with the status quo since it gives them enormous control rights. There is little hope for extensive privatization until at least some stakeholders get very strong incentives to move away from the status quo.

Second, because the stakeholders have enough effective control to veto any changes, no restructuring can take place. That means no layoffs, no wage restraints, no plant closures, and no management changes until a way of resolving conflicts between stakeholders is found. The local governments, the workers, and the managers can always use their political and economic influence to stop any changes that do not meet their wishes, and their wishes are inconsistent with restructuring. Like privatization, restructuring cannot proceed under the current situation.

To achieve privatization and restructuring, the Russian government must find ways to provide very strong incentives for the existing stakeholders to move to a governance structure that is consistent with fast privatization and restructuring. This objective suggests a two-pronged strategy, which we discuss in this section. First, enterprises should be commercialized or corporatized so that they are separated from the government and their formal governance structure becomes more clearly established. Second, stakeholders should receive strong command and financial incentives, in the form of shares and privatization proceeds, both to preserve the assets of the corporations today and to accede to privatization. Some steps in this direction have already entered the government's program; others are still being debated. It makes sense, therefore, to lay out the issues behind this high-pressure approach to privatization.

12.4.1 Corporatization

In the last two years, many control rights over the assets of state enterprises have been transferred to their managers. In many cases, these managers enjoy their new power and independence and are in no rush to privatize. When they do consider privatization, it often is spontaneous privatization that completely entrenches them at the helm. In addition, the Russian privatization program transfers the control over the privatization of many enterprises to the local governments. Many of the local administrators view this control as the right to manage the state enterprises rather than privatize them. Today, Russia is in the grave danger that firms will move toward local administrative control rather than private ownership.

The first essential step to prevent this tide is mandatory commercialization (or corporatization) of all the enterprises. This means that, within six months, all large state enterprises should be converted into joint-stock companies with publicly traded shares and boards of directors. Initially, all the shares would be held by the central government, but, as the privatization process unfolds over time, they will be given away or sold to the various stakeholders and investors. The board of directors would initially consist of the representatives of GKI, the managers, the representatives of the workers, bankers, and perhaps others involved with the corporation. After privatization, it would be elected by shareholders as in any private company. The idea is to make the state companies resemble private companies from the start. Such mandatory extensive commercialization has been advocated by Lipton and Sachs (1990) first for Poland and more recently for Russia.

Immediate corporatization accomplishes some of the goals of organizing corporate governance and resolving conflicts before privatization. To begin, it creates boards of directors charged with a fiduciary responsibility to maximize the wealth of the shareholders. These boards will serve several functions. First, because of directors' liability, directors will at the least try to prevent the blatant theft of assets by the managers. In some cases, directors will even provide more stringent checks on the management. In contrast to spontaneous privatization, boards of directors institutionalize the possibility of replacing the managers and thereby prevent complete entrenchment. Second, boards become a formal mechanism whereby the relevant stakeholders can exchange information and views. The workers' representatives will both be informed about the affairs of the companies and have the opportunity to express their positions formally. When they can do that, they are less likely to resolve conflicts through strikes. Finally, and perhaps most important, boards formalize the fact that shareholders—not the workers or the local governments—own companies and therefore have the formal right to run them. Disputes are resolved by votes on the board rather than by other means. The hope is that this approach will also reduce the destructive competition for rents.

Corporatization also creates tradable shares in the companies and hence outside shareholders. Initially, the shares will be owned by GKI, which will reinforce the central government's ownership claim. As we discuss below, some shares will immediately be allocated to the workers and the managers, which will clarify their ownership claims as well and provide them with some incentives to increase the value of the company. Other shares will be sold over time, which will create outside shareholders with value-maximizing objectives. Perhaps even better, the stage is set for GKI to sell control of some of these companies through a sale of controlling blocks of shares. By creating a potential market in the shares of state companies, corporatization moves companies a step closer toward privatization.

Unfortunately, the realization that corporatization redistributes control rights has not escaped the managers and the local government officials. Boards of directors and outside shareholders are not their idea of independence. Initially, this lobbying has derailed mandatory corporatization, and conversion into a joint-stock company was made voluntary. More recently, the government realized that giving (or even selling) shares to the workers and to the public as a whole cannot proceed without corporatization. This pressure to distribute shares—rather than an interest in governance—has lead the government to include mandatory corporatization of large companies into the privatization program. In that program, all large companies must convert into joint-stock companies by September 1992, which means issuing shares as well as appointing boards of directors.

12.4.2   The Workers

To avoid massive resistance to privatization, the government must pay off the workers. It is important not only to give workers stakes in their companies to make them feel like owners right away but also to provide them with strong incentives to want to see privatization accomplished. At the same time, GKI must deal with a legitimate and important concern that worker control is inconsistent with efficient corporate restructuring. The privatization program is a significant compromise in that it gives the workers substantial ownership and returns from privatization without giving them control.

Specifically, the privatization program gives workers 25 percent of the shares of the state companies for which they work, up to a certain ruble limit (approximately R 7,000 in March 1992). Initially, these shares will be nonvoting and will also pay a fairly high dividend. The idea behind making shares nonvoting at the beginning is to prevent worker control before firms are privatized. The law allows workers to trade shares from the start. The idea is in part to enable the workers who want cash to benefit from this transfer immediately and in part to limit the eventual voting power of the workers. There remains a serious question—still unaddressed—of how workers will be given tradable shares unless all large firms corporatize immediately.

The government is still debating the question of whether workers' shares should ever become voting. The correct answer is yes—for several reasons. First, workers' shares will become an important part of the float of publicly traded shares in the companies and may help active shareholders accumulate large stakes. If the shares are nonvoting, active shareholders will not be interested in them. Second, in countries with undeveloped securities regulation, nonvoting shares typically sell at large discounts to voting shares, even if the nonvoting shares have dividend protection. The reason for this is the large benefits that those in control can appropriate for themselves. In nonvoting shares sell at large discounts, the workers will be extremely disappointed in privatization and either resist it or demand further concessions.

But perhaps the most important concern about worker ownership is that voting shares will enable the workers to get significant representation or even control of the board, which will prevent any restructuring of the company. Worker representation on the board will probably be extremely beneficial to most Russian companies. The law provides for some worker representation on boards during the interim period before privatization. If such representation continues after privatization as well, workers will be better informed about the true financial situation of the company and will therefore be more likely to go along with the required tough restructuring steps. Board representation also gives workers a voice, which is a better way for them to be heard than through strikes and political action. At least in the near term, most dramatic changes in Russian companies will have to be made with the consent of the workers, and board representation is the most attractive way of gaining such consent.

At the same time, complete worker control of boards can prove disastrous as workers prevent restructuring from taking place and decapitalize companies. But it is hard to believe that, even with 25 percent of the votes, the workers will control the board. Some workers, particularly the poorer and the more redundant ones, will probably have sold their shares already. Some of the best workers might not even vote for directors who oppose restructuring. And the management might get the votes of the outside shareholders and the GKI if alternative directors do not want companies to change. In sum, giving workers votes and some board representation has a lot of advantages and few risks.

For these reasons, workers should have an option to convert their nonvoting shares into voting shares as soon as the government gets rid of enough shares. For example, when government ownership falls below 50 percent, the workers get the conversion option. Giving them this option also has the advantage that some workers will choose the dividend advantage of the nonvoting shares and will not convert. At the same time, the workers who want to sell their shares will convert and sell them at higher prices. In equilibrium, only a few workers might actually convert their shares and keep them so as to vote against restructuring. It might be better to have more worker representatives on the board than the workers could actually elect.

These grants of shares to the workers give them something regardless of whether privatization is accomplished. To give workers an extra incentive to favor privatization, the law provides them with further benefits. The workers get 10 percent of the government's privatization proceeds. They also get the option to buy 10 percent of the shares of privatized companies at a 30 percent discount to book value, which in most cases is a trivial fraction of true value. Importantly, getting anything out of these programs requires that the government's stake fall below 50 percent. One hopes that this will provide enough of a privatization sweetener. The Russian privatization program thus gives the workers the dual incentives that are required to get them to go along with privatization and to pressure other stakeholders to do likewise.

12.4.3 Local Governments

In the former Soviet Union, tensions between governments are not restricted simply to those between the former Soviet republics or those between local governments in Russia and the central Russian government. Tensions also exist between city and republic (*oblast*) governments, *oblast* and central Russian, and many other layers. In particular, Russia has several ethnic republics on its territory that are laying claim to the property on their territories and threatening to declare independence from Russia if these claims are not respected. In this section, we use the term *local governments* generically and focus on their relationship with the Russian center.

The strategy toward local governments should co-opt them into supporting privatization and relinquishing their control rights over firms. Given that their claims are often as strong as those of the workers, they will not be cheap to convince. At the same time, they should not be given shares, no matter when these shares become voting, since this strategy makes them large shareholders with a substantial interest in active control. While workers' shares are dispersed, local government shares are concentrated. In many cases, local governments would use their ownership rights to derail privatization and to continue managing the state firms. For this reason, the only feasible way to pay off local governments is by giving them privatization proceeds rather than shares.

Fortunately, the Russian privatization program recognizes this and is in fact extremely generous to the local governments. It gives them both a chunk of privatization proceeds and a role in privatization, but not shares.

The program divides firms into those under federal, *oblast,* and municipal jurisdiction. The exact division is still being negotiated. One proposal is to classify as federal only firms with more than 50,000 employees, or more than R 200 million book value, or otherwise large or strategic, for a total of about 2,000 enterprises. Municipal enterprises would be the ones that sell only to highly localized markets, and the rest would be *oblast* level. In all likelihood, pressures from the ministries will expand the list of federal enterprises.

Having classified firms, the Russian program gives *oblasts* and municipalities the responsibility to privatize the enterprises under their respective jurisdictions and assigns to the Russian government the right to privatize the federal ones. It is not clear who retains ownership in the meantime. Not surprisingly, the question of how much management rights the local governments actually have has become the most important point of disagreement between them and the center. The center wants to keep management to a minimum, while many localities are more interested in management than in privatization.

The law gives local governments several privatization techniques to choose from, including auctions and competitions. The latter allow sales based on criteria other than price. The book value is used as the reserve in these auctions and competitions. The law also specifies ways of dividing privatization revenue between the federal, *oblast,* and local governments. The principal objective of this division is to prevent conflict in the allocation of firms between levels, which would arise if the split of privatization revenues varied greatly depending on who privatized the firm. One important source of tension in the choice of privatization techniques has been the insistence of some local governments that they be able to exclude nonresidents from participating in auctions for small firms. This preference is driven mostly by the desire to keep auctions thin and so to collect more bribes. While this conflict has not been resolved, the center has been caving in to this pressure from local governments. Whatever the final outcome, giving the local governments a substantial financial incentive to privatize has been the cornerstone of the Russian privatization program.

This decentralized approach to privatization has several advantages. First, it provides local governments with substantial financial incentives to privatize. It also greatly reduces the burden on the central government of finding some privatization arrangements for a large number of enterprises. Since the managers and the workers are likely to get along with the local governments better than they do with the center, they are more likely to find an acceptable solution. Last but not least, the transfer of control over privatization of some firms to the local governments eradicates the role of the ministries in these privatizations virtually completely.

The greatest difficulty with privatization from below is that local governments may simply refuse to privatize and try instead to keep control over firms. After all, the bureaucrats in the local governments get bribes and presents only as long as they keep control over firms. In fact, many local governments have expressed a clear view that they will privatize sometime in the future but in the meantime have to manage the firms for the benefit of the local populations. If privatizations in some areas become successful, even the recalcitrant local governments might see the benefits of privatization in the regions that have moved fast and so feel compelled to follow suit. Competition between regions for foreign investment and for domestic funds might also accelerate privatization. Yet probably the strongest pressure toward privatization might be the desire of the workers and the populations of these areas "to get their cut," which will force many of the local governments to privatize so as to satisfy their voters.

A second problem with privatization from below is corruption. While the coffers of the local governments benefit from privatization, the pockets of the bureaucrats do not. Pushing privatization down to the local level will create tremendous corruption problems, as the local bureaucrats try to get a cut. This problem is rendered much worse by the fact that the law allows the local governments to use criteria other than price for privatization. Why not, then, sell a firm cheap in exchange for a promise to build a park in the city, or procure food for the town, plus a bribe? In fact, it is often in the interest of the local governments to choose privatization schemes that commit firms to doing things for localities rather than maximizing privatization revenue. To some extent, this problem is smaller when localities keep a lion's share of privatization proceeds. Even then, the potential for corruption is truly enormous.

While local control spells corruption everywhere in the world, some steps can be taken to reduce this problem. Most important, nonprice methods of allocating firms should be restricted where possible, and auctions (including auctions where each buyer must meet certain terms) should be used instead. Auctions reduce corruption relative to more discretionary forms of sale. Second, the government should require the maximum publicity about firms that are being privatized. Some transparency will prevent the blowup of the privatization process as corruption becomes exposed.

All things considered, putting more pressure on the local governments to privatize is highly desirable. Starving the local government budgets by not allocating funds from the center might provide them with a strong incentive to try to raise money, including by means of privatization. In addition, pressure from the workers is likely to be extremely important since workers in state enterprises represent many of the voters in the local elections. For this reason as well, generosity toward workers in accomplished privatizations is desirable.

12.4.4   Managers

Enterprise managers can easily sabotage privatization by refusing to cooperate with either the buyers or the government, and their claims are therefore the most important to respect. Most managers have considerable control over assets now and will retain most of it no matter what form privatization takes. The privatization program recognizes the power of the managers by giving them the right to choose privatization plans for their companies. The options among which they can choose include auctioning off the shares after corporatization, the sale of a control block to a large investor (through some competitive process as well), or a worker-management buyout. If the company is privatized through a worker-management buyout, as most companies undoubtedly will be, the managers will be completely in charge. But, even if the company is privatized through a substantial investment by a foreign or a domestic buyer, in almost all cases these buyers will seek the cooperation of the incumbent management both to privatize and to run the firm. In this case as well, the control rights of the incumbents will be largely preserved.

Managerial control is not as bad as is commonly supposed. The Western literature is fixated on the non-value-maximizing conduct of corporate managers. Most of that conduct results from having excess cash flows to waste (Jensen 1986). At least in the near future, free cash flow will not be nearly as large a problem for the Russian firms as outright theft. Moreover, even with all its imperfections, control by the managers is much less evil than the control of either the workers or the local governments. When the Western literature criticizes managerial control, the usual comparison is to active governance structures, such as large shareholders, banks, or takeovers. The emergence of these active governance structures is unlikely in Russia in the near future. Moreover, the gains from these structures are much smaller than the gains from replacing worker or government control with managerial control. In short, managerial control is not a very severe problem (although it is best to avoid governance structures that completely entrench the managers, such as closed companies). If anything, the best prospect for a rapid restructuring is a transfer of most control rights to the managers and active outside shareholders, as opposed to the workers and the local governments.

Because the managers have such strong control rights, they are unlikely to get shut out from the corporate cash flows, no matter what the public sentiment against them is. In worker-management buyouts, they are likely to get nontrivial ownership stakes. If companies are bought by outsiders, they will get finder's fees, bonuses, severance pay, or ownership stakes anyway. In all these cases, the managers have a substantial financial interest in the success of privatization since, particularly after prices are liberalized, their ability to profit from continued government ownership is not likely to be as great as their ability to profit from privatization.

The greatest danger is that in some companies, particularly the rich ones, managers might get enough benefits from their current control that they do not want to privatize at all. The oil companies, for example, can now retain enough earnings that they can buy all the equipment and expertise they need, without privatization or even joint ventures. The managers of these companies can consume tremendous perquisites now, yet risk a substantial loss of control if these firms are privatized. At the same time, it is not clear that they can get many shares of such valuable companies in the case of privatization. As a result, these managers might simply prefer the combination of state ownership and substantial earnings retention.

To provide further incentives to privatize, the government can enhance the managerial ownership of cash flows through stock options and other means to make it more politically acceptable. In fact, some companies have begun to institute small management-ownership schemes. Unfortunately, compared to what the managers can get for themselves from spontaneous privatization or management buyouts at ludicrously low prices, these schemes offer them fairly little. It is much better to be more generous to the managers in legal and open privatizations than to face the consequences of a mass spontaneous privatization.

12.4.5   Branch Ministries

The one stakeholder whom the Russian government probably should fight rather than appease is the branch ministries. The workers, the managers, and the local governments seem to be united in trying to diminish ministerial control since it directly conflicts with their rights. Moreover, from the long-run-efficiency viewpoint, any control by the ministries is bad for the simple reason that the ministries are a substitute for market transactions and giving them a role would reduce the role of the market. In particular, privatization is strictly against the interests of the ministries. If the ministries get control rights, they would use them, not to facilitate transactions, but rather to entrench themselves.

Of course, as we have already mentioned, the ministries still have some control over enterprises and voting power in the government. Excluding them from the privatization process will be costly. The current privatization recognizes this and concedes to the ministries in two important respects. First, they will be able to review and perhaps reject privatization plans for large federal enterprises. Second, some of the shares will be distributed along the vertical production chain, as the ministries like. So far, the government has resisted giving a large role in its privatization program to sectoral privatization plans that will be developed by the ministries. Resisting the sectoral ministries on this and other issues might well be worth the fight, for the ministries have no real interest in long-run decentralization and efficiency.

12.4.6   The Public

One important stakeholder whom we have not discussed so far is the public, which includes several important categories of people who do not benefit from the free handouts or subsidized sales of shares. The public includes pensioners, students, invalids, and others citizens supported directly by the state budget. The public also includes doctors, teachers, professors, and others who do not work at firms that will be privatized. Perhaps most important, the public includes the army, which is very hungry and very angry. All these members of the public have some political power and want to benefit from privatization like everyone else. They are represented in Parliament, are ready to demonstrate in the streets, and, in the case of the military, offer a potentially much greater threat to the government. Like every other privatizing country, Russia must give something to the public for privatization to succeed.

The privatization program incorporates a voucher scheme similar to that used in Czechoslovakia. In this scheme, members of the public will be given individual vouchers that will give them claims to shares of privatizing companies. Individuals will be able to sell these vouchers for cash, to turn them over to mutual funds that will use them to buy shares of privatizing companies, or even to use the vouchers to bid for shares directly. While the government is very sympathetic to the idea of having private mutual funds to collect or buy vouchers, it is resisting the idea of Polish-style state-sponsored mutual funds, which might prove difficult to separate from the government in Russia. Details of this voucher scheme remain to be worked out, and it is likely to be introduced late in 1992. The government feels the urgency of at least announcing some future giveaway to the public to avoid resentment of privatization.

12.4.7 Summary

In this section, we have outlined some strategies of the Russian privatization program. These strategies invite the workers and the local governments to give up their control rights, allocating them to the managers and the new investors. But, even if all the steps described in this section are taken, conflicts over privatization and restructuring will remain. Nonetheless, the legislation should continue to move in the direction of providing compensation for the stakeholders in return for cooperating in privatization.

12.5   The Future of Privatization

With a high probability, there will be very little privatization in Russia in the near future. Too many local governments, ministries, and even enterprise managers are opposed to privatization, and it is much easier to stop privatization than to move it ahead. Nonetheless, in many regions, the pressure to privatize from below will be high enough that some privatization, particularly of small firms, will take place. In this section, we discuss what will be the likely privatization scenarios. We consider small-scale privatization (meaning that of firms to be privatized by the local governments) and large-scale privatization (meaning that of firms to be privatized by the Russian government, separately).

12.5.1   Small-Scale Privatization

Some manufacturing firms, as well as many shops, bathhouses, and movie theaters, will be privatized locally. These firms will be sold on some terms, although not necessarily to the highest bidder. It is virtually certain that the management and the employees of these firms will be substantially involved in these sales. In some cases, particularly of smaller or of unprofitable firms, the employees and the managers will get together and simply acquire the firm in an auction or a management buyout. They will subsequently try to find partners to help them with restructuring, and perhaps even do it themselves. In fact, some auctions of shops have successfully taken place in Nizhny Novgorod in March 1992, with many more still to come.

Prices paid in these transactions are likely to be very low. The starting values in the auctions and competitions are book values of assets, which because of fast depreciation and a rapid inflation are usually only a trivial fraction of firm values. Moreover, there will not be much competition for most of these assets. First, local governments are not required to conduct auctions and so will probably use less transparent privatization techniques. If their efforts to restrict participation in auctions succeed, in many cases the local governments might simply be able to decide the winners of the auctions themselves in exchange for bribes. Second, the managers and the workers will obviously strongly oppose competition for the assets if an MBO is an option. If outsiders are involved, they will become partners of the MBO organizers rather than making competing bids. With little competition and low starting values, equilibrium prices will be low. The bureaucrats will get bribes to grease the wheels of this process and are therefore likely to go along. In this way, the local governments will give up control rights in exchange for payments to the bureaucrats, a nontransparent procedure but one that works. Small-scale privatization will not raise much money.

Some of the money for the worker-management buyouts will undoubtedly come from the cash reserves of the firms, which typically are not accounted for completely in the calculations of book value. The Russian law explicitly allows the use of these cash reserves for the purposes of buying firms from the state. In fact, many firms have been preparing for this strategy by accumulating cash reserves. In addition, if the credit policy allows them to do so, many MBOs will use bank loans to acquire the firms. The banks lending to these activities are likely to be the so-called private banks, which in fact take the deposits from other state enterprises and lend them out, usually for trade. Given the low prices in the worker-management buyouts, these loans will in most cases be repaid in a few months. In the cases where the WMBO organizers need additional funds, they will probably turn to some of the existing businessmen to participate in the acquisitions. This strategy will be most prevalent in firms that can profitably produce some goods for the local market or for export. For example, many of the stores in Moscow are attracting such investments because their retail space can be used for selling imported consumer goods as well as whatever these stores have been selling traditionally. The firms that attract such outside money will restructure most rapidly and efficiently, in part because the managers will have large shareholders breathing down their necks. These WMBOs with the participation of outside money are most similar to the typical Western MBO.

Very few of the smaller firms will be sold outright to buyers who are not insiders in the firms. A few auctions will be won by outsiders. Sometimes, outsiders will pay local bureaucrats higher bribes than the insiders do and will gain control in this way. These cases will be the exception rather than the rule since the built-in procedures strongly favor the insiders. Similarly, foreigners will rarely get involved in smaller firms, except through joint ventures with the insiders, since typically these firms are too small and too unlikely to export in the short run to interest them. Overall, small-scale privatization will be a slightly more transparent and regularized version of the spontaneous privatization that has already begun in Russia.

12.5.2   Large-Scale Privatization: Who Will Be the Buyers?

Some of the intermediate and large enterprises in Russia are too large and have too much capital per worker, even at book value, to be privatized through worker-management buyouts. Even if the sector ministries get their way and the suppliers and customers are allowed to participate in the MBOs, the combined resources might still be insufficient to buy out the largest companies. Also, since the largest companies are being privatized from the center, their privatization will require considerably more transparency to avoid bad publicity. Transparency, of course, also raises prices as long as they are not pinned to book values. Nor will it be easy to conduct MBOs with the participation of local investors since again there is simply not enough private capital in Russia today to acquire more than a few of its large enterprises. The most likely alternatives for small-scale privatization are often not open for large-scale privatization.

One potential hope for large privatization is foreign buyers. Unfortunately, the foreign buyers are interested in many natural resource industries in Russia, but not much else. Even when they are interested, they face several obstacles. First, current laws require the agreement of too many people, including the local government, GKI, the sectoral ministries, and the Committee on Foreign Investment, for an acquisition by a foreigner to take place. With so many approvals required, most proposals are likely to be rejected or sink in infinite negotiations, like VAZ. Second, Russia still lacks laws regulating business activity in general and foreign investment in particular. Except in the sectors where foreigners can take stuff out of the ground fast and export it, the absence of laws will slow down foreign investment. Third, in many cases, the managers of the Russian companies are not eager to give up control to foreign investors. Since these investors will often insist on control, few actual privatizations to foreigners might actually be accomplished.

The difficulty of finding buyers for large companies suggests that Russia will need to use its large-scale voucher privatization scheme aggressively to allocate the shares of the largest firms to the public. The success of this scheme will depend crucially on the technological feasibility of introducing vouchers as well as the possibility of running auctions in which both vouchers and cash can be used to bid (perhaps for different blocks of shares). If these technological difficulties can be overcome, the voucher scheme will become the central element of the Russian privatization. If technological problems become too severe, the government will move to a simpler method of allocating shares to the public, perhaps through state-sponsored intermediaries such as the mutual funds used in Poland. As of this writing, the details of the voucher scheme in Russia are too vague to be discussed more concretely.

12.6   Conclusion

In this paper, we described privatization as a redistribution of existing control rights over company assets between its stakeholders. To get the stakeholders to agree to this redistribution, they need to be compensated in terms of dividends and privatization proceeds. We have discussed some schemes of providing this compensation to the workers, the managers, and the local governments, the three principal forces that might oppose privatization. While these schemes will not stop all resistance to privatization, they might well reduce it. Luckily, the Russian privatization program in most instances tries to reconcile conflicts between stakeholders.

It is impossible to tell how fast privatization will proceed in Russia. Many bureaucrats, politicians, and managers oppose it and have enough political clout to slow it down. Even after privatization, restructuring need not come. Despite all these concerns, it is obviously essential to push for privatization and to grease the wheels when they turn slowly.

References

Boycko, Maxim, Andrei Shleifer, and Robert W. Vishny. 1993. Privatizing Russia. *Brookings Papers on Economic Activity* 2.
Coase, Ronald. 1960. The problem of social cost. *Journal of Law* and *Economics* 3 (October): 1–44.
Grossman, Sanford, and Oliver D. Hart. 1986. The costs and benefits of ownership: A theory of vertical and lateral integration. *Journal of Political Economy* 94, no. 4 (August): 671–719.
Hart, Oliver D., and John Moore. 1990. Property rights and the nature of the firm. *Journal of Political Economy* 98, no. 6 (December): 1119–58.
Jensen, Michael C. 1986. The agency cost of free cash flow, corporate finance, and takeovers. *American Economic Review Papers and Proceedings* 76, no. 2 (May): 323–29.
Lipton, David, and Jeffrey Sachs. 1990. Privatization in Eastern Europe: The case of Poland. *Brookings Papers on Economic Activity*, no. 2:293–333.
Shleifer, Andrei, and Robert W. Vishny. 1992. Pervasive shortages under socialism. *Rand Journal of Economics* 23, no. 2 (Summer): 237–46.

Comment   Jacek Rostowski

The authors describe one of the key microeconomic problems of the Russian economy: the failure of property rights over the vast majority of nonhuman assets to be properly defined. Instead of clearly defined owners there are stakeholders whose rights to decide what to do with assets are unclear. Moreover, there are no clear procedures about what to do if stakeholders disagree. As a result, by Coase's theorem, assets are used inefficiently. Therefore, privatization is seen above all as a way to define property rights.[1] However, because privatization takes time, stakeholders are motivated to undertake action that will increase their claims during the privatization process, even if these actions reduce the value of the assets being contested. This is what I call *property rights–seeking behavior.* It is rational to pursue such behavior as long as its costs—in terms of the resulting value destruction that is borne by the stakeholder concerned—are smaller than the expected benefits.

Shleifer and Vishny believe that the Russian privatization program, which transforms managers and workers into (minority) shareholders and grants local authorities an important share of privatization proceeds, will work to neutralize the opposition of these key groups to privatization. Also, by providing an initial definition of property rights, the scheme is likely to reduce destructive property rights–seeking behavior, as it is worth engaging in such behavior only if one's expected increase in wealth (compared to the allocation imposed by the state), less the costs of achieving it, is positive. Without such an "external" definition, some stakeholders may get nothing if they fail to assert their claims through destructive action. Nevertheless, it remains the case that, if the allocation of property rights resulting from the Russian government's privatization program is very different from that which corresponds to stakeholders' perception of the allocation that would result from a period of property rights–seeking behavior, such behavior is still likely to take place. A key question is therefore how close the proposed Russian allocation is to such a "perceived equilibrium" allocation?

An alternative approach would be to find an "uncontestable" allocation—one that, once made, could not be resisted by stakeholders, even if it were not necessarily the same as the equilibrium allocation. Given the strength of egalitarian and "workerist" sentiments in Russia, I believe that such an allocation would be one in which the bulk of the shares in most state-owned enterprises (SOEs) was given to the employees.[2] Such an allocation need not ex-

---

1. Privatization could also be used to allocate assets to those who need to make ex ante investments in the human capital that is complementary with these assets, along the lines of Grossman and Hart (1986). Privatizers would thus attempt to achieve an allocation of property rights as close to the efficient as possible. However, the authors do not pursue this interesting strand in their analysis far.

2. Exceptions could be made for natural monopolies such as railways and power transmission.

clude the other stakeholders. Central and local governments could retain their stake in each enterprise in the form of shares that would be nonvoting as long as they remained in public hands but that would recover their voting rights when sold.[3] Each share sold by employees would require the simultaneous purchase of a proportionate number of public-sector shares. Managers would obtain shares as employees and also often be able to use their prestige and greater understanding of the business to convince workers to agree to management buyouts.

This approach abolishes all ownership rights held by local and central government at a stroke, giving these rights to a group that ought to be capable of defending them in practice. It is far from clear that the supervisory boards of commercialized firms advocated by the authors, which would consist of representatives of the State Property Agency (GKI), managers, workers' representatives, and banks, would have the power to resist the local authorities. Given the extremely dangerous propensity of local governments in Russia to replace the old branch ministries as the controllers of the activities of state enterprises on their territory, such an "intraenterprise revolution" is vital. The experience of Eastern Europe suggests that the only force within the enterprise capable of standing up to the planning bureaucracy is the workers.[4] However, it is critical that the shares should become the property of employees as individuals (and not as members of a collective) and that they should from the start be tradable (i.e., "closed" companies must be banned).

A number of advantages relating to privatization technique stem from the approach that I am suggesting. First, the authorities are not obliged to organize auctions of enterprises (as is foreseen in the Russian program) but can leave the choice and organization of the privatization technique to the enterprise itself. While auctions would continue to be possible, trade sales, flotations, and management buyouts could now also be used. Given the "administrative fragility" of the Russian state, this is a not inconsiderable advantage. More important, under the Russian scheme, GKI has to decide on whether and how to break up the enterprise before privatization. It seems plausible that the managers and workers in the enterprise will know better how to do this, and the "employee-centered" scheme gives them the incentive to do it relatively efficiently.

Furthermore, the profitability of SOEs typically collapses after macroeconomic stabilization in post-Communist economies.[5] Many loss-making enterprises will be impossible to sell. Domestic and foreign capitalists will be willing to pay only very small amounts for marginally profitable enterprises, which may require a large injection of capital and a huge reorganization and restruc-

---

3. To the best of my knowledge, the originator of this proposal is Tomasz Stankiewicz of Warsaw University, the deputy minister of privatization of Poland.
4. If the workers decide to allow themselves to be led by the managers in determining the firm's policy, that can be all to the good.
5. In Russia, it seems to have collapsed before stabilization.

turing effort if they are to have a long-term future. Unlike in the auction-based scheme, employee-owners can help resolve this problem by increasing the capital of the firm by admitting outside capitalists. Sale to foreign investors becomes far harder to oppose on nationalist grounds when the sellers are the workers rather than the government. The employee-centered approach also ensures that, whatever the profitability of the firm, there always exists a group of owners whose future is bound up with the enterprise for at least a time. And, unlike worker-managed firms, employee-owners do not have the disincentive to invest that results from the knowledge that the enterprise will ultimately be privatized, with the proceeds going to the state.

Last, but far from least, Polish experience since 1990 shows that, even in the almost complete absence of divestment of organized businesses by the state, one can have extremely dynamic private-sector development as long as the commercial property market is decontrolled and SOEs have the right to sell their physical assets. Capitalists prefer to buy (or hire) the assets and work force they actually need and to combine them in ways that correspond to their requirements rather than to take over organized businesses created in completely different circumstances and adapt them. There is some concern that the Russian auction-centered approach to privatization will make it harder for SOEs to sell their physical assets, as a result of a desire by the authorities to prevent insiders from stripping the assets of SOEs at the expense of the formal owner (the state). The employee-centered approach, like worker management in Poland, frees the enterprise to do as it sees fit with its assets.[6]

Reference

Grossman, Sanford, and Oliver D. Hart. 1986. The costs and benefits of ownership: A theory of vertical and lateral integration. *Journal of Political Economy* 94, no. 4 (August): 671–719.

Discussion Summary

Jan Svejnar argued that a lack of human capital would make it difficult to hire enough qualified board members to implement the corporatization proposal. *Andrei Shleifer* responded by noting that many of the board members would come from the current group of managers.

Simon Johnson discussed the role of managers in Ukraine. He said that the transfer of control rights from ministries to managers has led to greater efficiency. He noted that, in Kiev, managers effectively control the local govern-

---

6. Part of the proceeds of the sale would go to the state, in a proportion corresponding to its share in total ownership. This is a good reason for keeping the share of the state low on privatization via distribution to employees.

ment and the workers by using side payments. He noted, however, that, while many managers have effective control of the firms they operate, they do not have the ability to sell those control rights legally. Finally, he predicted that the next step for Ukrainian managers will be to undertake leveraged management buyouts.

Richard Layard suggested that the Russian government should undertake a mass privatization plan. He said that Shleifer and Vishny's corporatization plan would actually create hurdles for the privatization process since worker-controlled board members would prevent rapid restructuring.

Michael Dooley suggested that in addition to the four groups that Shleifer and Vishny had identified—the central government, local governments, workers, and managers—the bureaucrats in state-owned banks would also try to grab control rights of newly privatized firms. Dooley argued that the lack of a private capital market would enable the banks to make this demand.

Dmitri Vasiliev also suggested that Shleifer and Vishny had ignored some important participants in the privatization debate. He highlighted the roles of the army and the new business class.

13   The Logistics of Privatization in Poland

Andrew Berg

Privatization remains the most important outstanding item on the agenda of radical reform in Poland. The "big bang" reform program was designed to stabilize the hyperinflation, free prices, liberalize trade, and restructure the foundations of the economy toward a market system. An integral part of this restructuring was to be the rapid privatization of the state-owned enterprises (SOEs), which overwhelmingly dominated the nonagricultural economy.

In fact, little privatization of SOEs has taken place.[1] This is not due to a lack of ideas about how privatization should be accomplished; there has now developed a minor industry in which economists propose and discuss privatization programs.[2] Nor is it due to a lack of trying; the Polish government has attempted to implement several methods of privatization. This paper will supplement the discussion about privatization strategies with a review of the actual attempts to implement them. By doing so, it should become clearer why so little privatization has actually occurred.

Two themes emerge. First, although much of the debate has focused on opti-

The author thanks Kevin McDonald, Tony Levitas, his friends and colleagues at the Ministry of Finance, the Ministry of Privatization, and Jeffrey D. Sachs and Associates for many useful discussions, and especially Zanny Minton Beddoes for her invaluable help. He has also benefited from the remarks of conference participants. Mistakes and misjudgments remain his own.
    1. In this paper, I do not address the dramatic success that has been achieved in the growth of the private sector, particularly in construction, trade and other services, and the transfer of shops to private hands. These developments have resulted in an increase of the share of the private sector in GDP to more than half by the middle of 1992. In industry, however, the share was still only about 19 percent. The vital topic of reform and privatization of the financial system is also not addressed here. For a fuller discussion of how privatization of state-owned enterprises fits into the general problem of economic transformation in Poland, see Berg and Blanchard (chap. 2 in vol. 1).
    2. For discussions of Polish privatization, see, e.g., Dabrowski (1991), Dabrowski, Federowicz, and Levitas (1991), Gruszecki (1991), Kawalec (1992), Szomburg and Lewandowski (1990), and Winiecki (1992). For more general contexts, see Aslund (1990), Fischer (chap. 7 in vol. 1), Frydman and Rapaczynski (1992), Kornai (1991), and Stark (1990).

mal privatization schemes, in practice the issue has proved to be how to execute a minimally acceptable and feasible program. It is common to discuss privatization in terms of a set of goals, such as speed, effective ownership, equity, fiscal stability, avoidance of excess dependence on foreigners, and low cost. The problem, however, seems to be not how best to reconcile competing goals but rather how to accomplish anything at all. What is striking in Poland is that, more than two years into the radical "big bang" program, the vast majority of state enterprises have undergone no ownership transformation; instead, the highly unsatisfactory initial structure has been maintained: the workers control but do not own the enterprises.

If the current situation in the state-enterprise economy were satisfactory, this lack of action would be easier to understand. The current pattern of control of state enterprises, however, gives little cause for complacency. As economic theory would suggest, the evidence implies that these enterprises are generally performing poorly. And, despite the huge budget deficits, political pressure is growing to help these enterprises with subsidies, looser credit, and trade protection.[3]

The second theme is that the initial conditions and constraints have shaped what has been attempted and what has taken place. Section 9.1 isolates three constraints: the usual set of institutional weaknesses common to most LDCs, special problems associated with the revolutionary "rules of the game," and the existing pattern of ownership rights. Section 9.2 examines privatization efforts to date. Section 9.4 concludes.

13.1   The Constraints on Privatization

Poland shares with LDCs a set of well-known characteristics that make privatization difficult. They include a lack of well-developed capital markets and related institutions such as banks, insurance companies, a functioning judicial system to resolve civil disputes, and property registries; a shortage of skilled and experienced personnel; weak administrative capacity, including a shortage of infrastructure such as copy machines and telephones; a difficult macroeconomic environment; and state enterprises in generally poor financial condition. In addition, Poland's efforts to date have brought out a further set of problems whose influence is harder to appreciate but equally pervasive. This is the fact that the situation with regard to the rules of the game, in the broadest sense, is revolutionary. Laws are either new or newly enforced after decades of dormancy. Customs and traditions of behavior, especially the bureaucratic, are widely recognized as inappropriate to the new environment, while new practices have not yet developed. Two points should be emphasized here. First, I am not referring to some "socialist psychology" where individuals are no

---

3. For more discussion of these issues, see Berg and Blanchard (chap. 2 in vol. 1). For a discussion of restructuring problems in state enterprises, see McDonald (1992).

longer capable of responding to incentives.[4] Second, the problem is not predominantly that the laws themselves do not exist but that they have never been enforced. Most of the commercial code and bankruptcy law, for example, dates from the 1930s (see Gray 1991).

The problem lies rather in the lack of institutional development and in the complexity of the decisions involved in privatization. The habits and traditions that lower transaction costs by substituting for rigid rules do not exist.[5] As a result, where rules are broken, especially in privatization transactions, corruption is suspected.[6] Thus, each minor piece of a transaction, such as the publication of a request for tender offers, requires the signature of the head of a department, who may be criminally liable if there turn out to be mistakes in the advertisement. The result is that the Polish bureaucracy is in effect on a "work-to-rule" strike.[7]

The final and most important constraint on the privatization process is the initial structure of ownership rights. Understanding this requires a brief discussion of property rights in the state-owned enterprises. Polish state enterprises should not be confused with state-owned corporations in the West: they are not joint-stock corporations whose shares are controlled by agents of the state Treasury. They are also not administrative units of the bureaucracy. They are unique legal entities, subject to their own specific structures of ownership and control, with as much political legitimacy as almost any institution in Poland (see Breitkopf, Gorski, and Jaszczynski 1991; Dabrowski, Federowicz, and Levitas 1991; and Frydman and Wellisz 1991).

Poland began decentralizing decision making to the enterprise level in the 1950s, but the point of departure for the current situation is the 1981 State Enterprise Law, which in an emended form is still in effect. This law defined a state enterprise as "an autonomous, self-managed and self-financing unit, possessing personality at law," and gave to the self-management bodies, which are democratically elected workers' councils, the power to appoint the managing director, allocate profits, and plan production. The government kept only the power to create and liquidate enterprises, placing it in the hands of the branch ministry or "founding organ" responsible for the particular enterprise.

This legal self-management was strongly qualified in practice by the nature of the "shortage economy." The central administration and the management retained real independent power, partly through the fact that the shortage econ-

---

4. Where bureaucratic institutions are not involved, and where individual incentives are appropriate, such as in the small private sector, entrepreneurs are starting businesses in the hundreds of thousands.

5. On how ideology, customs, and tradition reduce transaction costs, see North (1981).

6. There is no direct evidence of actual corruption in privatization. However, there have been well-publicized scandals involving foreign debt management ("the FOZZ affair"), loopholes in certain import tariffs ("the alcohol affair") and large-scale check kiting and related bribery of government officials ("the Art-B affair"). These have served to heighten an already high sensitivity.

7. A type of industrial action, common in public unions prohibited from more overt strikes, whereby all rules and regulations are followed blindly and no actual work gets done.

omy made personal contacts in the government and with other firms critical for the functioning of the firm in order to obtain inputs, subsidies, tax relief, and so on (see Kawalec 1992; and McDonald 1992). The administration and the Party thus retained central roles in appointing and influencing management. In the late 1980s, as reform continued and central planning receded, the power of the workers' councils and managers vis à vis the state grew.

The critical point was reached in 1989 and 1990 with the collapse of the Communist regime. The financial relation between the state and the enterprise was clarified. The only remaining Treasury claim on profits was in the form of a proportional income tax and a "dividenda" payment based on the book value of capital in 1983. All remaining profits were left to the enterprise. The enterprise was still ultimately owned by the state, but most important aspects of ownership had by now been carefully and clearly allocated to the self-management bodies.

The final collapse of the old state structure at the end of 1989 and the beginning of 1990 led to a strong affirmation of the power of the workers' councils. New councils, elected in early 1990, proceeded to pass judgment on management in about half the firms, replacing some 40 percent of the managers reviewed.[8]

The growth in the stake of workers in the firm was more than a legal phenomenon. The shock troops of the Solidarity revolution were the industrial workers, and the front line in the confrontation between the state and the people was the shop floor. As a result, the sense of attachment of workers to their enterprise should not be underestimated. For example, 45 percent of workers surveyed in 1987 and 67 percent in 1989, and 63 and 77 percent of managers, respectively, were in favor of selling shares to workers, despite the fact that most workers did not "support private initiative" (CBOS 1989) in large state enterprises. Privatization of large enterprises to workers was also the most popular type of privatization among the entire population. For example, 80 percent of respondents to another survey agreed that "shares of privatized state enterprises should always be sold first to their workers" (CBOS 1990).

The upshot of this process is that workers are now the dominant force controlling the state-owned enterprise. Despite this power shift toward workers, however, management often maintains significant power because of information advantages or close contacts with suppliers, foreign partners, or even the government and because workers' councils may be passive or co-opted.[9] This granting of some sort of a stake in the firm to insiders has the advantage of creating a certain incentive for those who have the information to make efficient decisions.

8. Help-wanted advertisements can be observed in Polish newspapers in which workers' councils announce that they are looking for experienced, skilled managing directors.

9. There are often two, or even three, plant-level unions active in the enterprise, sometimes in conflict with the workers' council. As a result, the Polish press speaks of the firm being lost in the "Bermuda Triangle" of management, the workers' council, and the unions.

The situation is more complicated that the description given above implies. In addition to workers and management, the state retains significant power in the enterprise. While it has largely given up control of the enterprises, it has not relinquished the legal right to dispose of the assets of the enterprise. The need for ministerial approval of important transactions such as privatization or formation of a joint venture confers influence. The government also retains some of its traditional power through control over the banking system and the budget. Finally, many enterprises are in arrears on taxes, giving the state the power to force the firm into liquidation, as described below.

This confused control structure results in feeble decision making in the enterprise. The relative power of the various players (management, the workers' council, the unions, the government, and possibly creditors such as state banks) varies widely from enterprise to enterprise. In general, the end result, however, is that any one of the stakeholders can block change, while concerted action requires consensus. One implication is that, in smaller enterprises, the insiders are more likely to cooperate and actively carry out adjustments, whereas in large firms internal conflict and passivity are more common (see Dabrowski, Federowicz, and Levitas 1991; and McDonald 1992).

This peculiar ownership and control structure has unfortunate implications for privatization:

1. The current situation is extremely dangerous and probably unstable: real wages are rising, and profit rates have declined to the point where aggregate net profits were negative in the fourth quarter of 1991, with direct implications for the budget, both because of lower accrued taxes and because of enterprise arrears to the government. The budget deficit for 1991 was running at 4.5 percent of GDP, and arrears equaled 85 percent of this deficit. Taxes on wage increases in excess of government-established norms constituted the largest component of these unpaid liabilities. Prospects for the 1992 budget are worse.

2. The withdrawal of the state has left current insiders with a powerful informational advantage over the government as well as a strong incentive to try to preserve their current rights during privatization. One potential *positive* implication is that those who control the firm have the information and some of the incentives to behave efficiently. The looming threat of disenfranchisement through privatization weakens these incentives and encourages irresponsible behavior.

3. Insiders will resist disenfranchisement except where the firm is in financial distress. The government finds itself making promises of financial and other support in its effort actively to privatize firms.

The next section reviews the experience to date in the privatization of state-owned enterprises.

13.2   Privatization Efforts to Date

13.2.1   Spontaneous Privatization

Given the constraints outlined above, it is not surprising that the first occurrence of privatization was instigated and controlled by insiders. With the relaxation of government control over the enterprise in the late 1980s, and as the end of the Communist era appeared, management found opportunities to privatize profits through so-called *nomenklatura* privatizations. In a typical transaction, the management and perhaps ministry officials would participate in a new private company that would enter into a joint venture with the state enterprise. Transfer pricing and other terms of the joint venture would ensure that profits would be transferred to the private company.

Condemnation of these sorts of deals was widespread, and one of the Solidarity government's first reforms in late 1989 made liquidation of a state enterprise mandatory in the event that "over half of the enterprise's assets are composed of shares, other equity in joint-stock companies, or bonds, or have been transferred in usufruct to other parties on the basis of civil contracts" (Breitkopf, Gorski, and Jaszczynski1991). The increased power of the workers' councils and unions also resulted in a curbing of *nomenklatura* privatizations.

As the power in the firm has shifted from the *nomenklatura* to the stakeholders described above, a related form of spontaneous privatization has developed. In this case, assets are transferred to private hands with the agreement of all interested parties, which would normally include workers and managers. For example, one wholesale distribution enterprise, with several hundred employees, was largely dismantled and began to operate in private hands, probably without any transaction registered as *privatization.* The gas station was leased to employees, the trucks were sold, and a private company was using the parking lot and some of the office space. The arrangements may or may not have been legal, but probably no one with any power to interfere was unhappy. In another case, a warehouse that was part of a state farm was being used by a local farmer to store animals prior to export, as part of a major private operation. The state employee in charge of the warehouse was also an employee of the private company.

By its nature, this sort of privatization is hard to observe, much less measure. It is probably economically efficient. If it is significant, it represents an important qualifier both to the claim that little privatization has taken place and to the statistical evidence on the decline in employment and output in the state sector. Informal estimates from recent surveys suggest that perhaps one-third of enterprises have engaged in some sort of partial asset transfer to the private sector and that virtually all the assets from the burgeoning private sector come from the state sector.[10]

---

10. I am indebted to Tony Levitas for sharing preliminary results from current work in Poland. I rely heavily on his information both here and later, when I discuss outcomes in liquidated enter-

It is not clear that this sort of privatization can form an important part of the overall process. It appears to be difficult to arrange in the larger state enterprises. The privatization of an asset in such an enterprise requires an arrangement within the company for distribution of the gains. If the asset is well defined (a pig farm belonging to a shoe factory, e.g.), it may be a natural outcome for those working with the asset to appropriate it. For integral parts of the factory, however, the internal coalition may be difficult to form. In one case, a private company in Gdansk leased workshops and hired workers from one of the large state-owned shipyards at much higher (presumably efficiency) wages. This arrangement was halted by the workers in the state enterprise, who apparently objected on grounds of equity.

13.2.2   The Law on Privatization of State-Owned Enterprises

The alternative to spontaneous privatization is active government intervention to privatize. The government gained the legal power to begin privatizing state enterprises with the passage of the Law on Privatization of State Enterprises on 1 August 1990 (see Center for Privatization 1990), and this continues to define the context for privatization in Poland.[11]

This law was the culmination of a long and acrimonious debate. Initially, at the end of 1989, the government envisaged universal *commercialization* of state enterprises (Polish terminology for the legal conversion of state-owned enterprises into joint-stock companies owned by the state Treasury and subject to the commercial code). The government hoped to privatize these commercialized firms rapidly, primarily through initial public offerings. There were several justifications for this approach: the desire to generate widespread share ownership for sociological and political reasons; a strong attachment to Anglo-Saxon-type capital markets, itself partly due to the influence of aid-financed investment bankers and financial market specialists; and, more generally, the feeling that the valuation and sale of assets was the only "civilized" approach. The government's intentions to commercialize "from above," without workers' council approval, generated strong resistance, and the plan was abandoned. This was partly simple interest-group politics in the Sejm (the lower house of Parliament) and partly a widespread fear of nationalization, based on concerns that the state would run the enterprises no better than it had in the past and that Solidarity might take on characteristics of the former regime if given power over the enterprises.[12]

---

prises. For further discussion of measurement of the private sector and some estimates of biases in the measurement of output and consumption during transition, see Berg (1992).

11. For a useful description of privatization mechanisms in Poland, see Madigan (1992).

12. The main alternatives to the government plan in the Sejm were variations on the idea of worker self-management. Gruszecki (1991) argues that, while there was some real attraction for the worker-management/employee-stock-option-type plan, a dissatisfaction with the government approach of selling enterprises generated much of the resistance. In the end, and after some twenty-four versions, the final draft still assumed the case-by-case commercialization and sale of enterprises.

The law envisages two possible paths for the privatization of an enterprise. The first, *capital privatization,* was intended in general for large enterprises. The second, *liquidation,* was intended for smaller enterprises and will be discussed below. The first step in capital privatization is commercialization. This step normally requires the approval of the workers' council, the management, and an assembly of employees.[13] With commercialization, a board of directors is appointed by the representative of the Treasury (now the minister of privatization). The workers appoint one-third of the board. The 1981 State Enterprise Law no longer applies to commercialized enterprises. In particular, the workers' council loses its powers, and the management is responsible to the board.[14] After commercialization, the Ministry of Privatization (MOP) is responsible for privatization of the enterprise. The workers are given the right, however, to buy up to 20 percent of shares at half price, subject to a limit on the total discount equal to one years' wage.

The second major path of privatization envisaged in the law is liquidation.[15] Here, the basic idea is that the enterprise decides to privatize, the branch ministry responsible for the enterprise agrees, the MOP concurs, and the liquidation is implemented by the branch ministry. The state enterprise ends its legal existence, and there are three possible outcomes for the assets: (1) The assets are sold piece by piece by the responsible ministry. (2) A new company is created between the Treasury and a private investor. (3) The management and employees create a private firm and lease the assets (and the liabilities) of the enterprise from the Treasury.[16]

13.2.3   Implementation of the Privatization Law

Commercialization

Commercialization is the necessary first step to capital privatization. Table 13.1 gives the number of firms commercialized by size facts and table 13.2 a sectoral breakdown. Some 244 enterprises have been commercialized since the law was passed (as of the end of 1991). These represent about 10 percent of employment in the national economy. The government strategy has been to associate commercialization directly with privatization, so, while the con-

13. The law did provide that a majority of the Council of Ministers and the prime minister could compel an enterprise to commercialize without workers' council approval. This power has not been exercised to date. For explanations of this aspect of the law, see *Prywatyzacja* (Ministry of Privatization), nos. 1, 4 (1991).

14. A later addition to the law allows the loosening of wage controls in an effort to encourage commercialization.

15. Confusingly, the State Enterprise Law of 1981 also envisages "liquidation" of state enterprises that are delinquent on certain tax payments. This distinct type of liquidation will be discussed separately below.

16. The new private company must be created according to the commercial code, with a paid-in capital equal to at least 20 percent of the book value of the state enterprise. The law also defines some of the terms of the lease. For legal commentaries on this aspect of the law, see Prywatyzacja, nos. 2, 3 (1991). For further explanation, see esp. Madigan (1992).

Table 13.1   Number of State Enterprises Commercialized and in Liquidation as of 31 December 1991

No. of employees	Liquidations via 1981 State Enterprise Law				Liquidations via 1990 Privatization Law				Commercialized	Total
	(1)	(2)	(3)	(4)	(1)	(2)	(3)	(4)		
Total	442	5	2	534	24	15	338	416	244	1194
<200	324	4	0	371	15	8	159	190	8	569
200–500	75	0	1	99	6	4	117	144	52	295
>500	43	1	1	64	3	3	62	82	184	330

Source: Ministry of Privatization, Warsaw.
Note: Means of liquidation: (1) via sale of property; (2) via contribution into company; (3) via leasing; (4) total.

Table 13.2   Number of State Enterprises Commercialized or in Liquidation by Industrial Sector as of 31 December 1991

		Enterprises Transformed					
Sector	Total No. of Remaining State Enterprises	Liquidated		Commercialized		Total	
		No.	%	No.	%	No.	%
Industry	3,009	255	8.5	201	6.7	456	15.2
Construction	1,367	271	19.8	30	2.2	301	22.0
Agriculture	1,833	174	9.5	1	.1	175	9.5
Forestry	51	1	2.0	2	3.9	3	5.9
Transportation	529	62	11.7	7	1.3	69	13.0
Communication	5	1	20.0	0	.0	1	20.0
Trade	608	126	20.7	1	.2	127	20.9
Other	826	60	7.3	2	.2	62	7.5
Total economy	8,228	950	11.5	244	3.0	1,194	14.5

Source: Ministry of Privatization, Warsaw.
Note: The percentages indicate the ratio of number of transformed enterprises to the number of remaining state enterprises.

straints discussed above have influenced this process as well, I will not focus on them, except to summarize some tentative conclusions.

First, it was not difficult to find board members. A training program developed within the MOP has succeeded in producing enough candidates. There is no direct evidence, however, that boards intervene actively. MOP officials complain that important decisions require their direct intervention. It appears that boards tend to become advocates for the enterprise instead of agents of the owner (the Treasury).[17] Second, the enterprise and the government tend to

17. For this reason, the placing of representatives of creditors, such as banks and other enterprises, on the boards of commercialized companies is being considered.

feel that the state is newly responsible for the enterprise. This is a logical result of the increased ownership rights of the government and an outgrowth of the implicit or explicit promises that the government makes to enterprises in its efforts to get them to commercialize.

Third, some evidence points to an increased passivity in the enterprise. There is apparently a fear on the part of the management that, since the government is now responsible for finding buyers, foreign partners, and so on, it is not a good idea to risk strikes or other disruptions that might be caused by restructuring. The fact that the MOP will actively structure any eventual privatization means that the management has much less chance of benefiting from, for example, a joint venture than if it could negotiate and conclude the deal itself.

The First Five IPOs

In the year after the passage of the privatization law, the government focused its energies on the preparation of companies for initial public offering (IPO). The idea was to make the first privatizations so successful that the process would "snowball" and up to 100–200 enterprises could be processed and sold every year. However, the experience with the first five IPOs convinced almost everyone that additional methods of privatization were necessary.

The selection of companies was a long and politically difficult venture, in which a list of twenty companies in January 1990 was winnowed down a final five. These companies, with 23,000 total employees, were chosen as the best candidates by Western and Polish consultants, on criteria of quality of management, financial soundness, ability to export, and so on. They were offered to the public in November 1990. The five enterprises were successfully sold, although the subscription period had to be lengthened and a state-owned bank allowed to purchase shares in order to avoid undersubscription in some issues. Ultimately, 130,000 shareholders bought shares worth $31 million. The offering of five large companies simultaneously has to be considered a success considering the environment, but these transactions were expensive and, more important, required tremendous allocation of government human resources.

The achievement of actually privatizing five companies in the Polish situation and, in the process, creating some of the institutions of a capital market was remarkable. But the success has been mixed. Since the initial offering, at least two of the five have got into in serious difficulty, as real appreciation of the zloty and the elimination of CMEA (Council for Mutual Economic Assistance) trade have hit them hard. Share prices have fallen below the offering price in four of the five companies. The boards do seem to function reasonably well. But these boards have a high concentration of scarce talent, such as the president of a new development bank and department directors from the MOP. The companies still appeal to the MOP for help when in trouble as well, cashing in on implicit or explicit promises of support.

In a larger sense, the failure of the IPO approach was clear and acute. While certain technical details could be better worked out in the future, nothing suggested that there would be a "snowball" acceleration of IPOs; the next round would clearly be as hard as the first. While some capacity had been built, the transaction cost was unsustainable, and public enthusiasm had fallen in response to the poor stock market performance. After all, only five had been done. Nonetheless, the government continued to carry out public offerings, and, since 1990, there have been another five full or partial public offers, in which some $33 million worth of shares have been sold. (For a list of all firms privatized through capital privatization, see app. table 13A.1.) In addition, there have been another sixteen enterprises privatized through auctions and tender offers. As table 13A.1 shows, the total value of shares sold in these sixteen enterprises was about $142 million, with the companies valued at $228 million. The largest of these were sold at least in part to foreign investors.

The IPO approach has thus proved to be extremely slow. Advocates of alternative approaches had already provided the reasons why the program could not be the primary vehicle for privatization. Until the end of 1990, however, there were always those who argued that the process was about to accelerate drastically. It is thus instructive briefly to look at the reasons for the slow pace of public offers.

The novelty and risk of the procedure compelled the government to promise good returns to investors and health and success to the companies involved. This made doing due diligence (verifying the health of the company, checking the balance sheet, etc.) even more arduous than the difficult environment would imply. The fact that afterward there would be diffuse ownership, together with the political exposure of the project, made it necessary to carry out any restructuring prior to privatization. The "snowball" concept exacerbated these problems by raising the stakes enormously.

In addition to the need to value the firm, all sorts of details slowed the process down. For example, the legal determination of all the land-ownership claims and tax liabilities of the enterprises was a necessary prerequisite for privatization and required close cooperation from a large number of government bureaucrats unaccustomed to making legal statements. In addition, in some cases, complex "unofficial" claims against the enterprise needed to be unraveled prior to privatization. For example, an enterprise might have been providing free central heating to the local town for many years. The future of this relation would have to be negotiated prior to privatization.

Sales to foreign investors illustrate many of the same problems as IPOs. In particular, they highlight the different agendas and relative bargaining power of insiders and the MOP. Managers are often the best equipped to locate and negotiate with foreigners. They know their own business and often the industry and may have long-term relationships with the foreign partners. They are generally interested in preserving and strengthening their company, perhaps under workers' council pressure. They may also be looking for some sort of "golden parachute" from the investor. The typical large direct foreign investment in the late 1980s, the joint venture, was thus often a sort of *nomenklatura* privatization.

The MOP recognized the inherent conflict of interest involved when managers negotiate deals for state enterprises and called for major foreign investments to take place through capital privatization, with the Ministry of Privatization taking an active role in the negotiations and making the final agreement. This did not prove effective. Managers have the incentive to negotiate quick and cheap deals, but ministry bureaucrats do not. Given the sums of money involved, the difficulties in valuation, and the fact that the need to sell to highly risk-averse foreign investors lowers the price, very few bureaucrats are willing to take the responsibility for deciding to accept an offer. Moreover, they face steep obstacles in overcoming the insider power of managers to conduct legitimate tender procedures.[18]

As a result of these problems, many more deals have been announced than negotiated, and the big transactions have by and large not yet happened.

The Sectoral Approach

As a result of the difficulties with IPOs and the resultant demand for alternatives, and because of the difficulties the MOP had in coping with potential foreign investors, the "sectoral privatization" approach gained favor in 1991. This was intended to speed up the process and deal efficiently with the many problems with the IPOs and individual trade sales. The idea of sectoral privatization was simply to process capital privatizations, especially trade sales to foreign investors, one industry at a time instead of one firm at a time. Thus, one financial adviser could be used for a sector instead of a firm (see Hermann 1990). There were five factors encouraging this approach:

1. A simple economy of consulting and ministerial resources was possible. Handling a sector would be only slightly more difficult than handling one firm. The economies of scale come in several forms: (*a*) Marketing of companies to potential investors is more efficient. Industrial trade shows can be visited, advertisements in trade journals can be combined, and so on. (*b*) Industry studies, both domestic and foreign, are a necessary part of a serious single-company analysis. (*c*) Someone must oversee each consultant contract within the MOP. It helps to have one contract for several companies. As discussed above, the difficulty in finding a person able and willing to accept responsibility for a deal cannot be overestimated. The sector approach was to provide structure and help for MOP officials.

2. The bargaining position vis à vis the foreign investor was seen to be

18. For example, at one point, the MOP wanted to conduct a competitive tender for an important enterprise with two interested foreign buyers, one Japanese and one British. After a long and disastrous meeting between ministry representatives and the management, on the one hand, and the Japanese potential investors, on the other, the Japanese went home for good. Only then did the ministry officials notice that the management team was wearing the company ties of the British firm.

stronger. The investor could no longer go from company to company seeking the best deal.

3. The bargaining position vis-à-vis the company would be stronger. The MOP is equipped with perhaps more information than the managers themselves and can explain why the firm needs to be a part of the privatization. The ability to sit down with representatives of the entire industry and threaten them that if they do not get on board, they will lose out to their colleagues and competitors has turned out to be effective in getting firms to volunteer.

4. Sectoral studies could in principle help inform industrial policy.

5. Certain policies that affect all the firms in an industry could in principle be carefully formulated and applied, such as treatment of environmental liability.

Sectoral studies are under way in some twenty sectors. One, in the detergents sector, has been more or less completed. This project was initiated because of foreign expressions of interest in particular companies. After some nine months, the result has been that most of the firms involved in the study have been dealt with in some fashion. The best three were sold for what ministry officials perceived to be much better prices than would otherwise have been obtained. Other sectoral projects have resulted in studies with little other action so far, although perhaps forty transactions are in some stage of preparation. Five transactions have been carried out as of the end of 1991, all trade sales to foreign investors.

In general, however, the goals of the sectoral approach have yet to be realized. Heavy reliance on foreigners and consultants may have caused a public backlash against selling companies "too cheaply" to foreigners. More generally, it remains a question whether much can be done except to sell good companies to foreigners, something that Western investment banks do know how to do. On balance, while the sectoral approach seems to be a sensible way to conduct some foreign trade sales and can provide some useful information to the ministry, it is not in itself going to accelerate greatly the overall privatization process.

Privatization through Liquidation

Liquidation is the second main path of privatization envisaged in the 1 August 1990 Privatization Law. It was designed to facilitate a decentralized and "bottom-up" process, whereby interested enterprises could take the initiative to privatize themselves,subject to certain constraints, but with the possibility of lease financing from the Treasury.

This type of privatization has been by far the most common, despite receiving much less attention in the public (and especially foreign-language) debate, and although the MOP resources devoted to this path have been relatively minimal.[19] Although the law allows for three mechanisms for liquidation, in prac-

19. This is in part because small firms, typically the ones that undergo this sort privatization, represent a relatively small part of Polish industry. For example, the largest 413 enterprises employed in 1989 account for 45 percent of all workers in industry.

tice 81 percent of transactions have followed the leasing method: the creation of a new private company whose shareholders are the workers and managers and that leases the assets of the state enterprise. This follows from the "bottom-up" nature of the process: insiders try this, in general, only if they want to own their firm. (Tables 13.1 and 13.2 above present the size and sectoral breakdown for liquidated enterprises.)

In a typical transaction, the management and workers of a small and promising firm decide to privatize. They hire a consultant, approved by the MOP, who does a valuation of the company. The legal status of the assets and liabilities of the state enterprise is determined (land ownership etc.). When the responsible branch ministry and finally the MOP agree, the liquidation begins. The workers and managers form a new company and put in the start-up capital as required by the law. Often a "rich uncle," perhaps a foreign investor, helps provide the money. If no one objects, such as rival claimants for the assets or the local government, the MOP is likely to approve the liquidation. These transactions require months of strenuous effort, although, unlike capital privatizations, most of the work is done by the enterprise or the consultants it hires.

An important uncertainty exists as to how many of these deals have actually been completed. Some 416 liquidations have achieved final ministerial approval. However, only 154 have reached the final step, in which the state enterprise is crossed off the books. It appears that a variety of problems can arise to complicate the final closure of the deal. First, property claims turn out to be multiple and conflicting, or at least difficult to disentangle.[20] Second, the new private company, which may already be operating and benefiting from the state-enterprise assets by the time the ministerial agreement is given, may try to renegotiate the terms of its lease.

There are some potential problems with these liquidation privatizations. The companies may be overleveraged if the initial valuations were too high. The companies may be betting that the government will not want to reclaim the assets or that they will be able to appropriate the assets before this happens. The anecdotal evidence of excessively burdensome leases may, of course, reflect managerial attempts to force renegotiation of terms. The ministry has been worried, however, that the enterprises would be so burdened by debt payments that they would not be able to invest.

Important early evidence suggests that firms that undergo this type of privatization engage in active and positive restructuring. They change pay scales, reduce the work force, find partners, and so on. This seems to happen through-

---

20. An example of the kind of tangled property claims that can cause problems may illustrate the point. A private-sector supplier of plumbing (the "toilet king") during the late 1980s gained control over the parking lot to a major hotel outside a major town. He apparently made a deal according to which he supplied fixtures to the hotel in return for some sort of concession to the (only available) parking lot. He is currently charging a few dollars to each hotel guest to park there. This hotel could not be liquidated without first clarifying the legal status of this contract.

out the process, not only at the end, implying a confidence that the assets will eventually be privatized.

There are few signs of social or political resistance to these transactions, perhaps as a result of its "bottom-up" nature, although some people in the MOP are bothered by the idea that insiders are appropriating state assets too cheaply. In conclusion, this is a privatization method that seems to accommodate itself to existing stakeholders. With the caveats mentioned above, it seems to be proceeding fairly rapidly, without enormous ministerial effort.[21]

Bankruptcy

The second most common path to the transformation of a state enterprise, after liquidation and worker/management buyout, is liquidation according to the State Enterprise Law of 1981, a form of bankruptcy. This method is intended for firms that are in arrears to the government, which thereby gains the legal right to appoint a liquidator to sell off the assets and pay off creditors. A liquidator has begun work on some 534 mostly small firms, with an average employment of about 250, since the passage of the privatization law in 1990. Only a few of these liquidations have been completed.[22]

There is also a German-style bankruptcy law that gives creditors or the firm the option to begin bankruptcy proceedings in court. Given the general macroeconomic climate and financial outcomes in state enterprises, one would expect a large number of these bankruptcies. It is outside the scope of this paper to discuss why, in practice, virtually none have occurred, but the logistical and institutional difficulties involved in applying long-dormant laws are overwhelming.

Mass Privatization

The inclusion of a discussion of mass privatization in a paper concerned with the experience of privatization is somewhat premature, as no companies have actually been privatized through this method. The constraints discussed in this paper have, however, shaped the ongoing preparation of the program.[23]

---

21. One attractive alternative to the worker/management leasing approach for small companies would be simply to hold an auction. A desire to avoid excessive leverage, to find active outside owners, and to get better prices led the ministry to try this approach in 1991. Very few auction transactions have been carried out. Often, only one bidder has emerged, and this sole bidder may turn out to be a manager from the firm or a partner in the consulting company that handled the valuation. Examples like this help explain why some in the ministry consider that the most appropriate firms for auctions are the ones that come to the ministry begging for help, desiring only to avoid bankruptcy: these are the firms that the insiders do not much want and that therefore will not take care of themselves.

22. Tables 13.1 and 13.2 above present the size and sectoral breakdown for enterprises liquidated through the 1981 State Enterprise Law.

23. Discussion of the design of large-scale free giveaway privatization programs has a fairly long history, however. Among the many papers on free giveaways in Poland are Szomburg and

Therefore, the following briefly outlines the program as it appears to be developing, reviews some of the choices that have been made, addresses unresolved questions, and then asks why it has taken so long to implement.[24]

1. The program aims to involve some 200–600 companies, at least initially. A plausible estimate would be that these companies will average about 1,000 employees per company, so even this first tranche could amount to more than 10 percent of employment in industry. These companies will be commercialized over the next few months (some 150 have already been completed). Thirty-seven Polish consulting companies coordinated by a major international accounting firm are preparing informational packets on each enterprise to be involved in the program.

2. Ten to twenty financial intermediaries ("funds") are to be created. The funds will be joint-stock companies under the Polish commercial code, similar in some respects to American closed-end mutual funds. Their shares will be distributed to the Polish population, the ultimate owners. Their initial board will be appointed by the MOP. The first shareholder's meeting will be held and the board subject to reelection perhaps after the 1992 books are audited, in 1993.

3. The funds will choose and sign contracts with fund management companies, with the assistance of the MOP. The fund managers will have responsibility for all day-to-day management of the fund and its portfolio. The management contracts will contain strong incentive clauses to minimize dependence on initial valuations.

4. Each fund will be the lead shareholder in some ten to twenty companies, holding a 33 percent stake, and will hold much smaller pieces, say 2–3 percent, of many more enterprises. The method of distributing the companies to the funds has not been made clear. It may involve some sort of auction (for "bidding points," not real money) or a random allocation.

5. Workers in the enterprises involved will receive free of charge 10 percent of the shares in their firm (up to a limit of one year's wage worth of equity at book value).

6. The funds will be able to buy and sell shares in their portfolios soon after they begin operation, subject to approval of the Anti-Monopoly Commission. They will be responsible for appointment and oversight of board members for the companies in their portfolio. They will be given special responsibility for the companies in which they are the lead shareholder.

7. The mechanisms for the transfer of the shares of the funds to the population are still under active discussion and investigation. One plausible option

Lewandowski (1990), Lipton and Sachs (1991), and Frydman and Rapaczynski (1992). Implementation had been prepared in earnest since S. G. Warburg was appointed adviser on mass privatization to the MOP.

24. At the time of writing, the timing for the program was still uncertain, as the enabling legislation was before Parliament.

involves the creation of a single "program share" that would represent one share in each fund in the program. These shares would be distributed to the population (or sold for a small fee) and would be tradable over the counter. When a large number (for example, twenty) of the shares are taken to a licensed broker, they would be registered and "broken out" into the individual fund shares, which would be traded on the stock exchange. Dividends would not be distributed and proxy voting disallowed until the shares had been broken out. This potential solution has the advantage that it significantly reduces transaction costs associated with trading, payment of dividends, shareholder relations, and so on in the initial period.[25] Shares in the funds may be distributed somehow as an alternative to wage or pension payments for public-sector employees.

This brief description suggests that a large number of issues remain undecided. Among the more important questions are how to guarantee sufficient autonomy of management companies, how to manage trading of the large number of shares and, possibly, dividend payments, and how to handle the incentive contract if the fund decides to terminate the current fund management contract prematurely.

Many important questions appear to have been settled, however. I will concentrate on one: the "top-down" versus "bottom-up" creation of the funds. A central question faced early in the design of the program involved whether the funds should be created by the government or whether they should be allowed to develop spontaneously. Approaches similar to the current Czechoslovak approach were actively discussed in Poland. In this type of plan, vouchers are distributed to the population, who then are encouraged to choose an intermediary institution in which to invest the voucher. The intermediary, competing with other intermediaries for the voucher, can choose the enterprise of its choice for the initial investment.

The decision to reject this idea in Poland was made to minimize complexity. It was decided that the construction of a system that could reliably and in a reasonably fraud-free way distribute and redeem vouchers would be costly and risky, and perhaps impossible. The benefits of a more spontaneous creation of intermediaries by individuals were not considered to be worth the risk of large-scale confusion, chaos, and fraud. The ministry decided that relying on tested and reputable fund-management companies in the early stages would be more reliable than trusting the uninformed choice of voucherholders. In this model, shareholders would exercise choice later, as their share in the funds became tradable.

A potentially unfortunate upshot of this choice, however, and perhaps the major reason for the cautious approach taken so far toward mass privatization plans, is the risk of excess "centralization" perceived by some (such as, e.g.,

25. Of course, if it were politically acceptable randomly to allocate each citizen to one specific fund, this would further simplify the process.

Frydman and Rapaczynski 1992).[26] The government essentially creates the funds at first and by default must appoint the first board of directors, who are subject only to the indirect discipline of diffuse shareownership and legal obligations. It was judged that this would be an effective way of leveraging scarce government energies and that it would be possible to create a small number of quality boards.

Related to the "top-down" nature of fund creation is the need to decide on the structure of the intermediaries. If voucherholders simply decided with whom to invest, the government could avoid deciding whether the funds should more closely resemble holding companies, mutual funds, venture capital funds, or whatever. In the event, the proportion of shares going to the funds as outlined above was judged to provide a sufficiently active owner while avoiding some of the risks of excessive concentration of power.

Most of the other outstanding implementation issues can be worked out through pragmatic and careful analysis of options and discussion with potential fund managers. Three, however, are arguably more serious. Until now, the ministry has not used its powers to force the commercialization of state enterprises. Instead, it has relied on enterprises to volunteer for commercialization and specifically for mass privatization. Given the above discussion about incentives for insiders to attempt to preserve current rents where they exist, a concern about negative self-selection is logical.

It is not entirely clear that all the difficulties associated with capital privatizations have been resolved for mass privatization. One of the goals of mass privatization is to avoid having to construct each privatization separately, but some firm-specific issues may have to be addressed. For example, it may be necessary to unravel unclear property claims and decide on the disposition of social assets currently controlled by the enterprise. Another example is provided by the problem of environmental liability. Blanket indemnification for past damages usually requires an environmental audit at the time of transfer of assets, a time-consuming process. On the other hand, the absence of indemnification may expose the funds to excessive future risk.

The final question concerns the political acceptance of foreign involvement and of the program in general. Recent events, and some survey results, suggest that understanding and acceptance have grown and that the new Sejm is seriously addressing itself to remaining questions. Furthermore, the difficult situation for state enterprises has muted objections to temporary "centralization" of control and has perhaps focused debate on how to improve the situation for the state enterprises. On the other hand, the recent elections have witnessed some

26. The current, somewhat decentralized control structure has some advantages that could be threatened by a strengthening of direct government responsibility for the firm. There is the risk that the firms become even more passive than they currently are as workers and managers wait for the government to "save" them. Finally, the budget might come under even greater pressure if the government were less able to claim that it had no responsibility for wage setting in a given state enterprise.

resurgence of nationalism and doubts about foreign involvement in the economy. At the time of writing, mass privatization seems to have renewed political momentum and a good chance of going forward.

Why, then, is mass privatization taking so long to set in motion? On the one hand, the program has numerous potential advantages in light of the constraints mentioned above. It avoids some of the problems of valuation, finds owners for a huge number of firms, includes free distribution to insiders, but also prevents them from taking all the assets. It should mobilize resources in a decentralized way to restructure large numbers of enterprises, leveraging ministry energy through the funds. On the other hand, it is both a novel and a complex operation, involving to date some four foreign advisery firms, tens of Polish consulting companies, and much technical and political effort. Legal, economic, and political issues have to be carefully coordinated. Many decision makers felt a strong disinclination to increase government involvement in the enterprises, after years of struggling for decentralization. Difficult choices have presented themselves at each step in the design of the program. The alternative of taking a little more time to reflect and gather information has always been attractive. The lack of examples has been decisive in encouraging this extra care.[27] The program also has an important all-or-nothing feature: the critical mass of companies included needs to be large enough that the value of the fund shares is not ridiculous. Finally, such a complex plan requires the several ministries, political leaders, and the population to mobilize behind a basically confusing agenda.

13.3 Conclusion

Two years after the "big bang," 11 percent of Polish state enterprises have been commercialized or privatized. This paper has reviewed attempts at implementing privatization in Poland. In doing so, it has highlighted how difficult the process is and explained some of the reasons for this difficulty. The overthrow of the Communist regime, marketization of the economy, and legal and political revolution have changed all the "rules of the game," and in this environment the complexity of the privatization task overwhelms administrative capacity. Moreover, privatization requires a widespread rearranging of ambiguous property rights. It is not clear who owns the firm, who is responsible for liabilities, and in particular what power remains with the state. The result has been a confused political debate, a paralyzed bureaucracy, and enterprises whose workers and managers control the enterprise without any certain long-term stake in the firm.

We can characterize privatization strategies into three broad categories. The first, followed by Poland in 1990, stresses the careful creation of capital mar-

---

27. Stabilization programs are also complex and risky to implement. However, the existence of various worked-out examples simplifies the design of a new program.

kets and case-by-case "top-down" privatization of state enterprises. This has essentially failed. The second emphasizes the organic growth of the private sector, perhaps augmented with spontaneous privatization (see Kornai 1991). It may indeed be that the Polish economy will evolve over decades into a market economy without privatization of the large state enterprises. Indeed, the private sector is growing at a phenomenal rate, and liquidations of small enterprises seem to be proceeding fairly rapidly. The deep risks of this strategy are now evident, however. The deteriorating financial situation of state enterprises is leading to large and growing budget deficits. A macroeconomic relapse would endanger the growing private sector just as it threatens to move into manufacturing.

The third broad strategy is exemplified by the mass privatization program and emphasizes large-scale and widespread free distribution of equity through intermediary institutions. Much preparatory work has now been done, and implementation should soon begin, although parliamentary support has not yet been forthcoming. It is possible that this novel approach, designed with East European constraints in mind, may succeed where traditional methods have failed.

In retrospect, excess caution has been exercised in choosing the best possible scheme for mass privatization. It is difficult to imagine a plan whose implementation would have left the situation in the state enterprises worse than it is now. It may have been possible early on to act decisively and avoid much of the fragility of the current economic and political situation. A window of opportunity may have closed: the political honeymoon of the post-Communist era is over, and the financial predicament of the state sector continues to worsen. It is possible that the political system will manage to provide an environment that allows the private sector to continue to grow steadily. Unless mass privatization takes place, however, the risk of continued economic and political stability will be great.

Appendix

Table 13A.1   **Individual Enterprises Privatized through Capital Privatization as of 31 December 1991**

Name of Enterprise	Value (billion Zl)	Method of Sale	Value of Shares Sold (billion Zl)
Exbud S. A.	112.00	IPO	50.40
		Public tender	34.00
Slaska F-K Kablis S. A.	70.00	IPO	58.10
Prochnik S. A.	75.00	IPO	60.00
Tonsil S. A.	120.00	IPO	60.00
Krosno S. A.	132.00	IPO	66.00

Table 13A.1   (continued)

Name of Enterprise	Value (billion Zl)	Method of Sale	Value of Shares Sold (billion Zl)
Fampa S. A.	87.50	Public tender	77.00
Zminowroc	30.00	Leveraged buyout	30.00
Budokor Sp. Zoo.	52.80	Leveraged buyout	42.20
Norblin S. A.	40.00	Public tender	32.00
Polam Pila S. A.	223.03	Public tender	178.42
Pollena	330.00	Public tender	220.00
Wolczanka S. A.	75.00	Contract, IPO, Public tender	48.00
Swarzedz S. A.	100.00	IPO	70.00
Huta Szkla	54.00	IPO	3.90
Zywiec S. A.	200.00	IPO	154.00
Ekomel Sp. Zoo.	5.73	IPO	4.60
E. Wedel S. A.	687.50	Public tender	275.00
		IPO	83.20
Mostostal S. A.	99.75	Auction	69.82
Famet S. A.	35.00	Auction	25.00
Pol-Baf S. A.	40.00	Public tender	38.50
Techma Sp. Zoo	7.00	Public tender	3.60
Krakbud Sp. Zoo.	10.60	Public tender	8.50
Kaprinz Sp. Zoo.	4.5	Public tender	2.40
Pollena	165.82	Public tender	119.97
Pollena S. A.	71.60	Public tender	57.28
Alima S. A.	209.18	Public tender	125.51

Source: Ministry of Privatization, Warsaw.
Note: IPO = initial public offering; public tender = public tender of enterprise or portion thereof (this normally refers to a "trade sale" to foreign investors).

References

Aslund, A. 1990. How to privatize. Stockholm Institute of East European Economics. Mimeo.
Berg, A. 1992. The radical transformation of a social economy: Poland, 1989–1991. Ph.D. diss., Massachusetts Institute of Technology, Department of Economics.
Breitkopf, M., M. Gorski, and D. Jaszczynski. 1991. *Privatization in Poland.* Warsaw: Friedrich Ebert Foundation.
Center for Privatization. 1990. Act on the privatization of state-owned enterprises. Warsaw.
Centrum Badan Oponii Spoleczne (CBOS). 1989. Propozycje przeksztalcen stosunkow wlasnosci w opinii robotnikow i kadry kierowniczej przedsiebiorstw (Proposals to transform ownership in the opinion of workers and managers in enterprises). Warsaw, June.

186   **Andrew Berg**

————. 1990. Jak prywatyzowac polska gospodarke (How to privatize the Polish econ-
omy). Warsaw, June.
Dabrowski, M. 1991. Privatization in Poland. *Communist Economies and Economic
Transformation* 3, no. 3:317–25.
Dabrowski, J., M. Federowicz, and A. Levitas. 1991. Polish state enterprises and the
properties of performance: Stabilization, marketization, privatization. *Politics and
Society* 19, no. 4:403–37.
Frydman, R., and A. Rapaczynski. 1992. Privatization and corporate governance in
Eastern Europe: Can a market economy be designed? In *Central and Eastern Eu-
rope: Roads to* growth, ed. G. Winckler. Washington, D.C.: International Monetary
Fund and Austrian National Bank.
Frydman, R., and S. Wellisz. 1991. The ownership control structure and the behavior of
Polish firms during the 1990 reforms: Macroeconomic measures and microeconomic
responses. In *Reforming Central and Eastern European economies: Initial results
and challenges*, ed. Vittorio Corbo, Fabrizio Coricelli, and Jan Bossak. Washington,
D.C.: World Bank.
Gray, C. 1991. The legal framework for private sector development in a transitional
economy: The case of Poland. Working Paper WPS no. 900. Washington, D.C.:
World Bank.
Gruszecki, T. 1991. Privatization. Warsaw: Stefan Batory Foundation.
Hermann, K. 1990. Sectoral privatization. Warsaw: Ministry of Privatization. Mimeo.
Kawalec, S. 1992. The dictatorial supplier. In *The unplanned society*, ed. J. Wedel. New
York: Columbia University Press.
Kornai, J. 1991. The principles of privatization in Eastern Europe. Harvard Institute of
Economic Research Discussion Paper no. 1567. September.
Lipton, D. and J. Sachs. 1991. Privatization in Eastern Europe: The case of Poland.
Brookings Papers on Economic Activity, no. 2:293–333.
McDonald, K. 1992. The tap-dancing rhinoceros: Transformation of the Polish econ-
omy at the enterprise level. ITCA Europe. Warsaw: Mimeo.
Madigan, J. 1992. Privatization methods and strategy. Warsaw: International Privatiza-
tion Group. Mimeo.
North, D. C. 1981. *Structure and change in economic history*. New York: Norton.
Stark, D. 1990. Privatization in Hungary: From plan to market or from plan to clan.
East European Politics and Society 4, no. 3:351–92.
Szomburg, J., and J. Lewandowski. 1990. Property reform as a basis for social and
economic reform. *Communist Economies* 1, no. 3:257–68.
Winiecki, J. 1992. Privatization in East-Central Europe: Avoiding major mistakes. In
The emergence of market economies in Eastern Europe, ed. C. Clague and G. Raus-
ser. Oxford: Blackwell.

Discussion Summary

Tom Kolaja discussed many of the practical problems that have handicapped
the privatization process in Poland. First, he noted that the Ministry of Privatization has had difficulty attracting qualified personnel because of large wage
differentials between the private and the public sectors. Kolaja said that private
consultants earn ten to twenty times as much as equally qualified state employ-

ees. Second, Kolaja noted that many of the high-ranking officials in the ministries have come from the reform movement and hence have limited professional experience as politicians or bureaucrats. Third, he said that civil servants are criminally liable for any mistake they make during the privatization process. This explains why many decisions are avoided or delayed by being passed up the ministerial hierarchy. Finally, Kolaja observed that costly uncertainty has been generated by a lack of coordination among the myriad Polish regulatory agencies.

Kolaja also discussed the proposed program of mass privatization. He supports this approach, but he noted two potential hurdles that it will face. First, the Polish ministries must clarify whether and how environmental liabilities will be carried over from old to new firms. Second, the ministries must establish how much control the new owners will have. For example, he wondered whether the new owners will be able to carry out mass layoffs.

Jacek Rostowski noted that commercialization is often initially perceived by managers as a means by which firms can acquire additional government support instead of as an intermediate step to privatization. He cited examples in which newly commercialized firms had requested favors from the government officials who were serving on their boards. Rostowski warned that it usually takes at least two years before the boards of these commercialized companies start functioning in ways that correspond to the boards of Western firms.

Simon Johnson contrasted the Polish and Czechoslovak privatization experiences. First, he noted that the Czechoslovak voucher program had provided a much more successful "packaging of capitalism" than had been achieved by the various Polish privatization programs. Second, Johnson said that, in Czechoslovakia, all managers had been forced to submit privatization plans, thereby giving the privatization process a strong start.

Kalman Mizsei noted that delays in the privatization process in Czechoslovakia, Hungary, and Poland have been very costly to the governments because the market value of enterprises has fallen significantly during the last three years. He added that privatization programs should include an aggressive effort to attract foreign capital, as is currently being done in Hungary. He also praised Hungary's support for "self-privatization," a program in which privatization of small- to mid-sized firms is achieved with minimal interference by the State Property Agency.

Mark Schaffer suggested that the Kornai strategy for privatization—organic growth of the private sector without active efforts to privatize state-owned firms—might be a more successful strategy than the proposed plan of mass privatization. Schaffer warned that mass privatization may not solve the problem of growing demands for government subsidies and bailouts; newly privatized state firms will still generate such demands. Moreover, Schaffer stressed that the program of mass privatization will be fairly complicated, time consuming, and costly.

Stanley Fischer wondered whether the paper had taken a view that was overly pessimistic. He suggested that potential changes in the commercialization laws, of the type proposed in the paper by Andrei Shleifer and Robert Vishny (chap. 12 in this volume), would improve the prospects for commercialization. *Geoffrey Carliner* wondered whether Kolaja's comments were also too pessimistic. He asked if Kolaja's description of the difficulties plaguing the Ministry of Privatization was intended to suggest that privatization company by company has been a total failure.

Jeffrey Sachs argued in favor of privatization programs that work more quickly than the company-by-company approach that Poland has used so far. Sachs pointed out that the failure of the Polish approach was predicted. There were not enough skilled people in the privatization ministries to privatize each of the 3,000 industrial firms in Poland on a case-by-case basis. Sachs argued that the Poles need a privatization system that will operate more quickly, even if this leads to a less controlled and careful privatization process. He emphasized that case-by-case privatization is politically painful and extraordinarily time consuming and that it leads to charges of corruption with every deal. By contrast, a more aggressive program in which firms are turned over to insiders would operate quickly through a relatively decentralized mechanism and would align the interests of workers with the privatization process.

Andrew Berg responded to Schaffer's criticism of mass privatization. Berg conceded that there are unresolved questions about whether the new investment funds will insulate the government from demands for subsidies from newly privatized firms. However, Berg emphasized that the newly privatized firms will have the right allocative incentives with regard to whatever resources they end up controlling. Berg argued that it is much better to give resources/subsidies to an enterprise that is using them efficiently than it is to use subsidies to preserve structures that really should die.

14   The Treuhandanstalt: Privatization by State and Market

Wendy Carlin and Colin Mayer

To date, most of Eastern Europe has pursued privatization through markets: auctions, vouchers, mutual funds, and stock market flotations have all been widely advocated. The state has been viewed as an impediment whose involvement in the enterprise sector needs to be terminated at the earliest opportunity. There is one exception. Despite having an unusual abundance of managerial and financial resources, responsibility for restructuring East German enterprises has fallen on a state agency, the Treuhandanstalt (THA). This paper is an exploration of the way in which the THA has undertaken its function and of the lessons, if any, that it provides for the rest of Eastern Europe. We are not concerned here with the process of German unification and the course of events that rendered the vast majority of East German industry unprofitable (see, for example, Akerlof et al. 1991; Sinn and Sinn 1991; Dornbusch and Wolf, chap. 5 in vol. 1). This paper focuses on how the THA has engaged in restructuring and privatization in a situation in which the majority of tradable-sector jobs were under immediate threat.

The authors are grateful for the assistance of the Treuhandanstalt and several German banks in the preparation of this paper. They have benefited from the advice and suggestions of numerous individuals; in particular, they wish to thank Luqman Arnold, Andrea Boltho, Patrick Bolton, Robert Bischof, Gottfried von Bismarck, Jenny Corbett, Jane Darby, Christian Engell, John Flemming, Stephen Frowen, Bunt Ghosh, Andrew Glyn, Richard Gardner, Helmut von Glasenapp, Irena Grosfeld, Ulrike Grünrock, Horst Gruner, Frank-Christian Hansel, Andreas von Hardenberg, Oliver Henning, Horst Hillig, Wilfried Hübscher, Eberhard Kaiser, Kurt Kasch, Jan Klacek, Dieter Knoll, Claus Köhler, Marita Kraemer, Harald Kroll, Thomas Möller, Klaus-Peter Müller, Bernd Neubauer, David Peate, Joanna Place, Peter von Richthofen, Winfried Rosenkranz, Eberhard Rühle, Patrick Sandars, Gottfried Schega, Paul Seabright, David Soskice, Frank Stille, Rainer Stitterich, Benedikt Thanner, Horst Urban, Sigurt Vitols, and Karin Wagner. They wish to thank the Institute of Economics and Statistics in Oxford and the Wissenschaftszentrum in Berlin for their generous hospitality. Ian Zilberkweit provided imaginative and resourceful research assistance. The project was supported by the Centre for Economic Policy Research in London under its program on Eastern Europe funded by Ford Foundation grant 910–0383 and by the Stimulus Plan for Economic Sciences (SPES) program of the Commission of the European Community (grant E/90100033/PRO).

189

Section 14.1 describes the principles and methods by which the THA operates. These include extensive restructuring of enterprises prior to privatization, identification and evaluation of potential purchasers, and imposition and monitoring of conditions relating to sales of enterprises.

Section 14.2 describes the THA in operation. It discusses a case of a restructuring and privatization of a heavy industry *Kombinat* in Leipzig. This provides valuable insight into the significance that the THA attaches to considerations other than sale price, the procedure by which the THA evaluates social as well as private benefits, asset disposals, the formation of management and supervisory boards, and the interaction of the THA with Western firms, banks, and regional governments.

Section 14.3 turns to the central question: Why is the involvement of the state not just an unwarranted interference with market processes? The THA offers some clues. It is clear that considerations other than sale price have been crucial in privatizations: foremost among these are employment and regional/industrial policy. The attainment of these objectives has required nonmarket forms of restructuring. This can be seen by contrasting the operation of the THA with three market alternatives: simple auctions of enterprises, auctions with employment subsidies, and conditional auctions with employment and investment requirements attached. The interaction between employment and investment requirements in attaining the objectives of privatization is an important limitation on market processes.

Market transactions are limited in other ways. Allocating control of an enterprise through sales involves competition for ownership by purchasers of shares. This ensures appropriate patterns of ownership and control only where all potential purchasers have access to capital on equal terms. This is clearly not the case in Eastern Europe: domestic credit is severely constrained in relation to that available to overseas purchasers. It is therefore far from evident that market sales allocate ownership and control appropriately.

In addition to the attainment of the social objectives of employment and regional policy, there is a second basic issue: How can distortions created by credit constraints be avoided? East Germany offers only limited guidance on this. Even in the country that is commonly associated with the most industrially oriented banking system in the world, there is little evidence of financial support for East German enterprises. To date, the distinctive feature of East Germany is that enterprise control has not been retained within East Germany; privatizations have virtually exclusively involved transfers of ownership and control to Western enterprises. However, there is evidence that this may be on the point of changing, and East Germany provides important insights into how the process of privatization can be associated with debt financing and hence the retention of local ownership and control.

To many, the experience of East Germany will appear to be of only limited relevance to other countries. The abundance of managerial expertise and financial resources in West Germany sets East Germany apart from the other

East European countries. On the other side of the coin, monetary union created problems that were specific to Germany. East Germany is therefore regarded as a case of its own.

Section 14.4 argues that this judgment is too quick. The resources and problems may be different, but the objectives and requirements for their successful attainment are similar. East Germany illustrates the pitfalls of restructuring and privatization and the process by which they can be contained. This involves a gradual transfer of control from central agency to private enterprise. The paper concludes that retention of domestic control does not require an initial abundance of domestic managerial resources.

14.1 The Treuhand's Method of Privatization

14.1.1 Supervisory Boards

The creation of the Treuhandanstalt predates economic union between East and West Germany. Ownership of all state-owned enterprises (SOEs) was transferred to the trust agency in March 1990. SOEs with more than 2,000 employees were converted into AGs (German public stock corporations) and smaller SOEs into limited-liability companies (GmbHs). When the West Germans took over and reorganized the Treuhand, they were the owners of some 8,000 enterprises with a total employment of about 4 million (Kühl 1991, 682). They assigned smaller enterprises (with fewer than 1,500 employees) to regional subsidiaries of the THA and the larger enterprises to the industry-based divisions of the THA in Berlin. We do not discuss the privatization of very small businesses such as shops, kiosks, and pharmacies.

The Treuhand is a public agency with a supervisory board (the *Verwaltungsrat*) in which important interest groups in Germany are represented: the federal government (economics and finance ministries), state (Länder) governments, the Bundesbank, the commercial banks, major West German firms, the trade unions, and, to signify the importance of non-Germans in privatizations, two European businessmen.

One of the THA's first tasks was to ensure that all its enterprises with more than 500 employees had a supervisory board (*Aufsichtsrat*). These boards have a similar composition to the *Verwaltungsrat:* there are "shareholder" representatives from local government, banks, and other companies. "Employee" representation is established by law at one-third of the supervisory board for firms with fewer than 1,500 employees and half for larger firms. Chairpersons of supervisory boards are drawn from among the shareholders' representatives on the board and have casting votes in the event of a tie between shareholder and employee representatives.

Table 14.1 records the source of supervisory board members and chairpersons in East German firms. A large majority of both representatives and chairpersons come from Western (usually West German) companies. West German

Table 14.1   The Origin of "Shareholder" Representatives and Chairpersons of
              Supervisory Boards of East German Enterprises

	Supervisory Board Members (%)	Supervisory Board Chairpersons (%)
Other companies (mostly West German)	60–70	80
Banks (West German)	20–25	20
Local government	10–15	—

Source: Data supplied by the THA, September 1991.

banks account for one-fifth of both seats on boards and chairpersons. Local
governments have some representation on boards but do not hold any chairper-
son positions.

Supervisory boards oversee the formulation and implementation of restructuring plans. They discuss proposals with senior management of East German
enterprises, suggest modifications, and monitor their implementation. They are
a source of management expertise providing East German managers with advice and assistance. They have the power to dismiss management where necessary and are instrumental in bringing in new management. Supervisory boards
assist East German firms in making contacts with Western (usually West German) firms and help create markets for East German products.

Table 14.2 reports that most new managers come on consultancies and short-
term contracts from West German firms. Between one-fifth and one-quarter
are active managers of West German firms, and between one-twentieth and
one-tenth are retired managers.

14.1.2   Valuation and Evaluation of Enterprises

All THA enterprises were required to submit an opening balance sheet in
deutsche marks and a business plan to the Treuhand. The original intention of
the THA had been to establish independently audited balance sheets for its
enterprises and to offer enterprises for sale, providing potential buyers with
this balance sheet and the business plan. A key problem emerged quickly and
led to a change in strategy: in the absence of a market for real estate in East
Germany, the book value of enterprise property was too low, with the result
that property developers tried to purchase enterprises purely for the expected
capital gain on land.

The valuation problem revealed a deeper concern in the Treuhand with "un-
conditional" sales of firms: the THA was interested not simply in securing the
highest price for the enterprise but in transferring ownership to a purchaser
who would continue to operate the business.

The THA carried out an evaluation of the potential viability of each of its
enterprises in a market economy. It set up a team of eighty top West German
managers (*Leitungsausschuß*) to evaluate opening balance sheets and restruc-

Table 14.2   New Managing Directors of Treuhand Firms from West Germany

Consultants and managers on short-term contracts (%)	70
Active managers (%)	20–25
Retired managers (%)	5–10

Source: Data supplied by the THA, September 1991.

Note: Of 8,786 THA firms surveyed in 1991, there were 23,673 Eastern and 2,631 Western managers in the "most senior" management positions (reported by Mayhew and Seabright 1992, 118).

turing plans of each of its enterprises and to indicate how profitability could be achieved over the next two to three years. Restructuring plans included required reductions in employment and changes in products and processes.

The Treuhand team made a judgment as to whether an enterprise could be restructured successfully and assigned the enterprise to one of six categories (Carlin and Mayer 1992, 329). Enterprises assigned to categories 5 and 6 were judged not to be capable of successful restructuring and were destined for closure.

Balance sheets had to be adjusted to ensure that the 70 percent of enterprises categorized as "potentially viable" had a chance of survival. In particular, liabilities incurred by the enterprises to the state bank under the central planning system had to be written off. The method adopted by the THA was to compare projected turnover, assets, and liabilities of East German enterprises with equivalent firms in West Germany. The capital structure of these West German firms was used as a yardstick for the THA enterprises. Old debts were written down so as to create a "confirmed" balance sheet (the so-called *festgestellte Bilanz*), which gave the THA firm a fair chance of survival for two to three years (for a worked example, see *Informationen,* no. 5:8–9 [THA 1991a]). THA officials estimate that about three-quarters of the DM 106 billion in old debts will be written off through this procedure.

14.1.3   The Terms of Sales: Price, Employment, and Investment Guarantees

Contracts for sales include guarantees by purchasers of minimum levels of employment and investment in an enterprise as well as a sale price. Penalty clauses are written into contracts that specify the THA's share of capital gains in enterprises sold within five years of their privatization and payments due to the THA if the investment and employment guarantees are not fulfilled.

Negotiations over sales prices involve discussions about employment and investment guarantees; discounts on sales prices are made on a per job and per deutsche mark of investment guaranteed basis. From discussions with Treuhand officials, it appears that the reduction in the sales price per job guaranteed has increased over time from DM 12,000–15,000 to up to DM 50,000 in recent deals. This is consistent with data showing sales revenue received by the THA per job guaranteed declining from DM 23,100 to DM 16,600 from the first to the second half of 1991. Over the same period, investment guarantees per job guaranteed have risen from DM 75,100 to DM 115,000. This is consistent with a trend toward jobs being made more secure (data supplied by THA officials, 1991).

The imposition of employment targets reflects the obligation placed on the THA by the government to take account of the social costs of unemployment. For example, the THA takes DM 300,000 per job as the opportunity cost of permanent unemployment for large chemical enterprises, and it incorporates this into comparisons of the costs and value of liquidations and privatizations (McKinsey & Co. 1991, 2–7).

The THA official in charge of the sale of a particular enterprise takes the restructuring plan of the firm drawn up by the incumbent management and the supervisory board and forms a view (often with the assistance of outside management consultants) of the maximum number of jobs that can be saved. Buyers for the enterprise are sought by the management and the THA. Employment targets are paramount, and enterprises can be sold for an effective negative price. This is achieved by combining a sale price of DM 1.00 with investment grants to purchasers. (The number of DM 1.00 sales has declined since balance sheets have been adjusted and debt written off.) In exchange, the purchaser makes investment and employment guarantees.

The submission to the management board of the THA (the *Vorstandsvorlage*) sets out the terms of the proposed disposal of the enterprise and the business plan of the purchaser.

14.1.4   Restructuring Prior to Privatization

East German enterprises faced intense competition in their domestic market immediately after German economic and monetary union on 1 July 1990. On the basis of an analysis of input-output data, Akerlof et al. (1991) estimated the expense in ostmark of major East German enterprises (the *Kombinate*) earning a deutsche mark in Western markets. They found that less than 10 percent of employment in these enterprises was viable in covering even short-run variable costs.

This cost problem was exacerbated by the collapse of the CMEA (Council for Mutual Economic Assistance) and the Soviet Union as a purchaser. It is estimated that between 900,000 and 1 million industrial jobs were dependent on sales to former command economies (FCEs), with more than half going to the Soviet Union (*DIW Wochenbericht*, no. 12 [1991]:127). Fourteen percent of East German industrial output was sold to FCEs. The much faster than expected loss of markets to the East underlined the importance of restructuring.

The huge East German *Kombinate* were typically organized along product lines with plants scattered across East Germany. Incumbent managers saw the supply of output to the Soviet Union as providing the rationale for keeping *Kombinate* (comprising up to twenty enterprises) together as a unit. Synergies within *Kombinate* were regarded by managers as the source of their enterprise's competitiveness in supplying the Soviet market.

To avoid widescale collapse through bankruptcy, the THA initially provided 100 percent guarantees for liquidity credits to all enterprises. Guaranteed loans were granted across the board without any evaluation of the risk of default. The amount of loans guaranteed was expected to cover 40 percent of forecast losses in the enterprise sector. Enterprise managers perceived a relatively hard budget constraint and responded by cutting employment. Table 14.3 records reductions in employment in THA-owned enterprises to the end of 1991. Total employment in THA-owned firms has declined by 65 percent, of which 23 percent is attributed to employment guarantees in firms that have been sold (i.e., jobs that have been saved) and 42 percent to job shedding and closures. Since the completion of the evaluation of potential viability at the end of 1991, the THA has stopped all guaranteed loans to enterprises in categories 5 and 6; enterprises in these categories are now required to secure bank loans without THA guarantees.

The loss of Soviet markets encouraged the Treuhand to break up *Kombinate* into legally separate enterprises; the view was that buyers for the huge industrial holding companies could not be found. By the autumn of 1991, plans were in place for reducing the number of holding companies by one-third and the number of subsidiaries of holding companies by two-thirds (THA 1991c).

Despite its motto—"Privatization as the best form of restructuring"–the THA has been actively involved in restructuring. It has become increasingly evident that large industrial conglomerates must be broken up if viable firms are to emerge. Management and, in some cases, supervisory boards have frequently obstructed the breaking up of the old structures. As owner of the enterprises, the THA can dismiss the supervisory board. In addition, a new law was introduced in 1991 to enable the THA to separate subsidiaries of holding

Table 14.3   **Reduction in Employment in THA-Owned Firms (thousands)**

	Employment in THA Firms	Fall in Employment	Of Which, Accounted for by Employment Guarantees in THA Firms Sold	Accounted for by Labor Shedding and Closures[a]
1 July 1990	4,000			
1 January 1991	2,979	1,021	201	820
1 July 1991	2,310	669	338	331
1 January 1992 Forecast	1,404	906	391	515
Total		2,596	930	1,666

Source: Calculated from Kühl (1992) and data supplied by the THA.

[a]This is an approximation obtained by subtracting jobs guaranteed from the total reduction in employment in THA firms. Note that, in some contracts, the number of jobs guaranteed rises over time.

companies from the parent enterprise and to enable subsidiaries to take the initiative for separation from the parent (Heimpold, Kroll, and Wilhelm 1991, 36–40).

The Treuhand had decided on the closure of over 700 enterprises even before the completion of the classification exercise described above. More than four-fifths of closures are being carried out using a form of liquidation that places priority on salvaging viable parts of the enterprise rather than on meeting the claims of creditors (Carlin and Mayer 1992, 329–30). The liquidation team is maximizing the number of jobs saved or created on the sites of enterprises being closed.

14.1.5 The Privatization Record

In the year and a half since the West Germans took control of the THA, they have succeeded in disposing entirely of over one-third of their enterprises (table 14.4). Over one-quarter of these have been closed or wound up. The total number of enterprises that are or were owned by the THA has grown since Union by virtue of the splitting up of firms discussed above. Nearly one-quarter of THA firms have been sold to the private sector—nearly one-quarter of which have been sold to East Germans as MBOs (management buyouts). As table 14.4 indicates, the role of foreign buyers has been very limited.

Table 14.4   Sales and Disposals of Enterprises by the Treuhandenstalt

Status of Treuhand Firms as of the End of 1991	Number	% of Total THA Enterprises
Firms disposed of in their entirety[a]	4,594	41.9
Sold to the private sector	2,700	24.6
Of which, sold as MBOs[b]	646	5.9
Of which, sold to foreigners	248	2.3
Reprivatized (returned to previous owners)	527	4.8
Transferred to local authorities	250	2.3
Being closed	865	7.9
Other (wound up through closure, merger, or splitting up)	252	2.3
Enterprises still to be disposed of[c]	6,376	58.1
Majority owned by private sector	615	5.6
Majority owned by THA	5,706	52.0
Total enterprises that are or were owned by the THA[d]	10,970	100.0

Source: Calculated from data supplied by the THA.
[a]Includes enterprises for which transactions have been decided but which may be incomplete.
[b]A further 248 parts of enterprises have been sold as MBOs.
[c]Note that the Treuhand announces as its "headline" figure for privatizations the total of all firms for which it has sold at least a part. By the end of 1991, this number was 5,210.
[d]This number frequently changes, as enterprises are split up and reorganized.

Table 14.5 indicates that the distribution of privatizations by size of enterprise has been very even. As would be expected, MBOs are concentrated in smaller enterprises.

14.2   From *Kombinat* to Private Firm: The Case of Baukema Kombinat

The active involvement of the THA in privatization is illustrated by the case of a former *Kombinat*. This case is used to highlight the creation and activities of the supervisory board; the role of management, supervisory board, and the THA in developing a restructuring plan and identifying and evaluating potential buyers; the splitting up of large enterprises by the THA; the social cost/benefit analysis conducted by the THA and the negotiation of sale price, employment, and investment guarantees; and the behavior of incumbent management under THA ownership.

14.2.1   Background

The Baukema Kombinat was created only in 1987, in what turned out to be the last wave of industrial reorganization in East Germany. It was formed from two distinct groups of enterprises: first, the original Baukema Kombinat, which was a Leipzig-based holding company with its origins in construction machinery, and, second, the Gisag Kombinat, which at the time was an East Germany-wide foundry enterprise with 33,000 employees and its headquarters on the outskirts of Leipzig. Baukema Kombinat took over the core of Gisag (employment of 6,000), located in the Leipzig area.

An early decision of the Treuhand supported by the Baukema board was to separate out the foundries from the rest of Baukema's activities. The grouping together of foundries with construction equipment had no industrial logic, and the organizational structure of Gisag and Baukema had remained fairly separate. In the case study, attention is focused on the foundry side of the business, that is, on Gisag.

Table 14.5   The Size Distribution of Privatizations and MBOs (data as of the end of October 1991)

Employees per Enterprise	% of Enterprises That Have Been Privatized	MBOs by Size of Firm %
<100	11.0	74.1
101–500	14.9	20.9
501–1,000	15.9	.7
>1,000	13.0	0
Unknown	21.1	4.4

Source: Carlin and Mayer (1992, table 5, 332).

14.2.2   The Future of the Foundry Industry and of Gisag

The formal separation of the foundries, centered around the large Gisag AG enterprise, from Baukema AG and their direct attachment to the THA occurred in September 1991—six months after active THA engagement with Baukema began. As soon as Gisag became an AG in May 1990 (before Union), the management sought the advice of the West German foundry association and of the Dresdner Bank (Gisag's *Hausbank*) regarding suitable candidates for the supervisory board. The president of the West German Foundry Association, Eberhard Möllmann, accepted the chairman's position on the supervisory board.

From the outset, the restructuring of Gisag was viewed within the context of the future of the entire foundry industry in East Germany. The starting point for the East German foundry industry was the requirement that it compete with West German suppliers. The structural change undergone by the West German industry since the 1950s was taken as indicative of the required changes in East Germany and in Gisag itself. Fundamental change was required in the scale and composition of foundry output and in the size of enterprises. For example, in a speech at Gisag, Möllman pointed out that the number of foundry firms in West Germany had fallen by 60 percent between 1960 and 1990, with no increase in the average size of the remaining plants. Three-quarters of all West German foundries have fewer than 200 employees. In terms of Gisag, for example, the extrusion foundry had sufficient capacity to supply the entire German market. In 1991, 300,000 tons of output were produced by the East German industry using only 25 percent of available capacity. In Möllmann's view, output from East German foundries could rise to 400,000 tons by the end of the decade.

One of the Gisag foundries cast the components for the tracks of all Warsaw Pact tanks. This order was canceled, and the steel foundry employing 800 workers was closed down completely in the first quarter of 1991. Orders to the other foundries had collapsed with the drop in manufacturing output in East Germany. For example, one of the foundries made crankshafts for Trabants. Production of these cars ceased in May 1991. The finance director stressed the problems with securing orders in current conditions in which the future of the enterprise was uncertain. Customers felt that they had no security of supply.

14.2.3   Management under THA Ownership

Management remained unchanged from pre-Union days, with the exception of the appointment of a personnel manager (from West Germany). From May 1990, the managers spent a considerable amount of time undergoing training. The finance director spent time in Hanover with Salzgitter AG and in Augsburg with Preussag shadowing managers. He learned profit and loss accounting, how to calculate costs and utilize investment planning techniques. The only notable change in the internal organization of the management of Gisag was the increased relative dominance of the finance side as compared with the traditional emphasis on technical/production management.

14.2.4   The Strategy to Sell Gisag

The board of Gisag decided to appoint an expert on the casting industry in Europe (an American, found through the West German casting federation) to assist with finding buyers for Gisag or parts of it. Originally, the managers had taken the view that Gisag should be kept together and should offer the full product palette (steel, iron, shell mold, etc.). At the end of 1990, the philosophy changed as the size of the problem became more evident. Gisag management came round to the idea that the only way of saving any of the foundry business was to split it up. This was partly influenced by the U.S. industry expert and by the supervisory board chairman, Möllmann.

The Treuhand official assigned to the Baukema/Gisag case was a highly experienced West German manager who had been brought in to the Treuhand through the German chancellor's initiative. He engaged a management consultancy to carry out an assessment of Baukema and Gisag. The THA encouraged the use by Gisag AG of the industry expert in particular to try to persuade companies with foundries in West Germany to move with their markets to the East. This reflected recognition of the central problem facing Gisag: how to find a market for its products.

14.2.5   Restructuring and Privatization

By September 1991, two alternative strategies for the Gisag enterprise had been identified by the Treuhand. The choice was to break up the enterprise and sell off the foundries individually or to close the enterprise. The THA made calculations of the cost to them of each of these proposals.

Option 1: Closure. It would cost DM 180 million to close Gisag AG down and sell the assets at liquidation value. No permanent jobs would be saved. The costs of closure include only the direct costs to the enterprise—for example, the *Sozialplan* (cost of redundancies = DM 2,000–5,000 per employee)—and not the costs to the economy as a whole (e.g., unemployment benefits).

Option 2: Privatization. It would cost DM 208 million to privatize the foundries successfully. Successful privatization in this case entails two foundry firms in West Germany (operating in inner-city sites in Frankfurt and Ingolstadt) relocating to the main Gisag site in Leipzig and bringing their orders with them. A Swedish firm is interested in buying the most modern of the foundries (which was built before reunification to supply Volkswagen's engine plant). Another could be sold to a consortium of distributors (from Italy, France, and the United Kingdom) that wanted to establish some production capability. Although the most modern foundry is expected to attract a positive price, the price will be low reflecting the excess capacity in the European foundry business. The other foundries could not be sold at a positive price, and this resulted in the negative price for disposing of the foundry business as a whole. The Treuhand would pay grants to the purchasers of foundries, including reimbursement for their anticipated losses, amounting to DM 37 million. The foundries would be sold for DM 1.00.

Under option 2, purchasers would make investment guarantees of DM 77 million. They would guarantee 980 jobs (out of a current 3,600) as against none under option 1. Thus, 980 jobs would be saved at an additional cost of DM 28 million (i.e., a cost per job of DM 28,000).

The management board of the THA had to decide if this was worthwhile. If the THA were simply a private holding company, then it would adopt option 1 without question. One of the relevant considerations was the external effect of the existence of a foundry industry in Leipzig under option 2. Part of the additional costs required to make privatization possible (i.e., of the cost of option 2) is the outlay required to prepare the site for the operation of the privatized foundries. With one exception, the existing foundries will be demolished and new facilities installed. The buyers get the site for nothing, and their start-up losses are covered. The companies will invest DM 77 million themselves in new facilities. A large part of the investment guaranteed by one of the purchasers would take the form of orders for an independent THA company that makes foundry plants.

In view of the positive external effects of retaining the foundry business and the social costs of increased unemployment, the THA asked the city of Leipzig and the *Land* of Sachsen to contribute to the cost of implementing option 2. A contribution of DM 30 million was sought. To date, DM 10 million has been committed by Leipzig.

The THA adopted option 2 in November 1991. This empties Gisag AG of content—it is simply a shell owning ancillary property, such as nineteen blocks of flats, a hotel, etc. It will be put into liquidation and the assets sold. Additional buyers are being sought for the remaining bits and pieces. Small MBOs on the main Gisag site have been encouraged. To September 1991, five small MBOs had occurred, resulting in employment of 250. A railway siding and line linking the outer Leipzig site to the Leipzig main railway station was sold for DM 100,000; a West German partner was involved in this MBO.

Key features of the sales contract between the THA and one of the purchasers of a Gisag foundry are shown in table 14.6. Of note is the inclusion in the contract of detail concerning the purchaser's existing business and the future business at Gisag.

15.2.6   The Treuhand's Role in the Restructuring

The role of the Treuhandanstalt in restructuring the former *Kombinat* can be summarized as follows:

- Spinning off the foundries from Baukema AG (this has involved the Treuhand taking over the losses of the foundries directly and undertaking closer monitoring of Gisag);

Table 14.6   Elements of the Sales Contract for a Gisag Foundry

The purchaser operates a foundry in *x* [in West Germany] with approximately 600 employees and has particular knowledge and experience and an important market share in the casting industry.

The purchaser will continue to operate the foundry [at Gisag] . . . and on the same location after the renewal of the area . . . by the seller [THA] will erect a *y*-foundry with modern competitive technology with a capacity of *z* tons and providing a level of 200 rising to 600 permanent full-time jobs, investing a total of DM 40 million.

If the purchaser sells or transfers the land . . . to a third party before the 31 December 1993, then the purchaser must transfer 80 percent of the proceeds to the THA.

The purchaser will continue the business of *y*-casting and expand it in the following way: the purchaser will by the end of 1993 have invested at least DM 20 million in the *y*-foundry, in particular for the procurement and installation of a new large molding plant, and by the end of 1995 a further DM 20 million.

If by the end of 1993 there are not binding orders for the investment of DM 20 million, then the purchaser must pay the THA the difference between the value of such orders and the DM 20 million. . . . The purchaser will provide quarterly reports to the THA on the actual and planned investment.

The purchaser is obliged to provide at least the following number of full-time jobs and to report employment at the end of each quarter. . . . If this obligation is not met, then for each missing job the purchaser must pay the THA for the period of the missing employment per month a penalty of DM 2,000 . . . [up to] DM 2,500. . . .

The penalties do not apply only when the nonemployment of workers comes about through force majeure or through the failure of the THA to provide the essential services.

Source: THA.

• Restructuring Gisag AG by separating out the foundry activities from the other Gisag enterprises (e.g., foundry plant construction);
• Evaluating the costs of closure (option 1);
• In conjunction with management, identifying buyers for the individual foundries (option 2);
• Securing the retention of foundries in Leipzig (this involved separate negotiation with potential purchasers for each foundry);
• Seeking to persuade *Bund, Länder,* and local government to contribute to the costs of pursuing option 2 (the higher-cost option to the Treuhand) on the grounds that its social cost is lower once account is taken of the employment, regional, and industrial implications;
• Winding up the remaining activities of Gisag through a liquidation team.

14.3   State versus Market Systems of Restructuring

The distinguishing characteristic of East German privatizations is the close involvement of a state agency, the Treuhandanstalt, in the restructuring of firms prior to privatization. The German government has not sought to privatize enterprises at the earliest opportunity; instead, considerable emphasis has been placed on two considerations, employment and industrial/regional policy. The THA's guidelines for the privatization of enterprises state that account should be taken of the following: the continued operation and modernization of the business by the purchaser; securing employment; effects on the viability of suppliers from East Germany; contribution to the economic strength of the area around the enterprise; the future contribution to tax income (THA 1991b). The Gisag case illustrates these concerns quite clearly. By delegating control to an agency whose objectives include broader social criteria, the German government was redressing the balance between its interests as owner and its function as guardian of the East German productive sector. Inevitably, conflicts arise between these objectives, and these have been reflected in disputes between the Finance Ministry and the Economics Ministry over policies pursued by the Treuhandanstalt.

An impediment to privatization comes from emphasizing these broader considerations. Were it the case that the THA merely wished to maximize the proceeds from sales or dispose of assets at the earliest opportunity, then it would be difficult to dispute the proposition that an auction of assets would have been a more appropriate mechanism. However, once other considerations become relevant, the design of an auction becomes more complex. Essentially, an auction represents the interests of only the owners of the enterprise (namely the state), not other stakeholders, such as employees and local communities.

One possibility would have been to have invited tenders to bid for enterprises that had employment subsidies attached; such a procedure could have internalized the social value attributed to increased employment. There are two problems associated with employment subsidies. First, the development of industries in particular areas of East Germany is part of a broader industrial policy. There are externalities across firms in their decisions to locate in particular areas: the willingness of one firm to locate is dependent on the decision of others. The internalization of such networking considerations is not easily achieved through either simultaneous or sequential auctions.

Second, employment decisions can be reversed at low cost to employers but potentially at high cost to employees, local communities, and dependent suppliers and purchasers. Thus, although the state could have provided employment subsidies in the form of an ongoing subsidy that changed in line with employment rather than in the form of a discount on the initial purchase price, the costs to other stakeholders could not have been avoided. The Treuhandanstalt has clearly placed considerable emphasis on the quality of jobs, that is, on how secure they are as well as on how many are saved. Penalties could have been attached to shedding labor, but that would have introduced a third consideration into the auction process alongside price and employment subsidy, namely, the creditworthiness of purchasers. Penalties are of little value if employers go into liquidation. Problems of enforcing contracts are likely to be particularly acute for foreign firms whose assets cannot be seized in the event of default on employment obligations.

As a consequence, the THA has sought combinations of employment *and* investment guarantees from prospective purchasers. On the assumption that there are sunk costs associated with capital expenditures and that there is complementarity between investment and employment, investment guarantees introduce an element of irreversibility into employment decisions that employment subsidies on their own cannot achieve. For example, suppose that an investment subsidy of DM 50 million is paid on an expenditure of DM 100 million and that this is just sufficient to ensure a zero net present value on a private valuation. If, at the end of the five-year contractual period, the present value of the asset is DM 25 million, then the investment will be retained, provided that the realizable value of the asset has fallen more than 75 percent below its purchase price.

One example of where the THA has applied this principle is in relation to microelectronics. The THA has had interest in one particular site from a Far Eastern manufacturer that wishes to build a new microelectronics factory with a capital expenditure of DM 300 million and another buyer who is interested in the site as a depot for storage and the loading and unloading of lorries. The THA is inclined toward the first offer because of the greater commitment that the capital expenditure demonstrates. Likewise, bidders are more likely to be successful where they promise to build new factories rather than renovate old ones because of the greater sunk investments associated with the former.

As in the case of employment subsidies with penalties for labor shedding, sales that are conditional on investment requirements involve credit evaluations of the ability of the purchaser to sustain the operation of its investments. The THA therefore looks carefully at the nature of potential purchasers. One example of where the credit evaluation failed was in the microelectronics industry. A West German firm established a GmbH with DM 100,000 to purchase a THA firm and then threatened to put the GmbH into bankruptcy if the contract was not altered to its advantage.

Several of the functions of the Treuhandanstalt can be seen as a response to the above problems with auctions: the evaluation of the viability of different parts of an enterprise; the assessment of the social as well as private value of the maintenance of operations; the stipulation of investment and employment requirements; and the careful analysis of prospective purchasers (table 14.7).

However, there is one aspect of the operation of the Treuhandanstalt that the above does not capture, and that is the emphasis that has been placed on the creation of supervisory boards. To date, their function has essentially been limited to managing the transition process. Members of the supervisory board monitor and evaluate the incumbent management; they advise in the formulation of restructuring plans; they assist East German firms in establishing contacts with Western firms and finding outlets for their products in the West; and they help the THA find prospective purchasers. Important though these

Table 14.7   Market Alternatives to the Treuhandanstalt

Market Process	Problems
Simple auction	Does not allow for social/private divergence in values of employment and industrial/regional policy
Auction with employment subsidy	Reversibility of employment decisions. Credit evaluations required to enforce penalties. Does not internalize cross-firm externalities arising from regional and industrial effects
Auction with investment and employment requirements	Credit evaluation of prospective purchasers is necessary

functions are, to date they have been transitional in nature. Once a company has been successfully sold in whole or in part, then the supervisory board and the holding company are frequently disbanded, as the Gisag case illustrates.

Over the last year, a more permanent role for the creation of supervisory boards has emerged. To date, banks have provided little finance to East German enterprises that has not been guaranteed by the Treuhandanstalt. There has been some risky lending associated with small-scale MBOs. Recently, West German banks have shown increased interest in providing both risky debt and some equity capital (see Carlin and Mayer 1992, 340–41). The significance of this is that, once East German companies are able to raise finance without selling all their equity to Western firms, then the creation of enterprises that are owned and controlled by East Germans becomes feasible. Of course, this has already occurred with small-scale privatizations; however, large-scale privatizations have to date usually involved wholesale purchases by Western firms.

Credit constraints are the main reason why sales to Western firms are almost unavoidable in the initial stages of privatization. However, it would be wrong to conclude that the *availability* of finance is the constraint on the development of East German enterprises. The reason why interest is now being shown by West German banks in lending to East German firms is that viable companies are beginning to emerge. The monitoring and control functions of supervisory boards have been central to this development. Through their position on supervisory boards, banks accumulate valuable information on the quality of prospective borrowers. Banks are therefore just at the point of being confident that they can identify sound investments. When this happens, the role of the supervisory board will extend crucially beyond mere assistance with the transition process to the creation of self-sufficient enterprises. An early statement of the guidelines for the privatization policy of the THA states that, in assessing offers, the continuation of the business if possible as an independent enterprise unit should be taken into account (THA 1990, 3). As the next section explains, this self-sufficiency may be of even greater significance to the rest of Eastern Europe than it is to East Germany.

14.4 The Relevance of the Treuhandanstalt Experience to the Rest of Eastern Europe

There are several important respects in which the privatization problem in East Germany differs from that in the rest of Eastern Europe. On the negative side from the German perspective, economic and monetary union has made much of the East German enterprise sector uncompetitive. For many firms, the costs of restructuring to achieve commercial viability in the unified German economy exceed the expected present value of the restructured firm (to a private owner). On the positive side, East Germany has access to all the resources associated with one of the most highly developed economies in the world. These resources include transfers from the federal government,[1] institutional structures, legal systems, accounting and bankruptcy laws, training and apprenticeship schemes, management, and finance. The East German experience may therefore be felt to be of only limited significance for the rest of Eastern Europe.

While not denying the existence of these differences, many of the problems that the THA has been attempting to tackle are probably of even greater significance in the rest of Eastern Europe than they are in Germany. The two that will be discussed here are industrial policy and ownership and control of enterprises. Much of the activity of the Treuhand can be viewed as an attempt to reconcile the interests of individual firms with those of regions and industries as a whole. In particular, the emphasis on investment and employment conditionality was viewed as a response to problems of reversibility of corporate policies that act against the local or industrial interest. That concern becomes more relevant when one is talking about whole nations rather than regions of an economy.

While investment requirements can be used as a method of committing purchasers to take account of broader interests in relation to assets under negotiation, it cannot bind purchasers to the longer-term interests of localities in relation to investments that have not yet even been contemplated. In other words, there is no system of investment and employment requirements that can effectively ensure congruence of interest of firms and nations in long-term corporate strategy. That is why nationality of ownership matters. What the German system of corporate ownership and control largely through the supervisory board has been very successful in doing is internalizing the externalities that exist across firms within a nation.

The implication of this is that, in the long term, an important function of the Treuhandanstalt has been to integrate East Germany into the German pattern of ownership and control. Control is gradually being devolved from the Treuhandanstalt via supervisory boards to German industry and banks. In contrast,

---

1. For an assessment of the cost of the Treuhand, see *DIW Wochenbericht,* no. 7 (1992): 63–68; and Carlin and Mayer (1992).

auctions merely transfer ownership to those who have the best access to financial resources. In the case of Eastern Europe, that means Western firms: credit constraints on East European investors prevent control from being retained domestically. The solution is not simply to provide finance; what is required is the development of self-sufficient organizations. Once credible enterprises have been created, then finance will flow naturally. What is lacking are the mechanisms by which autonomous enterprises can be created.

One of the lessons to be learned from the Treuhandanstalt experience is that the establishment of control structures does not require preexisting managerial resources. As the previous sections have mentioned, East Germany has often simply purchased managerial and supervisory services from mainly West German firms. They could equally well have come from any country. The social obligation felt by West German managers and banks may have allowed East German firms to purchase their services at below-market rates, but that is all. The purchase of foreign services does not involve the loss of ownership and control because there is no investment; finance is only raised once the necessary management skills have been acquired, and then funds can be purchased in the form of debt rather than equity with no effect on ownership and control.

The central objection to market sales therefore is that they fail to create appropriate control structures before finance is raised. The lesson that the Treuhandanstalt can provide is how these control structures can be established without allowing the abuses of state control to persist.

14.5   Conclusions

To date, the Treuhand has secured employment guarantees for 1 million of the initial 4 million employees in THA firms. The criteria by which this performance should be judged are unclear, and it is not the purpose of this paper to evaluate the success of the Treuhand. Instead, the paper has the more limited aim of examining how the THA has sought to sell firms subject to employment, regional, and industrial policy constraints imposed by the government. Auctions, be they simple auctions, auctions with employment subsidies, or auctions with investment and employment conditions attached, cannot readily attain those objectives. Instead, the functions of the Treuhandanstalt can be understood as a response to the problems associated with auctions.

Six central functions of the Treuhand have been identified. It establishes the social value of firms; it disposes of uneconomic activities; it creates supervisory boards; it finds prospective buyers; it evaluates them; and it imposes investment and employment conditions.

These functions lend the Treuhandanstalt an important role in managing the transition process. In the last part of the paper, a longer-term effect of the East German approach was suggested. The creation of supervisory boards and the training of East German managers are gradually permitting the evolution of self-sufficient enterprises that can raise debt finance externally while retaining control over operations. In the longer term, the Treuhandanstalt is therefore devolving control not only to Western enterprises but also to East German firms themselves.

The transition issues and the reconciliation of social objectives of employment and regional policy are as relevant to Eastern Europe as they are to East Germany. The longer-term issue of ownership and control is probably of greater relevance to the rest of Eastern Europe: in the German case, control remains within Germany; in other countries, control may not be retained domestically. The approach of the Treuhandanstalt suggests that effective corporate control structures can be created without adequate managerial resources being available domestically.

References

Akerlof, George, Helga Hessenius, Andrew Rose, and Janet Yellen. 1991. East Germany in from the cold: The economic aftermath of currency union. *Brookings Papers on Economic Activity,* no. 1:1–87.

Carlin, Wendy, and Colin Mayer. 1992. Restructuring enterprises in Eastern Europe. *Economic Policy,* no. 15:311–52.

Deutsches Institut für Wirtschaftsforschung. 1991/1992. *Wochenbericht* (Berlin).

Heimpold, Gerhard, Harald Kroll, and Manfred Wilhelm. 1991. Privatisierung in den neuen Bundesländer—Bestandsaufnahme und Perspektiven (Privatization in the new federal states—stocktaking and perspectives). Forschungsreihe, no. 14/91. Berlin: Institut für angewandte Wirtschaftsforschung.

Kühl, Jürgen. 1991. Beschäftigungspolitische Wirkungen der Treuhandanstalt (Employment policy effects of the Treuhandanstalt). *WSI-Mitteilungen* 11:682–88.

———. 1992. Abgeschwächter Personalabbau in Treuhandunternehmen (The decline in personnel in Treuhand firms diminishes). IAB Kurzbericht, no. 2. Nürnberg: Institut für Arbeitsmarkt- und Berufsforschung der Bundesanstalt für Arbeit.

Mayhew, Ken, and Paul Seabright. 1992. 'Incentives and the management of enterprises in economic transition: Capital markets are not enough. *Oxford Review of Economic Policy* 8:105–29.

McKinsey & Co. and Arthur D. Little, for the Treuhandanstalt. 1991. *Unternehmenskonzepte für die Großchemie (Leuna, Buna, Bitterfeld, Wolfen): Abschlußbericht* (Business plans for large enterprises in the chemical industry [Leuna, Buna, Bitterfeld, Wolfen]: Final report). Berlin.

Sinn, Gerlinde, and Hans-Werner Sinn. 1991. *Kaltstart: Volkswirtschaftliche Aspekte der deutschen Vereinigung* (Jump start: Economic aspects of German unification). Tübingen: J. C. B. Mohr (Paul Siebeck).

Treuhandanstalt. 1990. Leitlinien der Geschäftspolitik der Treuhandanstalt (Guidelines for the business policy of the Treuhandanstalt). Internal document. Berlin.

———. 1991a. *Informationen: Wirtschaftsnachrichten aus der Treuhandanstalt* (Information: Economic news from the Treuhandanstalt). Berlin.

———. 1991b. Richtlinie für die Privatisierung von Betrieben (Guidelines for the privatization of enterprises). Internal document. Berlin.

———. Zentrales Beteiligungscontrolling. 1991c. Entflechtung (Deglomeration). Internal document. Berlin.

Comment   Wilhelm Nölling

The very interesting paper presented by Wendy Carlin and Colin Mayer has two objectives. On the basis of a case study, they paint a clear picture of the complex tasks facing the Treuhandanstalt, which started with over 4 million employees and was thus the largest holding ever to exist. Carlin and Mayer then discuss the important question of the significance of this "German model" for the other countries of Eastern Europe.

The key role of the Treuhandanstalt was and is to cushion the destructive effects of the 300 percent or more appreciation and total exposure to worldwide competition. Its activities are greatly influenced by the following factors: (*a*) the millions of property restitution claims lodged by West German citizens; (*b*) the strong investment incentives that are being financed directly out of public funds from West Germany and the EC; (*c*) the terrible environmental pollution caused by East German industry; (*d*) the fact that wages increased so rapidly; (*e*) the continued movement of skilled labor to the West; and (*f*) the lack of accountable ownership, which means that there is no effective control of the use of public funds.

At present, the functions of the Treuhandanstalt are as follows: monitoring whether the conditions imposed on enterprises that have already been privatized (e.g., employment and investment obligations) have been fulfilled; closing enterprises that cannot be restructured; and privatizing as well as maintaining and restructuring, the remaining portfolio of Treuhandanstalt enterprises. A new approach, however, is being contemplated, consisting of three additional methods: (1) allowing bids for whole sectors, such as furniture; (2) involving investment firms, banks, and insurance companies (privatization would then rest with them); (3) founding so-called *Managementgesellschaften,* in which the THA would have only a minority interest (it would be their job to privatize or to consolidate certain parts of the Treuhand portfolio).

Carlin and Mayer mentioned three alternatives to THA policy. These are straightforward auctions, auctions with the provision of employment subsidies, and auctions with provisions for investment and employment guarantees. Finally, they argue that current THA practice is superior to these alternatives.

Auction and participation models have so far not been put into practice, first, because these models were proposed too late in the day and, second, because there were hardly any East German enterprises that offered credible profitability prospects. In addition, the participation model has intrinsic technical difficulties such as time-consuming valuation procedures, denomination of shares, the question of to whom to distribute shares (the issue of social justice), and the guaranteeing of dividends. There is a real danger that such securities would prove worthless and that the whole idea of participation would be regarded as fraudulent.

Guided by experience, theoretical considerations, and an awareness of the vast scope and time scale required in order to approach privatization, the Treuhandanstalt adopted the only rational and economically feasible approach left open. Nonetheless, the task of adjusting policies in the second half of 1991 proved quite difficult. (1) It came as a surprise to many of us when the Treuhandanstalt conceded that it no longer aims to privatize all enterprises in full but is willing to retain minority ownership. In a large number of cases, it has indeed retained a minority stake—something that it had previously refused to do. (2) The THA greatly intensified its efforts to sell to foreign investors and regionalized its operations. (3) Reluctantly, the Treuhandanstalt agreed to participate in special job-creation schemes and training organizations created within the enterprises it administers. Carlin and Mayer fail to examine this aspect, even though it has major implications for the labor market as well as for overall policy (i.e., with regard to the postponement of closures).

In their paper, Carlin and Mayer focus primarily on the role of the Treuhandanstalt in reconstruction. This could lead to the false impression that the Treuhandanstalt generally accords greater priority to reconstruction than to privatization. The Unification Agreement commissions the Treuhandanstalt to "restructure along competitive lines and privatize the former state-owned enterprises." This, however, does not imply any preordained sequence on the part of the government. The Treuhandanstalt has consistently given priority to privatization. It has not tired of emphasizing this fact and has acted accordingly.

If the Treuhandanstalt were to devote major efforts to restructuring, it could easily become a lasting repository for inefficient enterprises—and a bottomless pit for state subsidies. Even under the present policy, the Treuhandanstalt has no choice but to incur gigantic debts that will prevent the stabilization of government finances for years to come.

In view of the large number of enterprises still awaiting privatization in East Germany, there is no alternative but to privatize as much as possible as quickly as possible. A factor that is often overlooked is that the Treuhandanstalt is not in a position to evaluate, monitor, and revise vast numbers of business development plans.

Is "retention of domestic control" an important criterion? In my view, this approach has numerous pitfalls: (i) Enterprises that can be rescued (including those currently making losses) should be transferred immediately to private ownership. Investors whose capital is at risk will take a more realistic view of the necessary restructuring tasks. Investors who reach the wrong conclusions lose *their own money*. The deferment of privatization merely places an added burden on state finances and slows down the restructuring process. (ii) In view of the four decades during which East Germany had no real experience of private ownership of the means of production, there are only three economically viable options for achieving effective local ownership and control: management buyouts; the subsequent sale of residual stakes held by the Treuhandanstalt to the local population; and the restitution of business enterprises to their former owners. (iii) The emergence of large numbers of new small- and medium-sized companies—which could gradually develop into larger units—will help strengthen the local industrial base in the former East Germany.

What are the prospects? (1) As referred to earlier, privatization has proceeded at a fairly rapid pace in certain branches. (2) An increasing number of companies whose products are no longer in demand in East Germany and/or whose markets disappeared with the collapse of the CMEA (Council for Mutual Economic Assistance) are being closed down. (3) Some 5,700 companies are still waiting for action to be taken and are uncertain about whether they face closure. This year, the Treuhandanstalt intends to keep up the rapid pace of privatization achieved in 1991. However, this will prove an even more difficult task as it is reasonable to assume that the companies with the best business prospects have already been privatized. (4) The Treuhandanstalt will continue to hold companies that are in the red within certain branches or regions, either because there is reason to be optimistic about the prospects of reorganization or because current employment or regional policies weigh against closure. In such cases, huge subsidies are required in order to fund technological modernization and/or update training and management as well as to reorganize auditing and to cover losses.

On the basis of these perspectives, it appears that, on the one hand, the tasks of the Treuhandanstalt have become more difficult and complex while, on the other, its work in particular regions or branches could soon be completed—or indeed has already been completed.

Privatization in Eastern Europe and the Lessons of Privatization in East Germany

Privatization does not seem to have made major progress in Eastern Europe. In these countries, we are still witnessing the very earliest stages of privatization. By contrast with East Germany, the economies of the East European countries are not in such a desolate condition or state of collapse because they are not subject to the fatal overnight exposure to worldwide competition. This leads me to conclude that the governments in these countries have more time to enact privatization policies than was available in East Germany. However, the uniqueness of the East German economic reforms lies in the existence of a common language, a common heritage, and the maintenance of many family ties as well as the massive transfer of management skills in the private and public sectors. These are all important advantages that do not pertain elsewhere.

What recommendations can be made on the basis of the German experience? (1) The motto must be, Privatize at virtually any cost. In other words, privatize as much as possible and as quickly as possible. With regard to enterprises that are not yet privatized and that are deemed to have potential, the same policy should be pursued as in East Germany. (2) As in East Germany, the necessary conditions for privatization must be created and made viable in the truest sense. Market-oriented structures must be developed—in particular, clear legislation on property rights and the creation of free-market controls and institutions as well as the removal of investment and wage structure disincentives. Large state-owned enterprises must be divided up and reorganized. (3) As far as lessons for East Europe's privatization are concerned, I would like to emphasize the following. We are all well aware that these countries need wider access to Western markets as well as massive debt relief. Unless these absolutely necessary conditions are fulfilled, it is difficult to conceive that new, stable, market-oriented, capitalist economies will become established in our lifetime.

Discussion Summary

Colin Mayer agreed with Wilhelm Nölling's suggestion that companies should be moved out of Treuhand control as fast as possible. Mayer emphasized that the Treuhand has pursued this goal while simultaneously trying to minimize the associated social cost of the economic restructuring.

Jan Winiecki criticized the recommendations for the rest of Eastern Europe that the authors had drawn on the basis of the Treuhand experience. He said that the Treuhand's supervisory boards had been so successful because they were populated with West German managers. Such highly skilled supervisory boards could not be replicated in countries like Poland. Winiecki concluded by proposing several lessons that the authors had not noted. He said that the Treuhand had demonstrated the advantage of splitting companies and financially restructuring them before privatization.

Andrew Berg and *Stanley Fischer* also suggested that many of the Treuhand's most successful features would be difficult to replicate in the rest of Eastern Europe. Berg emphasized that the Treuhand has the benefit of having relatively easy access to West German financial capital. Fischer stressed the Treuhand's access to West German financial and managerial expertise.

In response to the warnings about the difficulty of replicating the Treuhand's success in other East European countries, Mayer said that these countries could hire the necessary trained personnel from the West. Moreover, he noted, this hiring would be limited to the extent that such personnel would be needed only for some of the positions on supervisory boards, not for day-to-day management of the companies in question. He emphasized that only 10 percent of the managers of East German firms have been brought in from West Germany and that, to date, almost all the MBOs (management buyouts) have been implemented by East German managers.

András Simon noted that the principles of the Hungarian State Property Agency are similar to those of the Treuhand. In particular, both bodies have been given the tasks of opening up balance sheets, commercializing companies, creating control structures, and setting up viable restructured firms. However, he noted that there are also contrasts between the German and the Hungarian approaches. In Hungary, there is less emphasis on implicit employment subsidies because the relatively low real wage suggests that the unemployment problem will be less severe. In addition, the Hungarians have not implemented a policy of debt cancellations.

Simon identified two fundamental problems in Hungary that suggest that the privatization process in Hungary will evolve more slowly than that in East Germany. First, Hungary faces logistical constraints because it does not have access to resources like those in Germany (e.g., trained personnel and a working body of commercial laws). He estimated that, on their own, these logistical constraints put Hungary two or three years behind East Germany. Second, Hungary lacks a social structure that could support a capitalist economy. Hungary has neither savers nor entrepreneurs. He said that Hungary needs a class of risk takers who are willing to manage firms in which they have a personal stake. He estimated that creating a "capitalist society" will take five to fifteen years.

Jeffrey Sachs suggested that the record of the Treuhand did not bode well for other East European countries like Poland. He noted that East German restructuring has taken place in the best possible circumstances: the German government is relatively strong and immune from local politics, and Germany has a very successful monetary policy with a completely independent central bank. Even with these advantages, Sachs noted, the restructuring of East Germany has been accompanied by substantial rent seeking, exemplified by state subsidies that have been channeled through institutions like the Treuhand to support and validate rapid East-West wage equalization. Sachs noted that this outcome may be satisfactory in Germany, where it is possible each year to transfer 75 percent of East German GNP from West Germany. But this option is not available to other East European countries, which have weak governments that face enormous demands on very limited resources. Sachs concluded that the Treuhand structure did not adequately immunize the state from political pressure.

Rudiger Dornbusch responded to Sachs by noting that the policy of wage equalization was actually a deliberate social strategy and hence did not reflect badly on the restructuring process. *Janet Yellen* offered a different twist on this argument. She suggested that one of the interesting attributes of the Treuhand is that the agency has enabled the German government to mask the scope of the massive transfers that are taking place. Yellen said much of the Treuhand's costs arise off budget, like allowing newly privatized firms to sell off land. She believes that the German public would resist transparent expenditures as large as the hidden costs that the Treuhand is accepting. Dornbusch also suggested an unusual strength of the Treuhand. Because the agency uses a variety of mechanisms, it cannot be accused of choosing exactly the wrong one. He noted that, elsewhere in Eastern Europe, the debate over which mechanism is precisely right has enervated the privatization process.

Philippe Aghion suggested that it may be optimal to have more than one privatization agency. Increasing the number of agencies decreases the likelihood of regulatory capture. However, with too many agencies, economies of scale are lost. Aghion conjectured that there may be an optimal number of agencies that balances these two effects.

Jacek Rostowski said that Mayer's conclusion that the Treuhand has pursued a strategy that minimizes the social cost of restructuring was a "Panglossian ex post rationalization." Rostowski suggested that the Treuhand has been successful because it has taken the easy path of distributing the gains from privatization unevenly.

Mayer concluded the discussion by arguing that pragmatic institutions like the Treuhand may end up performing better than hypothetically optimal institutions devised by economists.

15 The Economics of Bankruptcy Reform

Philippe Aghion, Oliver Hart, and John Moore

Following the rapid demise of socialism, East European countries have been grappling with the question of what kind of market economy is best suited to their future needs.[1] Should they incorporate capitalism wholesale, and, if so, which kind: American, European, Japanese, or some new version? How should problems of the transition be handled? What kinds of institutional structures and laws are most appropriate for their situation?

This paper is concerned with an aspect of this last question: the choice of bankruptcy law. The decision facing East European countries on this question is both important and far from straightforward. It is generally recognized by economists and lawyers in the West that bankruptcy law has an important role to play in ensuring a timely resolution of the problems of insolvent or financially distressed firms and a socially efficient disposition of such firms' assets. Yet both practitioners and academics are dissatisfied with current Western procedures, which are thought either to cause the liquidation of healthy firms (as in Chapter 7 of the U.S. Bankruptcy Code) or to be inefficient and biased toward reorganization under incumbent management (as in Chapter 11 in the United States). Nor is there any consensus about how to improve these procedures. Thus, it is far from obvious that East European countries should simply pick "the best available Western procedure" (whatever that may be).

In this paper, we describe a new bankruptcy procedure that we believe

The authors thank Stuart Gilson, Leo Herzel, Bengt Holmstrom, John Kihn, Shan Li, Lynn LoPucki, Jay Ritter, Roberta Romano, Andrei Shleifer, Jeremy Stein, David Webb, Philip Wood, and two referees for their help and comments. They acknowledge financial support from the National Science Foundation, the United Kingdom Economic and Social Research Council, and the International Financial Services Research Center at the Massachusetts Institute of Technology. This paper is reprinted, with a new appendix, from *The Journal of Law, Economics, and Organization* (8, no. 3 [1992]: 523–46), © Oxford University Press.

1. Throughout the paper, *Eastern Europe* is used as shorthand for *Eastern Europe and the former Soviet Union*.

avoids some of the main pitfalls of existing procedures. While the stimulus for this proposal comes from the current situation of East European countries, we should emphasize that the proposal is potentially just as relevant for Western countries that are trying to improve existing procedures. We should also point out that our procedure is designed to be effective in the new post-transition-to-capitalism Eastern Europe, rather than being concerned directly with the transition process itself.

Our procedure is a simple one. First, when a firm goes bankrupt, all the firm's existing debts are canceled, and an individual—a judge, say—is appointed to supervise the procedure. This individual has two immediate tasks: task A is to solicit cash and noncash bids for all or part of the "new" firm (which at this juncture is all equity); task B is to allocate rights to the equity in this new firm among the former claimholders. These two tasks could be carried out in parallel and completed within a prespecified period of time: for example, three to four months. After this, the new shareholders—that is, the former claimholders who now hold shares—vote on which bid to select. The successful bid may be a cash bid (which corresponds to a liquidation or a sale of the firm) or a noncash bid. Noncash bids allow for reorganization and/or recapitalization of the firm as a going concern. For example, the old managers might propose that they keep their jobs and that each current shareholder receive a share in the postbankruptcy firm. Or the same financial arrangement might be offered by a new management team. A third possibility is that management (old or new) might induce some leverage in the postbankruptcy firm by proposing to borrow from the capital market and to offer each current shareholder a combination of cash and equity in the (leveraged) firm. After the vote, the firm exits from bankruptcy.

In essence, our proposed scheme is a decentralized variant on Chapter 7, in which noncash (as well as cash) bids are allowed and ownership of the firm is homogenized (to all equity) so that the owners can decide (by vote) which of the bids to accept.[2] However, insofar as noncash bids allow for reorganization/recapitalization, our proposal can also be viewed as a decentralized version of Chapter 11, in which conflicts of interest among different claimant groups are avoided through the homogenization of ownership.

We think that our procedure strikes the right balance between liquidation and reorganization. Unlike Chapter 7, the procedure gives claimholders the option of maintaining the firm as a going concern if the company's bad fortunes are the result of bad luck rather than bad management. Unlike Chapter 11, the procedure creates a (roughly) level playing field in which incumbent management is not advantaged in the reorganization process.

The paper is organized as follows. In section 15.1, we examine the need

---

2. What is less essential to our scheme is the precise mechanism by which rights to equity in the firm are allocated (task B). The main version of our procedure uses an allocation scheme developed by Lucian Bebchuk (1988). In sec. 15.5, however, we present some alternative mechanisms for allocating equity.

for a statutory bankruptcy procedure. In section 15.2, we discuss a number of procedures that either are used in practice worldwide or have been proposed in the literature. In section 15.3, we lay out our new procedure. We assess our scheme in section 15.4. In section 15.5, we present some alternative mechanisms that might be used for allocating equity. In section 15.6, we discuss certain key ancillary issues, such as claims disputes, the treatment of secured creditors, and the need for debtor-in-possession financing. Finally, in section 15.7, we raise some questions concerning the feasibility of our scheme in the current environment of Eastern Europe. In an appendix, we briefly survey what is happening now in two of the countries of Eastern Europe—Hungary and Poland.

15.1   The Role of Bankruptcy Procedure

It is generally accepted by lawyers and economists that the state has an important role in enforcing private contracts. The point is that, while ex ante two parties may find a contractual arrangement mutually beneficial, ex post one of them may have an incentive to breach. Thus, it is in the interests of both parties that a third party—the state—have the power to enforce contractual performance or to compel the breaching party to compensate the victim by paying money damages.

A debt contract is a particular kind of contract where one party, the debtor D, borrows money from another party, the creditor C, and in return promises C a (typically larger) payment in the future. If D defaults (i.e., breaches), C has two main remedies at his disposal (outside bankruptcy). First, in the case of a secured loan, C can seize the assets that serve as collateral for the loan. Second, in the case of an unsecured loan, C can sue D and can call on the clerk of the court (or the sheriff) to enforce the court's judgment, possibly by selling the debtor's assets (see Baird and Jackson 1985, 2).

This method of debt collection seems fairly uncontroversial when there is only a small number of creditors or when the debtor has sufficient assets to cover his liabilities.[3] However, problems arise if there are many creditors and the debtor's assets are less than his liabilities (i.e., he is insolvent). Under these conditions, as Jackson (1986) among others has emphasized, creditors will waste resources trying to be first to seize their collateral or to obtain a judgment against the debtor. Also, this race by creditors to be first may lead to the dismantling of the firm's assets and to a loss of value for all creditors if the firm is worth more as a whole than as a collection of pieces.

Given this, it is in the collective interest of creditors—and society too—that

---

3. An exception should be mentioned. This is where the debtor is an individual whose wealth would be reduced to close to zero if creditors could seize his assets. Part of (personal) bankruptcy law is concerned with providing such individuals with protection from their creditors. In this paper, we are interested in the debts of firms, not individuals, and so will not deal with this issue directly.

the disposition of the debtor's assets be carried out in an orderly manner, via a centralized bankruptcy procedure.

Of course, in an ideal world, there would be no need for the state to set up its own bankruptcy procedure: individuals could do it by themselves. That is, a debtor who borrows from a creditor could specify as part of the debt contract how his assets will be divided among various creditors (and the debtor himself) in the event of a default or insolvency. Writing such a contract is likely to be very difficult and costly, however, particularly since the debtor may acquire different types of assets and new creditors as time passes, and it may be very hard to specify how the division process should change as a function of such developments. Moreover, in practice, contracts like this are not written.[4] Thus, it seems likely that many parties will choose to take advantage of the bankruptcy mechanism provided by the state; moreover, even if, by some chance, a substantial number of parties choose to make their own arrangements, society must still deal with those parties who make no arrangements at all.[5]

15.2 Existing Bankruptcy Procedures

We turn now to bankruptcy procedures that either are used in practice or have been proposed in the literature. It is useful to classify them under four broad headings: (1) auctions, (2) structured bargaining, (3) administration, and (4) automatic financial restructuring.

15.2.1 Auctions

If the only problem with a standard debt collection scheme were that it led to inefficient "grab" behavior by creditors, then the obvious solution would be for a trustee or receiver to supervise the sale of the firm's assets and distribute the proceeds according to the priority of creditors' claims. This is essentially a description of Chapter 7 in the United States and of U.K. bankruptcy law prior to the 1986 Insolvency Act.[6]

A widespread concern with a Chapter 7–type proceeding, however, is that viable companies will be sold off at a substantial discount in a piecemeal liquidation. Some law and economics scholars (e.g., Baird 1986) have argued that this concern is misplaced because there is nothing to stop someone bidding for the company as a going concern: if the whole is really worth more than the

---

4. This may be because current laws do not allow parties to opt out of the state's bankruptcy procedure.

5. Of course, it does not follow from this that the costs of providing a bankruptcy mechanism for firms in financial distress should be paid for out of general taxation; arguably, firms that want to take advantage of such a mechanism should be forced to pay a fee (presumably before they get into financial distress!).

6. The German bankruptcy code also has the flavor of Chapter 7 in that it favors liquidation over reorganization. A debtor firm can avoid liquidation only if at least 35 percent of its creditors can be repaid *in cash* and the reorganization plan is approved by three-fourths (in value terms) of the unsecured creditors (see Mitchell 1990).

parts, then a bid for the whole will dominate a set of independent bids for the parts. These scholars have gone on to argue that, because of this, Chapter 7 is indeed the best bankruptcy procedure: it is simple, it avoids protracted bargaining and litigation, and it leads to an efficient outcome.[7]

While the argument of these scholars has some merit, the conclusion that a competitive auction will inevitably lead a firm to be sold to the highest-willingness-to-pay bidder at its (maximized) value is extreme. Auctions work well if raising cash for bids is easy and there is plenty of competition among bidders. However, even in the most advanced Western economies, these conditions often will not be met, and they are even less likely to be satisfied in Eastern Europe.[8]

Consider first what we shall call the *financing problem*. Imagine that a huge company like IBM were put on the block. (In Eastern Europe, where markets are less well developed, similar problems could arise with a much smaller company.) Say that the expected present value of IBM's earnings is $100 billion. Would any bidder be prepared to offer this much for the company? The answer to this question might well be no. One way to raise $100 billion is to approach a large number of small investors through what is in effect a public offering, but this is likely to be difficult given the time scale of an auction like Chapter 7. A more practical way is to raise the money from a few large institutions/investors (possibly with a view to going public later). The problem with this strategy is that (at least in the short run) these investors will be bearing substantial risk and so will be prepared to buy IBM only at a discount.[9]

We should emphasize that the financing problem that we are identifying here is not to do with management having private information about the firm's value (and being unable to verify it to the market). Rather, it is to do with the transactions costs associated with assembling a suitable group of investors to be risk bearers for the new firm. But notice that there is a natural group of risk bearers

7. Some scholars would push the argument for Chapter 7 still further. The piecemeal liquidation value of a firm may sometimes exceed its going-concern value. This could happen if the firm is inefficiently large but managers have been unwilling to split it up, possibly because they enjoy the perquisites of power. A Chapter 7 auction is then a good way of realizing value for creditors and shareholders.

8. One might ask why it matters how much shareholders and creditors receive in an auction as long as the firm's assets end up in their highest-value use. There are two reasons why shareholder and creditor receipts do matter. First, the more the firm's claimants receive in bankruptcy states, the more the firm's claims will sell for initially, and the greater the incentive the firm's founders will have in setting up the firm. Second, in the absence of a competitive auction, the winning bidder may not be the highest-value user of the firm's assets; that is, a competitive auction serves an important screening role in ensuring that the assets are indeed transferred to their best use.

9. The costs of financing a cash bid are akin to the costs of an initial public offering (IPO), which can be significant. For example, Ritter (1987) investigates two quantifiable components of the costs of going public: direct expenses and underpricing. From a sample of firms that were taken public by investment bankers in the United States during 1977–82, he finds that these two costs together averaged between 21 and 32 percent of the realized market value of the securities issued, depending on the type of IPO. The underpricing effect can be attributed to the risk aversion of issuers/investment bankers, in conjunction with various forms of asymmetric information (see, e.g., Rock 1986).

at hand: the former claimants (who were, after all, the previous risk bearers). Transactions costs would be reduced if bidders could reach this group directly by offering them securities in the postbankruptcy company. This is not allowed for in cash-only auctions like Chapter 7, but it is a key feature of Chapter 11 (see below) and also of the procedure that we propose in section 16.3.[10]

A second reason for doubting the efficiency of a Chapter 7 proceeding concerns what we shall call the *lack-of-competition problem*. Although there may be many *potential* bidders who could in principle raise the necessary funds, not all of them may participate. Preparing a bid is a costly and time-consuming process.[11] Unfortunately, only the winning bidder will recoup his costs, and this deters entry. In fact, in extreme cases, it may be an equilibrium for just one bidder to enter the auction and win with a low price because all other potential bidders realize that entry would cause such a fierce competition that everyone would make losses.

As Shleifer and Vishny (1992) have recently pointed out, both the financing problem and the lack-of-competition problem are likely to be exacerbated to the extent that the natural bidders for a bankrupt firm are other firms in the same industry; these firms may also be suffering financial distress and may therefore find it hard to raise capital.[12]

15.2.2   Structured Bargaining

If auctions cannot be relied on, what are the other possibilities? Many countries have tried to provide a framework within which claimants can bargain about the future of the firm, that is, decide by structured negotiation whether it should be liquidated or reorganized. A leading example of this in the West is Chapter 11 of the U.S. Bankruptcy Code.

The details of Chapter 11 are complicated, but the basic idea is the following: claimholders are grouped into classes according to the type of claim they have; committees or trustees are appointed to represent each class; and a judge supervises a process of bargaining among the committees to determine a plan of action for the firm, together with a division of value. During the process, incumbent management usually runs the firm. An important part of the proce-

---

10. Note that we are not denying that managerial private information can also cause financing problems. For example, suppose that IBM's management knows that the company is worth $100 billion but the market does not. Then management may be unable to raise $100 billion to make a cash bid, and the company could be sold inefficiently. Unfortunately, it is not clear that this problem lies in the province of bankruptcy law (nor is it clear that the law can help). As we argued in sec. 15.1, the rationale for bankruptcy law is to deal with collective-action problems among creditors, yet this asymmetric information problem would arise even if there were a single creditor.

11. For a compelling account of the cost of a bidding process, see Burrough and Helyar (1990) on the RJR Nabisco leveraged buyout.

12. Shleifer and Vishny's point is supported by evidence from LoPucki and Whitford (1992, sec. IV), who find that, in the forty-three largest U.S. bankruptcy cases between 1979 and 1988, *all* asset sales were to existing companies, usually within the same line of business.

dure is that a plan can be implemented if it receives approval by a suitable majority of each claimant class: unanimity is not required.[13]

We believe that there are serious theoretical and practical problems with Chapter 11 (and similar procedures). At a theoretical level, Chapter 11 mixes two decisions together: the decision of who should get what (i.e., whose debt should be forgiven, and by how much), and the decision of what should be done with the firm (should it be liquidated or reorganized, and, if reorganized, who should manage it, and what should be its new financial structure). This latter decision creates an additional dimension of conflict. For example, senior creditors may press for liquidation (since they will then be paid off for sure), whereas junior claimants may hold out for reorganization (since they enjoy the upside potential but not the downside risk). There are already reasons to think that bargaining may break down when agents negotiate over a *given* pie (e.g., if there is asymmetric information among the agents); matters are merely made worse by having a further conflict of interest over *which* pie should be chosen.

In addition, placing decisions in the hands of representatives—and indeed the supervising judge—creates agency problems. Since individuals on shareholder and creditor committees own only a small fraction of the equity and debt themselves, they are unlikely to devote the socially efficient level of resources to figuring out what a good reorganization plan is. This may leave the one informed group—management—with considerable power to tilt the outcome of the bargaining toward reorganization (and the retention of their jobs). Judges too can use their supervisory powers to pursue their own agendas, which may be in conflict with the claimants' narrow objective of value maximization.

The empirical evidence appears to support the theoretical view that Chapter 11 is imperfect. We mention a few relevant findings. (i) Chapter 11 can take a great deal of time.[14] (ii) During this time, there can be a serious loss in value—because of managerial distraction, incompetence, or negligence; forgone investment opportunities; or a drop in demand (either because competitors be-

13. Specifically, for a plan to be agreed to, it must receive approval by a two-thirds majority in value terms (and a simple majority in number terms) of each debt class and a two-thirds majority of equity—although under certain circumstances a plan can be forced on a class (the cram-down provision).

A similar system to Chapter 11 operates in Japan. Reorganization plans are drafted by a trustee appointed by the court; the court can amend the plan in consultation with the interested parties; for a plan to be ratified, it must receive four-fifths of secured creditors' approval and two-thirds of unsecured creditors' approval (shareholders cannot veto); if the plan is not ratified, the company is liquidated (see Mitchell 1990).

14. Flynn (1989) finds that nearly two-thirds of Chapter 11 confirmations occur in the second and third years after filing. LoPucki and Whitford (1992) find that the largest bankruptcy cases ($100 million plus) spend an average of two to three years in Chapter 11. Gilson, John, and Lang (1990) report a similar figure for exchange-listed companies in Chapter 11 between 1978 and 1987.

have more aggressively or because customers lose confidence).[15] Also, suppliers may be unwilling to extend credit.[16] (iii) The procedure involves significant legal and administrative costs.[17] (iv) The procedure appears to be soft on management.[18] (v) Chapter 11 judges sometimes abuse their discretionary powers.[19]

15.2.3   Administration

An alternative to structured bargaining is to appoint a "benign dictator"— that is, to appoint an administrator who, through the court, has authority to decide which parts of the firm should be sold off and which parts (if any) maintained as a going concern. This is roughly the way the French system operates.[20] (It is also roughly the way Chapter X of the old U.S. Bankruptcy Act operated prior to 1978.) Administration avoids many of the costs of Chapter 11 and is far less likely to be a soft option for management (insofar as management is no longer in charge of the firm). However, a lot of power is placed in the hands of the judge and administrator, who may have little or no background or expertise in the firm's operations and little or no financial incentive to make the right decisions about the firm's future. We know of no systematic empirical work that evaluates the administration procedure, but there are certainly theoretical reasons for being skeptical about it.[21]

15. A spectacular example of loss in value is provided by Eastern Airlines, which suffered operating losses of around $1.6 billion while in Chapter 11 from March 1989 until January 1991 (see Weiss 1991). In examining the Texaco Chapter 11 bankruptcy (resulting from the Texaco-Pennzoil litigation), Cutler and Summers (1988) discovered losses of over $3 billion, which may be attributable to the costs of financial distress. Other studies of the (indirect) costs of financial distress include Altman (1984), Baldwin and Mason (1983), White (1983), and Wruck (1990).

16. Roe (1983, n. 2) cites the cases of Food Fair Inc., Wickes, and AM International, in which customers and, particularly, suppliers refused to trade with the companies after they had filed for bankruptcy, causing serious revenue losses. However, Chapter 11 also plays an important role in facilitating debtor-in-possession financing, whereby suppliers' credit is placed ahead of existing (unsecured) senior debt. (For more on debtor-in-possession financing, see sec. 15.6.4 below.)

17. In a sample of New York and American Stock Exchange firms that filed for bankruptcy between 1979 and 1986, Weiss (1990) estimated these direct costs to be 3.1 percent of the book value of debt plus market value of equity (measured prior to bankruptcy).

18. Gilson (1989, 1990), Gilson and Vetsuypens (1992), LoPucki and Whitford (1992), and Betker (1992) show that senior managers often suffer as a result of their firms entering Chapter 11. However, we think that the proper comparison should be between how these managers are treated in Chapter 11 and how they would have been treated in Chapter 7. In the latter, one can presume that far more of them would have lost their jobs (and far more quickly). So, *relative to Chapter 7*, Chapter 11 is likely to be a soft option.

19. Weiss (1991) argues persuasively that the presiding judge in the case of Eastern Airlines was quite determined to maintain the company in business despite huge losses incurred while in Chapter 11. LoPucki and Whitford (1992) cite the Chapter 11 bankruptcy cases of Johns-Manville and Evans Products to demonstrate the exercise of judicial power at the extreme.

20. Under the French bankruptcy law enacted in 1985, the court can accept a reorganization plan without the approval of creditors (or workers), provided that it best ensures the maintenance of employment and the repayment of creditors. (Note that these two objectives may be in conflict.) See Mitchell (1990).

21. Since 1986, the U.K. bankruptcy system has also made use of an administrator—although, compared to France, creditors have greater powers to reject the administrator's reorganization plan.

15.2.4   Automatic Financial Restructuring

So far we have discussed procedures that are used in practice. Another possibility, which has been suggested by some scholars, is that bankruptcy should merely trigger an automatic financial restructuring—for example, all debts could be converted into equity in some prespecified manner.[22] Then the decision whether to liquidate or reorganize would be left to management (possibly constrained by the market for corporate control).

We believe that this approach to bankruptcy is flawed because it ignores conflicts of interest between managers and shareholders. In practice, managers, who enjoy private benefits of control, may be unwilling to shrink or liquidate an unprofitable company of their own accord. Moreover, the market for corporate control may not work well enough to force them to do so.[23] Under these conditions, debt plays an important role in constraining or bonding managers to act in the interests of securityholders. Specifically, the managers of a highly leveraged firm face a choice: reduce slack, or go bankrupt.[24]

Of course, for the bonding role of debt to be effective, management must suffer a significant penalty for nonpayment of debts, that is, for going bankrupt. But, under an automatic financial restructuring, there is no penalty at all: managers are in effect allowed to postpone or cancel debts and to continue to run the firm as if nothing had happened!

The U.K. administration system is in a sense a cross between the French system and Chapter 11 in the United States. In the United Kingdom, a bankruptcy court issues an administrative order outlining particular goals to be achieved and appoints an administrator who takes control of the firm and, within three months, prepares a reorganization plan. Ratification of a plan requires approval by at least half (in value terms) of the (unsecured) creditors. In principle, the court could bypass a negative vote and proceed at its own discretion. However, in practice, if the vote is negative, the court either convenes another creditors' meeting or appoints a receiver who liquidates the firm (see e.g., Mitchell 1990; and Webb 1991).

22. For instance, using the scheme proposed by Bebchuk (1988). For more on Bebchuk's scheme, see below.

23. Even a very badly run firm may not be vulnerable to a (hostile) takeover. One reason is that a raider may have to share a large fraction of the takeover gains with shareholders of the target firm because (i) minority shareholders can free-ride on the raider's offer (see Grossman and Hart 1980) or (ii) rival bidders can free-ride on the information embodied in an initial offer and make a counteroffer. Hence, a raider may fail to cover the ex ante costs of making a bid. (The evidence does indeed show that most of the gains from a successful takeover accrue to shareholders of the target firm rather than to the acquiring firm [see Jensen and Ruback 1983].) Further factors deterring a raider are management's ability to engage in various defensive measures (lawsuits, poison pills, employee stock ownership plans) or, at the last moment, to carry out the actions the raider was planning to undertake.

An alternative mechanism for removing badly performing managers—or, more accurately, directors—is a proxy fight. However, incumbents have the upper hand in a proxy fight because (i) they can use company funds to fight their campaign, whereas an insurgent typically cannot, and (ii) there is inevitably an element of "the devil you know is better than the devil you don't" (the insurgent, after all, is not offering something tangible like cash).

Note finally that, in practice, large premiums of 30 percent or more are earned by shareholders of target firms in takeovers (see, e.g., Jensen and Ruback 1983). These premiums are consistent with the existence of substantial slack in target firms prior to a takeover.

24. On the bonding role of debt, see Grossman and Hart (1982) and Jensen (1986). For evidence that the bonding role of debt is important in practice, see Jensen (1986) and Hart (1993).

15.2.5   Summary

In sum, we see flaws in all four kinds of bankruptcy procedures that we have discussed. Auctions (like Chapter 7) can lead to inefficient liquidation at fire-sale prices. Structured bargaining (like Chapter 11) is unlikely to work with large numbers of claimants given that they have different objectives. Administration procedures (as in France) place too much control in the hands of one person, who may not have the necessary expertise. Automatic financial restructuring eliminates the bonding role of debt. Thus, it seems desirable to consider alternatives.[25]

15.3   A New Bankruptcy Procedure

A fully fledged analysis of bankruptcy would derive optimal bankruptcy procedure from first principles. Unfortunately, this is an extraordinarily difficult task, not least because, as we noted in section 15.1, in an ideal world there would be no need for a state procedure at all: debtors and creditors would choose their own bankruptcy procedure as part of an optimal debt contract.[26] What is really needed is a full theory of contractual incompleteness based on transactions costs, which we do not yet have. Thus, while we have tried to provide some foundations for our proposed bankruptcy procedure, what follows must be seen as quite tentative.

In broad terms, we think that a good bankruptcy procedure is one that meets two goals: goal 1 is that it maximizes the ex post value of the firm (with an

---

25. One argument that we have not dealt with runs as follows: why have a "good" bankruptcy procedure at all? After all, there is nothing to stop the interested parties from renegotiating to avoid bankruptcy. In fact, this is exactly what we see in prebankruptcy workouts between firms and their creditors. However, such workouts may fail—inter alia because of holdout and free-rider problems and asymmetries of information among claimants. In a study of the companies listed on the New York and American Stock Exchanges that were in severe financial distress during 1978–87, Gilson, John, and Lang (1990) found that workouts fail more than 50 percent of the time and are more likely to fail the larger the number of creditors (see also Gilson 1991).

In the last few years, "prepackaged" bankruptcies have emerged as a new hybrid form in the United States. These informal reorganizations—agreed on before entering into bankruptcy—avoid some of the costs of Chapter 11 but take advantage of the fact that within Chapter 11 a reorganization plan can be ratified by a smaller fraction of creditors than would be needed outside bankruptcy. (Hence a prepackaged bankruptcy may be easier to implement than a workout.) However, by no means all financially distressed firms can be rescued this way; as McConnell and Servaes (1991) conclude, "A pre-packaged bankruptcy . . . is not likely to be useful in resolving complex, litigious disputes among hundreds of creditor groups with sharply divergent interests—the kind we often see in a traditional, highly contentious Chapter 11 reorganization" (see also Gilson, John, and Lang 1990, sec. 2.3).

26. In an ideal world, parties can write "comprehensive" contracts. A comprehensive contract is one where, at the outset, everyone's obligations are sufficiently clearly stated that the contract never has to be renegotiated as the state of the world unfolds. (That is, if in equilibrium parties ever recontract ex post, then they could have built in the outcome of this renegotiation ex ante.) In the absence of comprehensive contracts—i.e., where contracts are "incomplete"—there will sometimes be occasion to renegotiate. In the present context, bankruptcy is a clear example of such an event.

appropriate distribution of this value across claimants); goal 2 is that it preserves the (ex ante) bonding role of debt by penalizing management adequately in bankruptcy states.

It is worth pointing out that goals 1 and 2 may be in conflict. For example, if 2 were the only issue, then there would be nothing wrong with a "nuke-the-firm" strategy: any firm that went bankrupt could simply be shut down. However, such a strategy may be disastrous in terms of 1: given the presence of uncertainty, even well-run firms will sometimes go bankrupt, and it would obviously be very inefficient to close them all down. Equally, if 1 were the only goal, incumbent managers might be retained a lot of the time on account of their special knowledge or skills, which would be bad in terms of 2.

We now outline our procedure. It is an attempt, first, to strike a balance between goal 1 and goal 2 and, second, to achieve a point on the "frontier" of feasible combinations—that is, to maximize ex post value, subject to an adequate amount of bonding.

15.3.1 The Proposed Procedure

At the outset, after the firm has declared (or been pushed into) bankruptcy, the firm's debts are canceled. The firm's creditors do not go away empty-handed, however; as described in task B below, they may well become significant shareholders. What matters is that the firm starts out life in bankruptcy essentially as a "new," all-equity company.

An individual—a judge, say—is appointed to supervise the process. The judge has two immediate tasks: task A is to solicit cash and noncash bids for the new all-equity firm, task B is to allocate rights to the shares in this firm. We anticipate that these tasks could be carried out in parallel and completed within a prespecified period of time; three months might be reasonable.

Task A: Soliciting Bids

The judge solicits bids for the firm's assets and proposals for the firm's continuing operations. That is, over the three-month period, individuals are encouraged to make cash bids for all or parts of the firm's operations; in addition, management teams (including the incumbent) are encouraged to make proposals for how to run the firm as a continuing entity.

In fact, it turns out that, in a formal sense, there is no real difference between a bid for the firm and a proposal to run the firm as a continuing entity, once we allow for *noncash* bids. For example, if management (either the incumbent team or a new one) proposes to maintain the firm as a going concern with an all-equity financial structure, this is equivalent to their making the following "bid" for the firm: "We are prepared to buy each share of the present firm for no cash down and one share in the (identical) postbankruptcy firm." Similarly, if management wishes to deviate from an all-equity financial structure for (future) tax or bonding reasons, it can arrange to borrow $D in the capital market and offer to buy each of the N shares of the present firm for $$D/N$ down and one share in the (leveraged) postbankruptcy firm. Another way for management to obtain leverage is to offer each shareholder a share *and* a bond in the postbankruptcy firm.

Thus, it is useful to think of the judge simply soliciting a variety of cash and noncash bids rather than a set of bids for the firm's assets on the one hand and a set of restructuring plans on the other.

Task B: Allocating Rights

Before the judge can allocate rights to the shares of the new (all-equity) firm, he must first determine who the firm's claimants were and the amounts and priority of their claims. For example, if the firm owed taxes to the government, is that claim senior or junior to a claim by workers for unpaid wages or for pension benefits? How do these claims compare in priority to a claim by a secured or senior debtholder? Where do trade creditors or future tort claimants fit into the picture? If the firm recently borrowed $1,000 for one year at a rate of interest of 10 percent but the rate of interest has now fallen to 5 percent, is this creditor owed $1,000 or $1,100/1.05?

These are complicated questions, which have to be answered currently in both a Chapter 7 and a Chapter 11 bankruptcy.[27] Since we have nothing new to say about the answers, we shall simply assume that some procedure is adopted (possibly existing U.S. procedure) for determining the amount and priority of all claims.

Thus, we suppose that the judge's deliberations will lead to the identification of n classes of creditors who were owed (in total) the amounts $D_1, \ldots, D_n$, respectively, with class 1 having the most senior claim, class 2 the next most senior claim, and so on. The firm's shareholders form the $(n + 1)^{th}$ class, with a claim junior to all others.

Having identified these classes, the judge can proceed to allocate rights to shares in the new (all-equity) firm. If the "true" value, V, of the firm were publicly known (i.e., were verifiable), then it would be easy to figure out the total (monetary) amount S_i each class i should get, based on absolute priority. The most senior creditors, class 1, should receive the smaller of the amount they are owed, D_1 and the total amount available, V; that is,

$$S_1 = \min(D_1, V).$$

Class i ($i = 2, \ldots, n$) should receive the smaller of the total amount they are owed, D_i, and the total amount available after class ($i - 1$) has been paid off; that is,

$$S_i = \min(D_i, V - S_1 - S_2 - \ldots - S_{i-1}).$$

Finally, the equityholders should receive anything that is left over; that is,

$$S_{n+1} = V - (S_1 + \ldots + S_n).$$

27. For a good discussion, see Baird and Jackson (1985).

Unfortunately, V is typically not known. However, Bebchuk (1988) has constructed a scheme that achieves absolute priority in spite of this drawback. Note that, although Bebchuk's scheme is ingenious, it may be regarded as too complicated in some circumstances. In section 16.5, we describe some simpler alternatives.

Bebchuk's scheme works as follows. The most senior class (class 1) is allocated 100 percent of the firm's equity (so, if an individual creditor in that class is owed d_1, he receives a fraction d_1/D_1 of the firm's shares); however, the firm has the right to "redeem" this claim (i.e., buy back the equity) at a price of D_1 per 100 percent—that is, for the amount this class is owed. Investors in the next most senior class (class 2) are given the *option* to buy equity at a price of D_1 per 100 percent; however, the firm has the right to redeem this claim at a price of D_2 per 100 percent—that is, for the amount this class is owed.[28] More generally, class i investors ($3 \leq i \leq n$) have the option to buy equity at a price of $(D_1 + D_2 + \ldots + D_{i-1})$ per 100 percent, but the firm can redeem this right at a price of D_i per 100 percent. Finally, shareholders (class $[n + 1]$) are given the option to buy equity at a price of $(D_1 + \ldots + D_n)$ per 100 percent.[29]

This completes the judge's second task, task B.

Once the three months are up, the judge reveals the bids arising from task A, and everyone can make an assessment of their worth (possibly with the help of some outside expert, such as an investment bank [see n. 35 below]). At this point, optionholders are given some period of time—a further month, say—to exercise their options. (During this period, there can be trade in equity and options, although the process does not depend on this.) At the end of this fourth month, some options will have been exercised, and others will not. The firm (i.e., the judge) uses the receipts from the options exercised to make redemptions—starting with the most senior claimants and working down the seniority until the receipts have been used up. These redemptions balance the options exercised in such a way that exactly 100 percent of the firm's equity is allocated at all times.[30]

The final step in the process is that the firm's equityholders (i.e., those people who hold equity in the firm at the end of month 4) vote on which of the

28. Shortly, we will explain when these options, and buyback rights, can be exercised.
29. For example, let $n = 2$, $D_1 = \$100$, $D_2 = \$200$; i.e., there are two classes of creditors who were owed $100 and $200, respectively. Let there be 100 people in each class and also 100 shareholders and 100 shares of the firm outstanding. Then the first class of creditors is given one share each, each member of the second class is given the option to buy one share for $D_1/100 = \$1.00$, and each shareholder is given the option to buy a share for $(D_1 + D_2)/100 = \$3.00$.
30. To continue our example from n. 29, suppose that, on the basis of the bids announced by the judge, the firm is generally perceived to be worth between $100 and $300. Then no shareholders will exercise their options, but all junior creditors will exercise theirs. The judge takes the receipts of $100 and uses the money to redeem the senior creditors' rights for $1.00 each, transferring their shares to the junior creditors. At the end of the process, all the equity is in the junior creditors' hands, and all the senior creditors have been fully paid off. The shareholders neither pay nor receive anything.
It should be clear from this example that Bebchuk's scheme preserves absolute priority in the following sense. If class i creditors ($1 \leq i \leq n$) are (fully) paid off, then this must mean that some lower class exercised their options. But then all creditors senior to class i are also (fully) paid off.

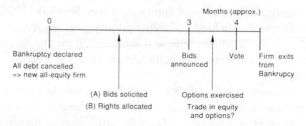

Fig. 15.1   Bankruptcy: Sequence of events

various cash and noncash bids to select. (Voting is on the basis of one share, one vote; in sec. 16.6.6, we discuss the voting procedure further.) Once the vote is completed, the firm emerges from the bankruptcy process.[31]

The sequence of events is summarized in figure 15.1.

15.4   An Assessment

In our view, one of the strengths of our proposal is that, in a precise sense, it embraces all the options currently available within both Chapter 7 and Chapter 11. In a Chapter 7 auction, anyone is free to make a cash bid for the firm; that is, liquidation and sale are both feasible. Our mechanism admits such outcomes too. Chapter 11 allows for the formulation of a reorganization/recapitalization plan. Any such plan is allowed for in our mechanism too because it can always be expressed in the form of a noncash bid. Thus, minimally, everything that is feasible within either Chapter 7 or Chapter 11 is also feasible within our proposal.

We believe that our procedure *improves* on Chapters 7 and 11. In section 15.2.1, we highlighted two problems with a cash-only auction like Chapter 7: the *financing problem* and the *lack-of-competition problem*. The major advantage of our proposal is that, by permitting noncash bids, it reduces (or even eliminates) the financing problem. The reason is that a bidder who is cash constrained or who does not want to bear the risk of holding a large fraction of the company shares himself, even in the short term, can share risks with the old claimants by offering them securities in the new company directly. In con-

31. Note that old claimants who become new shareholders in the firm do not have to remain as such. For example, a former trade creditor who becomes a shareholder can sell his shares once a market develops (and can vote with this prospect in mind).

Our procedure differs in an important way from the recent bankruptcy proposal of Bradley and Rosenzweig (1992). They suggest that, in the event of bankruptcy, the firm's equity should be transferred to creditors (unless the equityholders are prepared to buy out the creditors for what is owed), but they do not discuss how this leads to better management (or liquidation) of the firm. That is, they do not explain how a (possibly dispersed) group of creditors goes about replacing management. By contrast, in our scheme, the solicitation of cash and noncash bids, together with an automatic vote, provides a mechanism by which management can be removed. (For more on this, see sec. 15.4.)

trast, Chapter 7 requires an extra step: the bidder must raise *cash* from one group (the new investors) in order to pay another group (the old claimants).[32]

Our procedure does not deal directly with the lack-of-competition problem. However, allowing noncash bids is likely to mitigate it. Parties may be deterred from bidding given the cost of financing a bid. Noncash bids will help indirectly by reducing these costs. This is likely to raise the number of eventual bidders and therefore also to increase the competitiveness of the auction and the value of the winning bid.

Our procedure also improves on a structured bargaining procedure like Chapter 11 in a number of ways. Principally, we have substituted a simple vote by shareholders (whose interests are aligned) for protracted and complex bargaining among different claimant groups (whose interests typically conflict).[33] Also, agency costs are much reduced: our procedure leaves little or no discretionary power in the hands of the judge, management, or creditor/shareholder representatives.[34]

It is worth comparing our procedure to the automatic financial restructuring proposal discussed in section 15.2.4, whereby a firm's debts are canceled and market forces determine whether it should be liquidated. Such a proposal would leave incumbent management in place, unless and until it is removed. Our procedure is quite different. In our scheme, no one has the right of incumbency until specifically voted in by the shareholders: this is the prime purpose of having an obligatory vote.

We think that this feature of our scheme is crucial. In the course of normal business (*outside* bankruptcy), management is constrained in various ways. Aside from direct incentive schemes, managers (more precisely, directors) are subject to removal by a proxy fight or a takeover bid. As we mentioned earlier (see n. 23 above), both these mechanisms are—perhaps with reason—biased in favor of incumbent management. We think that, to maintain the bonding

---

32. Note that, in the main version of our proposal described in sec. 15.3, the old claimants are treated equally in the sense that each is offered (rights to) the same package of securities in the new company (some combination of equity, cash, and bonds, say). This is not essential, however. For example, one of the firm's previous creditors might be a large bank, which has a comparative advantage in monitoring the lower tail of the firm's cash earnings. It may be very inefficient for this creditor to be allocated a large amount of equity in the new company. There is a simple way round this problem, however. Management could propose a reorganization plan in which the bank agrees to become a large creditor of the firm, in return for selling back its equity to the firm. The only difficulty with this is that it can raise a conflict of interest: the bank, as a former creditor, will be able to vote on a deal from which it may well be benefiting substantially. We discuss ways of dealing with this kind of conflict in sec. 15.6.2.

33. It would be too strong to say that our procedure eliminates *all* conflicts of interest among claimants. Some claimants may be workers or other firms that have contractual relations with the bankrupt firm. These parties will be interested in more than just the market value of their equity and hence may have goals different from those of the average shareholder. We suspect that the resultant conflicts of interest are likely to be small relative to those between shareholders and creditors or among creditors in a standard Chapter 11 proceeding.

34. Except, of course, for the crucial role of the bankruptcy judge in deciding who is owed what and the relative seniorities of these claims.

role of debt, it is essential that incumbent management is not favored *within* bankruptcy. That is why the vote is important. The vote establishes a playing field that is at most flat and, we suspect, more typically, tilted in favor of outsiders. Incumbent managers have to persuade their shareholders to vote them back into office, probably against competition from a *cash* buyer. Shareholders, choosing between cash in hand and a noncash offer (of uncertain value) from the very management team that has just brought the firm to its knees, may well vote for the cash.[35] That is, except when it is clear that the bankruptcy was due to events outside management's control, incumbent management is quite likely to be booted out.[36]

There is a further aspect of the treatment of management that we should address. It might be argued that penalizing management harshly in bankruptcy is counterproductive since it will cause managers of financially distressed firms to delay filing for bankruptcy or to "go for broke"—that is, to engage in risky, but inefficient, behavior to stave off bankruptcy. People who take this position often go on to advocate a soft procedure like Chapter 11, which treats management relatively well. We are not persuaded by this argument. If the state-provided bankruptcy mechanism is harsh, it seems relatively easy for a firm to soften it ex ante. If those people choosing the corporation's financial structure wish to protect managers from the unpleasantness of bankruptcy, they can do so by choosing a low debt-equity ratio or by issuing senior debt to managers so that they receive something in bankruptcy states (a form of "golden parachute").[37]

In contrast, it is much more difficult for a firm to harden a soft bankruptcy procedure. Suppose, for example, that the statutory procedure specifies that incumbent management should be left in place for a minimum period of time. Consider some firm that wants to ensure that its own managers will be removed

35. This raises a more general issue. It may be unreasonable to expect (possibly quite small) shareholders to have the knowledge or incentive to assess noncash offers. One solution would be for the judge to hire an investment bank to value the various offers. The investment bank could also check whether the financing for each proposal is secure. (The bank's fees might be in the form of securities in the postbankruptcy firm.)

36. Note that the process of comparing cash and noncash bids that we have advocated is not completely unfamiliar in the corporate context. Firms that are undergoing leveraged buyouts (LBOs) face something similar. There the incumbent management team typically makes a bid to take the firm private. Other groups often show an interest too, and a subset of the board's disinterested (or independent) directors is charged with conducting an auction. At the end of this auction, the disinterested directors will approve one of the bids or decide that the status quo is better for shareholders (i.e., that the company should remain public).

The major difference between the LBO process and the one advocated here is that, in the LBO case, the bids are decided on by shareholder representatives while, in our case, they are decided on by the shareholders directly. (Even in an LBO, a decision to take the company private would have to be ratified by shareholders.)

37. Also, if a "harsh" procedure causes management to delay filing for bankruptcy for too long, then this problem can be mitigated by making it easier for creditors to push a firm into bankruptcy of their own accord—e.g., debt could have stronger covenants attached to it (which are more likely to be violated).

quickly in bankruptcy. The firm cannot achieve this by merely fine-tuning the existing procedure, since any attempt to remove management will, by assumption, not be respected by the courts. Instead, the firm will have to opt out of the statutory (soft) procedure and write its own private (hard) procedure; but, as we have argued in section 15.1, this may be very costly. Given this asymmetry—it is easier to soften a hard mechanism than to harden a soft one—our conclusion is that the state's bankruptcy procedure should err on the hard side rather than the soft.[38]

15.5   Simpler Methods of Allocating Equity

We have advocated using Bebchuk's relatively sophisticated—although conceptually not at all difficult—mechanism for allocating equity. Some people may argue that this mechanism is too complicated for practical purposes and that a simpler scheme should be found.

A useful way to explore this matter further is to begin by considering what happens in Bebchuk's mechanism if junior claimants (either junior creditors or shareholders) are cash constrained—so that they are unable to exercise their options when they perceive that the firm is valuable and the market for options is sufficiently underdeveloped that they cannot easily sell them. (This is likely to be a particular problem in Eastern Europe.)

At first glance, this may not appear to be a serious problem. For instance, if a junior securityholder (say, an old equityholder) has the option to buy equity at a price below what he considers it is worth but does not have the cash on hand to do so, then he could always borrow short term, offering the equity as collateral for the loan, and then sell the equity (at a profit) once the firm emerges from bankruptcy. However, this argument overlooks the fact that his perception of the future value of the firm's equity may not be shared by his potential creditors; if they are less optimistic than he is and he cannot offer them anything else by way of collateral, then he will not be able to borrow the cash needed to exercise his option.

But does it matter if options cannot be exercised? The net effect of a failure in the options "market" is to leave more equity in the hands of senior creditors than is warranted by the face value of their debt. Arguably, this redistribution of the firm's value (disproportionately into the hands of senior creditors) does not matter since claims have still been homogenized so as to remove the scope for ex post bargaining, and the new equityholders (mainly the old senior creditors) should therefore still vote for the best bid. Of course, there would appear to be some unfairness. But in principle this potential transfer of wealth from

---

38. However, as we argued at the start of sec. 15.3, a good bankruptcy procedure should strike a balance between penalizing management (in order to preserve the bonding role of debt) and maximizing the ex post value of the firm. That is why we do not advocate as harsh a procedure as Chapter 7. Our procedure is "softer" on management than Chapter 7 because management (along with anyone else) is free to make a noncash bid.

junior to senior claimants would be priced in the ex ante securities markets anyway, so the "unfairness" is more apparent than real.

This is an intriguing argument because it raises the larger question, Why should one bother using Bebchuk's mechanism when an even simpler rule could be used? Some possible alternatives are the following:

1. Once the bids (both cash and noncash) have been assembled, one or more outside investment banks could be employed to assess them and to estimate the value, V^e, of the best one. Shares could then be allocated according to absolute priority, taking V^e, as if it were the true value of the firm (i.e., as in Chapter 7, except that it is equity, not cash, that is being distributed). Shareholders would then vote to choose what *they* consider to be the best bid, just as in section 15.3.

2. As in alternative 1, except that the highest *cash* bid, V^c—which is an objective amount—is used in lieu of V^e as a basis for distributing equity.

3. Equity might be allocated in proportion to the *face* value of claims—with, say, x percent reserved for old equityholders, where $x \geq 0$ is some prespecified number.

4. An even cruder rule than 3 would be to allocate all the equity to senior creditors, regardless of the face value of their claims (indeed, this would be the outcome of our proposed scheme in the extreme case where no options were exercised because of cash constraints).

These four alternative rules are consistent with the basic features of our proposal: first, noncash as well as cash bids are allowed so that reorganization is given a fair chance; second, a homogeneous group of new equityholders is created who get to vote on the future of the firm; and, third, the old management faces the discipline of having to bid to keep their jobs. The sense in which these simple rules are inferior to our proposed scheme is that they may fail to preserve absolute priority: they typically give either too much or too little to junior claimants relative to senior. (In 1, e.g., V^e may overestimate the true value, V, of the firm, in which case junior claimants receive too much. In 2, V^c may be well below the value, V, of the best noncash bid, in which case junior claimants receive too little.) If cash constraints are not a problem, the strength of the Bebchuk scheme is that it is a market-based mechanism that preserves absolute priority. But, if one suspects that in practice the scheme would not work (and hence fail to respect absolute priority), then it may be better to opt for something simpler, along the lines of one of the above alternatives.[39]

39. Even if one were to opt for one of the alternative rules 1–4, there would be a strong argument for supplementing it with Bebchuk options: i.e., class 2 creditors could be given the right to buy out the most senior (class 1) creditors at price D_1; class 3 could be given the right to buy out both classes 1 and 2 at price $D_1 + D_2$; etc. This would at least give some power of redress to aggrieved individual junior claimants who feel that senior claimants are getting more than they are owed.

Readers may wonder why the preservation of absolute priority is important at all. Aside from the basic point that, ceteris paribus, it is always better to respect the provisions of private contracts, there are at least two other arguments. First, any discrepancy between what a class of claimants gets inside bankruptcy and what it gets outside bankruptcy could lead to inefficient rent seeking

15.6   Further Considerations

Of course many details of our proposal remain to be sorted out. In this section, we briefly raise some ancillary issues. We should stress that we do not have definite answers to a number of questions. There may be room for several answers, depending on the circumstances of the firm: indeed, one can imagine firms opting for different choices ex ante.

15.6.1   Claim Disputes

We have taken the view that a judge could fairly quickly decide on who is owed what and with what priority—say within three months. This may be too optimistic.[40] It can be argued that one advantage of a Chapter 7 sell-off is that the receipts can be safely held in some (interest-bearing) escrow account until such time as the conflicting claims have been resolved. By contrast, if the firm is to survive as a going concern, such delays could be fatal.

In practice, it matters just how big a slice of the pie is in dispute. If, for example, 90 percent of the prior claims can be decided on within three months, then the judge could proceed in the manner we have suggested, with these 90 percent of claimants being allocated equity/options (as if the disputed 10 percent do not exist). The 90 percent then vote.[41] Any *cash* that is generated—either as part of the winning bid or in the form of subsequent debt repayments/dividends—is held in an escrow account by the judge pending a resolution of the outstanding 10 percent of claims. Once resolved, successful claimants could be issued fresh equity in the firm according to the seniority and value of their claims (that is, the equity holdings of the original 90 percent would be diluted), and the cash held in the escrow account could be distributed appropriately. In short, the fact that certain claims are in dispute need not hold up the bankruptcy proceeding.

15.6.2   Dominant Voters

Left as it is, our proposal would be vulnerable to exploitation of the minority by a dominant shareholder. Suppose that, just prior to the vote being taken, someone ended up with more than half the shares. There are a number of ways in which this person could abuse his voting power. For example, he could vote to accept an artificially low cash offer from a second firm in which he has a

---

ex post—with some people bribing management into deliberately precipitating bankruptcy and other people attempting to forestall bankruptcy. Second, as shown in Hart and Moore (1990), the seniority structure of a firm's capital provides an important instrument for constraining management's ability to raise fresh capital; any arbitrary tampering with seniority rules within bankruptcy will typically reduce the flexibility of this instrument.

40. Douglas Baird (1992) suggests that much of a lengthy Chapter 11 proceeding can in fact be devoted to this issue.

41. There is no reason to suppose that the vote of the remaining 10 percent would be systematically different, given that they have the same objective: value maximization.

large stake. Or he could vote himself into control and sell the firm's assets cheaply to the second firm.

This problem is, of course, not new. It is a potential problem for any publicly traded company, and there exist laws to protect minority shareholders (boards of directors have fiduciary responsibilities). Indeed, under Chapter 11, minority creditors (within a class) need protection, in the form of equal treatment. However, it seems clear that existing law would not be able to protect minority interests under our bankruptcy procedure. The procedure would need to be amended in various ways—for example, to disallow voting by someone who has an interest in a bidder's firm. Another possibility would be (1) to grant a suitably sized minority of the shareholders the power to veto any winning bid that is a *noncash* bid (this would help prevent a dominant shareholder from voting in a bad noncash bid) and (2) to insist that a *cash* bid can be accepted only if it is the highest cash bid (this would help prevent a dominant shareholder from voting in a bad cash bid).

15.6.3   Secured Creditors

The issue here is the following: in bankruptcy, should the secured creditors of a firm be allowed to seize collateralized property? At present, U.S. bankruptcy law basically prevents such seizure, and we would not favor it either because it could lead to an inefficient dismantlement of the firm's assets through a "me-first" grab.[42]

We envisage that, in our proposal, a secured creditor might be treated much as he would be under present U.S. bankruptcy law. Namely, the value of the collateral is appraised; let this amount be S. Suppose that the level of secured debt is D. On the one hand, if the debt is oversecured ($S > D$), then the creditor is granted his full D in senior debt. On the other hand, if the debt is undersecured ($S < D$), then the creditor is given only S of senior debt; the remainder, $(D - S)$, is treated as unsecured (junior) debt.

15.6.4   Debtor-in-Possession Financing

The viability of certain kinds of bankrupt firms (such as retail stores) can depend crucially on management being granted debtor-in-possession financing, whereby suppliers' credit is placed ahead of existing (unsecured) senior debt. (This is often mentioned as an important role played by Chapter 11.) There is no reason why a comparable arrangement could not be used during the "four months" of our proposed bankruptcy process, with the judge's approval. In addition, for the sake of continuity, it is probably desirable to allow management to run the company during the bankruptcy process, under the supervision of the judge (again, as in Chapter 11).

---

42. Under present U.S. law, a secured creditor *may* be able to seize his collateral if he can demonstrate that the property is not necessary for the firm's reorganization and that it is worth less than the amount he is owed (see Baird 1992, sec. 8C). A comparable rule could be adopted under our procedure.

15.6.5   Partial Bids

We have tacitly assumed that the bids received are for the *entire* firm. In fact, bids may be for parts of the firm. The problem then arises as to how to deal with overlapping/inconsistent bids. Before a vote can be taken, a menu of coherent options has to be assembled.

We think that there is no alternative but to leave the matter of assembling "whole" bids in the hands of the judge and his or her appointed agents. It may well be necessary to solicit supplementary bids for parts of the firm, in order to package a whole bid. Although this seems messy, it should be noted that a similar difficulty is faced in a Chapter 7 proceeding: how to bundle/unbundle the assets of the firm so as to maximize cash receipts.

15.6.6   Voting Procedures

Another issue concerns the voting procedure per se. If there are only two bids, it seems natural to have a simple vote between them. However, with more than two bids, there are many possibilities. Shareholders could cast their votes for their most preferred plan, with the plan with the most votes being the winner; or shareholders could rank the plans, with the plan with the highest total ranking being the winner; or there could be two rounds, where shareholders rank the plans in the first round and there is a runoff between the two highest-ranked plans in the second round. One point to note is that thorny issues in voting theory (such as the Condorcet paradox) are less likely to arise in the present context, given that shareholders have a common objective: value maximization.

15.7   Implementing the Proposed Procedure in Eastern Europe

In this section, we raise some basic questions concerning the implementation of the above scheme in the context of Eastern Europe. Let us stress the following: we envisage that our procedure would apply primarily to the case of the (subsequent) bankruptcy of *new private* or *newly privatized* firms.[43]

A first source of difficulty in implementing our (or any other) bankruptcy procedure in East European countries lies in the insufficient number of qualified lawyers and judges. However, unlike both Chapter 11 and other systems outside the United States, our procedure attempts to minimize the need for lawyers by reducing the role of the courts to mainly supervisory functions. No decision or arbitration concerning a firm's future needs to be made by the courts as long as the bankruptcy procedure is followed by the firm's creditors and shareholders, and therefore no particular expertise in the firm's operations is required from either judges or lawyers.

In this respect, our procedure has the advantage of being potentially enforce-

---

43. Nevertheless, elements of our proposal might be of use for the purpose of debt restructuring and privatization of large state-owned enterprises (see van Wijnbergen 1992).

able using the existing judiciary system—that is, without having to introduce bankruptcy courts run by specialized judges. But it should be noted that the judge (or administrator) will need accounting skills in order to determine who had what claims, and of what seniority, in the insolvent firm. One solution during the transition phase could be for a well-established accounting firm not only to perform this task but also to allocate shares and options (Task B) and to supervise the process of exercising options. Foreign accounting firms that already operate in Eastern Europe could be used for this purpose.

As we have already suggested in note 35, outside experts could also be employed to evaluate competing bids on behalf of shareholders/voters. This may be particularly important in Eastern Europe, where, in the absence of smoothly operating capital markets, shareholders may have no other means of assessing noncash bids. Without outside evaluations, incumbent management would enjoy a considerable advantage in being able to "sell" their own bids to shareholders. Incumbent management would have more difficulty preventing a nominated team of outside accountants from gathering information about the firm's assets than it would concealing the information from individual shareholders. Accountants could also have an important role in ensuring that outside bidders have access to information about the firm. And of course there is very little that management can do to stop third parties from putting up cash or noncash bids.

In section 15.5, we discussed some simpler alternatives to Bebchuk's scheme for allocating equity. In Eastern Europe, it might be highly desirable to dispense with using Bebchuk's options, given the poor capital markets. Our first alternative may be especially attractive: namely, once the bids have been assembled, an outside expert (again, a foreign accounting firm?) assesses them and estimates the value, V^e, of the best one; shares are then allocated according to absolute priority, taking V^e as if it were the true value of the firm; and, finally, a vote is taken among shareholders to decide which bid to accept.

One concern about the adoption of our procedure in Eastern Europe is that the scope for making noncash offers might facilitate collusion among managers of mutually indebted firms. This is a particular worry in the current context, where interenterprise credits have substantially proliferated since 1988. In such a context, one could easily imagine the possibility of several firms, with sizable mutual debt obligations, becoming simultaneously insolvent. The managers of these firms could collude by making (and then voting in) noncash offers that maintain the status quo—thereby precluding potentially more efficient investors or management teams from winning. Incumbent managers would thus keep their jobs without any monetary transfer being made, in particular to compensate minority securityholders. (The drawback here relative to a straight liquidation procedure like Chapter 7 is that, in the latter, managers would have to be party to a successful *cash* bid in order to keep their jobs. But, as we have argued, Chapter 7 has serious limitations.) The kinds of devices that we put forward in section 16.6.1 to reduce the power of majority voters—for example, not allowing doubly interested parties to participate in the vote, or allowing noncash offers to be vetoed by a suitably sized minority of shareholders—may help eliminate collusion, too.

A further concern with implementing our procedure in the current environment of Eastern Europe is that it would burden state banks (which are the main creditors of most large enterprises in the East) with responsibilities in the reorganized companies, which they could hardly assume given their bureaucratic management structures and methods. (State banks are often unable to perform such operations as taking deposits, giving account balances, transferring money, etc., let alone evaluating projects and monitoring enterprises' managers.) We have little to say on this score. The commercialization and/or privatization of state banks would, of course, help, as would the setting up of adequate supervising institutions, such as banking commissions. (These changes are urgently required as part of the transition reform package anyway.) In addition, state banks could be obliged to sell the bulk of their equity to the private sector within a limited time period—say, five years—in order to avoid the possibility that the implementation of our procedure in the case of newly privatized firms with large state-bank creditors would lead merely to renationalization.

Appendix

In this appendix, we briefly look at what is happening now in two of the countries of Eastern Europe—Hungary and Poland. Unfortunately, we think that the bankruptcy procedures that these two countries have adopted are vulnerable to many of the criticisms that we have leveled against structured bargaining procedures like the U.S. Chapter 11 (see sec. 15.2.2). That is, bargaining among heterogeneous creditors is unlikely to be efficient, the creditors' representatives may not have the correct incentives, the procedure may be too soft on incumbent management, and judges and officials can abuse discretionary powers.

Hungary

The new Hungarian bankruptcy law (enacted in September 1991) obliges the leadership of an insolvent company to design a rehabilitation program for restoring solvency. In the case of state-owned enterprises, the leadership may consist of the general assembly of employees or the founding organization. In the case of private enterprises, it consists of the membership of the partnership or the general assembly of shareholders.

Within sixty days from the beginning of the bankruptcy proceedings, the debtor must convene a "compromise negotiation" meeting among representatives of the company's creditors. These representatives form a board of creditors, which ultimately decides either to accept or to reject the compromise agreement. Approval by *all* members of the board who are present is required for the rehabilitation plan to be approved and then ratified by the court. In the absence of any agreement within fifteen days, the court starts a liquidation procedure that is similar to the U.S. Chapter 7.

Poland

Whereas the Hungarian procedure provides a unified framework for dealing with state-owned and private companies, in Poland there exist several procedures to deal with insolvent firms.

The Law of State Enterprises (enacted in 1990) prescribed that, if a state-owned enterprise incurred a substantial loss that exceeded its reserve fund and, at the same time, the main creditor bank refused to extend credit, then the state owner/founding organization (local government, branch ministry, etc.) could either liquidate the enterprise or appoint a new compulsory management. This new management is given two years to rehabilitate the enterprise and thereby avoid its liquidation. Note that such a procedure clearly discriminates against claimholders (banks, trade creditors, etc.) who do not control the enterprise's parent agency. Also, the criteria for deciding between liquidation and appointing new management are left unspecified.

A modification of this procedure for insolvent state-owned enterprises has been adopted recently by the Polish Parliament, allowing the enterprise itself to initiate a process whereby the creditors would decide (only by unanimous agreement) whether to restructure/reschedule the enterprise's debt or to let the enterprise be liquidated.

In addition to the procedures outlined above, the new Polish privatization law enacted in July 1990 provides for "liquidations" that amount to the state leasing the insolvent enterprise's assets to new companies.

For insolvent private firms, the Polish authorities have rehabilitated the old Commercial Code of 1934. On declaring the firm insolvent, the relevant court appoints a trustee who supervises the property and management of the firm and also conducts settlement proceedings. To be enforceable, any settlement must be approved both by the court and by a majority of creditors representing at least two-thirds of the firm's debt obligations.

References

Altman, E. 1984. A further empirical investigation of the bankruptcy cost question. *Journal of Finance* 39:1067–89.
Baird, D. 1986. The uneasy case for corporate reorganizations. *Journal of Legal Studies* 15:127–47.
———. 1992. *The elements of bankruptcy.* New York: Foundation.
Baird, D., and T. Jackson. 1985. *Cases, problems, and materials on bankruptcy.* Boston: Little, Brown.

Baldwin, C., and S. Mason. 1983. The resolution of claims in financial distress: The case of Massey Ferguson. *Journal of Finance* 38:505–16.

Bebchuk, L. 1988. A new approach to corporate reorganizations. *Harvard Law Review* 101:775–804.

Betker, B. 1992. Management changes, equity's bargaining power and deviations from absolute priority in Chapter 11 bankruptcies. Ohio State University. Mimeo.

Bradley, M., and M. Rosenzweig. 1992. The untenable case for Chapter 11. *Yale Law Review* 101:1043–95.

Burrough, B., and J. Helyar. 1990. *Barbarians at the gate.* New York: Harper & Row.

Cutler, D., and L. Summers. 1988. The costs of conflict resolution and financial distress: Evidence from the Texaco-Pennzoil litigation. *Rand Journal of Economics* 19:157–72.

Flynn, E. 1989. A statistical analysis of chapter 11. Washington, D.C.: Administrative Office of the United States Courts. Mimeo.

Gilson, S. 1989. Management turnover and financial distress. *Journal of Financial Economics* 25:241–62.

———. 1990. Bankruptcy, boards, banks, and blockholders. *Journal of Financial Economics* 27:355–87.

———. 1991. Managing default: Some evidence on how firms choose between workouts and Chapter 11. *Journal of Applied Corporate Finance* 4:62–70.

Gilson, S., K. John, and L. Lang. 1990. Troubled debt restructurings: An empirical study of private reorganization of firms in default. *Journal of Financial Economics* 26:315–53.

Gilson, S., and M. Vetsuypens. 1992. CEO compensation in financially distressed firms: An empirical analysis. Working Paper no. 92–052. Harvard Business School.

Grossman, S., and O. Hart. 1980. Takeover bids, the free-rider problem, and the theory of the corporation. *Bell Journal of Economics* 11:42–64.

———. 1982. Corporate financial structure and managerial incentives. In *The economics of information and uncertainty,* ed. J. J. McCall. Chicago: University of Chicago Press.

Hart, O. 1993. Theories of optimal capital structure: A managerial discretion perspective. In *The deal decade: What takeovers and leveraged buy-outs mean for corporate governance,* ed. M. Blair. Washington, D.C.: Brookings.

Hart, O., and J. Moore. 1990. A theory of corporate financial structure based on the seniority of claims. Working Paper no. 560. Massachusetts Institute of Technology.

Jackson, T. 1986. *The logic and limits to bankruptcy.* Boston: Little, Brown.

Jensen, M. 1986. Agency costs of free cash flow, corporate finance and takeovers. *American Economic Review* 76:323–29.

Jensen, M., and R. Ruback. 1983. The market for corporate control: The scientific evidence. *Journal of Financial Economics* 11:5–50.

LoPucki, L., and W. Whitford. 1992. Corporate governance in the bankruptcy reorganization of large, publicly-held companies. University of Wisconsin. Mimeo.

McConnell, J., and H. Servaes. 1991. The economics of pre-packaged bankruptcy. *Journal of Applied Corporate Finance* 4:93–97.

Mitchell, J. 1990. The economics of bankruptcy in reforming socialist economies. Cornell University. Mimeo.

Ritter, J. 1987. The costs of going public. *Journal of Financial Economics* 19:269–81.

Rock, K. 1986. Why new issues are underpriced. *Journal of Financial Economics* 15:187–212.

Roe, M. 1983. Bankruptcy and debt: A new model for corporate reorganizations. *Columbia Law Review* 83:527–602.

Shleifer, A., and R. Vishny. 1992. Liquidation values and debt capacity: A market equilibrium approach. *Journal of Finance* 47 (September): 1343–66.

van Wijnbergen, S. 1992. Privatization in Eastern Europe. Washington, D.C. World Bank. Mimeo.
Webb, D. 1991. An economic evaluation of insolvency procedures in the United Kingdom: Does the 1986 Insolvency Act satisfy the creditors' bargain? *Oxford Economic Papers* 43:139–57.
Weiss, L. 1990. Bankruptcy resolution: Direct costs and violation of priority of claims. *Journal of Financial Economics* 27:285–314.
———. 1991. Restructuring complications in bankruptcy: The Eastern Airlines bankruptcy case. Tulane University. Mimeo.
White, M. 1983. Bankruptcy costs and the new bankruptcy code. *Journal of Finance* 38:477–504.
Wruck, K. 1990. Financial distress, reorganization, and organizational efficiency. *Journal of Financial Economics* 27:419–44.

Comment   Jeremy C. Stein

I found this to be a very interesting paper. I am not sure that I agree with the specific proposal the authors put forward, but I certainly agree with the premise—that one can do better than current Western bankruptcy procedures, particularly those associated with Chapter 7 and Chapter 11 in the United States. And I thought that the paper was extremely helpful in laying out the key issues that one must confront in trying to design a better system.

What the authors do is put forth some desirable properties of a bankruptcy system, measure Chapter 7– and Chapter 11–type procedures against these properties, and find them lacking. They then go on to try to strike a better balance. I will organize my comments in a similar way—I will start with the desirable properties. There are basically two types of criteria by which one might judge a bankruptcy system:

1. *Allocational efficiency.* This is obviously important—you want the right management team to end up running the firm after all the smoke clears. You do not want the firm to be liquidated if it is more valuable as an ongoing concern. And you also want a minimum of value destruction during the workout process.

2. *Distributional properties.* This in turn can be divided into two pieces:

(a) Is absolute priority observed? Many people, including the authors, seem to think that it is important to follow absolute priority. Why? First, it may be a good idea simply to uphold contracts, in order to remove a source of (idiosyncratic) risk and thereby make the securities ex ante more attractive. Second, deviations from absolute priority are likely to be associated with allocational inefficiencies—for example, once we are in Chapter 11, people may waste resources haggling over the allocation of the spoils. But it is not clear to me that observing absolute priority is an unmixed blessing. It can have costs, too, to which I will come back.

(b) Nobody should be able to buy companies at "fire-sale" prices, even if they are the best managers. This is particularly important in the East Europe context since it is unlikely to be a closed system—one must worry about the possibility that deep-pocket foreigners are the buyers, which is a welfare loss to the country and could have adverse political consequences. Although it is not really emphasized by the authors, I would worry about this criterion a lot.

So we have three things to keep in mind when evaluating a bankruptcy system: efficient allocation of resources, absolute priority, and the possibility for fire sales. Essentially, what Aghion, Hart, and Moore do is ask, How do Chapter 7 and Chapter 11 measure up against these sorts of criteria, and can we find anything that does better? However, before we make this comparison, there is a critical point to note: a large fraction of distressed firms never go into formal bankruptcy—they restructure out of court. In Gilson, John, and Lang's (1990) sample of U.S. firms, this fraction is about 50 percent. And the percentage of firms restructuring outside formal bankruptcy may be much higher in other financial systems—for example, in the Japanese or German systems, where there tends to be more closely held debt. Why is this critical? If out-of-court restructuring is pretty efficient, it is important to encourage it, and the incidence of such restructuring may be very sensitive to the rules of the game in the courts. Take a concrete example. Suppose that out-of-court restructuring involves deadweight costs of $1.00 and current Chapter 11 procedures entail costs of $10.00. Now suppose that we improve in-court procedures so that the costs are down to $8.00 but incentives are changed so that twice as many people wind up in court. As I will argue in a moment, this is not a totally improbable example, and it relates to the issue of absolute priority.

The basic problem that Aghion, Hart, and Moore see with Chapter 7 is a bias toward liquidation. They recognize that, owing to shallow pockets, information costs, etc., the auction mechanism is far from perfect. I agree and would just add my fire-sale-to-deep-pocket-foreigners concern. The good thing about Chapter 7 in their view is that it tends to observe absolute priority.

In contrast, Chapter 11 may have the (sometimes) good feature of preserving the business on an ongoing basis, but there are also serious problems. First, there may be an *excessive* bias in the direction of preservation of the business under current management—in a sense, not enough liquidation. Second, Chapter 11 appears to involve enormous costs of time and haggling. Another bad thing about Chapter 11 in Aghion, Hart, and Moore's view is that it is typically associated with large deviations from absolute priority.

Although I share their concern about costs and destruction of value, I am less sure that deviations from absolute priority per se are all bad. It is important to recognize that the potential for deviations from absolute priority will affect the restructuring behavior of a firm before it lands in court. From this ex ante perspective, deviations may be a good thing—metaphorically, a less sharp break between junior and senior claimants may help align interests and facilitate "good" behavior at the restructuring phase. For example, recent work by Asquith, Gertner, and Scharfstein (1992) shows that, when bank lenders are better secured, there is a greater likelihood that out-of-court restructuring will fail and the firm will wind up in Chapter 11. Essentially, when banks' priority status is well observed in Chapter 11, they do not seem to take any steps to avoid Chapter 11. Thus, the possibility of deviations may get banks to the bargaining table.

One can interpret Aghion, Hart, and Moore's proposal as an attempt to have the timeliness, reduced haggling, and absolute priority benefits of Chapter 7 while at the same time removing some of the bias toward liquidation. On a spectrum between the two, it strikes me overall as much closer to Chapter 7—basically, it is still an auction of the firm, with the one key difference being the noncash offers. (The Bebchuck allocation scheme is just a way of implementing absolute priority when there are "hard-to-value" noncash bids.) The idea of these noncash bids seems to be to overcome the bias toward liquidation—even if incumbent managers do not have deep pockets, Aghion, Hart, and Moore suggest that they can retain control with a noncash bid if they really are the best team for the job.

So what do I think? First, since I am less convinced about the merits of absolute priority, I am less drawn to the scheme—again, I am worrying about the ex ante effects of absolute priority on the ability to restructure out of court. Second, while I like the idea of a more flexible auction, I am unsure about how different it will be in practice. I have little in the way of evidence to go on here, but my instinct is that cash bids will have a pronounced edge in many cases, which brings us back to Chapter 7, and brings me back to my big concern about deep-pocket foreigners.

Let me attempt to be a bit more precise about this last point. We can ask the theoretical question, How does allowing a noncash bid enable us to accomplish anything that cannot already be accomplished with Chapter 7? Presumably, Chapter 7 is less than ideal because capital market imperfections make it difficult for certain cash-poor bidders to raise all the financing necessary to make an all-cash offer. In other words, because of incentive or information problems, the bidders cannot get anyone to accept the securities that they are offering in exchange for cash. Well, if this is the case, why will the current group of creditors be any different—why will they accept such securities instead of an all-cash bid?

Thus, if the shallow-pocket problem that plagues Chapter 7 is due to some real economic "blockage" (i.e., information or moral hazard problems), it is not clear to me exactly how Aghion, Hart, and Moore's proposal removes the blockage. So I see the proposal as effectively pretty close to Chapter 7, which troubles me a bit, particularly in the current context.

Is there a better option? Again, I agree with the basic premise that there ought to be something between Chapter 7 and Chapter 11 that does better. My own inclination would be to start working on the other end of the spectrum—to try to improve on the existing Chapter 11–type framework. Perhaps one might attempt to alter the rules of the road in Chapter 11 so that haggling costs and wastage of time are reduced. This might be accomplished by changing things in such a way as to reduce management's bargaining power, thereby forcing matters to a conclusion more rapidly. One concrete suggestion in this regard would be to reduce or remove the so-called exclusivity period of 180 days (in practice, it often winds up being much longer) when management alone has the right to make restructuring proposals.

References

Asquith, Paul, Robert Gertner, and David Scharfstein. 1992. Anatomy of financial distress. Working paper. Massachusetts Institute of Technology.
Gilson, Stuart, Kose John, and Larry Lang. 1990. Troubled debt restructurings: An empirical study of private reorganization of firms in default. *Journal of Financial Economics* 27:315–53.

Discussion Summary

Oliver Hart and *John Moore* started the discussion round by responding to the comments of Stein. Hart said that the introduction of noncash bids in the proposed bankruptcy procedure makes more of a difference than Stein had acknowledged. Hart noted that noncash bids would be particularly valuable in the likely case that a firm's original investors/creditors want to continue their association with the firm but are unable to raise the funds to make a cash bid. Moore criticized Stein's conclusion that the proposed new procedure is very close to the Chapter 7 procedure. Moore emphasized that the new procedure adds the step of converting the bankrupt firm into an all-equity firm before a bid for the firm is selected. He said that converting all the claimants into equityholders gives them a common objective and that allowing them to vote for the winning bid streamlines the selection process.

Jan Winiecki suggested that the proposed bankruptcy scheme could not be implemented efficiently during the current period of rapid economic transition. He said that a third of all state-owned firms should be forced into bankruptcy, and he warned that the East European countries have only a fledgling financial sector and very few individuals with financial skills. He said the East European governments will have to rely on "short-cut" bankruptcy and antitrust procedures during the transition period. He suggested that more sophisticated bankruptcy procedures, like the proposed scheme, could only be implemented five or ten years from now.

Andrei Shleifer warned of a shortage of judges interested in or capable of working in the area of commercial law. Shleifer also noted that whoever oversees the bankruptcy procedure may be subject to corruption. He suggested that management might bribe local administrators to discourage bids that would compete with a noncash management bid. This would mean that the proposed bankruptcy scheme would effectively end up leading to too few liquidations.

In response to the comments of Winiecki and Shleifer, Moore said that the shortage of individuals with financial skills and the possibility for corruption would also present problems for existing procedures like Chapter 7 and Chapter 11. He said that the proposed new scheme actually had the advantage that it minimizes both the amount of discretion that is given to administrators and the amount of financial sophistication that administrators are required to have.

Inderjit Singh questioned whether it is useful to force firms into bankruptcy because they cannot repay debts that were originally incurred for nonmarket reasons. He suggested that the authors consider the alternative of canceling debts so that the firms do not have to enter bankruptcy proceedings in the first place.

Jeffrey Sachs questioned whether most claimants are currently capable of acting as equity interests. He said that state-owned claimants, like banks, may act as a "vague morass of bureaucratic interests" rather than wealth maximizers. He noted that an absence of claimants with a real interest in wealth maximization would increase the possibility that competitive bids would not be sought out.

Michael Dooley suggested that the authors had overemphasized the difficulty of achieving coordination among the creditors. He noted that, in almost all cases, the government will hold most of the claims. Dooley asked the authors to suggest administrative rules for the state-owned claimants to follow when they exercise their voting rights.

Philippe Aghion responded to some of the questions. He asked Winiecki how he proposed to deal with the third of Polish firms that Winiecki said would need to go bankrupt. Aghion emphasized that the current Polish bankruptcy procedure would lead to extreme bargaining inefficiencies because the rules that determine priority are vague. In response to Shleifer and Sachs, Aghion noted that the existence of corrupt administrators and claimants with weak incentives compromises the efficiency of all bankruptcy procedures, not just the new procedure. Aghion concluded that the privatization of the banking sector would make any bankruptcy procedure, including the new procedure, more effective.

16   Private Business in Eastern Europe

Simon Johnson

Amid all the bad economic news from Eastern Europe in the past two years, there has been at least one consistent source of optimism—the rapid development of the private sector in some parts of some countries. But it remains far from clear whether this development will be fast or deep enough to carry these economies out of their recessions soon. It is also not fully clear why the private sector has developed faster in some places than in others.

The policy issues are important. Is there anything that a post-Communist government can do to speed up private-sector growth? Is there one type or path of economic reform that particularly stimulates the private sector?[1] Even in those countries where the private sector is relatively strong, can it provide the basis for a modern, industrial economy? These are important questions not only in Eastern Europe but also now in the former Soviet Union.[2]

This paper makes three main points that address these issues. First, comparative evidence reveals that the private sector is weak in the Czech and Slovak Federal Republic (CSFR) and much stronger in Hungary and Poland. Second,

The methodology used in the interviews reported here was developed with Piotr Strzalkowski and is part of a continuing project with him. His associates at MCR Research supervised both the interviews and the collection of information from other East European countries. Without their creative and inspired participation, this paper would not have been possible. The author would also like to thank three research assistants who very ably helped him collect and interpret data: Lloyd Melnick, Sapan Parekh, and Erik Whitlock. Helpful comments were provided by Peter Rutland, Kalman Mizsei, and Pawel Dobrowolski. The National Bureau of Economic Research generously financed the collection of cross-country survey information. Interviews with businesses in Poland were paid for with funds provided by the Fuqua School of Business, Duke University.

1. One of the arguments used in support of the "Chinese path" is that it helps nonstate enterprise to develop (McMillan and Naughton 1992, 4–6) and that this forces the state sector to become more competitive.

2. This paper will deal explicitly only with Eastern Europe. For an analysis of the emerging nonstate forms of enterprise in various parts of the former Soviet Union, see Johnson and Islamov (1991) and Johnson and Kroll (1991, 1993) and the references given there.

current government policies targeted at the private sector in all three countries are too similar to explain the difference in private-sector strength. Changes in taxes, credit conditions, and property reform have all proceeded along similar lines, yet the outcome in terms of private-sector performance has been quite different. Third, the most plausible explanation for differences in post-Communist private-sector performance lies with the different reform policies pursued by respective Communist regimes during their rule.

Continued private-sector growth is not surprising in Hungary, where the Communist regime allowed private-sector development on and off since 1968 and fairly consistently during the 1980s. However, economic reform in Poland is usually considered to have begun relatively recently, and the relative strength of its private sector needs further explanation. Therefore, I also provide more detailed evidence on the development of the Polish private sector, including the results of interviews conducted with a sample of private businesspeople in December 1991. In my assessment, the Polish entrepreneurs who have done well are those able to take advantage of the way in which economic reforms were sequenced from 1981 to 1991.

There is not a great deal of existing literature on the private sector of Eastern Europe. An excellent comprehensive survey of the private sector in East Germany and Poland up to the early 1980s is provided by Aslund (1985), and Seleny (1991) reviews the development of private business in Hungary, with particular emphasis on the 1980s. A number of papers have been written recently on the general situation of the private sector and the policies needed to stimulate its development, but most of these are general and do not contain much concrete detail. Important exceptions include an excellent review of the problems in the CSFR by Rondinelli (1991) and an interesting survey by Brandsma (1991). There are also some useful overview papers on the recent development of small business in the CSFR (McDermott and Mejstrik 1992; Capek 1990), Hungary (Hare and Grosfeld 1991; Galasi and Sziraczki, n.d.), and Poland (Piasecki 1991; Grabowski 1991; and Grabowski and Kulawczuk 1991b).

There has been surprisingly little empirical work based on interviews with entrepreneurs. At least one random-sample survey of private firms has been conducted in Gdansk, Poland (Grabowski and Kulawczuk 1991a), and an analysis of rural entrepreneurship in Hungary is available, based on data from the 1970s and early 1980s (Szelenyi 1988). Other studies have examined small, unrepresentative samples—such as interesting networks of private firms (see, e.g., Johnson and Loveman 1993). A World Bank comparative study of private manufacturing in the CSFR, Hungary, and Poland has also been announced, but its results are not yet available.

The remainder of this paper develops the three main points outlined above. Section 16.1 discusses the generic situation of the private sector under communism in Eastern Europe, and section 16.2 examines the available data on the development of the private sector in the CSFR, Hungary, and Poland over the past two years. Section 16.3 describes both the methodology and the results of our interview-based field research. Section 16.4 concludes with the important lessons. There is also an appendix that explains in more detail how our sample of Polish private entrepreneurs was selected.

16.1   The Private Sector under Communism

The story of the private sector under communism can be quickly told, in part because there is not much to say and in part because other authors have covered this ground thoroughly. This section provides information on how Communist regimes limited private activity because this is important for understanding the current situation of the East European private sector.

There were brief periods in which some Communist regimes tolerated a vibrant private sector, most notably during the New Economic Policy of the 1920s in the Soviet Union (Ball 1987; Kaufman 1962). There were also episodes of relative liberalization for private business, although these were usually followed by a crackdown. Perhaps the best example is Poland, where controls on private business were loosened in the immediate aftermath of various political crises—1956–57, 1965–68, 1977–80, and after 1982 (Aslund 1985, chap. 2). These cycles of policy reflected the tension between Communist ideology—which was opposed to any private-sector activity—and Communist governments' desire to maintain an adequate supply of goods and services. This same tension helps explain why there was frequently tolerance of so-called private plots in agriculture but also repeated clampdowns on this activity.[3] Communist regimes altered their economic policy toward the private sector in line with their current political policies. They had almost total control over their societies, and to crush the private sector they could use policy instruments that ranged from violent repression to altering tax rates. The simplest and most common policy was to declare most or all private activity illegal.

Even when legal, private business faced many constraints. Among the most significant were the difficulties associated with obtaining material inputs. Industrial supplies were hard to get, and the most desirable supplies were tightly controlled by state planning and supply agencies. Any private manufacturing operation, such as existed in the Polish handicrafts sector, relied on the state for its inputs and was therefore always vulnerable to a change in the political mood. In many cases, there were also restrictions on the use of labor by the private sector, usually in the form of statutory limits on the maximum number of employees in a private firm.

There were usually onerous taxes on private business. Tax rates were both high and unstable—it was hard to forecast future private-sector tax liability. In

---

3. The only significant private activity that remained in Eastern Europe by the 1970s was Polish agriculture, which was primarily private. However, both its supplies and its products were tightly controlled by state trading agencies.

some instances, important details of the tax regulations were not published, and local tax offices would have considerable discretion. Private businesspeople lived in fear of an investigation by tax inspectors with draconian powers.

Of course, the state tightly controlled the banking system. In all East European countries there was a monobank, so called because all functions of a central and commercial bank were effectively fused into one institution. This monobank oversaw all credit in the economy, with the goal of ensuring that it was allocated in support of the economic plan.[4] There were some supposedly independent cooperative banks, for example, for Polish agriculture, but in practice they were tightly controlled.

At the beginning of Communist rule, these regimes could seize any property they wanted.[5] As time went by and the political situation changed, the state became less inclined to use brute force against its citizens. There were exceptions, of course, and we know that the use of such force was seriously considered during 1989 by some East European governments. Communist states reserved the right to act with force against any perceived opposition, and the state's perception of what constituted opposition could change very rapidly. Actual and would-be private businesspeople were well aware of this fact.

In the mid-1960s, the private sector in Czechoslovakia, Hungary, and Poland was extremely weak and—with the exception of private agriculture in Poland—constituted a marginal economic phenomenon. In all three countries, we can consider the private sector as beginning from a similar starting point. Interestingly, as the next section shows, by the early 1990s there were significant differences among the private sectors in these countries.

16.2   Survey of Available Evidence

There is a lack of good data on the current situation of the private sector in Eastern Europe. Existing official statistical systems were constructed to monitor the performance of state enterprises, and they have been modified only slowly to measure new nonstate business. Unfortunately, Eastern Europe also lacks well-developed private sources of information, such as consultants' reports and local academics' research papers. While there are Western private consulting, accounting, and law firms operating in all three countries with the express purpose of providing detailed information on how to operate a (Western) private firm locally, we could not afford to buy the advice of these firms.

Our approach was to commission consultants' reports for each country.

---

4. The functioning of the credit system under communism is reviewed by Johnson, Kroll, and Horton (1993).

5. In some cases, this was not a legal right but simply the result of the state's coercive powers. For example, the property of some small firms was "nationalized" in Poland and Czechoslovakia illegally—i.e., this action was not legal even under the Communists' laws.

These reports were prepared during the fall of 1991 by independent researchers in each country, in the form of responses to a questionnaire.[6] As far as possible, all responses were checked by researchers in the United States against sources available here. Some inadvertent errors probably remain, and in addition we need to attach an important caveat to our description of tax rules. Tax regulations in these countries are currently very complicated and in flux.

Our survey covered Bulgaria and Romania, as well as the CSFR, Hungary, and Poland. However, the information provided for Bulgaria and Romania was less well documented and harder to check in the United States. Furthermore, it was clear that the urban private sector in Bulgaria and Romania was in a similar situation to that of the CSFR. Compared to Bulgaria and Romania, the CSFR is widely considered to have advantages—such as location and a strong industrial tradition—so we concentrated on the CSFR, reasoning that it should have the best potential for private-sector growth among those countries that ended the Communist era with only weak private business.

For each country I offer an organized set of facts. First and most important, I present all available information related to the number of private firms and the scale of their activities. Second, I review the current situation on a number of previous constraints that the Communists used to restrict the private sector. I answer the following questions. Is there now equal legal treatment of the private sector? Are there still shortages of inputs, and can all goods be freely exported and imported? Does the private sector have any tax advantages or disadvantages? Is there a banking system that is willing and able to lend to the private sector at reasonable rates of interest? Do private businesspeople have assets that they can use as collateral? More generally, what government policies are in place to help the private sector, and have they had any noticeable effects? I refer here not only to policies that are explicitly targeted at the private sector but also to more general macroeconomic policies that may have important indirect implications.

Third, I present evidence on a development that is proving important for the future prospects of the private sector—the privatization of shops and small firms. It is not the goal of this paper to explore in detail privatization plans, but it is a relevant issue to the extent that it creates new entrepreneurs or helps existing private businesses to expand.

I look first at the CSFR, using it as a benchmark because its private sector is so weak. This makes clearer the relative advantages and remaining problems that I examine for Hungary and Poland.

---

6. Simon Johnson drew up the questionnaire, and MCR Research contacted independent consultants in each country and supervised all the administrative arrangements. Consultants were paid only when they sent by fax a response to the questionnaire that satisfied MCR. Most of the information received was detailed and accurate and drew on local language sources that were not readily available outside that country. The sole exception was Bulgaria, where it proved impossible to find a reliable person. As far as possible, we checked the information provided with sources available outside the country and did not find any serious errors.

16.2.1   The Czech and Slovak Federal Republic (CSFR)

There were no legal private firms in Czechoslovakia—as it was then called—under the Communist regime. However, this situation changed rapidly after the "Velvet Revolution" of November 1989 caused the downfall of the Communist regime. By the end of 1990 there were a total of 488,000 "private firms," by 30 June 1991 this number had risen to 921,000 (*Tydenik hospodarskych novin*, 12 September 1991), and by the end of September 1991 there were 1.13 million (*Ecoservice*, 11 December 1991). This is an impressive rate of growth, but very few private firms—fewer than 5,000—were incorporated as of 30 June 1991.[7] The remaining "private firms" are actually individuals who are registered as engaged in business, of whom between 25 and 85 percent are estimated to have at least one other job.[8]

By 30 June 1991, the number of registered entrepreneurs in various sectors was divided into the following proportions: 27.6 percent in industrial production, 24.8 percent in construction, 17.2 percent in trade, 9.9 percent in nontrade services, and 20.5 percent in other sectors.[9] The same broad pattern is confirmed by the latest available statistics for registered entrepreneurs at the end of September.[10] The sectoral composition of the CSFR private sector seems fairly stable.

According to preliminary official statistics, small enterprises—defined as those nonstate and state firms with fewer than fifty employees—contributed only 1.92 percent of GNP in the Czech Republic during the first months of 1991. This share was even lower in the Slovak Republic—0.54 percent. The contribution of private firms was also low: 0.07 percent in the Czech Republic and 0.54 percent in the Slovak Republic. Better information will be available only when the tax data for 1991 are available in the spring of 1992.

The current situation of the CSFR private sector is fairly clear. There was a rapid growth in the number of private businesses after the political regime changed, but many of these "firms" represent only would-be entrepreneurs,

7. Ekonom (a CSFR economic news service) reported on 6 December 1991 that there were 2,811 "private firms" in the Czech Republic. This number must refer to incorporated firms, and we assume that there are fewer incorporated firms in the Slovak Republic. This suggests that our estimate of 5,000 incorporated firms is an upper limit.

8. Under law, there are two types of private enterprise in the CSFR. First, there is a private person who is registered as an entrepreneur by the local municipality. For some sectors, registration is possible only if the person can prove that he or she has special skills. Second, there is an incorporated company that may take one of three forms: a joint-stock company, a limited-liability company, or a partnership for which liability is not limited. All three forms require a minimum of Kčs 100,000 ($3,000) in paid-up capital.

9. Further data that confirm this picture were collected by CreditLine and published on 13 July 1991. According to this source, on 1 March 1991 there were 655,000 private firms, of which 28.9 percent were in industry, 25.7 percent in construction, 15 percent in trade, and 10.5 percent in services. "Services" comprised mostly tourist agencies—of which there were 3,500 in the CSFR—and consultancy.

10. The percentage of entrepreneurs registered in different sectors was as follows: industry, 26 percent; construction, 23 percent; trade, 20 percent; travel, 10 percent; and industrial services, 12 percent (Rutland 1992).

and the sum total of private activity is still rather insignificant. There appears to be an entrepreneurial spirit, but can it develop a more substantial private sector?

The answer to this question must depend on current conditions, which could either promote or hold back private-sector development. We need to look at government policy—especially macroeconomic, trade, and public finance policy—as well as the availability of credit and the effects of the privatization process on the private sector.

Very quickly after the November 1989 "revolution," the new government announced that private and state enterprises should now receive equal legal treatment. A constitutional amendment has been adopted, in the form of law number 100/91 Sb., which states that all owners are equal before the law. The government has repeatedly stated that it regards the development of small- and medium-sized private enterprises as essential for the success of the market economy.[11] There now really appears to be no difference in the rights of the private sector in the CSFR and in Western industrialized countries.[12]

Furthermore, the government has established a tight macroeconomic policy that has made possible a substantial degree of convertibility, allowed the liberalization of trade, and eliminated shortages.[13] According to a survey of top industrial managers conducted by the Federal Statistical Agency in April 1991, the supply of domestic raw materials and semifinished goods was considered satisfactory by 71 percent of respondents and unsatisfactory by only 14 percent.[14] As a further indicator of macroeconomic policy changes, unemployment—which was essentially zero in the Communist period—was 6.6 percent for the whole CSFR at the end of 1991. Unemployment was 11.8 percent in the Slovak Republic and 4.1 percent in the Czech Republic.

Most goods can be imported, subject only to certain duties that do not differ according to whether a firm is state or privately owned and that are not very high.[15] There remain, however, several restrictions on payments made abroad—the most important being that, while incorporated private firms can

11. See, e.g., the speech by Minister Dlouhy to the Federal Assembly, reported in *Hospodarske noviny*, 25 September 1991.

12. This statement should not be taken to mean that the whole system of private property already functions as in the West. Still to be resolved are important issues of privatization and the restitution of property seized by the Communists. The effects of these issues are dealt with below.

13. It is important to keep in mind that these shortages were never as severe in the CSFR as they were in Poland during the 1980s.

14. Only 47 percent of respondents were satisfied with the supply of goods from abroad, but, given the lack of import restrictions, this may just reflect expectations that were disappointed when the economy was opened up. Imported goods are expensive for CSFR firms and consumers.

15. An importer is liable to two taxes: first, a customs duty that is a percentage of the landed cost and that depends on the type of good (there are 5,190 different categories); second, a flat import duty (15 percent of the landed cost) that applies to all finished consumer goods. This duty is not charged on raw materials, machinery, and other productive inputs, and there is an exemption for a limited time for some goods—such as computers. In fall 1991 there were announced intentions to raise the customs duty on agricultural products, some electronics, and some textiles while the rates would be lowered on raw materials and spare parts.

purchase foreign currency with which to buy imports, individual entrepreneurs cannot.[16] Not surprisingly, there is anecdotal evidence that private individuals smuggle goods into the CSFR. As far as we can ascertain, there remain no significant export restrictions. In January 1991, there was still a small black market premium, not in excess of 10 percent—it is hard to know the precise rate because quotes on the street are often designed to attract foreign customers who can be cheated.

Nevertheless, the overall conclusion must be that the new government moved rapidly to establish general legal principles favorable to private business, to free prices, and to create supportive government agencies.[17] However, the government has also been criticized by entrepreneurs' organizations for not having done more, particularly on taxes and credit.

The current tax situation in the CSFR is difficult to specify precisely because the introduction of a new commercial code on 1 January 1992 was intended to change regulations significantly but was not preceded by detailed announcements. On many issues, the previous tax treatment of private business was murky, and the code—based on the German and Austrian models—is supposed to provide clarification. The tax regulations that follow represent our understanding of private-sector taxation at the end of 1991.

Self-employed individuals are exempt from the wage tax, which is a hefty 50 percent. Although there are no hard data, we suspect that a great number of the more than 1 million registered entrepreneurs are actually working for other people and are registered as self-employed only to reduce the cost of hiring them. One supportive anecdote is a private construction firm in Prague that, at the beginning of 1992, had 500 workers—all of whom were officially self-employed.

All firms, irrespective of ownership, face the same rates of turnover tax and social security tax, and all are quite restricted—compared to standard practice in the West—in the range of business expenses that they are allowed to claim as tax-deductible costs.[18] Incorporated private firms are subject to the same progressive corporate tax rates as state enterprises, although there are some advantages for joint ventures.[19] A significant number of the smaller joint ven-

16. An importing CSFR firm must present a valid invoice in order for a payment to be made abroad. However, the CSFR bank will not make the payment for three months if the amount involved is above a certain size—at the beginning of 1991, this was Kčs 1 million ($30,000), but, by mid-1991, it had been raised to Kčs 3 million ($90,000).

17. For example, there is now a Federal Agency for Mediating Foreign Economic Assistance, headed by a former World Bank staff member, and an Agency for Foreign Investment and Assistance at the Ministry of Industry. Active in providing training for CSFR managers are the British Know How Fund, USAID, USIA, and the Swiss Rotary Club.

18. The four basic levels of turnover tax are 0, 11, 20, and 29 percent. The social security tax depends on the level of salary, marital status, and number of children. For example, the social security tax on a monthly salary of Kčs 6,000 ($200) is 8.7 percent.

19. The rate is 20 percent for up to Kčs 200,000 ($6,000) of taxable corporate income, rising to 55 percent for more than Kčs 200,000 for a domestic company but only to 40 percent for joint ventures with capital investment above 30 percent of their paid-up capital. Joint ventures can also

Table 16.1   Personal Income Tax Rates in the CSFR

Annual Income (Kčs)	Tax Rate
0–60,000	15%
60,000–180,000	Kčs 9,000 plus 25% of taxable income over Kčs 60,000
180,000–540,000	Kčs 39,000 plus 35% of taxable income over Kčs 180,000
540,000–1,080,000	Kčs 165,000 plus 45% of taxable income over Kčs 540,000
1,080,000 and above	Kčs 408,000 plus 55% of taxable income over Kčs 1,080,000

Source: Consultant's report.
Note: Personal income tax is regulated by law no. 389/90 Sb. There are approximately Kčs 30.00 to $1.00.

tures are apparently disguised private CSFR businesses.[20] However, a bigger advantage exists for registered private entrepreneurs, who pay personal income tax on their earnings (see table 16.1) and who can claim accelerated depreciation for machinery and some other equipment if it is produced in the CSFR. They cannot, however, carry current losses into a subsequent financial year to offset future tax liability. This package constitutes only slight tax advantages for the unincorporated private sector compared with incorporated private firms and with state firms.

As part of the anti-inflation policy, there are limits on wages that are set by the Federal Ministry of Finance. The permitted rate of nominal wage growth was 9 percent in the first quarter of 1991 and 22 percent in the second quarter.[21] However, in the first half of the year, average wage growth was less than these ceilings allow—there was a real wage fall of about 20 percent. These wage regulations do not currently apply to firms with fewer than twenty-five employees.[22] Again, this represents a slight advantage for the small private sector.

Up to the end of 1991, there were no special incentives or credit policies to

apply for a two-year income tax holiday if earnings are retained in the CSFR and reinvested in privatization or in the development of a retail distribution network. Joint ventures can also apply for accelerated depreciation of capital equipment that is used for domestic production. Commercial banks and other financial institutions should pay 65 percent of their corporate income as taxes.

20. At the end of 1990, there were 1,236 joint ventures, and, by 23 July 1991 there were 2,937. In July, 84 percent of these firms had paid-up capital under Kčs 1 million ($30,000), and 1,187 had only the minimum required amount—Kčs 100,000. There were 22 large joint ventures with capital above Kčs 10 million ($300,000), representing 84 percent of total paid-up capital and 80 percent of all foreign capital in joint ventures. Most joint ventures were with CSFR legal or private persons—only 374 were with state-owned firms. This latter type of joint venture represented nineteen of the twenty-two large joint ventures and only 6 percent of joint ventures with capital less than Kčs 1 million ($30,000).

21. If the permitted wage growth rate is exceeded by more than 3 percentage points, there is a 200 percent tax on the extra payments to workers, and this tax rises to 750 percent if wages rise more than 5 percentage points over the limit.

22. On 25 September 1991, while presenting the government's program for 1992, Minister Dlouhy said that wages in the private sector should be the result of unregulated contracts between employer and employee.

promote small- and medium-sized firms.[23] Credit was available to fund the purchase of assets in the "small privatization" process, but at an interest rate that was not significantly below the usual rates. Recognizing the difficulties of the private sector, on 16 January 1992 the Czech Republic allocated Kčs 1 billion ($30 million) to help small businesses. This program will provide up to a 40 percent subsidy on interest rates and guarantees for 70 percent of the principal. Of course, it is too early to judge the effect of this initiative, but it is unlikely to stimulate the private sector quickly. Why is it so difficult to promote the private sector?

Part of the answer lies in the credit system. The CSFR's financial system is still dominated by state-owned banks. At the start of 1990, the monobank was dissolved and replaced in commercial banking by seven new banks—sometimes called *commercial banks*—although at the end of 1991 the largest of these banks still made almost 50 percent of all loans and the top three banks accounted for more than 80 percent of all credit. The banking system in the CSFR remains much more concentrated than in either Hungary or Poland, and, although most banks are due to be privatized in the spring of 1992, apparently there will not be further demonopolization.[24]

There has been some entry into this sector, but the newer banks still do not account for a large part of credit. By the end of 1990, there were twenty-five commercial banks, and, in August 1991, there were thirty-four banks. With the exception of seven subsidiaries of foreign banks, all thirty-four banks were either state-owned or joint-stock companies having a substantial state share.[25] There are also at least two smaller banks with the stated aim of financing small- and medium-sized firms.[26]

According to the new banking laws passed at the end of 1989, state commercial banks cannot raise capital from outside sources, even though their capital-asset ratio is rather low. The level of losses on bad loans may exceed these banks' own capital, and the banks are reportedly becoming more cautious.[27]

---

23. However, the Ministry for Economic Development in the Czech Republic has reportedly prepared a law that is intended to promote small- and medium-sized enterprises through changes in taxes and insurance conditions. Funds may also be established that will help provide private firms with collateral (*Tydenik hospodarskych novin*, no. 30 [1991]).

24. The current idea is to place 40 percent of bank shares through the coupon method and sell 10–15 percent to private foreign investors, with the state retaining the remaining shares.

25. Two examples of foreign bank investment are the subsidiary of Creditanstalt, with paid-up capital of $20 million and the creation of a joint venture between Societe General and Komercni banka Praha. Up to the end of 1991, however, most foreign banks seem primarily involved in consulting work.

26. These banks are Slovenska zarucni banka and Banka Bohemia—a joint-stock company with Kčs 70 million ($2 million) in paid-up capital and 52 percent of its shares owned by seven trade unions. Both banks say that they differ from other banks because they do not ask for private property as collateral. The Czech Union of Private Entrepreneurs is negotiating with the German Union of Private Entrepreneurs to borrow DM 100 million ($70 million) at 6 percent for two years. These funds would be used to create a special bank to promote small- and medium-sized firms.

27. One estimate is that, of Kčs 700 billion ($23 billion) total bank credit, between Kčs 100 and Kčs 200 billion cannot be repaid (*Banker*, no. 46 [December 1991]).

Table 16.2   Prices in the CSFR during 1991 (index with December 1990 = 100)

	Month						
	Jan.	Feb.	Mar.	Apr.	May	Jun.	Jul.
Food	133.1	131.8	129.1	128.0	127.9	127.3	127.2
Consumer goods	125.0	140.0	156.0	160.0	168.0	169.0	167.4
Services	110.0	113.0	114.0	121.0	126.0	141.0	140.9
Total CPI	128.0	132.0	141.0	143.0	147.0	151.0	149.2

Source: Tydenik hospodarskych novin, no. 36 (1991), from official statistics of Federalni statisticky urad.

This is reflected in the rising relative proportion of short-term loans, which were 28.1 percent of all credit at the end of 1990 but had already reached 36.2 percent by 30 June 1991 (*Tydenik hospodarskych novin*, nos. 19, 40 [1991]). On 30 June 1991, total credits issued stood at Kčs 662.9 billion ($22 billion), of which only Kčs 24.7 billion ($820 million) were lent to individuals and private business combined, and of which only Kčs 1.5 billion ($50 million) was reported as lent to private business (Brandsma 1991).[28]

Nominal interest rates—which are set by the central bank—fell during 1991, but real interest rates rose dramatically. Nominal loan rates were high at the beginning of 1991—up to 24 percent per year—but they fell steadily. For example, in September 1991, the discount rate was reduced from 10 to 9.5 percent, and the maximum interest rate that commercial banks could charge on credits was lowered even more sharply, from 19.5 to 17 percent. As table 16.2 shows, there were sharp price increases at the beginning of the year, and the high inflation in the first seven months of 1991 implied negative real interest rates. However, in the second half of 1991, prices were roughly constant— retail prices recorded an increase of only 45.3 percent for the whole year (*Hospodarske noviny*, 21 January 1992). Real interest rates must now be considered rather high and unlikely to encourage private borrowing.

Of course, the lack of loans to the private sector could also be due to the requirements of bank lending. In principle, borrowing from a bank is not too difficult. In order to obtain a loan, an entrepreneur has to produce evidence that he or she is either incorporated or registered by a local municipality. The entrepreneur must also specify his or her objectives and provide a business plan and all relevant financial data.[29] In most cases, private property is needed as collateral, and most banks prefer to secure their loans with real estate.

28. Because of the perceived problems with commercial banks, a second round of banking reform was supposed to begin in January 1992 and involve at least partial privatization of banks. However, this round of privatization has now been delayed. It is also unclear how privatization alone will strengthen banks' balance sheets.

29. Compared to Western industrialized countries, we would expect that a lower proportion of people in the CSFR know how to prepare a business plan. However, there are now educational programs in which these skills are taught.

256   Simon Johnson

Table 16.3   The Housing Stock in the CSFR (31 December 1989)

	CSFR	Czech Rep.	Slovak Rep.
No. of apartments	5,860,286	4,082,357	1,777,929
Of which (% shares):			
State	24.1	27.0	17.4
Cooperative	18.3	17.5	20.1
State enterprise	8.9	9.7	6.8
In private houses	48.7	45.8	55.7

Source: Hospodarske noviny, no. 52 (1990); Tydenik hospodarskych novin, no. 9 (1991); Federalni statisticky urad.

There is some private property that in principle could be mortgaged. Almost half the housing stock in the CSFR is privately owned—table 16.3 shows the distribution by type of ownership and republic—and most of this housing is presently unmortgaged. Does this mean that there is a fund of property that is available for use as collateral?

The answer is rather complicated because there is a strict tenancy law that makes eviction very difficult, even in the case of foreclosure. For this reason, banks do not usually accept private apartments as collateral.[30] Cooperative apartments are also quite unsuitable as collateral.[31] However, mortgage credit can be obtained against the security of some private houses, particularly second homes in rural areas.[32] Unfortunately, it is not possible to determine whether this potential collateral is in the hands of would-be entrepreneurs.

All this evidence suggests two conclusions. First, there are no remaining barriers to private-sector growth that could be rapidly removed by government action. Second, it is unlikely that the CSFR private sector will soon amount to a large part of the economy. There are plenty of people who want to be entrepreneurs, but it is difficult for them to expand rapidly, and there are no easy answers to their problems with the credit system.

This rather pessimistic conclusion does suggest a further question. Can the process of small privatization—especially the sale of shops—help the accu-

30. There are not many such apartments, even though, according to Czech law no. 283/90 Sb., municipalities are allowed to sell state-owned apartments to private persons. The process of housing privatization has been slowed down by restitution claims.
31. According to law no. 176/90 Sb., a member of a housing cooperative can transfer his or her rights and obligations to another person, provided that the housing cooperative agrees. The second person must then become a member of the cooperative. A cooperative apartment remains always the property of the cooperative, and a person can buy and sell only the right to use it.
32. Agricultural land remains predominantly nonprivate. According to official statistics, in 1988 there were 6,749,000 hectares of land in state and cooperative farms, and only 261,000 hectares were farmed by "self-producers," i.e., private farmers. There are not yet any official statistics concerning the privatization of land, even though some land has been obtained by former members of cooperatives. Still outstanding are most claims for the restitution of land seized after the Second World War.

mulation of capital in the private sector? Can the government promote private business by helping it acquire privatized assets?[33]

The privatization of retail shops and restaurants is governed by the so-called small privatization law, number 427/90 Sb. There are no official data on the number of shops affected, and estimates range between 70,000 and 130,000 for the whole CSFR (*Banker*, no. 46 [December 1991]). Almost all privatizations take the form of an auction, sometimes for full ownership rights, more often for a two-year lease.[34] Recently, there have also been auctions of five-year leases. Around 12 percent of all sales have been through "Dutch auctions," which are intended to facilitate sales in areas where demand for retail space is not great.[35] By the end of 1991, 19,500 units had been sold or leased in the CSFR, for a combined price of Kčs 25.5 billion ($800 million) (Rutland 1992). For most types of retail shop, the new operator or owner can freely choose the goods to be sold.[36]

Until the small privatization process began at the start of 1991, there were almost no private retail shops or restaurants. Small privatization continues but will not quickly transform the structure of the economy. Quite probably, the most attractive properties were auctioned first, and the pace of small privatization will slow.

Restitution has been resolved in principle by legislation, but important practical issues remain.[37] The only property that can be claimed is that which was nationalized or confiscated after 25 February 1948.[38] Restitution will either be through returning the original property or through a combination of cash and government bonds as compensation. By September 1991, 12,000 claims under law number 87/91 had been presented to the CSFR Ministry of Finance. Under these laws, there are deadlines by which claims must be made. However, the last deadline at this time—for claims on land—is 31 December 1992, so the restitution process is far from complete.

Even if these complications with small privatization are resolved, most CSFR production and employment remains concentrated in large firms, which

33. It is up to the Federal Ministry of Finance and the Republic Ministries of Privatization whether a particular firm should be treated as large or small and dealt with under law no. 91/91 Sb. or law no. 427/90 Sb., respectively.

34. The first time a set of property rights is auctioned, only Czech and Slovak citizens are allowed to bid. Foreigners can bid at subsequent auctions if the property rights are not bought in the first round.

35. See the statement by Minister Jezek in *Hospodarske noviny*, 1 October 1991. The term *Dutch auction* is used in the CSFR to describe an auction in which the asking price starts at book value and then falls until a purchase is made or until the minimum reserve price is reached. Dutch auctions have been used in less wealthy regions; in the center of Prague, there are no Dutch auctions, and the selling price has been on average thirteen times higher than the initial asking price.

36. An important exception is food shops—for one year after an auction or restitution there cannot be a substantial change in the type of goods sold.

37. Claims can be made under laws nos. 403/90, 458/90, 87/91, 229/91, and 137/91 Sb.

38. This effectively excludes firms that were confiscated after the Second World War because the owners were deemed to have collaborated with the Nazis.

the private sector is not in a position to purchase quickly. At the same time, the so-called large privatization has been delayed and has not generated rapid success. The CSFR faces a serious problem because of the size disparity between the very young private sector and the existing state sector. It is unlikely that the private sector can provide a significant share of output, particularly in industry, for some years. Unless large state firms are broken up into small, more digestible pieces, it is also unlikely that the existing private firms will be able to purchase a significant amount of privatized assets.

16.2.2 Hungary

Given the fact that the private sector has been developing in Hungary for a relatively long period—at least since 1982 and arguably since 1968—it might be expected that Hungarian official statistics would better cover the private sector than is usual in Eastern Europe. If anything, the opposite is true. Most disappointing is that there exist almost no official data that show directly the property form of an enterprise.[39] As a result, it is extremely hard to determine what is really private and what represents some reorganized form of state enterprise in Hungary.[40]

The available statistics on the number of firms are given in table 16.4. The Hungarian Statistical Office divides firms into a number of categories, which are represented in this table. First, there are five forms of state companies: enterprises, trusts, subsidiaries, joint companies (known in Hungarian as *Kozosvallalat*), and associations (known in Hungarian as *Egyesules*). Second, there are incorporated firms, which include both joint-stock companies and limited-liability companies.[41] Third, there are various kinds of cooperatives. There are also joint ventures with foreign partners and unincorporated businesses, neither of which are included in table 16.4.[42]

The most striking fact revealed in table 16.4 is the rapid rise in the number of limited-liability companies during 1990. This rise is confirmed by numbers that are available for the end of 1990, which show 18,317 limited-liability companies and 646 joint-stock companies (*Figyelo*, no. 39 [1991]).[43] As table 16.4 shows, by the end of June 1991, there were 28,059 limited-liability companies

---

39. The statistical office uses the term *private* to refer to individual entrepreneurs. The actual level of private capital in a company is nowhere measured.

40. This confusion is partly due to the fact that in Hungary, particularly between 1989 and 1990, state enterprises were able to initiate "spontaneous" privatization (Stark 1990). State enterprises never had this opportunity in the CSFR.

41. As far as we know, nearly all joint-stock companies so far have been established by state enterprises, but most limited-liability companies were founded by private individuals.

42. Sometimes three types of firms—joint-stock companies, limited-liability companies, and joint ventures—are classified together as *economic companies* (known as *gazdasagi tarasago* in Hungarian).

43. *Figyelo* (Observer) is a Hungarian economic weekly.

Table 16.4 Number of Hungarian Firms, by Institutional Form (excluding unincorporated firms)

	Dec. 1982	Dec. 1985	Dec. 1986	Dec. 1987	Dec. 1988	Dec. 1989	Sept. 1990	Dec. 1990	May 1991
State companies									
Enterprises, trusts	1,782	1,910	1,940	1,955	1,986	2,001	2,008		
Subsidiaries	25	254	345	397	391	398	373		
Joint companies (*Kozosvallalat*)	211	251	276	302	309	327	251		187
Associations (*Egyesules*)	45	57	61	69	78	105	198		201
Incorporated firms									
Joint-stock companies	19	62	74	137	116	307	594	646	784
Limited-liability companies (KFT)	...	...	...	...	451	4,485	15,560	18,317	28,059
Cooperatives									
Agricultural fishing and specialized agricultural cooperatives	1,387	1,350	1,340	1,337	1,333	1,333	1,392		
Other cooperatives	2,745	2,735	2,719	2,658	2,439	2,510	2,559		
Small cooperatives	145	762	1,278	2,154	3,108	3,233	3,191		
Other	...	535	545	588	600	470	576		
Total	...	7,916	8,578	9,597	10,811	15,169	26,702		

All data are for the end of the respective month.
Sources: Economic Trends in Hungary (Budapest: Gazdasagkutato Intezet, November 1990), except for May 1991 data, which are from *Heti Vilaggazdasag*, 19 October 1991.

in Hungary. By the end of 1991, there were between 52,000 and 53,000 incorporated businesses in Hungary.[44]

The growth in limited-liability companies provides a rough indicator for the development of private business, although some of these "new" firms may actually be previously existing firms which were legally registered for the first time.[45] We also know that, during 1990, 14,867 "economic organizations" were "founded"—although only 13,491 were classified as being "new"—while 632 were closed and 202 reported as having no legal successor (Central Statistical Office, Monthly Statistics, July 1991). Unfortunately, this source does not indicate either the property form or the sectors of those firms that opened and closed.

There has also been a rapid growth in the number of joint ventures in Hungary—in the first nine months of 1990, 2,225 new joint ventures were established.[46] There are obvious tax advantages to forming a joint venture, although the minimum required investment is quite high—Ft 50 million (about $650,000).[47] However, there are no statistics that reveal the extent of participation by the Hungarian private sector in these joint ventures.

The number of unincorporated firms has also risen. There are two kinds of partnerships in Hungary: ordinary partnerships, in which all partners have unlimited liability, and limited partnerships, in which "full" partners have unlimited liability but any "silent" partner has limited liability. On 31 December 1989, there were 5,769 ordinary partnerships and 1,125 limited partnerships, but, by 31 May 1991, these totals had risen to 10,869 and 9,537, respectively (*Heti Vilaggazdasag*, 19 October 1991).

It is surprisingly difficult to obtain statistics on the number of individual entrepreneurs in Hungary. One estimate is that there are over 300,000 such people.[48] Another informed source states there are 500,000.[49] We have not been able to obtain satisfactory confirmation of this number, and we recommend treating it with extreme caution.

These statistics suggest that there is a boom in the creation of new business in Hungary, and it is likely that much of this business can be considered to be

44. These numbers were provided by Kalman Mizsei in his comments on this paper at the conference.

45. It is well known that there has long been a vibrant underground economy in Hungary(see, e.g., Stark 1989).

46. A joint venture can obtain a 60 percent reduction in its taxable income during its first five years, and a 40 percent reduction subsequently, provided that it satisfies the following conditions: that most of its revenue is from selling goods or running a hotel that it built; that its registered capital exceeds Ft 50 million ($650,000); and that at least 30 percent of its capital is foreign. A joint venture can receive even more generous allowances if it operates in certain "important activities," which have been established by law.

47. The official exchange rate is Ft 76.00 to $1.00. In mid-1991, the black market rate was Ft 80.00 to $1.00.

48. This figure was given by Csilla Huvyadi in a presentation at the AEA meeting in New Orleans, January 1992. We have been unable to find a published reference.

49. This number was provided by Kalman Mizsei.

private. It makes sense that Hungary's private economy should be more developed than the CSFR's, not least because Hungary's comprehensive reform legislation was initiated earlier.[50] The most important legislation was the Company Law of 1988, supported by the Law on Transformation of 1989, which made it possible to establish new forms of enterprise—such as joint-stock companies and limited-liability companies. However, the sustained growth of the Hungarian private sector can be traced back at least to the reform legislation of 1982 (Seleny 1991).

The Hungarian government's policy is clear: the private sector is viewed as an essential part of the economy and at this time should receive some advantages. Whether these advantages are sufficient remains controversial.[51] There certainly appears to be no special, comprehensive program to help the private sector.

The prerequisites for private-sector growth are arguably in place. The macroeconomic situation has sufficiently improved, and, although there is still significant inflation, there are no longer any significant shortages.[52] Foreign trade is less controlled than in the past, and imports can be made by any kind of firm or by private individuals. However, trade is not completely free. There are tariffs, and about one-third of all agricultural products still require an export licence. About 10 percent of imports are still not liberalized, including raw materials, semifinished goods, agricultural products, and some consumer goods. There are also some quotas, for example, on cars.

There is no difference in the tax rates faced by private and state firms, for example, on turnover taxes.[53] There is a 40 percent tax on profits, and the social security contribution is 43 percent of an employee's gross wage.[54] However, there are some tax advantages for private firms in the form of allowances that reduce profit-tax liability. Every firm that is owned by private individuals receives a 50 percent reduction in its profit tax, but only during 1991–93. In addition, any firm that has at least 50 percent private ownership can obtain accelerated depreciation allowances.[55] There is a 40 percent tax on profits, but private individuals instead pay personal income tax. As is apparent from table

50. The most notable pieces of recent legislation were the Company Law (no. VI, 1988), the Transformation Law (no. XIII, 1989), the Law on State Property Agency (no. VII, 1990), the Act on Securities (1990), the Preprivatization Act (no. LXXIV, 1990), the Act on Direct Foreign Investment in Hungary (1990), and the Asset Policy Guidelines (decree no. 20, 1990, of the Hungarian Parliament).

51. For example, Kornai (1990) makes a strong case for more substantial assistance to the private sector, as a way to offset the continuing strength of the state sector.

52. Hungary still imports most of its oil from the former Soviet Union, and these deliveries have been less than the agreed-on levels. Therefore, there is a potential shortage of energy that can be linked to the disintegration of the CMEA (Council for Mutual Economic Assistance) and the problems inside the former Soviet Union.

53. The turnover-tax rates for services are 0, 15, and 25 percent, and for products they are 0 and 25 percent.

54. There is an additional tax that is intended to finance unemployment benefits. Employers pay 1.5 percent of gross wages, and each employee pays 0.5 percent of his or her gross wage.

55. There are also tax breaks for "important" investments in infrastructure and agriculture.

Table 16.5   Income Tax Rates in Hungary

Annual Income (Ft)	Tax Rate
0–55,000	0%
55,001–90,000	12% of taxable income over Ft 55,000
90,001–120,000	Ft 4,200 plus 18% of taxable income over Ft 90,000
120,001–150,000	Ft 9,600 plus 30% of taxable income over Ft 120,000
150,001–300,000	Ft 18,600 plus 32% of taxable income over Ft 150,000
300,001–500,000	Ft 66,600 plus 40% of taxable income over Ft 300,000
500,001 and above	Ft 146,600 plus 50% of taxable income over Ft 500,000

Source: Consultant's report.

16.5, paying personal income taxes is an advantage—as long as one's income is not too far above Ft 300,000 (about $4,000). Perhaps most important, the private sector is exempt from the controls on wage growth that are strictly enforced on the state sector. This difference in tax treatment enables private firms to pay higher wages and attract skilled labor.

The state monobank was dissolved at the beginning of 1987, and five new state-owned "commercial banks" were created.[56] However, within the banking system it is evident that there are still very close ties, in the form of outstanding loans and cross-ownership, between very large state firms and banks.[57] There are fears that the Hungarian industrial structure will begin to resemble that of Yugoslavia, where banks help firms find ways to keep their budget constraints "soft." However, a counterclaim can also be made—that Hungary is following the successful German model of allowing close links between banks and firms.

In order to obtain a loan, a Hungarian entrepreneur must demonstrate that he or she has a satisfactory business plan and also provide some collateral. The one serious problem appears to be that it is very difficult to obtain mortgage credit—to borrow against the security of an apartment or a house.[58] There is also relatively little private land in Hungary.[59]

Nominal interest rates also remain quite high. In the first quarter of 1991,

56. There are no special regulations on the kind of customers that these banks should serve, but one bank has tended to specialize in lending to small enterprises.

57. This is true, even though in total the state explicitly owns only 33 percent of financial institutions (National Bank of Hungary, *Annual Report*, 1990). Some observers are worried by the rapid growth in interenterprise credits in the state sector. In early 1991, this had reached Ft 200–300 billion ($3–$5 billion), which is about 10 percent of GDP and constitutes more than half of all the loans received by enterprises.

58. The reason for the lack of mortgage credit is unclear and requires further investigation, particularly as it is possible to buy and sell private apartments freely. About 80 percent of all housing is already privately owned. In all likelihood, there are complications caused by legal restrictions on eviction—as in the CSFR and Poland.

59. The state owns 30.8 percent of the land area, and cooperatives own 57.2 percent. So-called small producers operate on only 12.0 percent of the land (annual statistics, 1989). There does not yet appear to be a well-developed market for agricultural land, so it is not yet attractive as collateral.

the interest rates on loans with a maturity of one year were between 23 and 50 percent.[60] However, inflation remains quite high—prices rose 35.7 percent in the first half of 1991.[61] Nevertheless, according to official statistics, at the start of 1990, there was Ft 374 billion ($4.7 billion) in outstanding loans to individuals and to small enterprises—with total credit of Ft 1,704 billion ($21.3 billion) (National Bank of Hungary, *Market Letter*, no. 3 [1991]). There are, in principle, also special credits available to help individuals and private firms acquire assets in the privatization process, but up to the end of 1991 these credits do not appear to have been very significant.

The privatization process in Hungary has several elements that need to be mentioned here.[62] Under the so-called preprivatization law, the State Property Agency—to which I will refer by its Hungarian acronym, AVU—plans to privatize around 10,000 shops "by 1992." This form of privatization means precisely that individuals can purchase the equipment and stocks of shops but obtain only the right to lease the real estate (*Figyelo*, 14 March 1991, 4). These rights are to be sold in open auctions, and, if successful, this would affect about 20 percent of all state-owned shops.

There are some complications. AVU has been criticized for asking too high a price for the shops. Perhaps more important, however, is that, in most cases, a successful bidder pays some money to AVU for the right to lease the property but the actual lease payments must be made to the local government. These lease payments are fixed in advance, but often for a period less than the length of the lease. Financially pressed local governments have expressed their interest in sharply raising rents on privatized shops.

In summer 1991, there began a new program, called *self-privatization*, in

60. The average annual interest rates in each month were as follows: January, 33.1 percent; February, 34.2 percent; March, 34.8 percent; April, 35.2 percent.

61. Monthly inflation was as follows: January, 7.5 percent; February, 4.9 percent; March, 3.7 percent; April, 2.4 percent; May, 2.2 percent; June, 2.1 percent (National Bank of Hungary, *Monthly Review*, no. 4 [1991]). Inflation in the consumer price index was 17.0 percent in 1989 and 28.9 percent in 1990.

62. Hungary is the only East European country in which privatization is taking place under legislation that was passed when the Communists were still in control—the Law on Protection of State Property (January 1990). Privatizations are supervised by the State Property Agency, which became operational on 1 March 1990 (Whitlock 1990).

At first, privatization in Hungary was enterprise initiated, but, after the change of political regime, there was an attempt to use more active programs, in which the government sold assets. However, by mid-1991, there was dissatisfaction with the pace of privatization (see, e.g., *Figyelo*, 11 July 1991, 1). One estimate places the value of total assets at around Ft 2,000 billion ($32 billion) (Whitlock 1990). To the middle of 1991, under AVU (the State Property Agency) there have been only 160 "transformations." (Before privatization, a state enterprise must be transformed into either a joint-stock company or a limited-liability company.) These 160 enterprises are worth Ft 203 billion ($2.34 billion), but only fifty have been fully transformed (*Figyelo*, 11 July 1991, 13).

As a result, there are new initiatives, in the form of "preprivatization" and "self-privatization," which are described in the text, as well as plans to pass a new privatization law. The precise shape of this law is not yet clear, but it seems likely to differ from Poland's, in that there will probably not be either discounts for workers in privatized enterprises or free giveaway of rights to obtain shares.

which the AVU has selected eighty-four consulting companies to act as a type of owner for up to 600 small- and medium-sized companies—with asset values less than Ft 300 million ($3.8 million) and fewer than 300 workers.[63] By December 1991, there were more than 300 contracts signed or under negotiation between AVU and consulting companies, and 132 contracts had actually been signed (*Figyelo*, 19 December 1991, 18). It is also now possible for AVU to agree to a foreign bid on an enterprise without consulting the target company.[64] Whether allowing this form of hostile takeover speeds up privatization remains to be seen.

The Hungarian restitution process remains unresolved. Legislation was passed in April 1991, but it was deemed unconstitutional by the Hungarian Supreme Court because it excluded emigrés and people whose property was taken before June 1949 from restitution. The political debate over this issue continues.

According to current Hungarian legislation, there will not be restitution of property, but people can claim compensation for property seized after 8 June 1949.[65] This compensation will be paid in the form of a government bond with a three-year maturity (par. 5 of the 1991 Law on Compensation). This bond can be turned into a lifetime annuity or used to buy privatized property, such as farmland, apartments, and AVU privatized property. Trading these bonds on a secondary market is also permitted, but anyone other than the original bondholder can use the bond only to buy property privatized by AVU. Needless to say, the precise outcome of this process is still unclear.[66]

Although statistical problems make it hard to know the precise situation of the Hungarian private sector, there are indications that its growth has accelerated in the past two years. The incorporated private business sector has grown particularly fast. Unfortunately, there are no good numbers on private-sector employment, and estimates depend greatly on the number of workers employed by registered entrepreneurs. Our best guess is that the private sector employs between 650,000 and 1 million people, which implies that its share of urban employment is in the range of 15–25 percent. The future growth of

63. Some of these consulting companies are foreign, but all must be registered in Hungary. These companies must pay a fee to the government and leave the existing management in place, and they cannot simply liquidate the firm. Their goal is to sell the firm to the highest bidder, and they will receive a percentage share of the proceeds. However, the sale must take place within two years, or the asset will revert back to AVU. Hungarians refer to this as *privatizing privatization*, and the attractions of this approach are evident when one considers that AVU employs fewer than 100 people.

64. The first such case was that of the Gundel Hotel.

65. Under the Compensation Law, the maximum amount that a person can receive is Ft 5 million ($62,500) per piece of property (par. 4.3 of the law). Restitution remains very controversial—the Smallholders' party continues to campaign on behalf of former landowners. Some important opposition groups are against restitution.

66. This process is governed by law no. 25, 1991, which was only passed in September 1991. Claims must be submitted within ninety days of the law coming into force.

this sector is likely to be steady, with probably a slowdown in the rate of creation of new businesses.

16.2.3   Poland

Statistics on the number of firms in the Polish private sector are quite good.[67] However, in order fully to understand these statistics, it is necessary to appreciate the difference between *trade law companies* and *individuals* who operate as firms. Both limited-liability and joint-stock companies are trade law companies, which means that they have their legal basis in the amended 1934 Commercial Code.[68] In this paper, I refer to these companies by their common collective Polish name: *spolka*. Polish official statistics define a *spolka* as private when at least 51 percent is owned by private individuals, and table 16.6 shows the recent rapid growth in the number of private *spolki*.

Table 16.6 shows both companies founded with only "domestic" capital and those that were registered as joint ventures—at this time requiring a minimum investment of $50,000 in "hard currency."[69] The total number of joint ventures rose from 32 in 1988 to 429 in 1989 and 1,645 by the end of 1990. For most of the Communist period, it was not practically possible to create new *spolki*, but this changed after 1987 when the Communists tried to encourage some private business.[70] The number of incorporated *spolki* rose from 1,275 in 1988 to 11,693 at the end of 1989 and to 33,239 at the end of 1990.

The growth of *spolki* tells only part of the story of the Polish private sector. Many private entrepreneurs, even those with substantial businesses, prefer to operate as individuals.[71] There are several reasons for this. First, it takes only a few days to start an individual business because it is necessary only to complete a simple registration procedure; in contrast, forming a *spolka* is relatively complex and usually takes time.[72] Second, there is no minimum starting capital for an individual, whereas for *spolki* it is now Zl 10 million (about $1,000) for a limited-liability company and Zl 250 million (about $20,000) for a joint-

---

67. In the Polish statistical system, a company with at least 51 percent of its shares privately owned is defined as private.

68. A very good translation of the Commercial Code is now available: "The Polish Commercial Code: The Law as at 15th August 1991," translated by Roman Poplawski and published by the Polish Bar Foundation (Warsaw, 1991).

69. Not shown in table 16.6 is the number of *Polonia* firms, which were a forerunner of joint ventures in which only foreigners of Polish origin were supposed to participate. Although these firms attracted some attention when first formed, they were never a very significant part of the economy. *Polonia* firms numbered 46 in 1980, 683 in 1985, 689 in 1988, 727 in 1989, and 862 in 1990.

70. A few *spolki* existed under the Communists, but these had been created before the Communists took power, and they were subject to state control.

71. De jure, one principle advantage of *spolki* is that they have limited liability. However, interviews with entrepreneurs suggest that, in practice, individuals do not face unlimited liability.

72. A *spolka z.o.o.* (limited liability company) can be formed in a few weeks, but a *spolka akcyjne* (joint-stock company) takes significantly longer.

Table 16.6   **The Number of Private *Spolki* in Poland: Domestic and Joint Venture**

	31 December 1989	1 December 1990	30 June 1991
Industry			
Domestic	2,769	7,014	7,698
Joint venture	240	853	1,431
Construction			
Domestic	2,640	5,646	7,164
Joint venture	12	71	167
Agriculture			
Domestic	83	342	285
Joint venture	14	48	62
Forestry			
Domestic	10	36	39
Joint venture	3	4	5
Transportation			
Domestic	86	356	507
Joint venture	14	67	124
Telecommunication			
Domestic	18	56	80
Joint venture	. . .	5	7
Trade			
Domestic	1,759	8,661	12,598
Joint venture	32	198	475
Other branches of			
material production			
Domestic	2,979	7,098	5,837
Joint venture	80	258	296
Municipal economy			
Domestic	76	160	163
Joint venture	1	6	9
Nonmaterial production			
Domestic	1,273	3,870	4,145
Joint venture	33	135	264
Total	11,693	33,239	38,516
Of which, joint venture	429	1,645	2,840

Source: Consultant's report.

stock company.[73] Third, if the accounting is handled properly, there are fewer taxes on an individual entrepreneur than on a *spolka* (see below for more de-

73. Up to 1989, the minimum capital required to start a limited-liability company was Zl 1,000, which had been a significant amount in the 1930s but was worth only a few dollars by the late 1980s. It is not unusual to meet people who registered several *spolki* at that time, some of which may still be "sleeping"—if they are not active, then no taxes need to be paid.

Table 16.7   **Number of "Individual Entrepreneurs" in Poland**

	31 December 1990	30 June 1991	30 September 1991
Industry	334,613	339,291	348,803
Construction	165,541	165,428	170,618
Transportation	61,368	56,913	60,203
Trade	346,294	456,844	N.A.
Catering and restaurants	22,511	30,443	N.A.
Other material services	122,099	122,555	124,768
Nonmaterial services	83,066	100,923	111,629
Total	1,135,492	1,272,397	N.A.

Source: Consultant's report, based on statistics from the Polish Central Statistical Office.
Note: N.A. = not available.

tails). In addition, there was a one-year tax holiday that was available to individuals in 1990, as long as they were "newly" involved in wholesale trade.[74]

On 31 December 1989, official statistics reveal that there were 813,485 "unincorporated firms" registered, of which 482,020 were in handicrafts, 71,802 were in trade, and 259,663 were classified as *others*.[75] Fortunately, after this date, statistical information was published in a more detailed form, and table 16.7 shows the number of unincorporated firms (also known as *individual entrepreneurs*) at the end of 1990, halfway through 1991, and—for some sectors—at the end of the third quarter of 1991.

Table 16.7 shows growth, but perhaps not as rapid as might be expected—anyone who has visited Warsaw in the last two years can attest to the number of new firms that are apparent. In fact, as table 16.8 shows in some detail, during 1990 there were significant numbers of start-ups and liquidations of private firms.[76]

Some of these firms failed because, although they had prospered under the Communists, they could not adapt to the completely new economic conditions in 1990. For example, the category *handicrafts* represents mostly traditional private-sector activities, which were allowed to operate under the Communists. The "net balance" of firm creation in this sector—start-ups minus suspensions

74. The actual requirement was that the business was new at the address where it was registered. Not surprisingly, there is anecdotal evidence of businesses simply changing their addresses and people active in other sectors—especially retail trade—switching to be registered as wholesale traders.

75. Official statistics give the total number of unincorporated firms as 357,000 at the end of 1980, 418,000 at the end of 1985, 660,000 at the end of 1988, 814,000 at the end of 1989, and 1,136,000 at the end of 1990.

76. A suspended firm does not have to pay taxes but can be quickly reestablished. In interviews, entrepreneurs sometimes say that they currently operate one firm but that they have several more "sleeping." Some sleeping firms can be viewed as a form of tradable option. For example, in 1991, I was offered a sleeping firm that was exempt from taxation—because it had been properly registered as a wholesale trader before the end of 1990. Unfortunately, official statistics do not appear to record the number of sleeping firms that are reawakened.

Table 16.8   Start-Up, Liquidation, and Suspension of "Individual Firms" during 1990 in Poland

	Cumulative Totals, in Thousands (by quarter)			
	1–3	1–6	1–9	1–12
Total				
Start-up	66.9	174.7	314.1	516.2
Liquidation	33.7	65.6	102.0	154.0
Suspension	78.3	81.4	93.4	100.2
Handicraft				
Start-up	26.5	54.5	85.7	140.6
Liquidation	19.4	36.4	53.1	75.0
Suspension	42.4	43.5	46.2	51.1
Trade				
Start-up	27.3	91.0	180.9	300.7
Liquidation	4.4	10.9	22.5	41.9
Suspension	6.0	8.6	16.4	21.4
Services				
Start-up	13.1	29.2	47.5	74.9
Liquidation	9.9	18.3	26.4	37.1
Suspension	29.9	29.3	30.8	27.7

Source: Consultant's report, based on statistics from the Polish Central Statistical Office.

and liquidations—was negative in the first three quarters of 1990. The most striking contrast is with the trade sector, which is composed largely of entrepreneurs who entered this activity in 1989 and 1990. Table 16.8 shows a positive net balance of firm creation for this sector even in the first quarter of 1990, and this net balance rose rapidly during 1990.

The latest available data are for 30 September 1991, and they show totals of 44,226 private *spolki*, 3,512 joint ventures, and 1,365,644 individual entrepreneurs. Table 16.9 shows the sectoral composition of the individual entrepreneurs' activity, their employment; it also shows that about 200,000 of these firms have managed to qualify for tax-free status. The latest estimates are that the private *spolki* and joint ventures together employ 0.5 million people, in addition to the 2.5 million shown employed by individual entrepreneurs in table 16.9. The Polish urban labor force is about 12 million people, so these numbers imply that the private sector accounts for 25 percent of jobs outside agriculture.

This private-sector growth was not the result of particularly favorable government tax policies. In fact, Polish tax policies are very similar to those of the CSFR. Private firms face the same turnover and social security taxes as state firms. *Spolki* face a corporate income tax of 40 percent, although the effective

Table 16.9   **Number of Individual Entrepreneurs in Poland on 30 September 1991**

Sector	No. of Firms		Total Employment
	Total	Of Which, Taxed	
Industry	348,803	306,989	826,658
Construction	170,618	154,430	392,575
Transportation	60,203	59,493	74,575
Trade	514,778	393,838	797,772
Catering	34,845	29,973	83,981
Material services	124,768	122,353	143,953
Nonmaterial services	111,629	102,443	159,552
	1,365,644	1,169,519	2,477,751

Source: Consultant's report, based on statistics from the Polish Central Statistical Office.
Note: The second column shows the number of firms that were actually subject to taxation.

tax rate may be much lower.[77] State firms also pay 40 percent corporate income tax, but they are liable to two important taxes from which the private sector is exempt. First, there is the "excess wage tax," which penalizes firms paying wages above a norm set by the government.[78] Second, state enterprises must also pay a "dividend" to the government, based on the value of their fixed assets.

Individuals operating as a business must pay income tax and also a "leveling tax"—if the entrepreneur's annual income exceeds Zl 36 million ($3,000). The Polish tax rates are quite high, as can be seen from table 16.10.[79] In addition, the entrepreneur must pay a 20 percent "wages tax" and a social insurance contribution that is at least Zl 238,000 per month.[80]

Surprisingly, some strange Communist tax regulations still exist with regard to individuals operating in the "handicrafts" sector. For this sector, there is also a fixed tax per year, with a rate that depends positively on the size of the town in which the firm operates. The tax also depends on the number of employees—a tailor who works by himself in a town with more than 50,000 inhabit-

77. Polish entrepreneurs have found numerous ways to reduce their tax liability. One favored route is to have several companies, which employ each other as subcontractors and thus reduce their declared profit.
78. In 1990, there were bitter complaints from the private sector when it was subject to the same "excess wage tax" as the state sector. Private firms were fully exempted from this tax only in 1991, but anecdotal evidence suggests that they found ways to avoid it even in 1990.
79. A new, comprehensive income-tax system is supposed to have come into operation on 1 January 1992, but essential details are still not clear.
80. For example, a person earning Zl 36,000,000 (about $3,000) would be exempt from the leveling tax but would pay 20 percent income tax and at least 8 percent (Zl 2,856,000, about $260) in annual social insurance contribution. This implies an effective tax rate on private entrepreneurs of around 28 percent.

Table 16.10   Tax Rates for Individuals in Poland

Income (Zl)	Tax Rate
Income tax	
0–26,400,000	20%
26,400,000–52,800,000	Zl 5,280,000 plus 30% of taxable income over Zl 26,400,000
52,800,000 and over	Zl 13,200,000 plus 40% of taxable income over Zl 52,800,000
Leveling tax	
36,000,000–54,000,000	10% of taxable income over Zl 36,000,000
54,000,000–72,000,000	Zl 1,800,000 plus 20% of taxable income over Zl 54,000,000
72,000,000–90,000,000	Zl 5,400,000 plus 30% of taxable income over Zl 72,000,000
90,000,000 and over	Zl 10,800,000 plus 40% of taxable income over Zl 90,000,000

Source: Consultant's report.
Note: There are about Zl 11,000 to $1.00.
[a]Income up to Zl 36,000,000 per year (and per partner where appropriate) is exempt from the leveling tax.

ants must pay Zl 61,000 ($5.00) per month, whereas a neighboring tailor with five employees should pay Zl 858,000 ($78.00) per month.[81]

In the second half of 1990, there was a one-year tax holiday available to individuals in wholesale trade, but one of its main effects seems to have been to induce reregistration of already-existing firms. There were also some individual firms, created in September 1990, that were able to avoid paying customs duty.[82] Owing to a complicated legal situation, some wholesale trade companies opened in September and October 1990 are exempt from customs duties.[83]

There were some significant tax changes during 1991, which included allowing losses from one year to be included in costs for up to three years. There was also an increase in amortization allowances. However, more important, it remains possible to include almost all investment as a cost of production, as long as it can be bought in units costing less than Zl 1,000,000 (about $100).[84] For this reason, leasing is a popular method of obtaining capital equipment.

Turnover tax is currently 20 percent for production activities, 5 percent on trade, and 5 percent on services. However, there is a special turnover tax on imported goods that must be paid on the border. For some goods, state importers are able to pay lower tax rates than private importers.[85] There are strange

81. For example, the monthly fixed tax on a hairdresser with no employees is Zl 49,000 in towns with a population up to 5,000 people, Zl 55,000 if the population is between 5,000 and 50,000, and Zl 61,000 if the population exceeds 50,000.
82. This was the result of a very complicated legal situation.
83. Advertisements have appeared in newspapers that say something along these lines: "I have a company opened in September 1990, and I am looking for proposals."
84. For example, if you want a new set of office furniture, it is best to buy each chair separately.
85. For example, at the end of 1989, a private importer of gasoline paid a tariff of 40 percent, while a state importer only paid 20 percent.

anomalies in the turnover-tax system. For example, there is a 15 percent turnover tax on imported paper, but no turnover tax on imported books.

It is also readily apparent that the Polish banking system did not play a major role in private-sector development. The monobank was broken up at the beginning of 1989 and divided into nine commercial banks, each of which had a regional basis.[86] At least fifty private banks were created, but these remain very small. In December 1990, state banks were responsible for at least 97 percent of all credits.[87]

These banks are extremely inefficient in their transfer of money, particularly in and out of Poland. Simple transactions can take several weeks or even months. Many private importers who rely on a rapid turnover of goods have had to devise ways to send large sums of cash out of the country. Regulation of banking activities has also been unsatisfactory—this was most evident in the "Art-B" scandal of the summer of 1991, which resulted in the dismissal of the president of the National Bank of Poland and the arrest of the senior vice-president.[88]

Unfortunately, government credit policy has also not been able to help the private sector. Faced with an inflation rate that remained stubbornly high, the government has had to maintain quite high nominal interest rates. The benchmark National Bank of Poland refinance rate peaked at 432 percent per year in January 1990 and then fell steadily to 34 percent in June 1990. However, it rose again from October 1990 to February 1991, reaching 72 percent per year. By October 1991, it was down to 40 percent. Loan rates were usually about one-fifth higher than the refinance rate.

Calculating real interest rates when both nominal rates and inflation are high is difficult, but the following general conclusions are possible. Very high inflation meant negative real interest rates at the beginning of 1990, at the same time as nominal rates were shockingly high. In June 1990, monthly inflation was down to 3.4 percent (equivalent to 49 percent per year). Monthly inflation has remained in the 2–6 percent range since that time (annualized rates of 27–100 percent), which means that the real interest rate moves from positive to negative from month to month.

It seems likely the continued high level of nominal interest rates, combined with instability in the real rate, discourages private borrowing. Credits for private firms and individuals were 17 percent of total bank credits on 31 March 1991 and 21 percent on 30 September 1991. There is also anecdotal evidence

86. There are also six specialist banks, e.g., one for food processing and another for the financing of foreign trade.
87. There are plans to privatize these commercial banks, probably beginning with Bank Slaski and Bank Wielkopolski.
88. Art-B might be the only private firm that has benefited from the inefficiency of the Polish banking system. Art-B shifted money between banks rapidly in order to earn interest at several banks simultaneously—this mechanism is referred to in Polish as an *oscylator*. It was also able to obtain a large amount in bank loans that were not properly secured. The owners of this company subsequently escaped the country.

Table 16.11   Ownership of Polish Housing Stock (% shares)

	Cooperatives	State Enterprises	State	Private
Total	24.3	12.1	19.3	41.7
Urban	36.7	11.4	27.7	23.4
Rural	.5	13.5	3.1	76.7

Source: Statistical Yearbook, 1988.

of an informal market for loans in hard currency, which have the advantage of carrying a low, stable rate of interest.

Especially after the recent Art-B scandal, banks have become very cautious about lending to private firms and often require more than 100 percent security in the form of liquid assets—such as bank deposits. There is some available collateral in the hands of the private sector, principally housing. As table 16.11 shows, the private sector owns more than three-quarters of housing in the countryside and almost one-quarter in towns. In addition, these data are from 1988, and since that time some people have bought their cooperative apartments. Unfortunately, official housing statistics have become increasingly unreliable because, although it is permitted to buy and sell private and cooperative apartments, there are legal restrictions and tax regulations, which means that a great deal of this activity takes place in a disguised form.[89] Probably another 10 percent of the urban housing stock has become private through some form of market transaction. However, this progress should not be confused with plans to privatize "state" housing—controlled by local government—which have not yet produced significant results.

It is possible to borrow against the security of a private apartment, but banks require that no one other than the owner is registered as living there. This form of credit is easier to obtain in the countryside, but it still requires a lot of administrative work, and the property must be properly evaluated. State banks apparently do not welcome this kind of work.

Most agricultural land is privately owned. Official statistics for 1990 show individuals owning 76 percent of arable land, with state farms owning 18.6 percent and cooperatives having 3.7 percent. More than 3.5 million people work on private farms, while around 800,000 work on state and cooperative farms.

There has been some privatization of state assets, which has helped private-sector development. Efforts to sell state enterprises in auctions have definitely not been very successful. Instead, privatization by "liquidation" has been more widespread—by December 1991, at least 875 firms had undergone this pro-

89. The main problem is how to minimize the sales tax when an apartment changes hands. Various techniques are employed, including using fictitious names and "exchanging" apartments rather than selling.

cess, which usually means that they end up being owned by their employees. The employees have to provide 20 percent of the firm as a down payment and can buy the rest of the firm from the state in installments. However, these firms are relatively small, and the total amount of privatized firms so far probably accounts for no more than 5 percent of total assets of state firms.

The privatization of retail space has proceeded much more smoothly. Under the Communist regime, a large number of shops were in principle privately owned but in practice controlled by a state agency of some kind. Early in 1990, private owners were able to regain this property. In addition, from May 1990, newly elected non-Communist municipalities had the right to dispose of shops that had been state owned. Most of these municipalities were short of money, and this encouraged them to auction off the movable property of shops quickly, along with fairly short-term leases for the building—usually the leases are for a few years.[90] By the end of 1990, private firms operated 65 percent of all shops but only 27 percent of total retail space—some large cooperative and state stores remain. However, after the first six months of 1991, 75 percent of shops were privately run, and this accounted for 80 percent of retail sales. The total number of private shops in mid-1991 was 456,000, up from 346,300 a year before.

Although most agricultural land remained private during communism in Poland, there was substantial nationalization of urban property.[91] The situation with regard to reprivatization remains unclear, and there is not yet definitive legislation on this point.[92] However, it is relatively simple to recover property that was taken illegally by the Communists—that is, in breach of the Communists' own laws. Typical types of property are mills, buildings, land, and drugstores.

The Polish private sector appears to be doing well, although some problems definitely remain. Taxes are high, credit conditions are unfavorable, and privatization has been quite slow. Nevertheless, there continues to be rapid growth both in the number of private firms, incorporated and unincorporated, and in private-sector employment.

16.2.4   Comparison

In order to compare the relative importance of private-sector activity, table 16.12 gives data for estimated urban labor forces: 4 million in Hungary, 7 million in the CSFR, and 12 million in Poland. We use this measure rather than total population as the basis for comparison because around one-quarter of the Polish work force is in agriculture—the average total employment in Poland in 1990 was 16.5 million, but employment in agriculture accounted for 4.4

90. There have been complaints that municipal authorities raise rents repeatedly even when this is not allowed under the lease.
91. One estimate is that 20,740 enterprises were nationalized in the period 1945–59.
92. There remains debate about whether the 1946 Nationalization Act should be accepted as legitimate.

Table 16.12   Comparison of Current Government Prices

	CSFR	Hungary	Poland
General indicators			
Population (million)	16	10	38
Labor force (urban) (million)	7	4	12
No. of private firms:			
Incorporated	5,000	50,000	40,000
Unincorporated (million)	1.1	.4–.5	1.5
Sectors of private activity (% of registered entrepreneurs in a sector)			
Industry (%)	2–28	N.A.	26
Trade (%)	17	N.A.	38
Equal legal treatment?	Yes	Yes	Yes
Macroeconomic situation:			
Substantial convertibility	Yes	Yes	Yes
Black market premium	5%	5%	No
Liberal trade	Mostly	Mostly	Mostly
Shortages	No	No	No
Taxes			
Tax rates (%)			
Corporate income	20–55	40	40
Private income (see also	15[a]	4[a]	20[a]
table 16.13)	55[b]	50[b]	80[b]
Turnover	0, 11, 20, 29	0, 15, 25	5, 20
Social security tax (%)	8.7	43	45
Wage tax (per employee) (%)	50	. . .	20
Excess wage tax	Yes[c]	No[d]	No[d]
Tax advantages for private sector:			
Accelerated depreciation	Yes[e]	Yes	Yes[f]
Carry-forward losses	No	No?	Yes[f]
Tax credits	No	Yes	
Tariffs	15%[g]	Various	0%–40%[h]
Capital needed for limited liability	$3,000	$15,000	$1,000
Tax advantages for joint ventures	Yes	Yes	Yes
Minimum capital required for joint venture	Kčs 100,000 ($3,300)	Ft 50 million ($650,000)	$50,000[i]
Credit situation			
Dominant state banks?	Yes	Yes	Yes
Preferential interest rates?	No	No	No
Nominal interest rates in 1991 (%)	20	20–50	40–70
Inflation 1991 (%)	50	35	30–100
Private share of total credit (%)	< 5	25	< 21
Private housing (% share of total)	45	N.A.	40

Table 16.12   (continued)

	CSFR	Hungary	Poland
Privatization progress			
Large companies	Begins in spring 1992	Under way and gradual	Repeated delays
% privatized at end of 1991	A few[j]	10%[k]/25%[l]	< 10%
Shops and restaurants privatized (% of total numbers)	10	10	60–80
Restitution:			
Laws passed	Yes	Yes	No
Politics settled	Yes	No	No
Claims settled	No	No	No

Sources: Discussed in text and other tables.
Note: N.A. = not available.

[a]To $1,000	[g]Many exceptions.
[b]Top rate.	[h]Usually.
[c]200%–750%, but not if small.	[i]Valued in dollars.
[d]Yes for state-owned enterprises.	[j]Foreign deals.
[e]Restricted.	[k]Fully.
[f]Recent.	[l]Corporatized.

million (*Rocznik Statystyczny 1991*, p. 93, table 2 [174]). The fraction of labor working in Hungarian and CSFR agriculture is much lower.

In terms of the number of incorporated private businesses, Hungary clearly has the lead, with 1.3 incorporated businesses per 100 people in the urban labor force, while Poland has 0.3 and the CSFR only 0.1. But, in terms of the relative number of unincorporated businesses, the CSFR surprisingly has the lead, with 16 such firms per 100, while both Poland and Hungary have 13. However, we suspect that a large number of registered entrepreneurs in the CSFR are actually working for other people and declaring themselves to be self-employed as a way to avoid the wage tax. Unfortunately, it is very hard to know how much these different private sectors contribute to national output. One set of estimates for the share of the private sector in GDP is 14.7 percent for Poland, 16.6 percent for Hungary, and 3.1 percent for the CSFR (Brandsma 1991).[93] In terms of share in urban employment, we estimate that, in both Poland and Hungary, the private sector now provides 20–25 percent while, in the CSFR, it accounts for less than 5 percent.[94]

93. This same source estimates that the private sector contributes to GDP 8.9 percent in Bulgaria, 3.5 percent in the former East Germany, 2.5 percent in Romania, and 2.5 percent in the former Soviet Union.
94. Although it is not directly comparable to Eastern Europe's private sector, we should note that the small business sector in Western Europe contributes between 32 percent (in the United Kingdom) and 46 percent (in Germany) to GNP.

Our conclusion is that, compared to the CSFR, and implicitly to other post-Communist countries, the private sector is relatively strong in both Hungary and Poland. However, this strength is manifest differently in the two countries. We therefore have two phenomena to explain. First, why are Hungary and Poland ahead of the CSFR in terms of private-sector development? Second, why has the private sector in Hungary developed in a corporate form, whereas in Poland a much larger part is unincorporated?

Table 16.12 summarizes the different measures of government policy that were discussed above. With regard to macroeconomic policy and basic legal framework, all three countries are very similar. For example, all have substantially liberalized trade while still having—at the end of 1991—some trade restrictions. In all three countries, private business is now subject to a commercial code that draws heavily on the German-Austrian model and that is related to their prewar experiences.

Government tax policy cannot really explain the differences between these three countries. As table 16.12 shows, corporate income tax rates in all three countries are remarkably similar. Table 16.13 provides a comparison of the rates of taxation on individual entrepreneurs—we calculated the rate of tax that an individual must pay at various levels of income, converted into dollars. Table 16.13 suggests that tax rates are highest at all income levels in Poland, lowest for low incomes in Hungary, and lowest for mid-range incomes ($3,000-$5,000) in the CSFR. Of course, table 16.13 does not reflect other tax legislation, such as accelerated depreciation and the ability to deduct business expenses from taxable income. As we discussed above, it seems easiest to reduce taxable income in Poland and hardest in the CSFR—although the CSFR tax code is currently being revised to allow more deductions. Nevertheless, table 16.13 suggests the interesting conclusion that the Polish registered entrepreneurs have prospered, not because of favorable tax rates, but despite very high rates.

In terms of credit conditions, as measured by nominal and real rates of interest, it appears that the CSFR had an advantage, in the form of low real interest rates, during the first half of 1990, but now its real rates are very high. Unfortunately, we could not obtain information about the extent of credit rationing to private firms, and this may be more important than the posted lending rate. Hungary may have the best combination—nominal interest rates roughly in line with inflation and an established pattern of lending by some state banks to private firms. The continued instability of real and nominal zloty interest rates in Poland should probably be considered a major disadvantage.

Small privatization appears to be proceeding significantly faster in Poland than in either the CSFR or Hungary. This may be because there is not much capital in the hands of private business in the CSFR and because the auction process has been centrally controlled in Hungary. However, in our opinion, the successful auction of leases to shops is an effect rather than a cause of the strong Polish private sector.

Table 16.13   **Comparative Income-Tax Rates**

Income per Year in U.S. Dollars	Effective Tax Rate (%)		
	CSFR	Hungary	Poland
1,000	15	4	20
3,000	18	20	22
5,000	21	27	32
10,000	27	37	50
Top rate	55	50	80

Source: Author's calculations based on tables 16.1, 16.5, and 16.10.
Note: We used approximate exchange rates of Ft 80.00/$1.00, Kčs 29.00/$1.00, and Zl 11,000/$1.00.

Our comparative evidence has raised an important question. Why has the private sector been relatively successful in Poland? Economic reform in Poland began more recently than in Hungary and brought with it high inflation and other macroeconomic problems. How did the Polish private sector manage to grow in this environment? Is there something different about the Polish private sector?

16.2.5   What Is Different about Poland?

Why has the Polish private sector done relatively well in its unusual, unincorporated form? In our opinion, the answer lies in the way the Polish economy was reformed. The Polish private sector is the product of a particular sequence of events, primarily due to changing government policy.

The relaxation of controls over the private sector came earlier in Poland than in the CSFR. It is true that the new wave of *spolki* creation did not really begin until 1988, but since the mid-1980s there had been gradual liberalization of private economic activity—for example, at this time new cooperatives were created that were essentially private firms (Johnson and Loveman 1993).[95] There was a rapid growth in individual international trade by Poles—the government did not impose any restrictions on most people's travel.[96] In fact, it was quite common for young Poles to work in Western Europe for a few months each year.[97] Foreign travel was much harder for Hungarians and citizens of Czechoslovakia.

These experiences matter because it was in these small ways that Poles learned about nonstate business, acquired modest amounts of capital,and made connections with the outside world. Most important, it was possible to earn

95. Some of these firms were linked to the Solidarity movement, which at this time was illegal and "underground."
96. The government did restrict travel—usually by denying a passport—to people whom it regarded as its political enemies.
97. It is not uncommon to find well-educated people who worked as manual laborers at harvest time in France or Sweden.

very high rates of return on some imports. The best example is the case of computers, in which people could begin by buying computer equipment by mail order from abroad at a cost of a few hundred or thousand dollars, sell this equipment to state firms at prices that implied a return of several hundred percent, and by reinvesting in other computer-related imports accumulate— within a few years—hundreds of thousands of dollars.[98] There was a rapid accumulation of capital, both financial and human, that was unique to Poland.

The Communists also tried to rebuild some legitimacy by widening the scope of private-sector activity. In particular, the last Communist government—headed by Mieczyslaw Rakowski—passed legislation that by early 1989 had essentially removed all legal and most administrative barriers on the private sector.

However, these changes brought little in terms of visible benefits while the Communists retained power. Their macroeconomic policy was very unsuccessful and caused rapid inflation despite partial price controls.[99] The result was terrible shortages and grossly distorted prices (Lipton and Sachs 1990), a situation that exacerbated the supply problems of the private sector. Circumventing import controls helped private businesspeople make money on semilegal trade, but these controls constrained the speed with which this trade could develop.

The details of the political transformation and the construction of the economic reform of 1990 have been explored at length in other papers, and the main results are clear. Almost overnight, there was an end to shortages, and the zloty became convertible at a stable exchange rate.[100] It became possible to import freely, and private traders moved rapidly to do just that.

Two points are important. The first is that the reform program did not have to change much in terms of the legal treatment of the private sector. The most important steps had already been taken. Second, the stabilization of the economy and rapid liberalization of foreign trade had a major stimulative effect on the private sector.

As table 16.8 above shows, not all the private sector was favorably affected, and many firms that had prospered under the previous price system found themselves unable to survive at world prices. It is also true that the first quarter of 1990 showed only limited private-sector growth. But this growth soon became apparent—table 16.8 shows that the total net balance of individual firm creation improved every quarter in 1990.

98. The story of Polish computers is the subject of ongoing research by Piotr Strzalkowski and Simon Johnson.

99. For a model of the acceleration of Polish inflation, see Johnson (1991).

100. Strictly speaking, the zloty became convertible for legal persons only on current account— in order to obtain foreign currency, they had to present a valid invoice from a foreign exporter. However, the zloty was fully convertible for private persons at legal, private exchange offices (*kantors*).

16.3   Field Research

16.3.1   Methodology

It is very hard to provide a full explanation for the relatively rapid growth of the Polish private sector. However, the characteristics of Polish firms that have had some success may shed some light on this issue. Unfortunately, to this time these characteristics have nowhere been carefully measured. There are anecdotes, analyses of clusters of successful firms (e.g., Johnson and Loveman 1993), and some surveys of private firms that are based on samples that are biased—in the sense that they oversample firms that are doing badly. (These surveys cannot yet be cited.)

For this reason, we decided to collect our own primary data by interviewing private-sector entrepreneurs. In particular, we wanted to interview a representative sample of "active" firms.[101] We emphasize the word *active* because in Poland there are many registered firms that exist only on paper and that can hardly be considered the basis for sustained private-sector development.[102] The easiest way to construct a sample is to obtain a list of limited-liability and joint-stock companies because these must be registered with a court.[103] However, this would have implied ignoring those large and successful Polish private firms that, because of tax incentives, had registered as individuals engaged in wholesale trade in 1990.

Our personal experience with Polish entrepreneurs suggests that they select the property form that has the most favorable tax conditions at the time of start-up and that, if tax incentives switch, they are willing to reregister their firms. For these reasons, we decided not to use property form as a selection criterion for inclusion of firms in the sample. However, this created another problem—the population of Polish firms contains an enormous number of private individuals who have very small operations, and we did not wish these observations to dominate our sample.

For this reason, we chose to draw our sample from a very specific population—private Polish firms that advertise. In our opinion, firms that advertise are likely to be active. The details of how we obtained information on this population is contained in the appendix, which also describes how we divided our sample by sector of activity and ensured that our sample had the same

101. A short while ago, Polish entrepreneurs were unwilling to speak with outsiders. This situation changed at the beginning of the economic reform program. A good example is that, in 1990, the Central Statistical Office suddenly found that entrepreneurs became much more willing to respond to requests for information, and some also sent in long letters of comments.

102. For example, there are about 130,000 companies in Warsaw, a city with a population of around 1.8 million. This ratio of 7 companies per 100 inhabitants is rather high—the usual number in a Western city is around 4. However, many of these Polish firms do not operate on a regular basis.

103. This was the method used in one large study whose results we have read but that we are not yet allowed to cite.

Table 16.14   **Survey of Private Companies in Warsaw, December 1991: Breakdown of the 294 Interviewed Private Companies, by Sector**

Traditional services (mainly handicrafts)	60
Modern services (e.g., consulting, advertising, accounting, finance)	40
Production	85
Transport	8
Restaurants	4
Retail trade	20
Wholesale trade	76
Total	294

proportion in each sector as existed in the economy as a whole. Table 16.14 shows the sectoral composition of firms in our sample.

Selected firms were interviewed using a questionnaire with fifty-six questions, focusing on five sets of issues, each of which examines an important aspect of the firms' operations. We asked about several measures of the firms' size, the career of the entrepreneur, the sources of finance for this business, indicators of business strategy, and perceptions of the general economic environment in Poland.

16.3.2   Results

Because of space limitations, we provide here only some principal, overall results of our survey. More detailed results, broken down by sector, are under preparation for a separate paper.[104] For this paper, we have divided up responses between four tables, and we do not show answers to all questions, only those that most closely address the issues raised in this paper. The order in which responses are given is not necessarily the same as the order in which questions were asked.[105]

Table 16.15 shows several indicators of firm size that we chose to use. Most of the firms in our sample are quite small in terms of employment—only forty-three employ more than twenty people. At the same time, sixty-nine firms had turnover above Zl 1,000 million ($100,000) in 1990—a significant amount under Polish conditions. In almost all sampled firms, turnover was higher in 1991 than in 1990, although this is hard to evaluate because there was also substantial inflation during both years. In terms of profitability, there are really two poles: in both 1990 and 1991, sixty to seventy firms earned less than Zl 50

104. These sectors were constructed by Piotr Strzalkowski of MCR Research from his data base, in which there are seventy-six categories.

105. For example, previous experience of MCR Research suggested that entrepreneurs would answer questions about their finances, but only if they were asked after the interview was well under way—so they had already built a relationship with the interviewer. This idea appears to be confirmed by our results—a surprising number of entrepreneurs answered our financial questions very precisely.

Table 16.15   Descriptive Information for Sample

How many employees do you have?
  0–2 (81 cases)
  3–5 (78 cases)
  6–20 (92 cases)
  More than 20 (43 cases)
What was your turnover in 1990 (in millions of zloty, with about Zl 10,000/$1.00)?
  Up to 100 (48 cases)
  100–200 (18 cases)
  200–500 (29 cases)
  500–1,000 (28 cases)
  1,000–10,000 (44 cases)
  10,000–100,000 (21 cases)
  More than 100,000 (4 cases)
What was your turnover in 1991 (in millions of zloty, with about Zl 11,000/$1.00)?
  Up to 100 (35 cases)
  100–200 (9 cases)
  200–500 (24 cases)
  500–1,000 (34 cases)
  1,000–10,000 (84 cases)
  10,000–100,000 (30 cases)
  More than 100,000 (4 cases)
What were your profits in 1990 (millions of zloty)?
  Up to 50 (74 cases)
  50–100 (27 cases)
  100–200 (25 cases)
  200–300 (2 cases)
  300–400 (3 cases)
  400–1,000 (4 cases)
  1,000 and higher (29 cases)
What were your profits in 1991 (millions of zloty)?
  Up to 50 (63 cases)
  50–100 (34 cases)
  100–200 (19 cases)
  200–300 (15 cases)
  300–400 (6 cases)
  400–500 (6 cases)
  500–1,000 (9 cases)
  1,000 and higher (27 cases)
How many customers do you have?
  1 (7 cases)
  2–5 (28 cases)
  6–10 (21 cases)
  More than 10 (227 cases)
The market for your product(s) is:
  Local (65 cases)
  National (105 cases)
  National and foreign (54 cases)
  Only foreign (3 cases)

million ($5,000), while over thirty firms earned more than Zl 400 million ($40,000). Note that, while most sampled firms answered most questions, about half of all firms declined to answer questions about profits.

Without doubt, by Western standards most of these randomly selected "active" Polish private firms are small. However, table 16.15 shows that it is not correct to characterize them as tied to one state firm or as serving only a local market. The vast majority of all firms reported having more than ten customers, and in 105 cases entrepreneurs said that their market was "national." Surprisingly, fifty-seven of these private firms (19 percent of our sample) reported exporting some goods.

We were interested in the entrepreneur's family background because it has been suggested that this is an important factor in determining who becomes an entrepreneur. Table 16.16 shows some interesting evidence in this regard: in about one-third of all cases, the entrepreneur's family had run another business in the past ten years. Interestingly, however, only forty-eight respondents said that their firm was established "as a family tradition." We took this to mean that a family background in private business is conducive to entry into the private sector but not necessarily into exactly the same activity.

The vast majority of entrepreneurs replied that this firm was the result of either their initiative or that of a partner. Only five firms were spin-offs of some kind from another firm. However, about one-third of the entrepreneurs had worked in the private sector before establishing their own firm, and about the same number had held a management position in a state firm. This indicates that one-third of sampled entrepreneurs either held no previous employment or were workers in state firms.

According to the responses shown in table 16.17, most of the entrepreneurs started with money saved from earnings in Poland. In forty-two cases (14 per-

Table 16.16   The Entrepreneur's Background

Has your family run another business in the past ten years?
  Yes (101 cases)
  No (190 cases)
Was the company established:
  On the interviewee's and/or a partner's initiative?
  Yes (227 cases)
  On the initiative of another company?
  Yes (5 cases)
  As a family tradition?
  Yes (48 cases)
Did you work in private sector before establishing your own company?
  Yes (112 cases)
  No (155 cases)
Did you ever have a management position in a state firm or a cooperative?
  Yes (111 cases)
  No (166 cases)

Table 16.17   **Financial Information**

What was the source of your initial capital (respondents could give more than one answer)?
  Domestic earnings (214 cases)
  Earnings abroad (42 cases)
  Loans from family and friends (80 cases)
  Bank credit (34 cases)
Have you applied for credit in the past two years?
  Yes, successfully (71 cases)
  Yes, unsuccessfully (32 cases)
  No (183 cases)
If you obtained credit, was it:
  In zlotys?
  Yes (62 cases)
  In hard currency?
  Yes (13 cases)
Do you have any debtors (trade credit)?
  Yes (130 cases)
  No (162 cases)
Do you have any creditors (trade credit)?
  Yes (92 cases)
  No (200 cases)
How do you finance turnover (respondents could give more than one answer)?
  With own funds (256 cases)
  With bank credit (42 cases)
  With supplier credit (76 cases)
How do you use your profits at present (respondent can choose more than one answer)?
  To increase turnover (129 cases)
  To purchase fixed assets (143 cases)
  To pay dividends to shareholders (9 cases)
  To build reserves (46 cases)
  To make outside investments (stocks, bonds etc.) (21 cases)
  Other (72 cases)
If your profits increase, you will (respondent can choose more than one answer):
  Increase turnover (162 cases)
  Purchase fixed assets (126 cases)
  Stop using bank credits (34 cases)
  Increase inventory (48 cases)
  Make long-term deposits (17 cases)
  Increase financial reserves (48 cases)
  Buy securities (14 cases)
  Pay dividends (9 cases)

cent of the sample), they had savings from foreign earnings. About the same number of entrepreneurs started out with bank loans, and eighty people reported using some money from family and friends.

Interestingly, table 16.17 also shows that relatively few entrepreneurs have ever applied for credit—only one-third of our sample. These numbers indicate that two-thirds of Polish private businesspeople do not even try to borrow money. Many firms also operate without giving or receiving trade credit—162 interviewees said that their firms had no debtors, and 200 said that they had no creditors. Of those who had obtained credit, thirteen said that it was in hard currency.

Table 16.17 shows that most private firms reinvest their profits. Around half said that they used profits to increase turnover, and 162 said that they would do that if profits increased. Fixed assets are purchased out of profits by 143, and 126 would do the same with higher profits. Only twenty-one presently make investments outside the firm. Clearly, the growth of these private businesses is based on their own retained earnings.

Table 16.18 shows that most of these entrepreneurs consider their competition to be either other private companies or black marketeers. When asked to name the main three barriers to rising sales, limited demand was named by 163. More interesting, however, is the fact that—adding across the first-, second-, and third-named barriers—a lack of employees adversely affects thirty-eight firms (13 percent of the sample). We believe that this indicates both the lack of skilled labor in Poland and the fact that the Warsaw labor market is actually quite tight.

Very few of these firms use consulting firms or lawyers, but just under half use an accountant, at least part-time. The hiring of accountants is easy to explain—Polish tax regulations are complex, and one bookkeeping error could bring on a much-feared investigation by the tax authorities.

16.3.3 Analysis

The information from our sample of Polish firms confirms the broad picture of private-sector development that we outlined above. In addition, we have uncovered some data that confirm or clarify prevalent opinions about the Polish private sector.

Where did these private entrepreneurs come from? About one-third had families with business backgrounds. Most of them started their firms themselves, with their own money. Where did they get the experience and the capital necessary to do this? For about half, the answer is previous work in the private sector, and slightly more than a third had previous work experience as managers in the state sector. The liberalization of this sector under the Communists appears to have had useful, lasting effects.

The private sector provides its own capital. Most of these entrepreneurs do not borrow money, and their growth is based on reinvested profits. This is consistent with anecdotal evidence suggesting that the rapid growth of the Polish private sector since the beginning of 1990 was due to the existence of high rates of profit in some activities—particularly wholesale trade.

For all their successes, most Polish private firms remain small and compete mostly with other private firms. As expected, it is now apparent that some will continue to grow while others will remain small. But it is far from clear how fast firms can grow when that growth is based only on retained profits. Yet there is little credit available to the private sector, and the much-vaunted priva-

Table 16.18   **Strategy**

Who are your main competitors?
    Black marketeers (73 cases)
    Other private companies (153 cases)
    State owned companies (32 cases)
    Cooperatives (12 cases)
    Foreign firms (27 cases)
    Imports (34 cases)
    None (36 cases)
What are the three main barriers to increasing your sales (rank them in order)?
  First:
    Lack of orders (163 cases)
    Lack of employees (14 cases)
    Taxes (27 cases)
    Legal/administrative (14 cases)
    Other (53 cases)
  Second:
    Lack of orders (29 cases)
    Lack of employees (20 cases)
    Taxes (53 cases)
    Legal/administrative (35 cases)
    Other (27 cases)
  Third:
    Lack of orders (11 cases)
    Lack of employees (4 cases)
    Taxes (12 cases)
    Legal/administrative (12 cases)
    Other (24 cases)
How often do you use the services of lawyers?
    Never (130 cases)
    Sometimes (3–10 times) per year (72 cases)
    Once a month (12 cases)
    Several times a month (26 cases)
    Every day (50 cases)
Do you employ a bookkeeper?
    Yes (136 cases)
    No (153 cases)

tization program has so far had little effect on already-existing private businesses.

16.4   Conclusions

Our evidence has shown considerable differences among the conditions of the private sectors in the CSFR, Hungary, and Poland. The private sector has done well in Hungary, in part because there was a steady liberalization of the private sector over a long period. The Polish private sector has also done well, primarily because it was able to grow in the midst of an unstable macroeconomy. Private firms in the CSFR remain small and have a long way to go.

The recent history of economic reforms—in the last ten to twenty years—continues to shape the fortunes of the private sectors in these countries. At first this seems strange because their Communist regimes for the most part succeeded in imposing a very similar economic structure on all three countries.[106] Although further research is needed, our working conclusion is that the Communist economic reforms of the 1980s established—probably inadvertently—the basis for sustained Polish private-sector development. Reforms conducted at the same time in Hungary had similar—but probably more intentional—effects, but the form taken by the private sector in Poland and Hungary was rather different. What were the important differences between the Hungarian and the Polish economic reforms?

In Poland, there was much more liberalization of travel and informal importing. There was also, from the beginning of 1988, a much worse macroeconomic situation in which the government lost control over the inflation rate. Permissive legislation was introduced at the same time as there were enormous discrepancies between prices inside and outside Poland. It was individuals who made money and gained experience in this situation. Corporate forms were sometimes convenient, but they were never essential to private-sector development. Because the Hungarian economy remained more tightly controlled, similar "hothouse" conditions were never created, and private-sector development was more even paced.

This helps explain why the unincorporated private sector is stronger in Poland whereas the private corporate sector is more developed in Hungary. Individual enterprise is stimulated more by the availability of foreign travel and small-scale import opportunities. The relatively stable macroeconomic environment of Hungary means that more capital is needed to start a private firm, and this requires the use of a corporate form. Moreover, as our survey research shows, Polish entrepreneurs live and grow on internally generated capital, partly because the capital market is not well developed. The capital market is better developed in Hungary, and this permits larger-scale private enterprise. (However, in order to make a deeper analysis of the Hungarian private sector, we would need to conduct a survey similar to that in Poland.)

What is the secret of the relative success of the private sector in Poland? In part, it was the historical sequence of events. The Communists' partially reformed economy was a good place to learn how to do business. The economic reform program rapidly changed the economy, to the relative benefit of small, flexible firms that could adjust quickly. The achievements to date have been so remarkable that it is almost possible to speak of a Polish private-sector miracle. But one element is still missing: there is no bank credit at low nominal and real interest rates.

There are few obvious conclusions for the CSFR and other countries that

---

106. It is true that agriculture was never successfully collectivized in Poland, but we have not seen evidence that private agriculture was the basis for rapid growth in the urban Polish private sector. In fact, private farmers have been among the most vociferous opponents of the economic program that began in 1990.

abandoned communism before their private sector was significantly developed. Some of these countries now have similar policies as Poland but have not yet had such rapid growth. It makes no sense to suggest that they try to create a Polish-style "hothouse" because these conditions also involve terrible macro-economic imbalances—and these helped bring down the Polish Communist regime. The CSFR has little choice but to maintain its existing policy combination: attempt to hold down inflation, maintain an open economy, provide modest tax incentives, and keep credit reasonably priced. Some measures to provide special assistance to small business have worked in industrial countries and have already been proposed for the CSFR (see Rondinelli 1991). In essence, this implies trying to follow the Hungarian path of gradual and more steady private-sector growth, although without the Hungarian acceleration after 1989.

There has been discussion of various innovative ways to stimulate the private sector in post-Communist countries. A significant amount of unmortgaged private property exists in these countries. There may be legal changes that would allow an individual to sign away his or her protection from eviction—this would facilitate the development of mortgage credit. Policymakers are also aware that accelerating small privatization would definitely help put physical capital in the hands of private business. Furthermore, following successes in selling shops and restaurants, in Poland and Hungary measures have been taken to promote a separate track for the privatization of "small" industrial assets. However, given their current situation, it will be hard for the CSFR and other Communist countries to emulate the success of either Hungary's or Poland's private sector.

These conclusions suggest partial answers to the three questions raised in the second paragraph of the introduction. There are measures that post-Communist governments can and have used to accelerate private-sector growth, but the effectiveness of these measures depends on how much the private sector grew under the Communist regime. There are at least two paths to private-sector growth, one typified by Hungary and the other by Poland. In both cases, the results so far have been impressive, but it remains unclear whether they provide the basis for a modern, industrial economy.

Appendix
Sample Selection for Polish Entrepreneurs

Our full sample consists of 294 companies that were interviewed in Warsaw in the last three weeks of November and the first week of December 1991.[107]

---

107. Most of the detailed work described here was performed by Piotr Strzalkowski and his associates at MCR Research.

These companies were selected from a data base of about 3,000 firms that advertised themselves in the Polish press in the last two months of 1990. For obvious reasons, we were able to interview only those firms that were still in business at the end of 1991. Interviews were conducted by a team of twenty people, trained and supervised by MCR research.

The list of firms that advertise was obtained from *Gazeta Wyborcza*, which is available throughout Poland and has seventeen local editions. Three other newspapers were used: *Rzeczpospolita, Zycie Warszawa* (60 percent of the copies are sold in Warsaw), and *Kontakt*. *Kontakt* is not a popular daily but rather a specialized paper in which manufacturing firms advertise. It was included because manufacturing firms less often advertise in daily newspapers—most of this advertising is done by firms offering nonmaterial services, particularly trade.

In order to qualify for inclusion in the data base, a firm had to give in its advertisement its name, address, and telephone number. In many Polish advertisements, a firm gives only its phone number or its name and phone number. We judged these "firms" more likely to be one-off trade shipments, and we did not wish to include them in our sample.

Our category *traditional services* comprised primarily services in which private-sector activity had been allowed before 1990. These include automobile repair, miscellaneous repairs, shoemaking, tailoring, and carpentry. These need to be contrasted with *modern services*, such as consulting, advertising, accounting, and finance, which the private sector has started doing only recently. Our other categories of firms were production, transport, restaurants, retail trade, and wholesale trade.

With the data base prepared, we then consulted official statistics (published by the State Statistical Office, GUS) to determine the proportions of different sectors that should be selected for our sample. As far as possible, we attempted to achieve the same relative proportions of sectors in our sample as exist—according to GUS statistics—in the population of Warsaw private firms.

There is one feature of our sample that may seem at first strange. Our sample contains only twenty retail firms but eighty wholesale firms. The reason for this is simple—for some months in 1990, there was available a complete one-year tax holiday for anyone registering to do wholesale trade as a physical person and operating for the first time at a particular address. There is ample anecdotal evidence that many people, particularly retailers, were able to take advantage of this tax break.

Interviews were conducted by native Polish speakers, coordinated by MCR Research. Some firms in the sample were phoned at random to check that the interviewer had actually been there. These interviewers were experienced subcontractors of MCR Research and were instructed to ask follow-up questions when an answer was unclear and to build rapport with the interviewee—particularly with a view to extracting financial information.

References

Aslund, Anders. 1985. *Private enterprise in Eastern Europe.* New York: St. Martin's.

Ball, Alan M. 1987. *Russia's last capitalists.* Berkeley and Los Angeles: University of California Press.

Brandsma, Judith. 1991. Entrepreneurial development in Czechoslovakia. Paper prepared for the OECD Conference on Training for Entrepreneurship, Prague, 10 October.

Capek, Ales. 1990. Small firms in Czechoslovak economy. Prague: Czechoslovak Academy of Sciences, Institute of Economics. Mimeo.

Galasi, Peter, and Gyorgy Sziraczki. N.d. A review of developments in the organization and structure of small and medium sized enterprises: Hungary. Mimeo.

Grabowski, Maciej H. 1991. Entrepreneurship and the development of small and medium-size enterprises in Poland. Gdansk: Gdansk Institute for Market Economics, September.

Grabowski, Maciej H., and Przemyslaw Kulawczuk. 1991a. Financial study of the private firms in the Gdansk region. *Economic Transformation* (Gdansk Institute for Market Economics), no. 17 (July).

————. 1991b. Small firms in the last decade and now. *Economic Transformation* (Gdansk Institute for Market Economics), no. 17 (July).

Hare, Paul, and Irena Grosfeld. 1991. Privatization in Hungary, Poland and Czechoslovakia. Discussion Paper no. 544. Centre for Economic Policy Research.

Johnson, Simon. 1991. Did socialism fail in Poland? *Comparative Economic Studies* 33, no. 3 (Fall): 127–51.

Johnson, Simon, and Bakhtior Islamov. 1991. Property rights and economic reform in Uzbekistan. Working Paper no. WP 90. Helsinki: World Institute for Development Economics Research of the United Nations University, September.

Johnson, Simon, and Heidi Kroll. 1991. Managerial strategies for spontaneous privatization. *Soviet Economy* 7, no. 4:281–316.

————. 1993. Strategy, structure and spontaneous privatization. In *Changing political economy of privatization in post-Communist and reforming Communist states,* ed. Vedat Milor. Boulder, Colo.: Lynne Rienner.

Johnson, Simon, Heidi Kroll, and Mark Horton. 1993. New commercial banks in the former Soviet Union: How do they operate? In *Changing the economic system in Russia,* ed. Anders Aslund and Richard Layard. London: Pinter.

Johnson, Simon, and Gary Loveman. 1993. The implications of the Polish economic reform for small business: Evidence from Gdansk. In *Small firms and entrepreneurship,* ed. David Audretsch and Zoltan Acs. Cambridge: Cambridge University Press.

Kaufman, Adam. 1962. Small-scale industry in the Soviet Union. Occasional Paper no. 80. Cambridge, Mass.: NBER.

Kornai, Janos. 1990. *The road to a free economy.* New York: Norton.

Lipton, David, and Jeffrey Sachs. 1990. Creating a market economy in Eastern Europe: The case of Poland. *Brookings Papers on Economic Activity,* no. 1:75–147.

McDermott, Gerald A., and Michal Mejstrik. 1992. The role of small firms in the industrial development and transformation of Czechoslovakia. *Small Business Economics* 4:51–72.

McMillan, John, and Barry Naughton. 1992. How to reform a planned economy: Lessons from China. *Oxford Review of Economic Policy* 8, no. 1 (Spring): 130–43.

Piasecki, Bogdan. 1991. The creation of small business in Poland as a great step towards a market economy. *Economic Transformation* (Gdansk Institute for Market Economics), no. 17 (July).

Rondinelli, Dennis A. 1991. Developing private enterprise in the Czech and Slovak

Federal Republic: The challenge of economic reform. *Columbia Journal of World Business* 26 (Fall): 27–36.

Rutland, Peter. 1992. The small privatization process. Wesleyan University. Typescript.

Seleny, Anna. 1991. Hidden enterprise, property rights reform and political transformation in Hungary. Working Paper no. 11. Harvard University, Program on Central and Eastern Europe, June.

Stark, David. 1989. Coexisting organizational forms in Hungary's emerging mixed economy. In *Remaking the economic institutions of socialism: China and Eastern Europe*, ed. Victor Nee and David Stark. Stanford, Calif.: Stanford University Press.

————. 1990. Privatization in Hungary: From plan to market or from plan to clan? *East European Politics and Societies* no. 3 (Fall): 351–92.

Szelenyi, Ivan. 1988. *Socialist entrepreneurs: Embourgeoisement in rural Hungary.* Madison: University of Wisconsin Press.

Whitlock, Eric. 1990. Notes on privatization in Hungarian industry. June. Typescript.

Discussion Summary

Kalman Mizsei suggested that Johnson had exaggerated the contrast between the development paths of the Polish and the Hungarian private sectors. First, Mizsei said that, like Poland, Hungary recorded a dramatic boom in private-sector growth at the end of the 1980s. He noted that, by 1988, only 450 limited-liability firms had been established in Hungary; by 1991, 41,000 such firms were incorporated. Second, Mizsei emphasized that, like Hungary, Poland had a long history of liberalization under Communist rule. He cited the economic liberalization following the 1981 Polish political crisis, and he mentioned the prevalence of Polish "trade tourism" and employment abroad during the 1970s. Third, Mizsei argued that Johnson had overstated the relative importance of unincorporated private enterprises in Poland. However, Mizsei did highlight one area in which the Polish and Hungarian experiences have substantially differed. He noted that, under Communist rule, the second economy in Hungary had been oriented toward production, in contrast to the speculative focus of black market activity during Communist rule in Poland (e.g., illegal trade in foreign currency).

Mizsei discussed several financial issues that pertain to Hungary. He noted that lax bankruptcy laws have enabled private entrepreneurs to strip the assets of bankrupt firms. He suggested that Hungary's policy of giving preferential credits to individuals who purchase state assets generates pricing distortions and raises the likelihood of corruption. Finally, he said that the banking sector is taking an increasing interest in attracting deposits from and making loans to the private sector. He said that credits to the private sector represent 30 percent of the total credit in the portfolios of Hungary's three largest banks. He argued that the general issue of financial intermediation had received too little attention at the conference.

Mizsei also described the status of the Hungarian privatization agency, the

SPA. He said that, in 1991, the SPA reported $40 billion of foreign-currency sales, with $35 billion coming from foreign investors. He noted that, in response to political pressure to get a fair price for state assets, the SPA has insisted on sale prices that are often too high to attract any buyers. Finally, he said that the SPA has not finalized any of the privatization deals that the agency has initiated itself. He said that most of the deals that have been completed were initiated by state enterprise managers.

Mark Schaffer said that Johnson had not acknowledged the important role that the privatization of small-scale enterprises had played in the growth of Polish private-sector employment. He noted that, in 1990, the private sector recorded a net increase of over 500,000 jobs. Approximately 400,000 of these jobs appeared in private firms in the trade sector. At the same time, jobs in the socialized trade sector fell by 400,000, a one-third decrease for that sector. Schaffer concluded that these large employment shifts occurred because of the government's emphasis on privatizing small shops in the retail trade sector.

Lev Freinkman and *Jan Winiecki* supported Mizsei's argument that Johnson had exaggerated the contrasts between the paths of private-sector development in Poland and in Hungary. Winiecki noted that, in 1989, the last year of Communist rule, both Poland and Hungary recorded that employees of private firms accounted for 10 percent of total employment in the industrial sector. Winiecki also provided some details about the program of small-scale privatization in Poland. He noted that the term *privatization* is misleading since 98 percent of the firms were not sold but rather leased. He said that this has generated perverse incentives with regard to the maintenance of the leased assets.

Simon Johnson conceded that he may have overstated the contrasts between private-sector development in Poland and Hungary, but he argued that there were important differences. He agreed with Winiecki that the private sectors in the two countries looked remarkably similar in 1989. Johnson noted, however, that the two countries were very different in 1985, when Hungary had a strong second economy and the private sector in Poland was small and was not developing. Johnson suggested that Hungary's 1989 boom in limited-liability companies probably was driven by state-owned capital, not private entrepreneurs; the minimum capital required to start such a firm was roughly equivalent to $20,000. At the same time, it took only $5.00 to form a joint-stock company in Poland. Finally, Johnson argued that much of the Hungarian private-sector growth in the late 1980s reflected legalization of already-existing activities, while in Poland this source of growth was less important. During this period, Poland experienced more of an actual change in the level of private-sector participation.

17   Foreign Direct Investment in Eastern Europe: Some Economic Considerations

Kenneth A. Froot

With the radical transformation of East European economies has come a wave of interest in inward foreign direct investment (FDI). In the past two years, host countries have adopted completely new legal frameworks as well as institutions and agencies to encourage and approve of foreign investments. On the demand side, surveys suggest that almost two-thirds of multinational firms are interested in investing directly in Eastern Europe. Indeed, firms initially showed a keen interest in "beating out the competition" by attempting to invest there first. Some observers became highly optimistic that foreign direct investment inflows would soon be sufficient to fund large current account deficits.

Now that the initial euphoria on both sides has died down, countries and Western companies have scaled back their expectations. In spite of their increased interest in FDI, Western companies have on average invested relatively small dollar amounts. While the *number* of investments and joint ventures with foreigners for all of Eastern Europe has risen extremely rapidly to over 10,000, the average dollar amount per investment remains very small—about $150,000. The difficulties of setting up the investment and the uncertain status and direction of the transformation programs have led companies to slow the pace of entry and to downsize their expected participation. Today, it is hard to imagine that FDI will provide a major net source of funds to these countries in the near future. A more realistic view is that FDI's major financial contribution to Eastern Europe is to be one of intermediation rather than inflow.

It is undoubtedly true that the host countries of Eastern Europe badly need the technology, Western organizational experience, and financial depth and intermediation services that foreign companies bring. Yet the entry of foreign firms is also greeted with distrust—not unlike that seen in other countries that

The author is grateful to Ellen Lederman, Jeff Sachs, Jeremy Stein, and Ray Vernon for helpful conversations and to the Division of Research at the Harvard Business School for research support.

293

have experienced bursts in foreign investment. There are often-heard complaints that foreigners purchase assets at fire-sale prices, taking advantage of inexperienced or corrupt government bureaucrats or managers. Because it is frequently necessary to negotiate with former Communists and government apparatchiks, there is a sense of complicity between the worst parts of the old order and newer foreign entrants. Furthermore, foreigners often displace or are insensitive to original stakeholders in Eastern firms. Many argue that the actions of local domestic owners would be more in line with social interests than are the actions of foreigners. For example, foreign owners may be less concerned with the level of unemployment in a certain municipality than would be local (domestic) stakeholders. And there may well be short-run social and political gains to preserving employment and smoothing needed labor market adjustments over time.

The experience thus far with FDI has intensified the discussion of *how* best to get foreigners involved in the privatization process. One view is that foreign ownership should be explicitly limited and regulated by government, as in the case of, say, the Czechoslovak banking sector. Under this view, needed knowledge of Western technology, organizational skill, and business practice is to be purchased by domestics in fee-for-service kinds of agreements. In practice, many countries have already found that there is no shortage of Western experts ready to give advice on these matters. However, it is not clear that experts' interests are always adequately aligned with those of their advisees.

A second view is that foreigners—like domestic investors—ought to be encouraged to participate in auctions and that these auctions should either be part of the primary privatization process or take place after privatization occurs in the secondary market. In such a case, there would be little specialized treatment of foreign bidders, and competition, as the argument goes, would occur quite naturally between them. The highest bid would win. The difficulty here is that, in practice, little foreign competition actually tends to emerge. And auctions are easily subverted when there are few truly competing bidders—the highest bid may be a very low bid indeed. As I discuss below, even auctions that are highly competitive ex ante are, in the context of Eastern Europe, likely to be very imperfectly competitive ex post.

A third and very different model, one that is currently being pursued by Germany's Treuhandanstalt, is to involve a governmental agency directly in asset sales and restructuring. The activities of identifying and advertising assets, soliciting bids for their use, and then aiding in their restructuring and ultimate sale to foreign buyers might all be taken on by such an agency. Indeed, the Treuhand frequently uses whatever bargaining power it has to negotiate conditions on payment, current and future employment levels, the range of required production activities, and investment expenditures. It is not so interested in selling rapidly at the best available prices.

While the Treuhand's example is in many ways unsuitable for the rest of Eastern Europe (see Carlin and Mayer, in this volume), it raises the issue of government involvement in the privatization process specifically with respect to foreigners. Effective competition in foreign purchases may be limited to such a degree that government involvement is needed to improve competition and/or negotiate for a better deal from society's perspective. In these circumstances, privately run auctions may by themselves be a poor means of redistributing control to foreigners. Governments can take (and have taken) a number of steps to protect against this outcome by intervening in the privatization process. But these steps also come with costs—any interventionist strategy that gives discretion to government authorities is subject both to possible administrative lags and to corruption.

The story of Poland's brief encounter with sectoral privatization demonstrates many of these points. The sectoral approach evolved ostensibly out of the need to identify and characterize assets and provide information to a class of interested foreign buyers. Undertaking one sector at a time seemed to economize on the costs of research, of finding interested parties, and of informing the parties about the assets. It also allowed for the trading of certain employment and investment guarantees in return for ownership. For much of 1991, sectoral privatization was expected to become a major track in Poland's privatization program. But the effort now seems to have failed, partly because it was moving too slowly, but, more important, because of the possibilities for and suspicions of corruption throughout the program. This kind of handicap, from which the Treuhand does not suffer, will be a problem for every other East European country.

This paper argues that the treatment of foreign investment is an important consideration in the initial design of privatization programs. I look at how foreigners can be paired efficiently and competitively with assets and conclude that governments may need to intervene in the foreign privatization process in several ways. First, the terms on which sales to foreigners take place can be improved (*relative* to the terms of sales to domestics) by disseminating information on individual assets and sectors, by promoting FDI through various bilateral and multilateral agencies and rules-based approaches, and by clarifying, codifying, and enforcing domestic property rights.

As it will take time to do these things, foreign investment may often be encouraged too hastily. That is, a sequencing of foreign involvement to follow domestic privatization may be desirable. Such a delay in foreign investment would give domestic owners and the government time to disseminate information and provide for a relatively high level of competition in sales to foreigners. In addition, this sequencing would require foreigners to wrest control from a number of private holders. Such transactions are more likely to give greater bargaining power to domestics and less likely to be perceived as corrupt than similar transactions that involve only the government and a foreigner.

The advantages of slowing foreign investment do not, however, imply that domestic privatization should be slowed. Firms or assets that are intended for sale to foreigners can be rapidly privatized to domestics (with certain control

s being retained by the government) as the government-led process of in-
nation collection and dissemination begins. Governments therefore might
involved in actively delaying or restricting foreigners' initial participation
in direct investment while working to establish the conditions for active foreign
competition at a later date.

The next section outlines the evolution of (primarily) the Polish treatment
of foreign investors and argues that this evolution, however flawed it may be,
can be interpreted as a response to the naturally low initial levels of foreign
competition for domestic assets. Section 17.2 discusses various factors that
help determine foreign valuations of domestic assets. Section 17.3 then turns
to a more analytic examination of country bargaining power in the process of
selling assets that are costly to learn about. The point is to see how costly
learning affects the level of foreign competition and to explore various selling
and sequencing mechanisms that might help improve seller bargaining power.
Section 17.4 offers conclusions.

17.1 Recent Developments in Poland

This section describes very briefly some of the important developments in
Poland that affect foreign investment and the terms on which it takes place.

17.1.1 Changes in the Regulatory Framework

The treatment of FDI in Poland is in the process of evolving from an interventionist and discretionary system toward a rules-based framework. Prior to
the 1988 Joint Venture Law (which along with the 1991 Foreign Investment
Law continues to regulate foreign investments in Poland), FDI into Poland was
highly restricted. Foreign participation was limited to firms with fewer than
200 employees, and there were severe restrictions on profit repatriation, use of
foreign exchange, and export and import activity. Together, the 1988 and 1991
laws removed virtually all these restrictions In addition, the 1991 law removed
completely the 1988 law's application and approval processes (the 1988 law
itself liberalized these processes) and eliminated the regulatory authority of
the Foreign Investment Agency (FIA).[1]

The Polish FIA was abolished in part because it appeared that the discretionary nature of its approval process actually hindered FDI. As this process was
highly bureaucratic in nature, the true requirements for approval often remained vague and uncertain.[2] This discouraged foreigners from proposing
deals in the first place. Furthermore, the uncertainties associated with approval
were widely understood to create opportunities for corruption. Bureaucrats
generally have an interest in creating the appearance of uncertainty in order to
make their authority more valuable to applicants. The perceived opportunities

---

1. For additional details on the foreign-investment laws in Poland, see Spar (1991).
2. For details, see Maslankiewicz (1991).

for impropriety created fears among the FIA's staff of taking the lead on individual deals—a completed deal was likely to be accused of being a corrupted deal. The result was that no one on the Polish side wanted to pursue investment approval aggressively. Thus, to remove the discretionary nature of the process and to emphasize the importance of rules, the FIA was dissolved.

The evolution of tax policy is another example of the movement toward a rules-based approach. In the aftermath of the political changes in Poland, tax holidays were offered in the attempt to attract foreign investors. However, these benefits often took the form of tax competition with other East European countries (so they had a beggar-thy-neighbor aspect to them) and in any case did not stimulate foreign investment. Indeed, surveys show that many investors view negatively programs that meddle with foreign-investment taxation because of their discretionary nature. Foreign investors are often more comfortable being treated symmetrically with other host-country companies, even if it involves higher initial rates of taxation. Indeed, the 1991 law requires symmetry between foreign and domestic company taxation.

This movement away from discretionary bureaucratic decision making toward a legalistic rules-oriented system is evident in other countries as well. In many cases, detailed regulation of businesses (mandated by early legislation on direct investment) was carried out by low levels of the bureaucracy. Regulation was often perceived to be capricious and in some cases was even of dubious legal status. For example, Soós (1991) argues that the Model Joint Venture Statute issued by the Romanian Ministry of Foreign Trade contained prescriptions whose legality could easily have been questioned. This, combined with the many unpublished ministry directives, magnified the sense of caution with which foreigners approached Romania.

Overall, Poland and other countries have endeavored to lower the costs of foreign investment by moving to a simpler, more transparent rules-based system with less emphasis on bureaucratic intervention. In many cases, the laws and regulations have come to resemble those common in the West, particularly the EC (examples include recent tax codes, accounting principles, bank guarantees, etc.), which helps lower costs of adjusting to Poland.

17.1.2   Changes in the Methods of Foreign Privatization

Alongside the basic legal changes associated with FDI, the Polish government has sought several means of marketing and selling domestic enterprises to foreigners. The main responsibility for this effort resides with Poland's Ministry of Privatization. The ministry is divided into three sections: capital privatization (under which firms are commercialized); liquidation (under which firms are legally dissolved, allowing for their piecemeal sale); and mass privatization (under which a yet-to-be-created group of mutual funds will distribute shares to citizens). Many of the transactions involving foreigners are joint ventures, which may form in the aftermath of a liquidation or through the capital privatization track. In addition, foreign firms purchase assets in trade sales or

Table 17.1   **Joint Ventures, 1989–91**

	Poland	Czechoslovakia	Romania	Hungary	Bulgaria
1989	867	22	5	180	30
1990	2,799	1,550	1,502	4,400	140
1991:1	4,000	1,318	2,665	2,420	366

Source: Economist, 21 September 1991.

IPOs (initial public offerings), which are alternative outcomes under the capital privatization program.

While joint ventures are the predominant form of foreign investment *by number*, they are typically small transactions. By June 1991, there were already 4,350 joint-venture permits issued by the Foreign Investment Agency, but the average value of the total capital (of which any foreign contribution is part) was only about $150,000.[3] Table 17.1 reports the number of joint ventures in several countries through the first quarter of 1991. Table 17.2 shows the location of the foreign investors involved in joint ventures as well as the percentage of equity owned by foreigners.

While there was a good deal of excitement with joint ventures initially, that excitement has waned. In some respects, joint ventures do as much to hinder as to help the privatization effort. First, the terms on which foreigners enter are often perceived to be overly generous. The Polish Main Statistical Office reports that the average rate of return on *total* capital for joint ventures in 1990 was 86 percent. In many cases, foreigners' rate of return was much higher because foreign ownership positions are frequently obtained in return for technology and/or relatively small infusions of liquidity. To see this, we note that the average foreign financial contribution was about half the book value of the equity that foreigners received in return and that their share of total equity has averaged around 60 percent. Thus, an average foreign investor who contributed $30.00 would receive 60 percent of a firm with $100 in net worth. On average, one year later this venture had a net worth of $186, of which the foreign share was $112, a return of almost four times the initial investment of $30.00. Even with such high payouts, Polish firms often end up competing with each other for access to foreign resources, with the result that the transactions take place at prices that are probably close to domestic reservation values. Czechoslovakia and Hungary have had similar experiences with joint ventures.[4] Increasingly, there is concern that the joint-venture process leaves the country with little bargaining power.

A second reason that joint ventures are viewed ambiguously is that they

---

3. For more comprehensive data on Polish joint ventures, see Maslankiewicz (1991).

4. A commonly cited Hungarian example of underpriced selling to foreigners is that of a large light-bulb-producing firm in Hungary that was sold to one foreign group and then resold almost immediately at a 50 percent capital gain.

Table 17.2   Joint Ventures in Poland

Nationality of Foreign Investor		% Foreign Equity Ownership	
Germany	35.0%	100%	24%
Sweden	9.1%	91%–99%	7%
United States	7.6%	81%–90%	9%
Austria	7.1%	71%–80%	9%
Great Britain	7.1%	61%–70%	6%
Italy	4.7%	51%–60%	8%
France	4.7%	41%–50%	25%
Holland	4.6%	31%–40%	5%
Switzerland	3.2%	20%–30%	7%
Denmark	2.6%		

usually do not aid in the attempt to rationalize an industry's portfolio of assets. Naturally, foreigners pick the assets with which they would like to work. Because these assets are frequently part of a larger firm, the enterprise must liquidate in order to sell specific assets to the joint venture. In these circumstances, the government is left with the least-desirable assets and potentially explosive political problems (shutdowns of the only factory in a one-shop town, environmental cleanup, etc.). In the short run, there is a wedge between private and social values that arises from unemployment of resources (and all its associated political consequences). If the host country had greater bargaining power with the foreign entity, it would be able to require that the new venture deal with these problems.

Partly in response to these disadvantages to joint ventures, the capital privatization program began during 1991 actively to promote its "sectoral" approach to privatization. This approach briefly experienced a limited degree of success. Basically, the sectoral approach involves the identification and ultimate study of some 300 sectors across the economy. The basic plan is that in each sector a consultant is to be brought on to (1) identify companies operating in a given sector and analyze their viability and potential profitability, (2) assemble and prepare for dissemination the sectoral information and analysis, and (3) aid in the process of auctioning off the sectoral firms to interested foreigners. Each consultant is compensated through a retainer fee plus a contingency fee if the firms are successfully sold.

So far, approximately thirty-five sectoral studies are either in process or have already been completed. The means of choosing industries has so far been reactive: when a foreigner indicates a desire to purchase a firm, the Ministry of Privatization initiates a sectoral study. This typically takes about three months to complete, not substantially longer than a more narrowly focused bid evaluation.

The sectoral study serves several purposes. First, it gives the Ministry of Privatization representatives a reasonable basis for understanding the value of the assets and evaluating the offer. Second, it collects information on all similar facilities in Poland. This is often of use to bidding firms, which usually would not otherwise be able to consider a broad spectrum of alternative investments. It also forms the basis for a wider marketing effort, in which investment bankers and consultants advertise the assets to a wider audience. Third, the increased publicity generates enough competition to allow the pilot firm (and usually several others in the sector) to be sold off in an auction process. Auctions are characterized by reasonable levels of competition and also provide negotiating opportunities for the Polish government to adjust the sale terms based on deviations between private and social values (i.e., employment and investment guarantees can be negotiated).

Sectoral studies would seem to economize on the costs of accomplishing foreign investment. In addition to analyzing the assets and publicizing their sales, they create a safety net for firms involved in the auction process—losing bidders begin negotiations on another firm in the industry immediately after an auction ends. This goes a long way toward conserving on the effort that foreigners must expend to learn about and acquire assets in Poland.

Sectoral privatizations also help improve the host country's bargaining position with foreign firms. The likelihood is much higher that foreigner investors will be bidding against one another, and the possibility of foreign firms playing one host-country firm off against another is eliminated. The Ministry of Privatization is therefore in a better position to negotiate labor contracts, new investment guarantees, and other foreign "investment" requirements that (arguably) have high public returns for Poland.

Finally, sectoral privatizations help generate a game plan even for those firms that do not sell. That is, this approach to privatization usually involves some degree of simultaneous restructuring. Remaining firms (which are usually smaller) can be led through some sort of MBO (management buyout) process. Before letting go, however, the Ministry of Privatization can help rationalize their operations and direct their operations into different "niche" markets.[5] This process helps guarantee that the postprivatization industry structure has capacity smoothly distributed across various products. While competitive forces would ultimately achieve this type of industry structure (or do even better), these forces may be weak at first.[6]

There is also the argument that the negotiating process and direct government/foreign-investor contact required to make the sectoral approach work partly diffuses foreign perceptions of the costs of poorly defined property rights. To some extent, foreigners are educated in the process about the exact status of these rights. But perhaps more important, as the situation is fluid,

---

5. For example, in the detergent and soap sector, individual remaining firms were directed into hotel soaps and hospital soaps, respectively.
6. Such activities by the government have a ring of "industrial policy" to them and are often (rightly) criticized by economists in the case of the United States. However, in East European countries, the usual presumption that the existing allocation of capacity is nearly optimal obviously does not hold.

companies gain contacts within the government that understand their interests and keep them appraised of changes.

Initially, observers were critical of the sectoral approach, saying that it would repeatedly flood the market with waves of very similar companies. As a consequence, many were skeptical that the approach could improve host-country bargaining power, and the expectation was that prices would be low. However, this does not seem to have been the case thus far. In the recent sale of assets in the detergent sector, for example, the Ministry of Privatization received sales prices that were 2.5 times higher per ton of capacity (for smaller, somewhat less efficient firms) than did the Czechs, who have relied primarily on joint ventures. In addition to the higher prices, the auctions help lend an air of legitimacy to the selling process, creating a structure that promotes (what at least appear to be) arm's-length transactions.

Another criticism has been that the sectoral approach slows down the privatization process and takes energy away from the mass privatization effort. To the extent that this is true, the diversion must be balanced against the value of the information generated by the sectoral studies. I discuss alternative methods of combining mass privatization and sectoral studies in later sections.

But the sectoral approach's major problem—and the reason for its very recent demise—has been the opportunities for corruption that it affords. Consultants and staff were given considerable discretionary powers. By working closely with individual companies and groups of assets, and by virtue of their power to pursue "applied" industrial policies, consultants and staff often struck deals that were difficult for outsiders to scrutinize. (Indeed, there are accusations that files containing details of agreed-on deals have disappeared.) Germany's Treuhandanstalt has not fallen victim to these perceptions, partly because of the integrity of the German system.

In sum, Poland has made dramatic changes both in the legal basis for foreign investment and in the way in which enterprises are sold to foreigners. Some of these changes (e.g., the emphasis on the sectoral approach to privatization) can be interpreted as helping increase domestic bargaining power via-à-vis foreigners. All are at least partly driven by the need to lower the costs of foreigners learning about and investing in doing business in Poland and to raise foreigners' reservation prices for investing.

In the wake of the sectoral approach's demise, it is useful to remember that the earlier FDI tracks (e.g., joint ventures) were also not altogether desirable. It may be wise for Poland to make foreign investors wait for access and in the meanwhile spur on the progress of the mass privatization program for domestics. After these privatizations are completed, there would be room for a revamped sectoral approach, which could help market privately owned firms to foreigners. The informational advantages of the sectoral approach could in this way be retained, but, in these circumstances, the possibilities for corruption would be reduced, as private owners would be the primary counterparty in negotiations with foreigners.

17.2   Foreign Reservation Values

Next I turn to the puzzle of why foreign purchase prices appear to be so low in the first place. In general, one would expect foreigners to value East European assets far more highly than do East Europeans. In this section, I briefly discuss several of the determinants of foreign reservation values as well as the potential for policy-based measures to affect them. In the next section, I discuss the issue of foreign versus domestic bargaining power and how the design of the privatization process affects that power.

The simplest view of foreign reservation values is that they are generated by what foreigners would earn by acquiring East European operations. The overwhelmingly obvious presumption is that foreigners have better technology, more comprehensive experience with doing business in a market-based economy, better knowledge of and relations with suppliers and distributors, better risk-sharing capabilities, and much greater financial strength.[7] All else equal, these advantages should translate into a tendency for foreigners to pay more for East European assets than do domestic residents.

Foreigners may also be willing to pay more than domestics because they perceive an option value to establishing a "toehold" in the East European market. The aforementioned advantages that Westerners have are most valuable when the domestic economy turns out to be robust and grows rapidly. In such states, foreigners will be in a better position to expand sales and production rapidly than domestic firms that face capital and managerial talent constraints. To the extent that the level of uncertainty about these economies is high, this expansion option may be quite valuable.

Surveys of foreign investor sentiment suggest that this option value is important. Collins and Rodrik (1991) conducted a survey of multinational business focusing on attitudes toward investing in Eastern Europe. Businesses seemed to perceive that current investments gave them the ability to "beat out the competition" and "get to the market first"; indeed, these benefits of investment were ranked well above the benefits associated with low costs of production and a relatively skilled work force. Such perceptions seem to reflect the possibility that first-comers derive disproportionately large benefits from market access in certain states of the world and that, in these states, they will be in a privileged position to increase profits.[8]

However, not all forces tend to drive foreign reservation values above those

---

7. Naturally, financial strength would not matter in a world with perfect capital markets—i.e., markets in which firms do not face informational asymmetries and agency problems in their use of external financing. However, once such distortions exist, financial strength can be a source of competitive advantage. For an example of how this general idea can be applied to foreign direct investment, see Froot and Stein (1991).

8. To make sense of this story, one must also posit some form of barriers to entry at later stages. Such barriers could come from steep learning curves associated with the unique aspects of doing business in East European countries. For an example of a study that provides evidence of similar kinds of dynamic learning, see Teece (1976).

of domestic entities. For example, foreigners may suffer disproportionately from certain changes in policy, such as restrictions on dividend and profit repatriation, expropriation, controls on moving goods or foreign exchange across borders, etc. A political backlash against foreign involvement could easily motivate such policy changes (note the tenor of the discussion surrounding the relatively meager FDI inflow into the United States). This will be a particular problem if foreigners are held publicly responsible for poor macroeconomic performance or for firing workers at nonviable plants.

The penalty to foreign valuation created by the possibility of asymmetrical government policies can be mitigated in two ways. First, the government can take steps to negotiate contracts with foreign firms that stipulate how many workers must be employed, how much additional investment must be done over time, etc. Such contracts can help align private and social values. This is valuable to the country because it helps internalize the externalities associated with unemployment.

Second, governments may also endeavor to accomplish certain facets of the restructuring that foreigners would otherwise have to undertake themselves. This is again reminiscent of the Treuhandandstalt's attempts to undertake significant restructuring before privatization. Preprivatization restructuring can help guarantee that the foreign buyer will not be held responsible for the criticisms associated with plant shutdowns. Such a program may help countries precommit to eliminating certain forms of political risk from foreign investment, thereby ensuring that the interests of the government do not diverge radically from those of the foreign firm (which is when expropriation is most likely to occur).

It is sometimes argued that foreign reservation values are highest when the country is clearly committed to having a very high degree of foreign involvement (see, e.g., Wolfe 1991). The logic is that, in an economy with coordination externalities, multiple equilibria can arise. If enough firms pursue high-investment policies, then the country will experience rapid demand growth, which will in turn generate high returns on investment and support the initial high-investment policies. However, if firms pursue low-level investment strategies, then growth and returns on investment are sufficiently low to make it unprofitable for individual firms to invest more aggressively.[9]

With this in mind, some have argued that greater foreign participation makes the high-investment equilibrium more likely. This is likely to be a useful insight, especially in cases where foreigners perceive systematically higher returns on investment than do domestic entrepreneurs because of technological or financial advantages. However, it may well be that domestically owned firms are better at resolving the coordination problem that creates the multiplicity in the first place. Foreign-owned firms may make their decisions from all over the world and may not be particularly focused on the investment plans of other

9. For an example of such a model, see Murphy, Shleifer, and Vishny (1989).

firms in a given local economy. Therefore, even in the presence of multiple equilibria, it is not clear that greater levels of foreign involvement would cause higher growth.[10]

17.3   Selling Enterprises to Foreigners on Better Terms

There are obviously a number of good reasons why foreign and domestic entrepreneurs might have very different reservation values for East European enterprises and assets. But foreign reservation values are not the only—or perhaps even the major—practical concern in selling to foreigners. First of all, a country's total return from selling to foreigners may be high even if the pecuniary receipts are low: domestic residents may gain valuable technology and experience from a foreign presence in the economy. Some of the pecuniary returns may also come in the form of employment and investment guarantees that are valued more highly by the country. Second, the pecuniary receipts will themselves depend on the bargaining power of the country and the foreign investor in addition to the foreigner's reservation price.

The ability of the country to extract bargaining gains will be important when there is little effective competition among buyers. And competition will be inhibited by the presence of costs to potential bidders learning enough about enterprises (and about doing business in a country) to make bidding worthwhile. Such "costs of entry" are likely to be substantial.

A typical example comes from Sara Lee, Inc., which in mid-1990 was considering importing and/or producing hosiery in the East. Sara Lee chose Hungary—arguably the most promising and liberalized country for foreign investors at the time—as a potential investment site. But, after several trips by a number of senior executives and their aids, Sara Lee remained uncertain about its ability to do business there. There was confusion about the company's ability to import materials and repatriate profits, about the rules for ownership, and about the role of the State Property Agency in arranging for purchases. These explorations ultimately did yield a venture that Sara Lee considered worth pursuing—a $60 million investment (51 percent) in a Hungarian food company. But participation involved a complete reworking of Sara Lee's food and hosiery strategy in Eastern and Western Europe. Learning about the peculiarities of doing business in Hungary and integrating that into Sara Lee's overall strategy was costly. The whole process ate up far more top-executive time than that typical for comparably sized investments.[11]

Costly learning by foreigners can dramatically affect the terms under which East European assets should be expected to sell (if they sell at all). Reflecting their bias toward competition, economists usually envision some type of com-

---

10. There is some empirical work that demonstrates a positive correlation between growth and foreign direct investment inflows, but there is as yet little evidence on the direction of causality.
11. For more details, see Weiner (1990).

petitive auction mechanism for selling assets to foreigners. Regardless of the precise auction rules (Dutch, sealed-bid, English, etc.) and the distribution of information, it does not require many bidders to make the seller's reservation price largely irrelevant to the bidding. For example, in an open-outcry English auction with two bidders with (at least privately) known valuations, an asset will sell at (just above) the second highest bidder's valuation.[12] It usually goes without saying that competition among bidders raises the seller's bargaining power and the price the seller can expect to extract.

However, this conclusion no longer holds once there are costs to learning about the asset's value. The prospect of competition at the auction stage clearly disciplines a bidder's incentive to learn about the asset in the first stage. In such instances, sellers may actually gain by *eliminating* potential bidders rather than encouraging them to participate. I provide an example of a bidding model below in which an increase in the number of bidders does not increase the competitiveness of the auction.[13]

The practical point here is not so much that East European governments or enterprises will want to discourage potential foreign bidders from exploring investments in their countries. Rather, it is that the returns to increasing the universe of potential bidders may be surprising low (unless of course there is an attempt to economize on the costs of bidder information). In addition, whereas highly "redeployable" assets are thought to have relatively high liquidation values (redeployability implies a comparatively broadly based demand for a given asset), redeployable assets might be relatively more undervalued in actual East European auction sales, particularly when foreigners are the buyers. When there are costs to learning about value, having a large number of potential uses for the assets does not necessarily guarantee a high sales price.[14] The presence of costs to foreign bidding therefore strongly argues for more efficient information dissemination. Because this information is a public good, its dissemination may be best accomplished by a governmental agency or trade organization.

17.3.1 Auctions with Costly Participation: An Example

This subsection offers an example of an asset sale in which an increase in the number of bidders does not increase the seller's bargaining power.

Consider a simple two-stage process in which an asset is to be sold to the

12. When bidders are imperfectly informed about an asset's true value, they may use the seller's reservation price (if it is known) in determining their own reservation prices. For a simple overview and further citations, see Milgrom (1989).

13. Bidder elimination improves seller revenues in a number of models of both sequential and simultaneous bidding. In a sequential bidding model, an initial bidder may wish to make a preemptively high initial bid in order to ward off interest from other potential bidders. Fishman (1988) shows that, in such circumstances, the seller receives higher profits than when a preemptive bid does not occur and instead bidders compete in an auction.

14. A number of authors have stressed that redeployability is critical for determining an asset's debt capacity (see, e.g., Williamson 1988; and Shleifer and Vishny 1991).

highest bidder. In the first stage, each of N risk-neutral bidders may spend an amount c to learn their valuation of the asset. In the second stage, those who spend c compete in an open-outcry English auction. The variable c can be interpreted quite broadly as including the cost not only of learning about the specifics of an investment opportunity but also of general learning about the status of property rights and enforcement mechanisms in East European countries.

I start with the simplest situation in which individual bidder reservation values contain only a common component, v_c.[15] For now, I assume that it is common knowledge that $v_c = 1$. Bidders who pay the cost c are able to observe v_c.[16] It is common knowledge that the seller's reservation price, v_s, equals ½ and that the seller has no bargaining power in situations of bilateral negotiation: if only one bidder emerges with a reservation value greater than half, the sales price is the seller's reservation price. If more than one bidder arrives with a reservation value greater than half, then the sales price is equal to the realized common value, $v_c = 1$.

To get a sense for bidder strategies under these circumstances, note first that this example cannot support a pure-strategy bidding equilibrium. To see this, suppose that all N bidders decide to spend c and therefore to compete in the bidding. Competition in the auction will guarantee that the asset sells for a price of one, reducing to zero any expected gains from winning. However, since bidders must pay c to participate, their ex ante expected profits are negative. Individual bidders will therefore not wish to play, so the all-bidders-play outcome cannot be an equilibrium. Alternatively, it cannot be an equilibrium for bidders never to participate: if no bidders spend c to participate, a single bidder would have the incentive to deviate by paying $c < ½$, thereby keeping the expected profits from the auction of ½ all to himself.

The equilibrium to this game involves a mixed strategy, in which the nth bidder, with probability p_n, pays c and participates in the auction. (If no bidders arrive, the asset is not sold.) The nth bidder's expected profit from participating can then be expressed as

(1) $$\pi_n = p_n [E(v_c)\Pi_{j \neq n}(1 - p_j) - c].$$

In the symmetrical solution to the game, each bidder chooses the same probability of participating. Bidders will have an incentive to raise the probability with which they participate as long as expected profits are positive. As a result, expected profits in (1) are driven to zero, and the common probability of participation satisfies $(1 - p)^{N-1} = c/v_c$. Substituting, the expected profit, π, received by the seller is

(2) $$\pi = \frac{v_c}{2}\left\{1 + N\left[\left(\frac{c}{v_c}\right)^{N/N-1} - \frac{c}{v_c}\right] - \left(\frac{c}{v_c}\right)^{N/N-1}\right\},$$

---

15. The results are not importantly affected by whether v_c is known or random ex ante. I also allow for a random private component of value in the discussion below.

16. A related example can be found in Spatt (1989).

which is decreasing in N for $N > 1$. That is, eliminating bidders from this game *increases* the expected profit to the seller.

Essentially, bidders will participate only if they can expect to use the profits from winning the auction to amortize fully the costs of participating. All else equal, there must be *less* effective competition at the auction in order to justify the higher total learning costs associated with a larger number of bidders. (In the example above, this translates into a higher probability of an individual bidder making it to the auction alone.) More generally, when participation is costly, greater competition ex ante can be sustained only by effectively guaranteeing less competition ex post.

Costs of Bidding

There are several factors—besides the number of bidders—that help determine how "competitive" the selling-off process is likely to be. First, and most important, is the cost, c, of participating in the bidding. In the example above, if the costs of participation are removed altogether, then all N bidders participate in the auction, and the seller nets with certainty a profit of $v_c = 1$.

Bidding costs are particularly burdensome to expected seller profits because they are borne by each player individually. In the bidding game described above, suppose that the potential universe of bidders is ten. If there are no costs of participation, all ten bidders do bid with probability one, and the seller gets v_c. If, however, we introduce a cost of bidding equal to just 1 percent of the expected gain from winning the auction (i.e., $c/v_c = .01$), the probability with which bidders participate falls dramatically to .4. (Note that this implies that the expected number of participants in the auction is only four.) The addition of this 1 percent cost of bidding also lowers the seller's expected profit by 5 percent. Thus, even with small costs of entry, bidders compete in the auction much less frequently. This, in turn, has a relatively large negative effect on the competitiveness of the auction.

The magnification effect of small costs of bidding on seller profits implies that countries have a strong incentive to provide to all bidders information that is of common value. Continuing with the example above, if each bidder needs to obtain the same set of information in order to participate, then the country could itself obtain the information for 1 percent of the asset's value. By making this information public, the expected auction price rises by 5 percent—on net the country saves itself four times the costs of information.

Much of the learning about potential acquisitions in the East concerns the consumption of a public good. Foreign firms repeatedly report how difficult and time consuming it is to sort out the rules of the game, to understand the status (current and future) of property rights, and to determine who has the authority to do what. Simple promotional activities—such as the Hungarian government's early efforts to provide detailed information on large companies to major European banks, investment banks, and chambers of commerce or the Polish Ministry of Privatization's activities of studying and promoting individual sectors—have the potential to lower costs and increase the degree of competition facing foreign investors.

Seller Reservation Values

Because costs of participation make the auction mechanism imperfectly competitive, auction revenues depend importantly on the reservation price of the seller. In cases where seller reservation values are low relative to those of a relatively small number of bidders, seller reservation values will be particularly important to expected auction revenues.

It is important to clear up just what the seller's reservation value means in this context. If the seller has the option to retain control of the asset, then the reservation value depends on the cash flows that the seller would have received by holding on. As has already been discussed, there are reasons to think that these present values might be low, especially relative to those of foreigners. But in Eastern Europe there are many instances in which the present value of cash flows under the holder's control is irrelevant because the holder of the assets must sell. Even if the government and existing enterprises were able to manage the real assets of the economy in the coming years, the credibility of the transition to a decentralized market economy depends largely on the central authority's ability to divest its holdings of assets. Forced selling to foreigners could be avoided if the privatization goes through with only limited initial foreign involvement. In later stages, after firms have been privatized, the urgency to sell is reduced, and domestic reservation values will be higher.

Clearly, if there are factors (other than holding value) that prompt the seller to divest, the seller's reservation price need not equal the assets' value under the seller's control. These factors are evident in cases in which the government sells in response to political pressure. But they are also important in many other instances. Sellers of assets in Eastern Europe, whether they be governmental authorities or managers of firms or equityholders of recently privatized firms, often face severe liquidity constraints. They will view assets sales as a means of raising scarce cash.

This latter point is important because, in Poland, Hungary, and Czechoslovakia, the banking sector is extremely weak and securitization of assets (such as through public debt sales) is not likely to be practical for some time. Even if local banks are able to lend out domestically generated savings, credit allocation is likely to be poor. Recently privatized firms, for example, will find it necessary to sell assets, *not* because the assets are not useful or productive, but because they either need funds to service existing debts or wish to fund even more productive investments. Various levels of country governments, which will find it difficult to borrow for some time and which may not—or, because of slow growth, should not—raise taxes, will also have to resort to rapid asset sales. Thus, with the usual institutional sources of financial intermediation in such an underdeveloped state, asset sales become a disproportionately important source of liquidity.

The distorted importance of asset sales in supporting basic financial intermediation translates into a strong downward pressure on seller reservation prices. Such reservation values may be well below the value of the assets under the seller's control.

Private Information and the Value of Equity Retention

In the example above, the only source of potential bidder profits comes from the weak bargaining position of the seller. This weakness was manifest in the assumption that the seller receives a (relatively low) reservation price if only one high-reservation-price bidder arrives at the auction. However, expected bidder profits do not generally reflect bargaining power alone—they also reflect any private information about value that the bidder may have. The presence of private information increases the incentive for a given bidder to participate. This occurs because the auction requires the winning bidder to pay only the reservation price of the second highest participant. The greater is the dispersion of private-information values, the greater is this source of expected bidder profits.

Private information can be easily incorporated into the example above. Suppose that, instead of a common value, v_c, there is a private signal of value, v_n, $n = 1, \ldots, N$, which can take on the values of zero or one with equal probability.[17] By paying c, the nth bidder observes v_n and then competes in a second-price auction. The bidder enters the auction with probability p_n and has a reservation price higher than the seller with probability $p_n/2$. Thus, expected bidder profits become

$$(3) \qquad \pi_n = \frac{p_n(1 - v_s)}{2} \Pi_{j \neq n}\left(1 - \frac{p_j}{2}\right) - p_n c,$$

where $0 \leq v_s < 1$ is the seller's reservation price. In the symmetrical equilibrium, the common probability of participation is then

$$(4) \qquad p = 2\left[1 - \left(\frac{2c}{1 - v_s}\right)\frac{1}{N} - 1\right], \quad \text{if } c > \frac{1}{2^N};$$
$$= 1 \text{ otherwise.}$$

The seller's profits are now

$$(5) \qquad \pi_s = 1 - v_s - (1 - v_s)\left(1 - \frac{p}{2}\right)^{N-1}\left(1 - \frac{p}{2} + \frac{Np}{2}\right).$$

These results are similar to those above. The only real difference is that, with private information, the winning bidder expects to buy the asset at a price

---

17. The binomial distribution is chosen here for simplicity only and has little qualitative significance for the results. In addition, none of the results below are affected if we were to include both common and private value components in the example.

below his reservation value, even if there are other competing bidders. The possibility of positive expected profits means that sufficiently small (but positive) costs will not deter bidders from participating—expected profits can be strictly positive even when all N bidders participate with probability one. Thus, very small costs of bidding (in this case, $c < 1/2^N$) have no effect on the probability of participation and therefore no effect on seller profits. However, once costs reach a level such that the expected gains to a bidder from having the private information equal the costs of participation, $c = 1/2^N$, the situation discussed above applies. That is, small additions to the cost of bidding have large effects on the competitiveness of the auction and therefore lead to large reductions in the price that the seller can expect to receive.

Clearly, once bidders have private information, the seller is at an informational disadvantage. One way of overcoming this disadvantage—at least partially—is for the seller to retain a portion of the equity of the enterprise being sold. To see this, suppose that there are two risk-neutral bidders with privately known valuations, v_1 and v_2, that are independent draws from a common-knowledge distribution. In an English auction format with open outcry and no costs of bidding, the seller expects to receive the second highest valuation as the winning bid, $E[\min(v_1, v_2)]$, and the ith bidder, $i = 1, 2$, expects to profit by $E[\max(v_i - v_j, 0)]$. By selling only a portion of the asset, the seller can extract some of the high-value bidder's surplus. If the seller retains a fraction α of the asset, the seller's expected profits rise to become $E[\min(v_1, v_2)] + \alpha E[|v_1 - v_2|]$.

The use of equity retention to improve seller revenue demonstrates what Milgrom (1989) calls the "linkage principle," which says that it pays the seller to link his returns to any piece of private information the bidder may have. Naturally, it is best if the linkage occurs with respect to something that is *exogenous* to the bidder's actions—otherwise, there can be a moral hazard or principle-agent problem. For example, if the ultimate realization of value depends on future bidder efforts—which are *endogenous* from the bidder's perspective—then equity retention by the seller will act as a tax on bidder effort. All else equal, the presence of this tax will reduce the value of the asset.

While the positive effects of equity retention on bidder revenue seem intuitive enough, equity retention has a second, *negative* effect on revenue if there are costs of bidding. Greater seller expected profits come at the expense of expected bidder profits, and lower bidder profits reduce the ex ante incentives for bidder participation. The result is that equity retention lowers the average competitiveness of the auction, reducing the probability of participation from that given by equation (4) to

$$(6) \quad p = 2\left\{1 - \left[\frac{2c}{(1 - v_s)(1 - \alpha)}\right]^{1/N - 1}\right\}, \quad \text{if } c > \frac{1}{2^N}\left[(1 - v_s)(1 - \alpha)\right];$$

$$= 1 \text{ otherwise.}$$

Seller profits therefore rise to the extent that the seller retains a share α of equity in the asset but fall to the extent that lower bidder profits reduce the competitiveness of the auction. It is easy to show that expected seller profits are now

(7)
$$\pi_s = 1 - v_s - (1 - v_s)\left(1 - \frac{p}{2}\right)^{N-1}\left(1 - \frac{p}{2} + \frac{Np}{2}\right) +$$
$$\alpha(1 - v_s)\frac{Np}{2}\left(1 - \frac{p}{2}\right)^{N-1}.$$

Even though these two effects act in opposite directions, several unambiguous results emerge. It is possible to show that, for small costs of participation, retention of equity by the seller typically *raises* profits. The reason is that equity retention increases the perceived ex ante costs of bidding by a factor of $1/(1 - \alpha)$. By making costs sufficiently small, the resulting anticompetitiveness effect can be made small as well. But, even as costs go to zero, the positive effect on seller profits of equity retention does not. Thus, with small costs of bidding, equity retention improves the position of the seller.

Figure 17.1 helps us see the behavior of seller profits in these circumstances. The bold line represents profits from a direct auction with private bidder values. The line is convex because (as is the case with common values above) relatively small costs have a disproportionately large negative effect on seller profits. The larger the costs of participation become, however, the smaller is the effect on seller profits of a marginal increase in costs. The dotted line in

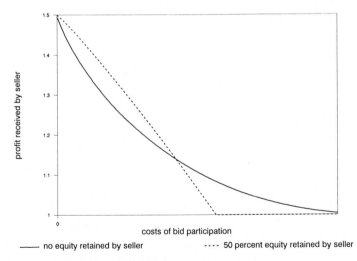

Fig. 17.1   **The effect on expected seller profits of equity retention by the seller in an auction with private bidder valuations**

the figure represents seller profits when part of the equity is retained by the seller. Note that equity retention mitigates the anticompetitive effects of costly participation when costs are small (relative, i.e., to expected bidder profits conditional on participating in the auction). When costs become large, however, the seller is made worse off if he retains some of the equity. Equity retention increases the ratio of bidding costs to bidding profits for given c; the result is a lower threshold level of c at which bidders refuse to participate with any positive probability. The less equity is retained, the smaller is the range in which equity retention leads to lower seller profits.

As in the case with no private information, sellers can raise expected profits through the ex ante elimination of bidders, provided that $c > 1/2^N$. This is true regardless of whether the seller plans to retain a portion of the equity. However, once costs are small enough or there are few enough bidders (so that $c < 1/2^N$), bidder elimination is no longer in the seller's interests. At this point, there are so few bidders that bidders expect to gain more from the bidding advantage conferred by the private information than they expect to pay to obtain it (c). Thus, because expected bidder profits are not dissipated through competition or bidding costs, bidders participate with probability one.

Figure 17.2 shows the effect on expected seller profits of an elimination of bidders. Figure 17.3 does the same when the seller is to retain half the asset's equity. Note that, regardless of the number of bidders, equity retention raises seller profits for small relative costs of bidding.

In spite of the potential theoretical benefits to equity retention, there are in practice a number of potential costs of such a policy. For assets that do not have legitimate private owners, complete divestment by the government may

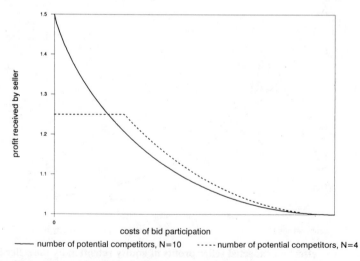

Fig. 17.2   Expected seller profits from an auction with private valuations and no equity retention by the seller

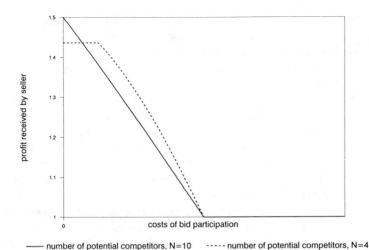

— number of potential competitors, N=10   ----- number of potential competitors, N=4

Fig. 17.3   Expected seller profits from an auction with private valuations and 50 percent equity retention by the seller

be a political goal. Minority equity retention by some form of centralized "development fund" is of questionable political viability.

17.3.2   Two-Step Sales to Foreigners

It would seem that holders of East European assets face a dilemma in realizing a high value when selling. The greater the share of the equity they retain, the more they expose themselves to political criticisms that privatization has failed. Yet, by selling a greater share, they suffer more from weak bargaining power and the imperfectness of the auction competition. However, the costs and benefits implied by this trade-off are not immutably fixed—they depend critically on who is selling the equity. In this subsection, I look at the ability of sellers to enhance their revenues by separating control from residual ownership and by selling the ownership of the assets in a two-stage process.

The first point to note is that a country's bargaining position can be strategically strengthened if foreigners must buy shares from a large number of small investors. These investors will have the incentive to free-ride on any common-knowledge improvements in operations and efficiency that foreigners bring. Since individual shareholders do not view their behavior as pivotal in a foreign acquisition, they will sell into a foreign tender offer only if the price is that which they expect under foreign management.[18]

To take a simple example, suppose that, under existing management, an uncommercialized East European firm is worth 100. Also, suppose that it is

18. The point that the free-riding of small shareholders reduces a raider's profits from taking over a firm was first made by Grossman and Hart (1980).

known that a foreign buyer could effect managerial and operational changes to make this firm worth 200 and that this amount is both observable and verifiable by third parties. If the government (or the firm's management) must bargain bilaterally with the foreign suitor, it can be expected to extract an amount between 100 and 200, say, 150. However, if the shares of the firm are widely dispersed, a public offer by the foreign firm of 150 would not be sufficient to induce small investors to tender. Each small investor—who perceives himself to have no effect on the offer's success—would reason that, by holding on, his shares would be worth 200, rather than the 150 received by tendering. That is, if investors are to tender their shares, they will demand in return the full value of the firm under foreign control. The free-rider problem therefore gives to small investors credible bargaining strength.

Many of the most popularly discussed privatization proposals include measures for widespread share distribution. However, in most cases, these shares are envisioned to be held in blocks by a limited number of investors: investment and pension funds, workers and management, some form of state development fund. These groups of investors are not exactly small, but holdings by even a limited number of investors will give the country much more bargaining power than would a single share owner. Greater bargaining power with foreigners may therefore be a little-stressed advantage of mass privatization policies that emphasize broad share distribution.

This advantage remains even if it is not practical to promote earnest foreign involvement quickly on reasonable terms. It takes time for the government to gather information and contact potential foreign bidders. However, even if the process of engaging foreign investors is slow, there are benefits to pushing quickly ahead with mass privatization. These benefits include not only the avoidance of ambiguities about ownership and control rights but also the ability to negotiate better with foreigners when the time comes. Thus, a two-step approach to firms that are ultimately to be owned by foreigners may be a good one.

In many ways, the actual terms paid by foreign acquirers are not so important politically as are the means by which the terms are determined. That is, there is likely to be suspicion about the legitimacy of insider transactions involving only government representatives and the foreign acquirer. Arm's-length transactions, or negotiated transactions in which representatives from the domestic firm also participate, would make corrupt transactions more difficult.

The economics of two-step foreign acquisitions can be taken one step further, to say something about the voting power of the shares that the government ought to distribute to small investors. To see this, suppose that the foreign firm in the example above receives observable (but not verifiable) private benefits of 40 from controlling the enterprise. (This is in addition to the 200 in value that foreign control generates.) These private benefits can arise from perks to management, from the multinational's increased ability to use transfer pricing to raise its profits, and from other nonpecuniary transfers back to the foreign parent (e.g., greater familiarity with Eastern markets and with the process of doing business in the East, option value of undertaking further investments, etc.). If the shares have full voting power (one share, one vote) and are initially distributed by the government to many different investors, the foreign firm will still succeed in acquiring the shares by making a tender offer of 200. In other words, small investors *do not* have bargaining power with respect to private benefits that accrue to the foreign firm.

However, this is not the case for the host government (or the firm's management). A central authority will have just as much bargaining power with respect to private benefits as it does with respect to verifiable benefits. So, in this example, it would make sense for the government to retain a "golden share" with special control privileges and to distribute nonvoting equity in the mass privatization stage. A foreign acquirer would then have to negotiate to obtain the golden share while acquiring at arm's length nonvoting shares. By employing this particular ownership/control structure, the host country will retain the full value of the verifiable component of foreign-firm value as well as a share (say, 50 percent) of the private benefits received by the foreign firm. Thus, total host-country gains are $200 + 40/2 = 220$—much greater than the $150 = 40/2 = 170$ that would result from a negotiation with the government for all the host-country firm's equity.

In practice, such a negotiation would let the government retain its ability to negotiate with foreign investors about future employment and investment spending. It may be that this form of expenditure by foreign firms has a relatively high social return so that it would be very costly for the government to give up its negotiating strength by selling all rights to enterprise control in the mass privatization phase.

17.4   Conclusions

This analysis of the behavior of country bargaining power leads to two types of prescriptions for encouraging FDI and improving the terms on which it takes place. First, it is clear that there are large returns to centralized efforts to collect and disseminate information about the assets and about how to operate them in the host country. If borne by individual bidders, such costs—even if they are small—can have large effects on the degree of foreign competition for domestic assets and on the revenues received by host countries.

Second, if the information acquisition phase takes time, it may be useful to go ahead immediately with some form of mass privatization. Privatization may be best accomplished if done quickly. Furthermore, privatization places a substantial number of shares in private hands so that interested foreign investors must negotiate for shares or purchase them in arm's-length transactions from a variety of private owners in addition to the government. This is likely to help guarantee better purchase terms and to contribute to a greater sense of fairness. To facilitate the government's ability to dictate nonprice terms (such as employment and investment guarantees), it may be useful for the government to retain some form of control through a golden share. Foreign investors would then have to negotiate for control while needing to tender for ownership of the economic up side.

References

Collins, Susan M., and Dani Rodrik. 1991. *Eastern Europe and the Soviet Union in the world economy.* Washington, D.C.: Institute for International Economics.

Fishman, Michael J. 1988. A theory of preemptive takeover bidding. *Rand Journal of Economics* 19:88–101.

Froot, Kenneth A., and Jeremy Stein. 1991. Exchange rates and foreign direct investment: An imperfect capital markets approach. *Quarterly Journal of Economics,* vol. 56 (November).

Grossman, S., and O. Hart. 1980. Takeover bids, the free-rider problem, and the theory of the corporation. *Bell Journal of Economics* 11:42–64.

Maslankiewicz, Jerzy. 1991. Foreign investment in Poland. Warsaw: Foreign Investment Agency, June. Mimeo.

Milgrom, Paul. 1989. Auctions and bidding: A primer. *Journal of Economic Perspectives* 3 (Summer): 3–23.

Murphy, Kevin M., Andrei Shleifer, and Robert W. Vishny. 1989. Industrialization and the big push. *Journal of Political Economy* 97 (October): 1003–26.

Shleifer, Andrei, and Robert W. Vishny. 1991. Asset sales and debt capacity. Working paper. Cambridge, Mass.: NBER, August.

Soós, Károly Attila. 1991. The changing role of joint ventures in the Central-Eastern European transition process. Institute for East-West Security Studies, July. Typescript.

Spar, Debora L. 1991. The political economy of foreign direct investment in Eastern Europe. Harvard Business School, November. Typescript.

Spatt, C. S. 1989. Strategic analyses of takeover bids. In *Financial markets and incomplete information,* ed. S. Bhattacharya and G. Constantinides. Totowa, N.J.: Rowman & Littlefield.

Teece, D. 1976. *The multinational corporation and the resource cost of international technology transfer.* Cambridge, Mass.: Ballinger.

Weiner, Steve. 1990. On the road to Eastern Europe. *Forbes,* 10 December.

Williamson, Oliver E. 1988. Corporate finance and corporate governance. *Journal of Finance* 43 (July): 567–92.

Wolfe, Holgar. 1991. Privatization and foreign investment in Eastern Europe. Massachusetts Institute of Technology, September. Typescript.

Discussion Summary

Pentti Kouri noted that, in practice, it is rare that there are too many foreign bidders in auctions of state assets. He criticized Froot's emphasis on this special case. Kouri also critiqued Froot's proposal for two-step sales to foreigners. Kouri said that the first step in this process, a rapid, wide-scale dissemination of equity to the general public, would severely restrict the government's capacity to implement a sensible industrial policy.

Kouri estimated that, in 1991, Eastern Europe and Russia jointly received approximately $1.5 billion dollars of FDI. Kouri said that this total was dominated by Czechoslovakia, Hungary, and Poland, each of which recorded roughly $500 million of FDI. *Kalman Mizsei* and *Mark Schaffer* suggested that Kouri's estimate for Hungary was too low. Mizsei said that Hungary received $1.2–$1.4 billion of FDI in 1991. *Anders Aslund* said that the 1991 FDI total for Eastern Europe and Russia was approximately $2.5 billion. Aslund also estimated that 30,000 foreign investments and joint ventures have been undertaken so far, three times the estimate given in the paper.

Simon Johnson noted that Western firms may learn about a business in Eastern Europe by sourcing from that firm. Western firms often use this knowledge to determine the potential profitability of investing in the Eastern firm. Johnson conjectured that this type of incidental information gathering reduces the cost of FDI for Western firms.

Andrew Berg supported Froot's proposal for two-stage sales to foreigners. Berg said that the government does not know enough about most state enterprises to conduct an effective program of sales to foreigners. After mass privatization, firms would be sold by private owners, who would probably have more knowledge about the asset.

Olivier Blanchard wondered why the extremely low wages in Russia had failed to attract a significant amount of FDI. Kouri responded that the ambiguous political environment and a lack of clarity in the laws on property rights have delayed the FDI process. Kouri also noted that, even after the political environment stabilizes and the laws are clarified, it will still take a substantial amount of time to complete the planning/negotiation stages of most foreign investment projects.

Geoffrey Carliner said that foreign firms could profitably invest in Russian firms that produce for the domestic Russian market. He noted that the foreign firms could repatriate their profits by purchasing the foreign exchange earned by the Russian natural resource export industry. Schaffer said that, unlike most of the East European countries, Russia will face great difficulty developing strong manufacturing export industries. He emphasized that, even before the collapse of the CMEA (Council for Mutual Economic Assistance), East Europeans were not buying Russian manufactured goods.

Aslund said that it is unlikely that FDI will generate substantial capital inflows to Eastern Europe and Russia during the next five to ten years. He noted that, historically, most liberalization and macro stabilization programs have been characterized by low levels of FDI during the first postreform decade. Aslund cited the cases of Spain and Mexico. He said that this kind of experience is likely to be repeated in Russia, with a possible exception in the energy sector. Aslund also noted that relatively high levels of FDI may be realized in Czechoslovakia, Hungary, and Poland because of the proximity of the large European export market.

Stanley Fischer supported the point that FDI will not play an important role in balance-of-payments financing in Russia and Eastern Europe. Fischer noted that Japan is currently the primary source of FDI and that most of Japan's FDI activity is focused in East Asia. Fischer also observed that, in Russia, there is some internal resistance to FDI. For example, many of the bureaucrats and managers who control the oil and minerals industries seem to believe that they can develop these assets without entering joint ventures with foreign firms. Finally, Fischer noted that the history of FDI in developing countries suggests that such deals work best when the FDI project itself generates the foreign exchange that the investing firm can repatriate as profit. Hence, FDI tends to occur only in export industries, suggesting that FDI cannot be relied on to restructure the overwhelming majority of industrial enterprises that manufacture products for domestic markets.

Jeffrey Sachs noted that, in Poland, there is popular resistance to sales of public assets to foreign investors; the current level of FDI activity reflects these internal constraints. However, there has not been any political resistance to joint ventures between private Polish firms and foreign firms. Hence, Sachs concluded that, if a program of mass privatization were implemented, the level of FDI activity would significantly increase.

Kenneth Froot concluded by noting that FDI cannot be counted on as an engine of growth in the near term in Eastern Europe and Russia. He observed that, historically, foreign firms have invested only in developing countries that have already demonstrated a consistent pattern of growth.

18 Foreign Trade in Eastern Europe's Transition: Early Results

Dani Rodrik

Integration into the world economy is one of the difficult tasks awaiting East European countries in transition. Three of these countries—Hungary, Poland, and (former) Czechoslovakia—have already traveled far along this road. Their economies have opened up dramatically, and trade with the West has expanded rapidly, while trade with the East has collapsed under the joint influence of the demise of the CMEA (Council for Mutual Economic Assistance) and the loss of Soviet markets. This paper discusses and analyzes the early results on the trade front in these three countries.

Integration into the world economy is one of the difficult tasks awaiting East European countries in transition. Three of these countries—Hungary, Poland, and (former) Czechoslovakia—have already traveled far along this road. Their economies have opened up dramatically, and trade with the West has expanded rapidly, while trade with the East has collapsed under the joint influence of the demise of the CMEA (Council for Mutual Economic Assistance) and the loss of Soviet markets. This paper discusses and analyzes the early results on the trade front in these three countries.

As we shall see, such an analysis is plagued by many uncertainties. Basic trade data are in some cases unreliable, and many other statistics are plagued by the inability of official statisticians to keep track of institutional changes and the expansion of the private sector. With many reforms taking place simultaneously and many shocks to contend with, it is difficult to discern changes that can be attributed to the trade reforms alone. Hence, few solid conclusions emerge.

The paper starts by reviewing the changes in trade policy since 1989 in Hungary, Poland, and Czechoslovakia. Then I present an overall evaluation of recent trends in trade flows, paying particular attention to the shortcomings of official statistics. The rest of the paper is devoted to groping for answers to four questions. How much trade reorientation from East to West has really taken place? How bad is the Soviet trade shock? What has caused the boom in

Susan Collins, Jeff Sachs, and Mark Schaffer have provided helpful comments. For assistance and information, the author is grateful to Ivan Angelis, Vladimir Benacek, Zdenek Drabek, Barbara Durka, Alain de Crombrugghe, John Earle, Peter Himl, Danuse Hinduliakova, Miroslav Hrncir, Jaroslav Jilek, Olga Jonas, Elzbieta Kawecka-Wyrzykowska, Jiri Kovar, Stanislaw Ladyka, Andrzej Olechowski, Brian Pinto, Jan Piotrowski, Milan Polak, Jan Svejnar, and Josef Zieleniec. This paper was written while the author was a national fellow at the Hoover Institution, to which he is also grateful.

319

exports to the West? Has import liberalization fostered price discipline and restructuring?

18.1   An Overview of Trade Policy Reforms

The three countries started their reform process from rather different initial points. In Hungary, considerable decentralization and market-oriented reform had taken place since 1968, with central planning largely discarded and enterprises already having a large degree of autonomy. In Poland, a similar, if more recent, process had been under way since the early 1980s. Czechoslovakia, by contrast, had retained most of the archetypal characteristics of central planning and of state ownership. Since 1989, the process of economic transformation has picked up considerable speed in Poland and Hungary and was started anew in Czechoslovakia.

Despite the differences in initial conditions and in the timing and speed of reforms, the trade regimes of the three countries looked quite similar by the end of 1991. In all three countries, trade is now demonopolized, and licensing and quotas play a very small role. Exchange controls have virtually disappeared for current account transactions. As in market economies, the main instruments of trade control have become tariffs and the exchange rate. Average tariffs are low relative to countries at similar levels of development (and in the case of Czechoslovakia compare very favorably with those of the industrialized countries). The exchange rate is managed in a "realistic" fashion, and the black market premium is contained well within 20 percent in Hungary, while it has virtually disappeared in the other two countries (table 18.1). In all three countries, some of the more important remaining quantitative restrictions (QRs) are those exercised in connection with the VERs (voluntary export restraints) imposed on them by the European Community, the United States, and some others. This irony highlights the dramatic liberalization that has taken place since 1989.

Appendix A provides a short summary of the main reforms and describes the current makeup of trade policies in each of the three countries (as of December 1991). Here, I emphasize only some of the main features and differences.

The major trade reforms in Poland and Czechoslovakia were undertaken simultaneously with their respective "big bangs"—at the beginning of 1990 in Poland and of 1991 in Czechoslovakia. Hungary's reforms were introduced in a more gradual fashion. Nonetheless, as mentioned above, the speed of reform appears to have had little effect on the end product. While the scope of licensing and QRs remains broader in Hungary, the difference is one of degree, not one of kind. Also, the other two countries have not been shy in tinkering with their commercial policies as circumstances have demanded. Czechoslovakia introduced a surcharge on consumer goods at the beginning of 1991, but then proceeded to reduce it when it became apparent that import demand had been

Table 18.1   Exchange Rates, Official and Parallel

	Hungary			Poland			Czechoslovakia		
	Off. (Ft/$)	Para. (Ft/$)	Prem. (%)	Off. (Zl/$)	Para. (Zl/$)	Prem. (%)	Off. (Kčs)	Para. (Kčs)	Prem. (%)
1988	50.4			431	1,979	359	14.36	33.40	133
1989	59.1			1,446	5,565	285	15.05	42.39	182
1990:1	64.0	95.1	49	9,500	9,476	−0	16.54	41.14	149
1990:2	64.9	90.9	40	9,500	9,713	2	16.62		
1990:3	62.9	77.7	24	9,500	9,502	0	15.99		
1990:4	61.0	71.4	17	9,500	9,590	1	22.67		
1991:1	70.3	82.5	17	9,500	9,471	−0	27.88	34.10	22
1991:2	75.9			10,394	10,416	0	30.32	31.80	5
1991:3	76.3			11,298	11,428	1	30.52	32.40	6

Sources: GUS (1991c); *Prague Post*, 23 November, 1991; World Bank (1991); and OECD (1991b).

Table 18.2   Share of Import Duties in Central Government Revenue (%)

Hungary:	
1990	5.7 (import duties only)
	7.5 (including all taxes on imports)
Poland:	
Jan.–Jul. 1991	5.8
Aug.–Sep. 1991	13.6
Czechoslovakia:	
1991:1–2	1.9 (import duties only)
	2.4 (import duties + surcharge)

Sources: OECD (1991b), GUS (1991c), RIFER (1991).

overestimated. Poland applied temporary tariff suspensions for items covering more than 50 percent of tariff lines, in part to ease inflationary pressures. In August 1991, it then introduced a new tariff schedule, with higher tariffs, when the real appreciation of the zloty and a growing budget deficit reversed the political pressures.

Tariffs average around 13–14 percent in Hungary and Poland (after the recent change there) and around 5 percent in Czechoslovakia. In Poland, the August 1991 change in the tariff schedule has helped more than double the share of tariff revenues in the government budget (from 6 to 14 percent). But some of this increase can be attributed to the decline in other tax revenues (particularly in enterprise taxes). In the other two countries, tariffs constitute a smaller share of budgetary revenues (see table 18.2).[1]

With respect to exchange rate policy, Poland's big bang devaluation on 1 January 1990 eliminated the parallel market premium overnight. This was achieved by raising the official rate to the level of the parallel rate. The exchange rate has remained unified since then (table 18.1). In Hungary and Czechoslovakia, the strategy has been somewhat different. In both these cases, unification has been more gradual and achieved in part by increases in the official rate and in part by a *decrease* in the parallel rate (as a consequence of the restrictive monetary and fiscal policies in place). This can be seen in the data presented in table 18.1. In Hungary, restrictive macro policies during 1990 helped squeeze the parallel market premium even though the official rate was constant. By the end of the year, the premium was below 20 percent. In view of the remaining restrictions on the convertibility of the forint, the remaining premium is modest and does not indicate a fundamental misalignment of the exchange rate. In Czechoslovakia, a similar downward movement in the parallel rate is also visible. A devaluation in December 1990 and highly restrictive

---

1. Foreign firms are an important constituency pushing for higher tariffs; they desire greater protection in exchange for direct investment. This has been especially marked in the auto sector.

macro policies in 1991 have led to the virtual disappearance of the premium by the second quarter of 1991.[2]

Compared to gradualism, instant exchange rate unification as in Poland may have had an important cost: the unification in Poland had to take place at the level of the parallel rate and may therefore have entailed overdevaluation. In general, the preunification parallel rate will be too depreciated in view of the macroeconomic stabilization measures to be put in place subsequently. Such measures can be expected to pull the parallel rate down by reducing aggregate demand. And, as mentioned above, this is what has happened in both Hungary and Czechoslovakia. Hence, the price paid by Poland for instant unification may have been overdevaluation. Whether this was a price worth paying to stop a developing hyperinflation is another question. I return to this issue below.

The real exchange rate has appreciated considerably in Poland since the big bang, as a consequence of continued, if reduced, inflation. The same has happened in Hungary also. Czechoslovakia, the country with the greatest degree of success in stabilizing the price level, has also had more success on this front: it has managed to maintain most of the real depreciation achieved by the devaluation at the end of December 1990. Real exchange rate indices are shown in table 18.3.

As a consequence of these reforms, there has been a substantial expansion of private activity in trade, especially on the import side. In Poland, close to half of imports and around 15 percent of exports were undertaken by private entities by late 1991 (up from 20 percent and 5 percent, respectively, in the first quarter of 1990). The number of private companies engaged in trade has mushroomed, from 2,809 in March 1990 to 12,598 in June 1991, an increase of 350 percent (Guzman 1991). In Czechoslovakia, the trade sector is the most buoyant one in terms of private activity. The number of registered private entrepreneurs in "commerce" has increased from 61,533 (12.6 percent of all registered entrepreneurs) at the end of 1990 to 222,804 (19.7 percent) at the end of September 1991. As we shall see in the next section, this mushrooming of private activity is causing problems for trade statistics.

Since the beginning of 1991, trade among the former members of the CMEA has been carried out in dollars and in accordance with the same principles as those that apply to trade with the West. The transferable ruble, in which trade was denominated prior to 1991, has been abandoned, save for the fulfillment of accounts left over from 1990: according to national statistics for the first three quarters of 1991, trade amounting to some 15 percent of the corresponding value for 1990 was still carried out in transferable rubles, but this trade is

---

2. Tourists were offered Kčs 36.00 to the dollar on the streets of Prague in November 1991, when the official rate was Kčs 28.00. (The transaction is illegal, unlike in Poland.) However, the gap apparently reflects overzealous entrepreneurial behavior, not economic fundamentals: the unsuspecting tourist receives a wad of bills that look like koruny but are actually Polish zlotys (with an effective rate of Kčs 0.10 to the dollar)!

Table 18.3   **Real Exchange Rate Indices**

	Hungary	Poland	Czechoslovakia
1988	100.0	100.0	100.0
1989	100.2	95.2	103.4
1990:1	89.8	122.7	110.3
1990:2	88.2	105.4	110.0
1990:3	81.2	89.7	96.2
1990:4	76.1	75.6	130.7
1991:1	73.3	71.0	119.1
1991:2		67.7	118.3
1991:3		69.3	118.9

Note: The real exchange rate is calculated by dividing the nominal exchange rate (home currency per dollar) by the CPI. An increase signifies a real *depreciation* of the home currency.

being phased out fast. The obligatory trade protocols of the past have now been replaced by indicative lists, covering much smaller quantities of trade. Soviet authorities initially prohibited all barter arrangements, but the prohibition was later rescinded, and there has been some revival in barter deals during the second half of 1991. The switch to dollar pricing for the bulk of trade has implied substantial terms-of-trade losses for East European countries vis-à-vis the Soviet Union. These losses will be discussed further below.

Last but not least, Hungary, Poland, and Czechoslovakia signed association agreements with the European Community in December 1991. Under the agreement, the EC recognizes the objective of these countries to become full members of the EC in ten years and has granted a number of important trade concessions. VERs on steel products are to be eliminated as of 1992. On products subject to variable levies (such as meat), the EC will undertake three equal cuts of 20 percent each year in duties and variable levies, and quotas will be increased (again in equal amounts) by 10 percent for five years. Quotas on textiles and clothing will be increased by 50 percent or more in 1992, with a complete elimination phased according to the MFA (Multi-Fibre Arrangement) regime to be negotiated in the Uruguay Round, but over a period not exceeding five years. These measures represent a substantial opportunity for the three countries in what is already their most important export market. In return, the East European countries are not expected to implement their tariff reductions until 1995.

18.2 Developments in Eastern Europe's Trade

Table 18.4 summarizes recent developments in the external trade of the three countries, as well as can be pieced together from national sources. The table distinguishes between trade with the formerly socialist economies (FSEs) and trade with market economies (MEs). With respect to the former, an immediate difficulty is the valuation of trade carried out in transferable rubles (TRs) prior to 1991 and the comparison of convertible-currency trade with TR trade. For 1989 and 1990, I have converted TR values to dollars by using the CMEA TR/ dollar rate set by the International Bank for Economic Cooperation (IBEC) (around TR 0.65/$1.00). Hence, the table presents changes in the implicit dollar value of trade with the FSEs. Where available, volume indices are presented also. The former East Germany has been included in the ME group in calculating the figures for 1991. While these data are subject to a number of problems (to be discussed below), some of the broad trends that they reveal are unmistakable.

First, there has been a rapid downward spiral in trade with former CMEA

Table 18.4   **Recent Trends in Eastern Europe's Trade (% change from corresponding period previous year)**

	Formerly Socialist Economy[a]		Market Economy		Total[b]	
	1990	1991[c]	1990	1991[c]	1990	1991[c]
Exports						
Value ($):						
Poland	−.4	−87.5	40.9	6.7	11.8	−1.8
Czechoslovakia	−18.9	−76.4	7.9	−1.2	−17.0	−13.3
Hungary	−17.3	−74.4	19.3	11.3	.8	.4
Volume:						
Poland	−13.3	−44.0	40.5	19.3[d]	13.7	−5.6
Czechoslovakia	−20.1	(−50.0)[e]	15.1		−5.9	−25.0[f]
Hungary	−27.0		13.0			
Imports						
Value ($):						
Poland	−25.6	−75.9	6.3	73.9	−2.5	64.7
Czechoslovakia	−7.3	−70.6	20.5	−24.9	−7.0	−23.6
Hungary	−9.8	−51.0	14.6	38.4	−.1	34.3
Volume:						
Poland	−34.1	−45.0	2.9	89.1[d]	−17.9	41.3
Czechoslovakia	−11.5	(−33.0)[e]	34.7		6.4	−28.0[f]
Hungary	−18.0		4.0			

Sources: GUS (1991b, 1991c), FSU (1991a), PlanEcon (1991), GATT (1991), and tables provided by the Embassy of the Republic of Hungary.

[a]For 1989 and 1990, dollar values are calculated by using the IBEC exchange rate between TR and dollars rather than implicit national cross-rates. For 1991, the former East Germany is included in market economies, and growth rates are calculated accordingly.

[b]Calculated by converting national currency values to U.S. dollars at period-average exchange rates. Owing to the difference between the IBEC and national cross-rates between TR and dollars, these figures are inconsistent with those for the FSEs in the first two columns of the table.

[c]January–September.

[d]EC only.

[e]PlanEcon estimate, for trade with the Soviet Union only.

[f]January–June.

trade partners. The cumulative decline in the dollar value of exports to the former CMEA since the beginning of 1990 has been on the order of 80–90 percent and is nothing less than monumental. Declines in volume terms are somewhat smaller, indicating a fall in (implicit) dollar prices in intra-CMEA trade. Soviet deliveries of fuels and raw materials have been severely disrupted. The volume of Soviet petroleum exports to East European countries declined by 23 percent in 1990 and is estimated to have declined by a further 53 percent in 1991 (IMF 1991a). As shown in table 18.5, the collapse of trade with the Soviet Union has been accompanied by substantial terms-of-trade losses. Poland's terms of trade with its former CMEA partners has deteriorated by 48 percent in the first nine months of 1991, and similar numbers are plausible for the other two countries also.

Second, some of the decline in trade with the East has been offset by an increase in trade with the West. Just to point out some of the more remarkable numbers in the table, Poland's exports to the West rose by 41 percent in 1990, while its imports were up by 74 percent in 1991. Hungary's imports from the West have increased by 38 percent in 1991, while its exports have been expanding at less remarkable but still healthy rates. Czechoslovakia seems to be an outlier, as both its exports and its imports appear to have fallen in 1991 after a respectable performance the previous year. However, this evidence is not borne out by the statistics of Czechoslovakia's trade partners: the latter show a continuation of the upward trend, rather than a reversal (see below).

The Czechoslovak case is symptomatic of a general problem with these statistics. As a consequence of the reforms discussed above and of the mushrooming of private traders in particular, a considerable part of trade appears not to be recorded. Previously, central statistical offices collected trade statistics directly from the small number of state trading organizations permitted to undertake trade. The demonopolization of trade has required new modes of data collection, which these countries have now introduced. But, at least in the

Table 18.5   **Terms of Trade (% change from corresponding period previous year)**

	1989	1990	1991
Poland	18.5	−17.2	−10.8[a]
In trade with CMEA	5.7	4.2	−48.2
Hungary	2.8	.1	N.A.
In trade with CMEA	3.6	7.6	−33.5[b]
Czechoslovakia	4.3	2.3	−27.7[c]
In trade with CMEA	6.1	2.5	N.A.

Sources: GUS (1991b), OECD (1991b), FSU (1991b).

[a]January–September.

[b]Midpoint of the estimates reported for Soviet trade in Oblath and Tarr (1991), based on 1990 quantities.

[c]January–June.

Table 18.6   **Comparisons of Home- and Partner-Country Trade Statistics (% change in dollar value of trade with market economies)**

	Exports		Imports	
Source	1990	1991:1	1990	1991:1
Poland:				
National statistics	40.9	16.3	6.3	68.8
IMF statistics	39.5	13.3	12.8	84.5
Czechoslovakia:[a]				
National statistics	12.9	−19.0	27.5	−32.3
OECD statistics	17.3	11.7	32.4	29.2
Hungary:				
National statistics	19.3	9.6[b]	14.6	38.0[b]
IMF statistics	15.5	5.9	23.4	16.2

Sources: Same as in table 18.4 plus IMF (1991b) and OECD (1991a).
[a]Trade with OECD only (including Yugoslavia).
[b]1991:1–2.

case of Czechoslovakia, these changes appear to have made statistics even less reliable in the short run.[3]

Table 18.6 compares official figures with those obtained from partner-country data. For Poland and Hungary, the partner data are the exports and imports reported by developed and developing countries in the IMF's *Direction of Trade Statistics* (*DOTS*). As *DOTS* does not give a separate entry for Czechoslovakia, I use the totals reported by OECD countries in the OECD *Monthly Statistics of Foreign Trade* in this case. In each case, exports (imports) of the East European country are matched with imports from (exports to) that particular country reported by these groups. As the figures show percentage changes, c.i.f./f.o.b. valuation differences should not affect the comparisons. However, since national statistics are converted to dollars at period-average exchange rates, some statistical discrepancies are possible on this account. Another source of discrepancy is due to the time that goods spend in transit (and during which they are recorded as exports by one country but not as imports by another). Finally, note that only the first quarter of 1991 is covered by the comparisons, as the most recent (aggregate) data available from IMF and OECD sources at the time of writing (December 1991) did not go beyond 1991:1.

On the export side, table 18.6 shows that the trends revealed by home and partner data are reasonably close to each other, with the striking exception of

3. The Czechoslovak monthly foreign trade bulletin puts it bluntly: "The data do not reflect real exports and imports in the reported period but only those exports and imports for which arrive [*sic*] completed proposals for customs procedure. . . . As a result of the above mentioned differences, the surveyed data in 1991 can be compared to the data of the previous year (1990) only for rough orientation" (Federal Statistical Office, *Foreign Trade* [Month 1991], 3).

Czechoslovak exports in 1991:1. According to Czechoslovak statistics, exports to the OECD fell by 19 percent in 1991:1, while OECD statistics show an *increase* of 12 percent. In the other two countries, increases in exports are somewhat higher according to official statistics, but the discrepancies are nowhere as large and can be accounted for by the factors mentioned above.

On the import side, home statistics almost consistently understate the increase in imports from the West and typically by nonnegligible margins. The growth of Poland's imports, for example, appears to have been twice as large in 1990 as was reported in table 18.4.[4] This is consistent with anecdotal evidence, such as widespread stories of enterprising individuals coming back from Germany with their cars full of consumer goods for resale at home. Since the bulk of private activity in trade has taken place in imports, it is not a surprise to find the discrepancies mostly on the import side. Once again, however, the magnitude of the Czechoslovak discrepancy is noteworthy: while the Czechoslovak statistics show a decline of 32 percent in imports from the OECD in 1991:1, the OECD statistics show an increase of 29 percent!

In view of the large discrepancies in Czechoslovak statistics, table 18.7 displays the comparative data at the level of individual countries. I have selected here important trade partners for which OECD data were available through the first half of 1991 so that we can also see whether the discrepancies extend beyond 1991:1. The answer seems to be yes. On the whole, both imports and exports appear to be greatly underreported in Czechoslovak statistics. Some of the discrepancies on the import side in particular are extremely large: while France reports an increase in exports to Czechoslovakia of 180 percent, Czechoslovakia's own statistics suggest an increase of only 2 percent!

What conclusions can we therefore draw from these comparisons concerning trade with the West? First, it seems evident that Czechoslovak trade statistics for 1991 are not reliable and hence that the 1991 declines in trade with the West reported in table 18.4 should not be taken seriously. Second, official statistics considerably understate the volume of imports from the West in all three countries. Third, while imports appear to have been increasing at impressive rates in 1991 (especially in Poland), export performance is not as solid in 1991 as it had been the previous year. In Poland, the 1990 export boom has fizzled out (and has been replaced by an import boom). In Hungary, a less impressive import boom is in place also, while exports have not expanded as rapidly in 1991 as in the previous year.

We finally look at trade balances, which are shown in table 18.8. Two points are noteworthy here. First, in all three countries, the balance with the FSEs (mainly the Soviet Union) deteriorated significantly in 1991, with surpluses in 1990 turning into deficits in Poland and Hungary and a small deficit growing sixfold in Czechoslovakia. These deficits reflect the deterioration in the terms

---

4. On the underreporting of Poland's imports in 1990, see also Berg and Sachs (1991), who, however, report a larger discrepancy.

Table 18.7   **Czechoslovak Trade with Leading OECD Partners, 1991:1–2 (% change from 1990:1–2)**

	Exports		Imports	
	CSFR Data	OECD Data	CSFR Data	OECD Data
Partner				
Germany	15.8	21.5	−22.6	6.0
Italy	19.0	19.0	28.8	33.6
Yugoslavia	61.8	72.1	−26.4	1.1
France	−11.4	−1.1	2.0	179.9
Netherlands	6.7	21.3	14.8	20.1
United Kingdom	−40.2	−13.0	−51.8	2.0

Sources: Same as in table 18.6.

Table 18.8   **Trade Balances**

	Formerly Socialist Economies	Market Economies
Hungary (Ft billion):		
1990	10.9	47.8
Jan.–Sep. 1991	−52.9	−57.0
Poland (Zl billion):		
1990	8,934	36,608
Jan.–Sep. 1991	−2,311	3,071
Czechoslovakia (Kčs billion):		
1990	−1.43	−6.59
Jan.–Aug. 1991	−8.26	9.62

of trade that followed the move to dollar pricing and the collapse of exports to the Soviet market. Unlike in previous years, these balances are now denominated in real money, that is, dollars. (It is still not clear how claims in transferable rubles that derive from previous surpluses with the Soviet Union will be settled.)

Second, each of the three countries has run a trade surplus with market economies during its program's first year (1990 in Poland and Hungary, 1991 in Czechoslovakia). Poland's 1990 trade surplus was particularly large, amounting to close to $4 billion. Moreover, in each of these cases, the surplus was entirely unanticipated. The Polish stabilization program had predicted a trade deficit in convertible-currency trade of $0.5 billion for 1990. Similarly, the 1991 Czechoslovak program had predicted a current account deficit of $2.5 billion. Hence, these economies have exhibited early on either an unexpectedly strong expenditure reduction or an unexpectedly strong expenditure switching, or both.

The standard economic prescription for a country that is undergoing a one-time transition cost is to run trade deficits for a while in order to smooth con-

Table 18.9   Partner Composition of Exports (%)

| Year | Eastern Europe[a] | | | EC | Others |
	EE5	Soviet Union	Total		
Czechoslovakia:					
1985	13.4	33.1	46.5		
1988	17.2	33.4	50.6	16.7	32.7
1989	16.7	30.5	47.2	18.2	34.6
1990	13.0	25.2	38.2	26.5	35.3
Jan.–Sep. 1991	13.0	19.4	32.4	40.1	27.5
Medium-run prediction[b]	10.8	14.3	25.1	46.3	28.6
Poland:					
1985	14.8	28.4	43.2	23.2	33.6
1988	11.8	24.5	36.3	28.3	35.4
1989	9.9	20.8	30.7	32.1	37.2
1990	6.8	15.4	22.2	47.2	30.6
Jan.–Sep. 1991	6.1	11.8	17.9	53.3	28.8
Medium-run prediction[b]	9.3	13.9	23.2	51.2	25.6
Hungary:					
1985	12.8	33.6	46.4		
1988	11.8	27.6	39.4		
1989	10.5	25.1	35.6	24.9	39.5
1990	8.0	20.2	28.2	32.2	39.6
Jan.–Sep. 1991			19.7	45.6	34.7
Medium-run prediction[b]	15.0	18.0	33.0	37.2	29.8

Sources: Rosati (1991), OECD (1991b), FSU (1991a), GUS (1991a).
[a]Excluding former GDR.
[b]From Collins and Rodrik (1991). See text for explanation.

sumption. Since these deficits have not materialized (at least until later on), the implication is that the early phase of the transition has been more costly than it need have been.[5]

18.3   How Much Trade Reorientation Has Really Taken Place?

The boom in trade with the West, combined with the collapse of intra-CMEA trade, suggests that a considerable amount of reorientation has already taken place in East European countries' trade patterns. Statistics using national exchange rates vis-à-vis the dollar and the transferable ruble seem to indicate that this has been going on for some time now. The figures show a nonnegligible reorientation of exports away from the CMEA and toward Western markets (the EC in particular) since the mid-1980s in both Poland and Hungary and since 1988 in Czechoslovakia as well (table 18.9). The basic trend is one of

5. A strong argument can be made that external financing was available for more borrowing than took place (see, e.g., "Poland Fails" 1992).

sharp reduction in the importance of other Eastern markets (mainly the Soviet Union), offset by an equivalent increase in the importance of the EC. Between 1985 and 1990, Hungary and Poland both reduced their shares of exports going to the Soviet Union by almost 14 percentage points; the shares of the EC meanwhile doubled. Czechoslovakia has undergone the slowest transformation, and the importance of Eastern markets remains much higher in this country than in the other two.

However, these pre-1991 figures are somewhat suspect. The reason has to do with the conversion rates used in translating exports in transferable rubles (TR) to the national currency. It is well recognized that national exchange rates against the TR have been rather arbitrary, rendering comparison of flows to the dollar area and the ruble area problematic. This in itself would not affect the trends in trade shares over time. But, in both Hungary and Poland, changes in the national exchange rates vis-à-vis the TR and the dollar have implied a depreciation of the TR against the dollar (Table 18.10). In part, these changes were motivated by the authorities' desire to discourage exports to the Soviet Union and to reduce trade surpluses in nonconvertible-currency trade. Consequently, the decline in Hungary's and Poland's CMEA trade is overstated relative to that in Czechoslovakia (where the cross-rate has remained more stable since 1985).

These considerations no longer apply to the trade figures for 1991, as the bulk of trade with the East began to be carried out in dollars in that year. These later figures show that former CMEA markets now receive less than a fifth of Polish and Hungarian exports and about a third of Czechoslovak exports. The share of the EC, meanwhile, is greater than 40 percent in all three countries.

These dramatic changes have occurred faster than predicted. Indeed, the decline in the Soviet and former CMEA markets has probably overshot the longer-run, steady-state market shares. Table 18.9 shows for each country a predicted regional distribution of exports at the end of the transition, taken from work that Susan Collins and I have done previously (Collins and Rodrik 1991). These predictions were obtained by updating an interwar (1923) trade matrix for these countries using information from the evolution of the trade of six comparator countries since then.[6] Since these predictions make no allowance for the hysteresis created by four decades of socialism and integration under the CMEA, a reasonable hypothesis is that they overstate the reorientation toward the West that will likely take place in the long run. However, in the case of Poland and Hungary, the 1991 results indicate that the realized reorientation has already surpassed those ambitious projections. In both countries, the share of the CMEA is lower and the share of the EC higher than the levels that our method yields as the most "reasonable" projections over the medium run.

6. The comparator countries are Germany, Austria, Finland, Spain, Italy, and Portugal. For a study based on the gravity model, see also Wang and Winters (1991), the results of which are broadly similar to those of Collins and Rodrik (1991).

Table 18.10   Implicit Ruble-Dollar Exchange Rates, Based on National Rates
                     (TR/$)

	Hungary	Poland	Czechoslovakia
1985	1.88	1.76	1.85
1988	1.94	2.21	1.44
1989	2.09	2.96	1.51
1990	2.30	4.52	1.79
ratio of 1990 rate to 1985 rate	1.22	2.57	.97

Source: Rosati (1991).

Impressive as they may be, these statistics do not really inform us of the extent to which enterprises have been able to shift sales from Eastern to Western markets, for these outcomes are also consistent with sharp reductions in the kinds of products exported to the East and sharp increases in products exported to the West, with no real reorientation of trade, save in a statistical sense. Evidence indicates that a considerable share of manufactured products previously exported to the East is unmarketable in the West, at any price. Examples are computer products that are several generations old and manufacturing activities specifically geared to Soviet standards (e.g., tramcars).[7]

In principle, it would be possible to see how much reorientation has taken place at the product level by examining highly disaggregated trade data. Here, I analyze somewhat aggregate product categories, exploiting the differences in the product composition of exports to the two areas.

I focus on Hungary and Poland, which are the candidates for the greatest reorientation. Tables 18.11 and 18.12 show the product composition of these countries' exports to the East and the West for 1990 and for either 1985 (Poland) or 1986 (Hungary). The data show large differences in product composition with respect to the two areas. Machinery has constituted almost half of Hungarian exports to the ruble area but less than 15 percent of exports to the West. Exports of raw materials to the West have been twice as important as exports to the East. In Poland, electroengineering products constitute three-quarters of exports to the East but less than a third of exports to the West.

Such differences allow us to check for reorientation of trade at the product level. If these countries have been successful at redirecting their Eastern exports to the West, we would see a certain convergence in the product composition of exports to the two areas. A quick look at the tables suggests that no convergence has in fact occurred since the mid-1980s, despite the remarkable decline in the overall share of exports to the East as discussed above. The shares of machinery and electroengineering exports to the West, in Hungary

---

7. For an argument that East-West trade is likely to remain small on account of the East's specialization in low-quality goods for which the West has little demand and no comparative advantage, see Murphy and Shleifer (1991).

Table 18.11   **Hungary: Product Composition of Exports by Area (%)**

	Ruble Area		Nonruble Area	
	1986	1990	1986	1990
Energy, elect.	.6	.3	3.4	3.3
Raw materials	22.3	20.8	38.9	43.8
Machinery	46.0	43.9	14.5	11.6
Ind. consumer	16.7	19.1	16.4	15.6
Food	14.3	15.9	26.9	25.7
Total	100.0	100.0	100.0	100.0

Source: OECD (1991b).

Table 18.12   **Poland: Product Composition of Industrial Exports by Area (%)**

	Ruble Area		Nonruble Area	
	1986	1990	1986	1990
Metallurgy	4.3	2.1	19.5	21.9
Electroengineering	74.2	76.2	30.0	29.2
Chemical	10.5	14.8	17.6	15.3
Mineral	.9	.6	1.8	2.5
Wood and paper	.9	.6	4.6	6.1
Light	6.3	3.0	9.5	9.2
Food	2.2	1.8	16.1	15.0
Others	.6	.9	.8	.8
Total	100.0	100.0	100.0	100.0

Source: GUS (1991a).

and Poland, respectively, were lower in 1990 than in the mid-1980s. Hence, there is no evidence that the overall increase in trade with the West was fueled by redirecting Eastern sales to the West or indeed that the latter played any role at all in the former.

To make this conclusion a bit more precise, table 18.13 shows an index of similarity of trade with the two partner groups. This index is calculated as $1 - \Sigma(\sigma_i^e - \sigma_i^w)^2$, where σ denotes shares of product categories in exports, i indexes product categories, and e and w stand for East and West, respectively. The index takes values between zero (completely dissimilar product composition of trade) and one (identical product composition). The index is calculated for the mid-1980s and for 1990. In addition, a hypothetical calculation is presented under the assumption that all the actual decline in trade with the East was diverted to the West. This hypothetical calculation shows the maximum value that the index would take if the reorientation from East to West had been complete. The following steps go into the calculation: (i) I assume a count-

Table 18.13   Index of Product Similarity in Trade in East and West

Hungary:		Poland:	
1986	.856	1985	.755
1990	.832	1990	.716
1990[a]	.949	1990[a]	.900

Source: Calculated from tables 18.11 and 18.12. See text for explanation.
[a]Hypothetical, with full trade diversion from East to West.

erfactual scenario in which exports to the East and West increase by an identical proportion, corresponding to the aggregate growth rate in exports. (ii) I calculate the "shortfall" in exports to the East in 1990, by product category, by subtracting the realized level of exports from the counterfactual level. (iii) This shortfall is then added to the exports that go to the West under the counterfactual scenario, to arrive at a hypothetical structure of exports to the West under full diversion.

The values of the indexes in table 18.13 bear out the previous conclusion from eyeballing the statistics. Not only do the values of the index come nowhere near the hypothetical values that they would take under the full-reorientation scenario, but they actually *decline* in both countries. While more disaggregated analysis could show some areas where diversion has occurred, the conclusion has to be that very little overall reorientation has taken place, even in the two countries where the shares of Eastern markets have exhibited the steepest declines. Moreover, a look at more recent export statistics for 1991 does not change these conclusions.

18.4 How Bad Is the Soviet Trade Shock?

The transition to dollar pricing in Soviet trade in 1991 and the sharp decline in exports to that market have wreaked havoc with the economies of all three countries. The effects show in many different ways. Alongside the collapse in exports has come increases in unemployment and reductions in profitability. Table 18.14 shows the Polish situation: industrial exports to the Soviet Union have fallen by 40 percent when evaluated at dollar prices implicit in the national cross-rate between the TR and the dollar and by more than 90 percent when evaluated at the former IBEC exchange rate. From the perspective of domestic activity and profitability, the former figure is perhaps the more relevant one, but even with that the decline in sales is very significant.

With the decline in enterprise profitability, the tax base of the government has shrunk. In Poland, the deterioration in the fiscal situation during 1991 can be attributed in large part to the reduction in enterprise taxes. In Czechoslovakia, fiscal revenues have also been reduced in the second half of the year.

Meanwhile, the increase in prices of raw materials and energy imports relative to prices of manufactured exports has implied a substantial transfer of income to the Soviet Union. The sharp increase in the (domestic) price of raw materials has also affected adversely energy- and raw-material-intensive exports to the West, in pharmaceuticals and petrochemicals, for example.

A comparison of economic outcomes in the Czech and Slovak republics highlights the devastating effect of the Soviet trade shock. Such a comparison is instructive because the two republics are quite different in the extent of their reliance on Soviet trade. As table 18.15 shows, the Czech Republic has twice the population and more than twice the income of the Slovak Republic, yet the volume of trade with the Soviet Union is comparable in the two republics. Exports to the Soviet Union are only 60 percent lower in the Slovak Republic, while the volume of imports is actually higher.

The greater orientation toward the Soviet market in the Slovak Republic finds reflection in a much worse economic performance compared to the Czech Republic. Starting from similar macroeconomic positions in mid-1990, output and employment trends in the two republics have diverged greatly. By the end of 1991, the Slovak unemployment rate was more than double the Czech rate, and the industrial recession was considerably deeper (table 18.15). The gap between the two regions has continued to widen since mid-1990, indicating (i) that the difference is intimately linked to the Soviet trade shock and (ii) that, as of the third quarter of 1991, the costs of the Soviet trade shock had not been fully paid yet.

Conceptually, the Soviet trade shock consists of three independent shocks that are frequently lumped together: a terms-of-trade shock, a removal of an implicit import subsidy in Soviet trade, and a market-loss effect. Appendix B discusses these shocks in a more analytic manner (see also Rodrik 1992).

Table 18.14   Poland's Exports to the Soviet Union ($ million)

	1990			Increase (%)	
	(A)	(B)	1991[a]	(A)	(B)
Fuels and power	126.5	937.4	82.8	−34.5	−91.2
Industry	1,837.7	13,617.4	1,102.1	−40.0	−91.9
Metallurgy	81.7	605.4	5.5	−93.3	−99.1
Electroengineering	1,354.0	10,033.1	666.5	−50.8	−93.4
Chemical	203.9	1,510.9	249.3	22.3	−83.5
Wood and paper	9.6	71.1	0.4	−95.9	−99.4
Light	153.9	1,140.4	44.9	−70.8	−96.1
Food processing	34.6	256.4	131.2	279.2	−48.8
Construction	66.8	495.0	51.5	−22.9	−89.6
Agricultural products	38.1	282.3	58.8	54.2	−79.2
Total	2,069.2	15,332.8	1,295.2	−37.4	−91.6

Note: Zloty values converted to dollars using (A) the official exchange rate (Zl 9,500/$1.00) or (B) the implied Zloty/dollar rate in trade with the ruble area (9,500 × 4.52/0.61).

[a]First three quarters multiplied by 4/3.

Table 18.15   **Comparison of Economic Performance in the Czech and Slovak Republics**

	Czech Republic	Slovak Republic	Ratio
Imports from Soviet Union (Jan.–Aug. 1991, Kčs million)	30,888	34,684	.89
Exports to Soviet Union (Jan.–Aug. 1991, Kčs million)	26,047	16,381	1.59
Population (million)	10,299	5,269	1.95
Money income of population (1990, Kčs billion)	361.1	163.8	2.20
Industrial output (same year, previous period = 100):			
1990:			
Apr.	97.8	102.7	.95
Aug.	94.8	96.8	
Dec.	94.1	89.4	
1991:			
Jan.	96.8	92.9	
Feb.	95.1	91.0	
Mar.	78.3	80.8	
Apr.	86.3	80.6	
May	76.6	68.8	
Jun.	89.7	81.6	
Jul.	71.3	64.4	
Aug.	72.0	65.7	1.10
Unemployment rate (%):			
1990:			
Apr.	.1	.1	1.00
Aug.	.3	.5	
Dec.	.8	1.5	
1991:			
Jan.	1.1	2.4	
Feb.	1.4	3.0	
Mar.	1.7	3.7	
Apr.	2.0	4.6	
May	2.2	5.4	
Jun.	2.6	6.3	
Jul.	3.1	7.7	
Aug.	3.4	8.7	.39

Sources: FSU (1991b) and Statisticke Prehledy (1991).

The first of these is a conventional terms-of-trade trade (TOT) shock. As pointed out earlier, with the transition to dollar pricing, border prices of exports have fallen relative to border prices of imports. The TOT shock has come about primarily because dollar export prices to the Soviet Union have fallen. Unlike what is often claimed, implicit dollar prices charged by the Soviet Union for oil and other energy exports have in fact not risen greatly: under the CMEA moving-average pricing mechanism, Soviet oil export prices had been *higher*

Table 18.16   **Pricing of Crude Oil Imports in Poland, 1990**

Source of Imports	Volume of Imports (million barrels)	Domestic Prices		Border Prices	
		Zl 1,000/Barrel	$/Barrel	TR/Barrel	$/Barrel
Soviet Union	55.5	27.61	2.91	13.32	21.83
Others	40.8	240.76	25.34	...	25.34
Total	96.3	117.96	12.42	...	23.32

Source: Own calculations from value and volume statistics in 1990 trade yearbook, using IBEC and Polish cross-rates between the TR and the dollar.

than world prices between 1986 and 1989 and became only slightly lower in 1990 owing to the jump in world market prices after the Gulf crisis in August.

Nonetheless, the *domestic* price of oil imported from the Soviet Union did increase substantially because the elimination of the TR removed a huge, implicit subsidy on imports from the CMEA area. The subsidy arose from the discrepancy between the internal cross-rate between the TR and the dollar and the rate used by the IBEC in translating a five-year moving average of world (dollar) prices into TRs. Compared to the IBEC rate of TR 0.61/$1.00 in 1990, the internal rates were TR 4.52, 2.30, and 1.79 in Poland, Hungary, and Czechoslovakia, respectively (table 18.10). Since the ruble was a lot cheaper domestically than externally, importers paid only a fraction of the dollar cost of the oil imported from the Soviet Union. Table 18.16 shows that, in Poland, where the implicit subsidy was largest, Soviet oil cost domestic users less than $3.00 a barrel, while the border price charged by the Soviet Union was TR 13.31 (i.e., $21.83). The second effect of the collapse of the CMEA, therefore, is the removal of an implicit import subsidy (and export tax) on trade with the Soviet Union, which I will call the *RS effect*. This is of course a positive shock, even though in the short run it has undoubtedly caused distress among enterprises dependent on cheap Soviet oil.[8]

The third shock arises from the reduction in the volume of export sales to the Soviet market. It involves the loss of rents earned previously from selling manufactured products to the Soviet market at prices that were on average double those that they would fetch in Western markets (see the figures in Oblath and Tarr [1991] and FTRI [1991, 135–37]). This market-loss (ML) effect operates independently from the TOT effect and would be present even if the terms of trade had not deteriorated. However, the deterioration has clearly squeezed the margin between dollar prices in the Soviet Union and those in world markets. So, in practice, there is a certain degree of arbitrariness in attributing the Soviet trade shock separately to the TOT and ML effects.

8. The import subsidy served the purpose of restraining ruble trade surpluses, which was a sensible objective as long as these surpluses were not convertible. For more details and a formal model, see Rodrik (1992).

Table 18.17   Estimates of the Soviet Trade Shock, 1990–91 (billions of dollars, unless otherwise noted)

	Poland	Hungary	Czechoslovakia
Basic data			
Imports from Soviet Union (1990) (A)	7.840	5.467	7.574
Changes in prices in Soviet trade (%):			
Terms of trade	−48.2	−33.5	−38.7
Export prices ($)	−46.4	−41.6	−43.6
Import prices (B)	−3.5	−12.2	−7.9
Ratio of ruble imports to exports (1990)	.687	.824	.949
Changes in prices adjusted for worthless ruble surpluses in 1990 (%):			
Terms of trade	−24.6	−19.3	−35.4
Export prices ($) (C)	−27.2	−29.1	−40.5
Price premium in Soviet market (%):			
1990 (D)	50.1	44.1	47.1
1991 (E)	3.7	3.3	3.5
Value of ruble exports to Soviet Union:			
1989 (F)	12.450	8.696	9.419
1990 (G)	10.794	6.348	7.526
Change in export volume to Soviet Union (%):			
1990 (H)	−13.3	−27.0	−20.1
1991 (I)	−44.0	−45.0	−50.0
Increase in domestic prices of energy (%) (J)	615.1	231.0	170.2
Value of energy imports from Soviet Union at domestic prices (K)	.801	.668	1.291
Reduction in energy use by subsidized users (%) (L)	27.1	11.5	8.2
Estimates of the Soviet trade shock			
Market-loss effect (ML) (1990), D × F × H	−.83	−1.05	−.89
Market-loss effect (ML) (1991), E × G × I	−.18	−.09	−.13
Terms-of-trade effect (TOT) (1991), A × (C − B)	−1.86	−.92	−2.47
Removal-of-subsidy effect (RS) (1991), ½ × J × K × L	.67	.09	.09
Cumulative 1990–91 shock	−2.20	−1.97	−3.40
(As % of GDP)	(−3.46)	(−7.82)	(−7.46)
Ruble trade surplus at domestic prices	.39	.30	.15
Cumulative 1990–91 shock at domestic prices	−2.59	−2.27	−3.55
(As % of GDP)	(−4.07)	(−9.01)	(−7.79)

Source: Rodrik (1992).

Table 18.17, based on Rodrik (1992), presents some estimates of the income losses suffered by the three countries on account of the TOT, ML, and RS effects.[9] Before discussing the results, three methodological issues deserve comment.

First, as mentioned above, it is not possible to draw an airtight distinction between the TOT and the ML effects in actual calculations involving discrete

9. For other (partial) estimates of these losses, the reader is referred to Berg and Sachs (1991), Oblath and Tarr (1991), and Kenen (1991).

(as opposed to infinitesimal) changes. If the TOT effect is calculated on the basis of base-year (1990) trade volumes, then, in order to avoid double-counting, the ML effect would have to be calculated using end-year (1991) margins between prices in Soviet and alternative markets. Alternatively and equivalently, we could calculate the TOT effect on the basis of 1991 trade volumes and use the 1990 price margin for the ML effect. The first option is followed in this table. Note also that the ML effect is calculated for both 1990 and 1991, as it was operative even before the transition to dollar pricing at the beginning of 1991.

Second, there is the issue of conversion from TRs into dollars. For calculating welfare costs, the appropriate valuation of trade is in terms of world prices. Using the IBEC exchange rate to convert TR values into dollars yields the implicit border prices (in dollars) used in Soviet trade (as explained in app. B). Using any other exchange rate (such as the internal cross-rate) would be inappropriate, in view of the pricing rules followed in CMEA trade, and would confuse the external terms of trade with an internal tax/subsidy scheme. That the IBEC rate may have been "unrealistic" in valuing the ruble too highly is beside the point in this context. Where East European countries are concerned, the trading opportunities among CMEA countries were defined by these "world" prices, no matter how inflated in dollar terms they may have been. One complication that arises, however, is the nonconvertibility of trade surpluses in TRs. We do have to adjust for the fact that ruble trade surpluses could not be redeemed at anything approaching the IBEC exchange rate. So the results in table 18.17 are based on the assumption that ruble surpluses in 1990 were in fact entirely worthless. This assumption calls for scaling down the "effective" dollar price of exports in 1990 by a factor that equals the ratio of recorded imports to exports (Rodrik 1992).

Third, the available data are incomplete and in some cases unreliable. In order to present a full set of estimates, I have occasionally had to rely on extrapolations, especially where Czechoslovakia is concerned (for details, see Rodrik 1992). So the results presented in table 18.17 are, at best, tentative. However, I have generally made the assumptions that would make the Soviet shock appear less costly. The results are therefore likely to represent a lower bound on the magnitude of the shock.

The numbers in table 18.17 show that the three effects combined amount to a huge loss of income (on impact) in the three countries, even on conservative assumptions—$2.2 billion in Poland, $2.0 billion in Hungary, and $3.4 billion in Czechoslovakia. These losses represent 7–8 percent of GDP in Hungary and Czechoslovakia and 3½ percent of GDP in Poland. Taking Keynesian multiplier effects into account, the Soviet shock could easily "account" for a large part of the cumulative decline in GDP in Hungary and Czechoslovakia during 1990–91. The shock plays a comparatively small role in Poland, as Soviet trade is less important in this larger economy.

It should be stressed again that these numbers are somewhat shaky and based on incomplete data. But, in view of the conservative assumptions made here, it is unlikely that revised estimates would change these conclusions greatly. Hence, there can be little doubt of the devastating effect of the demise of the CMEA in the short run.

18.5   What Caused the Boom in Exports to the West?

As discussed above, export performance in Western markets has been quite good in all three countries (provided that we rely on OECD statistics in the case of Czechoslovakia). In fact, this performance has been much better than most analysts had predicted on the basis of well-known problems with product quality and rigidities in enterprise behavior. What were the reasons for this?

Some of the contributing factors can be listed as follows. First, the external environment was very favorable. By the beginning of 1990, the EC had abolished its discriminatory quantitative restrictions on these countries' exports (except in the "sensitive" areas of agriculture, steel, and textiles). The remaining quotas were somewhat eased in 1990 and 1991. Further, domestic demand rose quite significantly in West Germany (by 5 percent in 1990, compared to a post-1973 average of 1.9 percent), a key export market for all three countries.

There were also important domestic reasons. Enterprise managers were aware of the need to reorient their sales from Eastern to Western markets in view of the coming collapse of the CMEA. Moreover, following price liberalization, enterprises came under pressure to unload their inventories, which had been at very high levels owing to special features of the previous policy regime. The pressure was magnified by a collapse in domestic demand, a byproduct of the stabilization measures put in place in all three countries. Finally, the trade reforms discussed earlier must have increased the profitability of exports to the West: import liberalization made available cheaper and higher-quality inputs, and devaluations served to increase the profitability of export sales.

Of these, only the collapse in domestic demand and the changes in trade policy (devaluation, in particular) qualify as serious contenders. The favorable external environment could have played at best a minor role. In view of the small volume of exports from East European countries, it is difficult to believe that these countries faced a serious external demand constraint. Hungary, Poland, and Czechoslovakia taken together accounted for just about 1 percent of EC imports in 1988 and 2 percent of German imports. With respect to quantitative restrictions, there can be little doubt that these restrictions were pervasive, especially in textiles and clothing and in steel. But, once again, their importance is limited since quotas were rarely binding. Some figures for Poland bear this out: only 68.7 percent of the EC quota in steel products was utilized in 1989, and similar ratios held for previous years also; in textiles, in only three out of thirty-three EC categories were quotas filled by more than 90 percent in

1989 (Synowiec and Rzeszutek 1991). The situation was similar for Hungary and Czechoslovakia as well.

On the supply side, the incentive to reorient sales from East to West was clearly in place in 1990. But, as I have already discussed at greater length above, the reorientation that has taken place so far appears to have been limited at best. As regards the unloading of inventories, the decline in inventories generally preceded the export response. In Poland, the sharpest reduction in inventories took place in January, when exports to the West actually fell.[10]

These considerations leave exchange rate policy and the domestic demand shock as the most important determinants of export performance. Both Poland and Czechoslovakia started their big bangs with substantial depreciations in the real exchange rate. And the collapse in domestic demand has exceeded 10 percent in both cases. In Hungary, meanwhile, the real exchange rate has appreciated somewhat during 1990 (table 18.3 above), and the reduction in demand has not been as marked as in the other two cases.

It is unlikely that either exchange rate policy or the demand shock alone could have been responsible for the export boom to the West. First, the effective real depreciations at the beginning of 1990 in Poland and at the beginning of 1991 in Czechoslovakia were smaller than the figures in table 18.3 suggest, owing to the presence of foreign-currency retention accounts in both countries prior to their big bangs. Enterprises were allowed to retain a share (40 percent in Poland and 30–35 percent on average in Czechoslovakia) of their hard-currency earnings from exports. Hence, exporters were partially able to obtain the more depreciated parallel rate even before the official devaluations. An appropriately calculated real exchange rate for exports would show a much smaller jump in both countries (for the Polish case, see Pinto [1991]). Second, the real rate has tended to appreciate after to the big bang. The appreciation was especially marked in Poland, where the fixed rate was eroded by a smaller-than-before, but nonetheless significant, inflation rate (table 18.3). By the third quarter of 1990, domestic prices had fully caught up with the exchange rate, as had domestic wages by the fourth quarter. These considerations undermine the importance of exchange rate policy and suggest that domestic demand may have played the key role. However, the Polish export boom has fizzled out in 1991, despite the continuation of the domestic slump. This outcome would be consistent with the sustained real appreciation of the zloty, suggesting that that boom had at least something to do with the devaluation on 1 January 1990.

In principle, we can discriminate between the two competing hypotheses as they have somewhat different empirical implications. If the increase in exports is due primarily to devaluation (or to the reduction in costs that arises from import liberalization), profitability across firms would be positively correlated with export orientation. If, on the other hand, the increase in exports is due primarily to the reduction in home demand, profitability would be *negatively*

---

10. For data on real inventories, see Calvo and Coricelli (1991, fig. 3).

correlated with export orientation. This is demonstrated in appendix C in the context of a simple model of firm behavior, with the firm assumed to be a price taker in world markets but a price maker domestically. When the increase in exports is a defensive move to compensate for the reduction in domestic sales, firms that increase their export shares the most will be the ones that suffer the greatest reductions in profitability in equilibrium. But, when the increase comes about because of an increase in export prices (or a reduction in input costs), higher export shares will go with higher profitability.

Table 18.18 shows profitability rates and export shares (in convertible-currency trade) for twelve Polish industrial sectors. Note that profits have declined in all sectors (except for food processing) while the export share has increased across the board. Table 18.19 shows the situation in Hungary for the enterprise sector as a whole. While overall profitability appears to have increased slightly in 1990, this can be attributed to a shift in the composition of exports from the East (where exports were less profitable) to the West (where they were more profitable). The profitability of exports to the convertible-currency area has actually fallen in 1990, while the export share has increased. The broad evidence, therefore, is more favorable to the demand-shock hypothesis.

We obtain the same conclusion from analyzing the variation across industries in the Polish case (shown in table 18.18). The correlation coefficient between the change in profitability and the change in export share is $-.43$ for the

Table 18.18   Export Orientation and Profitability in Polish Industry

	Exports to Convertible-Currency Area as a Share of Sales[a]		Cash-Flow Profitability[b]	
	1990	% Change from 1989	1990	% Change from 1989
Metallurgy	.34	129	.23	−17
Electromachinery:				
Metal	.40	119	.15	−19
Equipment	.39	75	.13	−39
Precision	.42	63	.18	−28
Transport equipment	.04	89	.02	−89
Electrical equipment	.31	65	.09	−39
Chemicals	.28	59	.19	−19
Glass	.42	96	.12	−61
Wood and paper	.71	482	.10	−57
Textiles	.28	107	.01	−98
Clothing	.31	71	.09	−49
Food processing	.48	15	.07	243

Sources: Mueller (1991, table 4) and Schaffer (in press, table 6).

[a]From a sample of 167 large enterprises.

[b]Cash-flow profit is defined as historical cost profit − nominal inventory accumulation + imputed depreciation.

Table 18.19   **Export Orientation and Profitability in Hungary (all enterprises and cooperatives)**

	1989	1990
% of net revenue[a] attributable to:		
Domestic sales	88.2	89.4
Ruble exports	4.2	2.5
Nonruble exports	7.6	8.1
Net revenue from all sales as a share of direct costs[b]	18.4	18.7
Net revenue from ruble exports as a share of direct costs for ruble exports	19.2	16.2
Net revenue from nonruble exports as a share of direct costs for ruble exports	31.4	26.1

Source: OECD (1991b).
[a]Sales revenue plus subsidies minus direct costs.
[b]Labor costs plus costs of material inputs plus marketing costs.

twelve industries included. That is, the industries that improved their export performance the most also suffered the greatest collapse in profits.

Hence, this evidence suggests that the demand shock may have been the predominant source of the export boom, with exchange rate policy playing a more secondary role. However, the evidence is weak and far from conclusive.

18.6 Has Import Liberalization Fostered Price Discipline and Restructuring?

The Polish and Czechoslovak big bangs encompassed trade liberalization alongside price decontrol in large part because the discipline of foreign competition was seen to be a crucial restraint on domestic enterprises. Since the industrial sectors of these economies are highly monopolized, one fear was that enterprise managers would use their new freedom to charge monopoly prices. Free trade would preclude such practices and obviate the need for a lengthy process of industrial restructuring before price liberalization could be launched.

In Poland, there is no evidence that this has worked. As table 18.20 shows, the inflation rate came down substantially after the price adjustments had worked themselves through in the first two months of 1990. However, inflation exhibited a considerable persistence at the rate of 3–5 percent a month for the rest of the year. Given the constant exchange rate, this implied a substantial loss in competitiveness through the end of the year and the first half of the next (see the real exchange rate index in table 18.3 above). Moreover, inflation was not confined to services and nontradables, as the index for industrial goods' prices in table 18.20 shows. Wages in fact rose slower than tradables prices, suggesting also that this was not a case of wage-push inflation (as in the similar

Table 18.20   Inflation in Poland: Change in Prices from Previous Month (%)

	CPI	Industrial Price Index		CPI	Industrial Price Index
1990:			1991:		
Jan.	79.6	109.6	Jan.	12.7	9.8
Feb.	23.8	9.6	Feb.	6.7	5.4
Mar.	4.3	−.2	Mar.	4.5	1.4
Apr.	7.5	2.1	Apr.	2.7	1.0
May	4.6	.6	May	2.7	1.6
Jun.	3.4	1.5	Jun.	4.9	3.1
Jul.	3.6	3.3	Jul.	.1	2.1
Aug.	1.8	2.9	Aug.	.6	1.6
Sep.	4.6	2.7	Sep.	4.3	1.6
Oct.	5.7	4.9	Oct.		2.1
Nov.	4.9	3.6			
Dec.	5.9	3.3			

Source: GUS (1991c).

Chilean experience with exchange rate–based disinflation during the late 1970s).

The question is, How can the prices of domestic tradables continue to rise in the presence of a fixed exchange rate, low tariffs, and no quantitative restrictions on imports? The only possible answer is that the unification of the exchange rate with the jump devaluation of 1 January 1990 took place at too high a level, that is, that the zloty was undervalued throughout much of 1990. The devaluation left domestic prices too low in dollar terms and left headroom for upward adjustment. Hence, it must have been the undervaluation of the zloty that put upward pressure on domestic prices.

In principle, it is not clear why the adjustment in prices could not have taken place in one jump. But in practice it is not difficult to see how enterprises would be adjusting in a slower fashion and groping around for the prices that the market would bear. Of course, once the undervaluation was eliminated, as it must have been sometime toward the end of the year at the latest, the pressure for inflation on this account should have subsided. The reasons for the persistence of inflation from this point on must be sought in other factors, such as the relaxation in fiscal and credit policies and the increase in wages in the second half of the year (see Calvo and Coricelli 1991).

That the zloty was undervalued throughout most of 1990 is evinced also by the huge, unanticipated surplus in Poland's trade balance and by the fact that the fixed exchange rate could be maintained until May 1991, even though the initial judgment had been that it would last for a few months only. Interestingly, not only did the Polish authorities not come under pressure to provide domestic firms with trade protection—after a radical trade reform and during a severe industrial recession—but they were in fact pressed to do quite the opposite. As mentioned in section 18.1 above, beginning in early 1990, a wide range of customs duties were suspended. Many of the imports involved were inputs for which no domestic competition existed, but the suspensions were also aimed at imposing price discipline through imports. The suspensions covered more than half of all tariff lines and served to reduce the effective tariff rate by half (from 10.9 percent in the first half of 1990 to 5.2 percent in the last quarter [Bak et al. 1991]).

Berg and Sachs (1991) report the results of a cross-sectional regression of changes in Polish industrial sales (by sector) on a number of variables, including changes in import penetration. For 1990, they find that imports did not have any (economically or statistically) significant effect on industrial sales. This is consistent with the argument that the zloty was undervalued and import competition was not a serious disciplining factor during most of 1990.

In 1991, with the continued appreciation of the zloty in real terms, the situation changed quite a bit. Since the first quarter of 1991, an import boom has been in place, especially in consumer goods (table 18.21). Enterprise profits have plummeted in light industries, which bear the brunt of import pressure. Consequently, pressures for protection have intensified, and the government has eliminated the suspensions and put in place a new tariff schedule with higher average tariffs (see app. A). However, it is clear from the persistence of inflation that free trade is still not stabilizing domestic prices.

Czechoslovakia's inflation experience has been different from Poland's. Table 18.22 shows the remarkable stabilization in Czechoslovak prices by the middle of 1991. The liberalization of prices has led to a textbook case of a one-time jump in the price level. Since July, prices have been completely stable (further adjustments in controlled prices in November have led to some increases not shown in the table, however). During the second half of the year, prices of many consumer durables (such as radios, televisions, and passenger cars) were in fact declining. Profits in manufacturing industry have deteriorated significantly throughout 1991, especially in consumer goods, although

Table 18.21   **Composition and Trends in Imports (corresponding period previous year = 100)**

	Total	Capital Goods	Raw Materials and Intermediary Goods	Consumer Goods
Poland:				
1990:2	75.9	86.3	70.0	101.0
1990:3	75.8	87.7	70.1	93.5
1990:4	82.1	89.0	76.9	97.0
1991:1	128.7	98.9	122.3	165.3
1991:2	143.5	153.1	118.2	226.6
1991:3	141.3	139.7	118.0	225.3
Hungary:				
1991:1–3	133.2	125.2	151.9	173.9

Table 18.22   Inflation in the CSFR: Change in Prices from Previous Month (%)

	CPI	Of Which:			
		Foodstuffs	Nonfoodstuffs	Services	Industrial Goods
1991:					
Jan.	20.7	25.9	19.2	6.5	
Feb.	6.8	1.0	13.6	3.6	19.3
Mar.	4.7	−2.2	11.4	1.5	−.2
Apr.	2.0	−1.6	3.9	4.8	2.9
May	2.0	−.5	3.5	4.2	1.7
Jun.	1.8	−.3	.5	12.8	−.8
Jul.	−.0	.4	−.6	.6	−.5
Aug.	.0	−.1	−.1	.6	.4
Sep.	.3				−.4
Oct.	−.1				.0

Source: Statisticke Prehledy (1991).

much of this is no doubt due to the loss of export markets in the former So-viet Union.

As discussed above, the devaluation of the koruna was cautious compared to the Polish case and did not aim to eliminate the black market premium at one go. The latter was achieved instead by a progressive reduction in the parallel rate as the domestic credit contraction took effect. In this sense, the Czechoslovak program was perhaps more conducive to importing price discipline from abroad. Nonetheless, the devaluation in December 1990 was still a large one (table 18.1 above), which left considerable room for an upward adjustment in domestic prices when price liberalization went into effect the following month. As in Poland, the pressures on tariffs were in the downward direction, not upward: the phasing down of the 20 percent surcharge introduced on consumer goods alongside the big bang took place more rapidly than anticipated.

There is of course another key difference from Poland. Inflation was never a serious problem in Czechoslovakia. Therefore, the stabilization program of 1991 did not have to concern itself with rooting out endemic inflation; it could be limited to minimizing the effects of a one-time price adjustment arising from decontrol. The inertial and expectational elements present in Poland were probably absent in Czechoslovakia. Hence, while the stabilization of prices in Czechoslovakia is consistent with the more gradual unification of the exchange rate, one cannot read too much into it.

18.7   Concluding Remarks

Briefly put, the tentative conclusions of this paper are as follows. First, the changes in trade policy have been quite dramatic, and all three countries have achieved a substantial increase in openness despite some differences in timing and speed. Second, judging by partner statistics, export performance has been impressive in all three countries, and import booms are under way in at least Hungary and Poland as well. Third, despite what the aggregate statistics show, there is no evidence that exporters have had any success in finding Western markets for the exports that they have lost in Eastern markets. The export boom is based on different kinds of products than those traditionally sold in the East. Fourth, the Soviet trade shock is very serious indeed, with real income losses (on impact) amounting to 7–8 percent of GDP in Hungary and Czechoslovakia and 3½ percent of GDP in Poland. Fifth, export performance can be attributed to exchange rate policy in part, but the collapse of domestic demand has possibly played an even more important role. Sixth, trade liberalization so far appears to have had little effect on price discipline among domestic enterprises or on industrial restructuring, thanks in large part to the substantial devaluations that have accompanied it.

Appendix A
A Summary of Reforms in Trade and Exchange Rate Policy[11]

Hungary

Foreign exchange system. The forint is not convertible to foreign currencies, but in principle foreign exchange is made available to importers automatically if the product is not subject to licensing. As a general rule, other transactions are subject to a foreign exchange license. The exchange rate is set on the basis of a basket of currencies, with the value of the forint adjusted against the basket at irregular intervals.

Tariffs. Tariffs averaged around 13 percent in 1991. Other charges apply in addition to tariffs: a 2 percent customs clearance fee, a 3 percent statistical fee, and 1 percent licensing fee if the imported item is subject to licensing.

Licensing and import quotas. Until January 1989, all imports and exports were subject to licensing. Continued liberalization since then has reduced the scope of licensing to imports covering less than 10 percent of total import value. There exists a consumer goods quota that covers fifteen product groups. The size of the consumer goods quota was tripled in 1991 to ($650 million from $200 million in 1990). There is also an advance import-deposit requirement for 100 percent of the value of the intended import.

Export measures. Restrictions apply on exports of steel (to the EC and the United States), sheep and sheep meat (to the EC), and textiles and clothing (to

---

11. Information reported in app. A has been obtained from World Bank (1991), GATT (1991), and other, national sources.

the EC, the United States, Canada, and Norway). Hungary maintains export subsidies on a number of agricultural products (including milk and dairy products, fruit and vegetables, and sheep meat).

Poland

Foreign exchange system. Since 1 January 1990, the zloty is convertible to foreign currencies for current account transactions. The exchange rate was held fixed against the U.S. dollar at Zl 9,500 from this date until 17 May 1991, after which the zloty was pegged to a basket following a discrete devaluation. On 14 October 1991, the zloty was put on a preannounced downward crawl (at the rate of about 1.8 percent a month). Another discrete devaluation took place in February 1992.

Tariffs. The average (trade-weighted) tariff rates were 8.9 percent in 1989 and 8.6 percent in 1990. During 1990 and the first half of 1991, tariffs were suspended on a wide range of goods (mainly raw materials, intermediate goods, and engineering products), pulling the average rate down. On 1 August 1991, a new tariff schedule was introduced, with eight basic rates from 0 to 40 percent, and suspensions were considerably limited. These changes have raised the average tariff rate to 13.6 percent.

Licensing and import quotas. Import quotas do not exist (save for certain alcoholic beverages), and licensing is limited to a few items.

Export measures. There are no export subsidies. Export restrictions apply on some "essential" goods for the domestic market and on goods subject to "voluntary" export restraints (textiles and clothing, steel, and sheep- and mutton-meat exports to the EC; textiles exports to the United States, Canada, Sweden, and Norway).

Czechoslovakia

Foreign exchange system. As of 15 January 1991, the koruna is convertible to foreign currencies for current account transactions. (There is a limit of Kčs 5,000 per person for travel abroad, however.) The value of the koruna is determined according to a basket of currencies.

Tariffs. Tariffs average around 5 percent, and 96 percent of tariff lines are bound under GATT. On 28 December 1990, a temporary 20 percent import surcharge was introduced mostly on foodstuffs and consumer goods. The surcharge was reduced to 18 percent and subsequently to 15 percent during the course of 1991.

Licensing and import quotas. Quantitative controls on imports are abolished, and only a few import licenses remain (on items such as drugs, weapons, and the like).

Export measures. There are no taxes or subsidies on exports. Almost 20 percent of exports remain subject to licensing. These cover weapons, "essential" inputs for domestic users (e.g., coal, cereals, and milk), and "voluntary" export restraints. The latter apply on metallurgical products (the EC), mutton (the EC), and textiles and clothing (the EC, the United States, Canada, and Norway).

Appendix B
The Anatomy of the Soviet Trade Shock

Understanding the Soviet trade shock requires understanding the mechanics of the pricing of imports and exports under the CMEA.

The domestic price of, say, crude oil, imported from the Soviet Union was determined in the following manner. First, a five-year moving average of world market prices (in dollars) would be calculated. Then this average price would be converted to TRs by using the IBEC exchange rate (which has varied in the range TR 0.60–TR 0.75/\$1.00). This price in TRs would then be the border price at which the oil was imported. The domestic-currency price would in turn be the TR price multiplied by the national exchange rate between the TR and the national currency. Hence, the domestic price (denoted P_m) would be

(B1) $$p_m = p_m^* \times e_{RS}^I \times e_R,$$

where P_m^* is the dollar moving-average price, e_{RS}^I is the IBEC rate (TR/\$), and e_R is the national exchange rate between the domestic currency (NC) and the TR (NC/TR). This can be stated equivalently as

(B2) $$p_m = p_m^* \times (e_{RS}^I/e_{RS}) \times e_s$$

where e_{RS} is the *national* cross-rate between the TR and the dollar (TR/\$), and e_s is the national exchange rate against the dollar (NC/\$). Note that e_{RS} is an implicit rate, obtained by dividing e_s by e_R. As mentioned in the text, the ruble was implicitly valued more cheaply than the IBEC rate in all three countries, so $(e_{RS}^I/e_{RS}) < 1$.

Export prices were determined in more or less the same manner:

(B3) $$p_x = p_x^* \times (e_{RS}^I/e_{RS}) \times e_s,$$

with the caveat that manufactured exports rarely had adequate comparators in world markets. So the border price set in TRs was more or less a negotiated price. Nonetheless, we can still use this (and the IBEC exchange rate) to define an implicit dollar price at the border, p_x^*. Note the important conclusion that the gap between e_{RS} and e_{RS}^I kept domestic prices of imports and exports cheap (relative to trade with the convertible-currency area), acting as an import subsidy and an export tax in ruble trade.

With the demise of the CMEA, pricing in Soviet trade has become the same as in any other trade. So import and export prices in domestic currency are now given by

$$(B4) \qquad\qquad P_m = p_m^{*\prime} \times e_s,$$

$$(B5) \qquad\qquad P_x = p_x^{*\prime} \times e_s,$$

where the prime indicates that posttransition world prices in dollar terms may differ from those prevailing earlier. (But, to save on notation, and with no loss of generality, e_s is assumed to remain unchanged.)

Comparing (B2)–(B3) with (B4)–(B5), we see that the move to dollar pricing involves two distinct effects. One, the terms-of-trade (TOT) effect, is the change from p_m^*/p_x^* to $p_m^{*\prime}/p_x^{*\prime}$. The second, the removal of the import subsidy (RS), is the unification of the cross-rate as e'_{RS}/e_{RS} effectively goes to unity.

The third shock arises from the gap between export prices obtained in the Soviet market, p_x^*, and those prevailing for comparable substitutes in world markets, p_a. Holding export prices constant, on every unit reduction of exports to the Soviet Union, a loss of $p_x^* - p_a$ is incurred on this account. This is the market-loss (ML) effect.

Appendix C
Discriminating between the Exchange Rate and Demand-Shock Explanations for the Export Boom

Consider a firm that has market power at home but is a price taker in its export sales. Let home demand be given by $q = a - p$, where p stands for the domestic price. The demand intercept, a, will proxy for demand shocks. The world price in domestic currency is given by e, which also stands for the exchange rate. Costs are given by $c(q + q^*)$, where q^* is exports. The firm's profits are

$$\pi = pq + eq^* - c(q + q^*)^2 = (a - q)q + eq^* - c(q + q^*)^2,$$

with the following two first-order conditions for domestic and export sales, respectively

$$a - 2q - 2c(q + q^*) = 0,$$

$$e - 2c(q + q^*) = 0.$$

Solving these two equations, we get the equilibrium values of q and q^*

$$q = \tfrac{1}{2}(a - e), \quad q^* = \tfrac{1}{2}\{e[(1 + c)/c] - a\}.$$

For home sales and exports both to be positive, we require

$$a > e > (a - e)c.$$

We assume that this condition is satisfied.

By substituting back into the objective function, we obtain the indirect profit function:

$$\pi(a, e, c) = (1/4)[(a - e)^2 + (e^2/c)].$$

The share of exports in total sales ($= \alpha$) is in turn given by

$$\alpha(a, e, c) = 1 - [(a - e)c]/e.$$

Note the various derivatives:

$d\pi/da = \frac{1}{2}(a - e) > 0,$
$d\pi/de = \frac{1}{2}[(e/c) - (a - e)] > 0,$
$d\pi/dc = -(1/4)(e/c)^2 < 0,$
$d\alpha/da = -(c/e) < 0,$
$d\alpha/de = ac/e^2 > 0,$
$d\alpha/dc = -(a - e)/e < 0.$

Now we can see how profits and the export share covary with changes in the exogenous parameters:

Devaluation: $de > 0 \rightarrow d\pi > 0$ and $d\alpha > 0.$
Reduction in input costs: $dc < 0 \rightarrow d\pi > 0$ and $d\alpha > 0.$
Reduction in home
demand: $da < 0 \rightarrow d\pi < 0$ and $d\alpha > 0.$

Hence, these shocks have different implications for the correlation between export shares and profitability. When the predominant shock is a fall in demand, we would expect firms that experience the highest reductions in profits also to experience the largest increases in export orientation. With the other two shocks, profits and export orientation are positively correlated.

References

Bak, Henryk, et al. 1991. Reintegration of Poland into Western Europe by internal and external liberalization. Working Paper no. 48. Warsaw: World Economy Research Institute.

Berg, Andrew, and Jeffrey Sachs. 1991. Structural adjustment and international trade in Eastern Europe: The case of Poland. Paper prepared for the *Economic Policy* Panel, Prague, 17–19 October.

Calvo, Guillermo A., and Fabrizio Coricelli. 1991. Stabilizing a previously-centrally-planned economy: Poland 1990. *Economic Policy*, no. 14 (April): 176–226.

Central Statistical Office (GUS). 1991a. *Handel Zagraniczny 1991* (Warsaw).

———. 1991b. *Informacje Statystyczne, Handel Zagraniczny* (Warsaw) (various issues).

———. 1991c. *Statistical Bulletin* (Warsaw) (November).

Collins, Susan M., and Dani Rodrik. 1991. *Eastern Europe and the Soviet Union in the world economy.* Washington, D.C.: Institute for International Economics.
Federal Statistical Office (FSU). 1991a. *Foreign Trade* (Prague) (various issues).
————. 1991b. *Quarterly Statistical Bulletin* (Prague) (September).
Foreign Trade Research Institute (FTRI). 1991. *Annual report.* Warsaw.
GATT. 1991. *Trade policy review: Hungary.* Vols. 1, 2. Geneva, July.
GUS. 1991a. *See* Central Statistical Office (1991a).
————. 1991b. *See* Central Statistical Office (1991b).
————. 1991c. *See* Central Statistical Office (1991c).
Guzman, Andrew. 1991. The best of times: The private sector in Poland. Harvard University. Typescript.
IMF. 1991a. The collapse of trade among the former members of the CMEA. Washington, D.C.: European Department.
————. 1991b. *Direction of trade statistics.* Washington, D.C., September.
Kenen, Peter B. 1991. Transitional arrangements for trade and payments among the CMEA countries. *IMF Staff Papers* 38, no. 2 (June): 235–67.
Mueller, Helga. 1991. Export performance of Polish enterprises during the transition process. Washington, D.C.: World Bank, September.
Murphy, Kevin, and Andrei Shleifer. 1991. Quality and trade. University of Chicago and Harvard University, August. Typescript.
Oblath, Gabor, and David Tarr. 1991. The terms-of-trade effects from the elimination of state trading in Soviet-Hungarian trade. Washington, D.C.: World Bank, May.
OECD. 1991a. *Monthly statistics of foreign trade.* Paris, September.
————. 1991b. *OECD economic surveys: Hungary.* Paris.
Pinto, Brian. 1991. Microeconomic response to the economic transformation program: Evidence from the largest polish SOEs. Warsaw: World Bank Resident Mission, September.
PlanEcon. 1991. *Recent Czechoslovak foreign trade performance.* Report. Washington, D.C., 24 October.
Poland fails to take up loans. *Financial Times,* 26 March 1992, 8.
Research Institute for Foreign Economic Relations (RIFER). 1991. *CSFR in International Economy Quarterly* (Prague), vol. 1, no. 2 (September).
Rodrik, Dani. 1992. Making sense of the Soviet trade shock in Eastern Europe: A framework and some estimates. Paper prepared for the World Bank/IMF Conference on the Fall of Output in Eastern Europe.
Rosati, Dariusz K. 1991. After the CMEA collapse: Is the Central European Payments Union really necessary. Working Paper no. 18. Warsaw: Foreign Trade Research Institute, May.
Schaffer, Mark. In press. The Polish state-owned enterprise sector and the recession in 1990. *Comparative Economic Studies.*
Statisticke Prehledy. 1991. *Monthly Statistics of Czechoslovakia* (Prague), no. 11.
Synowiec, Ewa, and Ewa Rzeszutek. 1991. Poland's trade with the European Community at the turn of the 1990s. Economic and Social Policy Series, no. 3. Warsaw: Friedrich Ebert Foundation, April.
Wang, Zhen Kun, and L. Alan Winters. 1991. The trading potential of Eastern Europe. Discussion Paper no. 610. London: Centre for Economic Policy Research, November.
World Bank. 1991. *Trade expansion program report on Czechoslovakia.* Washington, D.C.

Comment   Susan M. Collins

This paper provides a useful and informative survey of a number of key aspects of recent trade performance in Poland, Hungary, and Czechoslovakia. I agreed with many of the conclusions reached in the paper and found it quite interesting to read. However, there are a few areas where it seems to me that the paper misses some central points, leading the conclusions astray. I will discuss five of the main sections of the paper, pointing out my agreements and disagreements along the way.

The paper begins with a review of recent developments in trade policy in the three countries. Quite rightly, it emphasizes the dramatic shift toward liberalization in each country, although there have been differences in the speeds of liberalization. This section provides a very helpful summary of the key changes.

The paper then discusses recent trade performance. In particular, it shows the impressive increase in both exports and imports with the West. This discussion incorporates an appropriate skepticism of the available data, providing very interesting comparisons of figures from the countries themselves with figures from partner countries. It is worth making the point that, in 1989 and 1990, many analysts predicted that the East European economies would find it extremely difficult to increase exports to the West in the short run because there were supposedly very few products that Western consumers would wish to purchase. This line of thought led to extremely pessimistic forecasts of their external balances during transition. The actual export figures tell a very different story. Exports grew within the first few months of the new policy regimes. Of course, these experiences raise two questions. First, what accounts for the rapid export increases? Second, can they be sustained? I will return to these issues below.

One possible explanation for the very rapid surge in exports to the West is that enterprises simply reoriented exports that used to go to CMEA (Council for Mutual Economic Assistance) countries to market economies. The paper does a very nice job of debunking that hypothesis. It shows—not surprisingly—that the mix of products exported to the West has historically been quite different from the mix exported to the East. If trade had simply been reoriented, one would expect to see the discrepancies in the industrial composition narrow. However, there is no evidence of this at the aggregate industrial sector level. (Of course, there may have been reorientation of specific products.)

The paper then goes on to consider four explanations for the boom in exports to the West: favorable foreign demand, pressure to unload inventories, the collapse in domestic demand, and the increased relative profitability of exports owing to the devaluations and other policy changes. The first two are dismissed rapidly. I agree that demand from the market economies had not been a constraint; therefore, market conditions in the West cannot be the explanation for the dramatic surge. While the observed timing of inventory depletion and the export surges does not suggest that inventories are the key to the explanation, this connection warranted additional discussion in the paper. The larger the role that inventories played, the worse the prognosis for the increased exports to be sustainable.

Too much of the paper is then devoted to trying to distinguish between the demand collapse and the relative price explanations. First, it seems to me that this is a secondary issue, considerably less interesting and important than assessing whether the export surge can be sustained and how well exports in these countries responded to market signals at all during the early phase of their transitions. Second, the methodology used cannot adequately distinguish between these and alternative explanations of performance. I elaborate on this point below.

The approach is based on a simple model of profit-maximizing firm behavior in which all firms can choose between selling domestically as price setters or selling abroad as price takers. This model implies that a decline in domestic demand will give rise to a negative correlation between observed exports and firm profits since those firms experiencing the largest decline in domestic demand and thus in profits will increase exports most. However, a devaluation would give rise to a positive correlation between profitability and exports. Let me leave aside all the data issues and assume that we have accurate measures of profitability and exports (recall, however, that an earlier section of the paper emphasized that small private endeavors, which now account for an increasing amount of exports, are not adequately reflected in published statistics).

There are at least three problems with applying this model to Eastern Europe in transition. First, not all products are equally salable in the West. As the regime changes to allow additional sales to market economies, we should expect those firms producing goods most easily sold in the West to experience the smallest declines in profits and the largest rise in exports. This phenomenon could account for a positive correlation even without a decline in domestic demand. Second, the model implicitly assumes that firms have optimally allocated their sales between exports and domestic consumers before the shock (demand collapse or devaluation). Clearly, this need not be true of pretransition enterprises. Given an arbitrary allocation, it is difficult to interpret the changes observed at the beginning of the transition. Finally, it may not be accurate to classify East European exporters as price takers in Western markets for this purpose. Even though they account for a very small share of total Western consumption, it would not be surprising to find that they had reduced prices on a number of products in order to sell them quickly for Western hard currencies. If the East "dumped" products in the West, one would expect to observe a negative correlation between profitability and export volume, even if there had been no devaluation.

The last section of the paper argues that, contrary to some people's expectation, import liberalization has not been successful in disciplining price inflation, citing the persistence of inflation despite fixed exchange rates, low tariffs, and the removal of quantitative restrictions on imports. Here, I think that the paper focuses too much on the issue of discipline and not enough on the issue of price-system restructuring. In light of the experience with the slow reduction of inflation in the Southern Cone and other stabilization attempts, I do not find it at all surprising that Polish inflation persisted. But there is a second, and perhaps more interesting, explanation for the persistence of inflation. The economies in Eastern Europe are attempting to rationalize the structure of their price systems by importing prices from the rest of the world. The discrepancies in relative prices in socialist economies compared with comparable relative prices in market economies are well known. Thus, in some cases, the required relative price adjustments are enormous. It may well be that it is easier to achieve a massive price restructuring primarily through price increases than through nominal price decreases. If so, the restructuring would give rise to a general price inflation. It is interesting to note that Czechoslovakia, which had a price structure more in line with world prices than the Polish structure, has found inflation to be less persistent than Poland. The extent of price restructuring and the relation between restructuring and overall inflation are important topics that warrant additional analysis.

Discussion Summary

Kemal Derviş noted that state enterprises produce most of the goods that Poland exports. *Geoffrey Carliner* wondered whether state-owned firms have sufficient motivation and skills to expand this activity by seeking out new markets in the West.

Jeffrey Sachs made several comments. First, he noted that, at least in Poland, an "equalization tax" was used in internal markets to increase the price of Soviet imports. Moreover, the revenue from this tax was used to subsidize exports. Together, these programs undid the effect of the overvalued effective exchange rate of Poland vis-à-vis the Soviet Union. Second, Sachs said that it is not appropriate to compare a terms-of-trade loss, which is an income effect, to a reduction in real GNP, which is an output effect. Third, Sachs presented evidence supporting the thesis that the export boom was due largely to an aggressive policy of export expansion by East European industrial firms. He noted that World Bank economists have observed an explosion in the number of contacts between East European industrial firms and Western buyers/suppliers. Sachs also cited particular instances in which East European firms have produced new products exclusively for export to the West. Finally, he emphasized that only a small part of the export boom can conceivably be explained by depleted inventory stocks.

Richard Freeman suggested that Rodrik consider the economic performance of Finland as a benchmark for comparison with the East European countries. Freeman also wondered whether the East European import boom was being driven by consumption goods.

Mark Schaffer supported the consensus view that, at least in Poland, inventory depletion did not play an important role in the export boom. He said that, whatever the movements in inventories, the inventory stocks just were not large enough to account for the massive increase in exports.

Kalman Mizsei noted that, in most of Eastern Europe, and particularly in Poland and Hungary, pressure is mounting for the governments to reverse their programs of import liberalization. He said that many of the governments have already increased tariffs and quotas and temporarily suspended the liberalization process.

Sweder van Wijnbergen suggested that Rodrik look at the correlation between changes in sectoral markups and changes in sectoral import penetration. A strong negative coefficient would provide evidence that trade competition provides price discipline.

Dani Rodrik disagreed with Sachs's suggestion that the equalization tax completely offset the effects of overvalued exchange rates. Rodrik said that the equalization tax only partially mitigated the exchange rate distortions. To support this point, he noted that the effective price that East European enterprises pay for oil rose as a result of price liberalization. Finally, Rodrik agreed with Sachs that terms-of-trade effects are not directly comparable to GDP effects. However, Rodrik suggested that it is not clear which measure is more informative since both are problematic. The GDP measure understates the effect on incomes of the terms-of-trade shock, and the terms-of-trade measure needs to be scaled by a Keynesian multiplier.

Biographies (Volume 1 and Volume 2)

Philippe Aghion is official fellow at Nuffield College, Oxford, and senior economist at the European Bank for Reconstruction and Development.

Anders Aslund is director of the Stockholm Institute for Soviet and East European Economics at the Stockholm School of Economics.

David Begg is professor of economics at Birkbeck College, University of London.

Andrew Berg is an economist in the research department of the International Monetary Fund.

Olivier Jean Blanchard is professor of economics at the Massachusetts Institute of Technology and a research associate of the National Bureau of Economic Research.

Barry Bosworth is a senior fellow in the Economic Studies Division of the Brookings Institution.

Michael Bruno is professor of economics at Hebrew University and a research associate of the National Bureau of Economic Research.

Wendy Carlin is lecturer in economics at University College, London.

Geoffrey Carliner is executive director of the National Bureau of Economic Research.

Susan M. Collins is associate professor of economics at Georgetown University, a senior fellow of the Brookings Institution, and a research associate of the National Bureau of Economic Research.

Timothy Condon is an economist in the Central Europe Department of the World Bank.

Fabrizio Coricelli is professor of economics at the University of Siena.

Alain de Crombrugghe is assistant professor of economics at the University of Namur, Belgium.

Kemal Derviş is director of the Central Europe Department of the World Bank.

Peter Diamond is the Paul A. Samuelson Professor of Economics at the Massachusetts Institute of Technology and a research associate of the National Bureau of Economic Research.

Michael P. Dooley is professor of economics at the University of California, Santa Cruz, and a research associate of the National Bureau of Economic Research.

Rudiger Dornbusch is the Ford International Professor of Economics at the Massachusetts Institute of Technology and a research associate of the National Bureau of Economic Research.

Karel Dyba is the minister of economy of the Czech Republic.

Saul Estrin is associate professor of economics at the London Business School.

Stanley Fischer is the Elizabeth and James Killian Professor and director of the World Economy Laboratory in the Department of Economics at the Massachusetts Institute of Technology and a research associate of the National Bureau of Economic Research.

Richard B. Freeman is professor of economics at Harvard University and a research associate of the National Bureau of Economic Research.

Lev Freinkman is an economist in the Moscow office of the World Bank.

Kenneth A. Froot is professor of business administration at the Graduate School of Business, Harvard University, and a research associate of the National Bureau of Economic Research.

Roger H. Gordon is professor of economics at the University of Michigan and a research associate of the National Bureau of Economic Research.

Oliver Hart is professor of economics at Harvard University.

Simon Johnson is assistant professor of economics at the Fuqua School of Business, Duke University.

Tom Kolaja is an industry specialist in the Ministry of Ownership Changes of the Polish Government.

George Kopits is senior resident representative in Hungary of the International Monetary Fund.

Pentti Kouri is director of Kouri Capital in Greenwich, Connecticut.

Richard Layard is professor of economics and director of the Centre for Economic Performance at the London School of Economics.

Anthony Levitas is a Ph.D. candidate in political science at the Massachusetts Institute of Technology and a research fellow at the Center for European Studies, Harvard University.

David Lipton is deputy assistant secretary for Eastern Europe and the former Soviet Union, U.S. Department of the Treasury.

Colin Mayer is professor of economics and finance at City University Business School, London.

Kalman Mizsei is director of the Economic Focus Area and the Pew Economist in Residence at the Institute for EastWest Studies.

John Moore is professor of economics at the London School of Economics.

Wilhelm Nölling is president of the Landeszentralbank in der Freien und Hansestadt Hamburg, a member of the Central Bank Policy Council of the Deutsche Bundesbank, Frankfurt, and editor of *Hamburger Beiträge zur Wirtschafts und Währungspolitik in Europa*.

Boris Pleskovic is senior economist and deputy administrator, Research Advisory Staff, at the World Bank.

Dani Rodrik is professor of economics and international affairs at Columbia University, a research fellow of the Centre for Economic Policy Research, and a research associate of the National Bureau of Economic Research.

Jacek Rostowski is lecturer in Russian and East European economics at the School of Slavonic and East European Studies at London University, deputy director of the Centre for Research into Communist Economies, and an associate of the Centre for Economic Performance, London.

Jeffrey D. Sachs is the Galen L. Stone Professor of International Trade at Harvard University and a research associate of the National Bureau of Economic Research.

Mark E. Schaffer is a research fellow at the Centre for Economic Performance, London School of Economics.

Andrei Shleifer is professor of economics at Harvard University and a faculty research fellow of the National Bureau of Economic Research.

András Simon is professor of economics at the Budapest University of Economics.

Inderjit Singh is lead economist for the Transition and Macro-Adjustment Division of the Country Economics Department of the World Bank.

Jeremy C. Stein is associate professor of finance at the Sloan School of Management, the Massachusetts Institute of Technology, and a research associate of the National Bureau of Economic Research.

Lawrence H. Summers is undersecretary for international affairs, U.S. Department of the Treasury.

Jan Svejnar is professor of economics at the University of Pittsburgh and CERGE, Charles University.

Sweder van Wijnbergen is senior adviser in the Central Europe Department of the World Bank.

Dmitri Vasiliev is deputy minister of Privatization for the Russian government.

Robert W. Vishny is professor of finance at the University of Chicago and a program director at the National Bureau of Economic Research.

Jan Winiecki is executive director of the European Bank for Reconstruction and Development.

Holger C. Wolf is assistant professor of economics and international business at the Stern School of Business, New York University, and a faculty research fellow of the National Bureau of Economic Research.

Janet L. Yellen is the Bernard T. Rocca, Jr., Professor of International Business and Trade at the Walter A. Haas School of Business at the University of California, Berkeley.

Josef Zieleniec is a research associate of CERGE, Prague.

Contributors (Volume 1 and Volume 2)

Philippe Aghion
European Bank for Reconstruction and
    Development
6 Broadgate
London EC2M 2QS, United Kingdom

Anders Aslund
Stockholm Institute for Soviet and East
    European Economics
Stockholm School of Economics
Stockholm, Sweden

David Begg
Birkbeck College
University of London
7/15 Gresse Street
London W1P 1PA,
United Kingdom

Andrew Berg
International Monetary Fund
700 19th St., N.W.
IS-635
Washington, D.C. 20431

Olivier Jean Blanchard
Department of Economics
Massachusetts Institute of Technology
50 Memorial Drive
Cambridge, MA 02139

Barry Bosworth
The Brookings Institution
1775 Massachusetts Avenue, N.W.
Washington, DC 20036

Michael Bruno
Department of Economics
Hebrew University
Jerusalem, Israel

Wendy Carlin
Department of Economics
University College London
Gower Street
London WC1E 6BT, United Kingdom

Geoffrey Carliner
National Bureau of Economic
    Research
1050 Massachusetts Avenue
Cambridge, MA 02138

Susan M. Collins
The Brookings Institution
1775 Massachusetts Avenue, N.W.
Washington, DC 20036

Timothy Condon
Central Europe Department
The World Bank
1818 H Street, N.W.
Washington, DC 20433

Fabrizio Coricelli
Department of Economics
University of Siena
Piazza San Francesco 7
Siena 53100, Italy

Alain de Crombrugghe
Faculté des Sciences Economiques et
  Sociales
Namur University
Rampart de la Vierge, 8
B-5000 Namur
Belgium

Kemal Derviş
Central Europe Department
The World Bank
1818 H. Street, N.W.
Washington, DC 20433

Peter Diamond
Department of Economics
Room E52–344
Massachusetts Institute of Technology
Cambridge, MA 02139

Michael P. Dooley
Department of Economics
University of California, Santa Cruz
Crown College, Room 236
Santa Cruz, CA 95064

Rudiger Dornbusch
Department of Economics
Room E52–357
Massachusetts Institute of Technology
Cambridge, MA 02139

Karel Dyba
Ministry of Economic Policy and
  Development of the Czech Republic
CS-101 60 Praha 10
Czechoslovakia

Saul Estrin
Faculty of Economics
London Business School
Sussex Place, Regents Park
London NW1 4SA
United Kingdom

Stanley Fischer
Department of Economics
Room E52–274
Massachusetts Institute of Technology
Cambridge, MA 02139

Richard B. Freeman
National Bureau of Economic Research
1050 Massachusetts Avenue
Cambridge, MA 02138

Lev Freinkman
The World Bank
Ilyinka, 23, Entrance 10
Moscow 103132
Russia

Kenneth A. Froot
Dillon 23
Graduate School of Business
Harvard University
Soldiers Field
Boston, MA 02163

Roger H. Gordon
Department of Economics
University of Michigan
Ann Arbor, MI 48109

Oliver Hart
Littauer 220
Department of Economics
Harvard University
Cambridge, MA 02138

Simon Johnson
The Fuqua School of Business
Duke University
Durham, NC 27706

Thomas Kolaja
Ministry of Ownership Changes
ul. Krucza 36
00–525 Warsaw
Poland

George Kopits
Office of the Resident Representative in
  Hungary
National Bank of Hungary, Room 210T
1850 Budapest, Szabadságtér 8-9
Hungary

Pentti Kouri
Kouri Capital
19 Benedict Place
Greenwich, CT 06830

Richard Layard
Centre for Economic Performance
London School of Economics
Houghton Street
London WC2A 2AE
United Kingdom

Anthony Levitas
Center for European Studies
Harvard University
27 Kirkland Street
Cambridge, MA 02138

David Lipton
Department of the Treasury
1500 Pennsylvania Ave.
Washington, DC 20220

Colin Mayer
City University Business School
Frobisher Crescent, Barbican Centre
London EC4
United Kingdom

Kalman Mizsei
Institute for East West Studies
360 Lexington Avenue
New York, NY 10017

John Moore
Department of Economics
London School of Economics
Houghton Street
London WC2A 2AE
United Kingdom

Wilhelm Nölling
East-West Consulting Agency
Neuer Jungfernstieg 7
20354 Hamburg 11
Germany

Boris Pleskovic
Research Advisory Staff
The World Bank
1818 H Street, N.W.
Washington, DC 20433

Dani Rodrik
Department of Economics
Columbia University
420 W. 118th Street, 1312
New York, NY 10027

Jacek Rostowski
School of Slavonic and East European
    Studies
University of London
London W1P 1PA
United Kingdom

Jeffrey D. Sachs
Department of Economics
Harvard University
Littauer Center M-14
Cambridge, MA 02138

Mark E. Schaffer
Centre for Economic Performance
London School of Economics
Houghton Street, Aldwych
London WC2 2AE
United Kingdom

Andrei Shleifer
Department of Economics
Harvard University
Littauer Center 315
Cambridge, MA 02138

András Simon
Department of International Economics
Budapest University of Economics
H-1093 Budapest
Fövám tér 8
Hungary

Inderjit Singh
Transition and Macro-Adjustment
    Division
Country Economics Department
The World Bank
1818 H Street, N.W.
Washington, DC 20433

Jeremy C. Stein
Sloan School of Management
E52–448
Massachusetts Institute of Technology
Cambridge, MA 02139

Lawrence H. Summers
Department of the Treasury
1500 Pennsylvania Ave., N. W.
Room 3432
Washington, DC 20220

Jan Svejnar
Department of Economics
4M30 Forbes Quadrangle
University of Pittsburgh
Pittsburgh, PA 15260

Sweder van Wijnbergen
Central Europe Department
The World Bank
1818 H Street, N.W.
Washington, DC 20433

Dmitri Vasiliev
Ministry of Privatization
Moscow
Russia

Robert W. Vishny
Graduate School of Business
University of Chicago
1101 East 58th Street
Chicago, IL 60637

Jan Winiecki
Executive Director
European Bank of Reconstruction and
    Development
One Exchange Square
London EC2A 2EH
United Kingdom

Holger C. Wolf
Management Education Center
New York University
44 W. 44th Street, Suite 7–78
New York, NY 10012

Janet L. Yellen
Walter A. Hass School of Business
350 Barrows Hall
University of California
Berkeley, CA 94720

Josef Zieleniec
CERGE
FSV UK
Prague
Czechoslovakia

Author Index

Subject Index

Wages, Poland: increases in real, 114, 117; pension system based on final, 75–81; policy to curb growth, 116–17

Worker-management buyout (WMBO), Russia, 146–47, 158–59

Workers, Poland, 168

Workers, Russia: indicators of control gained by, 143–44; ownership stakes with spontaneous privatization, 147–48; payoff as incentives to allow privatization, 150–52